Library of Congress Control Number: 2020930790

Designed by Jack Chappell
Cover design by Justin Watkinson
Type set in Belwe/Agency/Minion

ISBN: 978-0-7643-6047-3
Printed in China

Published by Schiffer Publishing, Ltd.
4880 Lower Valley Road
Atglen, PA 19310
Phone: (610) 593-1777; Fax: (610) 593-2002
E-mail: Info@schifferbooks.com
Web: www.schifferbooks.com

For our complete selection of fine books on this and related subjects, please visit our website at www.schifferbooks.com. You may also write for a free catalog.

Schiffer Publishing's titles are available at special discounts for bulk purchases for sales promotions or premiums. Special editions, including personalized covers, corporate imprints, and excerpts, can be created in large quantities for special needs. For more information, contact the publisher.

We are always looking for people to write books on new and related subjects. If you have an idea for a book, please contact us at proposals@schifferbooks.com.

WAFFEN-SS TIGER CREWS AT KURSK

THE MEN OF SS PANZER REGIMENTS 1, 2 & 3 IN OPERATION CITADEL, JULY 5–15, 1943

Col. French L. MacLean
UNITED STATES ARMY (RET.)

SCHIFFER MILITARY
4880 Lower Valley Road   Atglen, PA 19310

Führer Order for Operation Citadel to the troops of the 2nd SS Panzer Corps on July 4, 1943:

"Just as he did in the last great war, the enemy will one day fail, despite everything. And the reason is this: The Russians were able to wrest an occasional success in the past due primarily to their tanks. My soldiers! You finally have better ones than they do."

—Adolf Hitler

Order of the commander of the Sixth Guards Army, opposing 2nd SS Panzer Corps, to his officers on July 5, 1943:

"Be careful, gentlemen; before you stand Hitler's guard."

—General Ivan Mikhailovich Chistiakov

Contents

Introduction 6
Acknowledgments 9
Dedication 11
Methodology 13

The Tiger Tank 16
Genesis 16
The Weapon 17
Doctrine 20
Tiger Killers 22
The Crew 26
Vehicle Recovery and Maintenance 29

Battle of Kursk Overview 31
Daily Battle Actions 43
Battle Rosters 81

Crew Member Biographies 91
13th (Heavy) Company 91
8th (Heavy) Company 109
9th (Heavy) Company 137

Analysis 150
Conclusions 163

Appendixes
Appendix 1: Kursk Battlefield Locator 179
Appendix 2: Crew Members Not Present for Duty 182
Appendix 3: Unit Field Post Numbers 183
Appendix 4: Waffen-SS Ranks 184

Photo Gallery 185
Endnotes 253
Bibliography 280
Index 284

Introduction

A company commander of a Waffen-SS Tiger tank company once said of his formidable vehicle: "It was like a wolf running wild amongst a herd of sheep."[1]

The Tiger (Panzerkampfwagen VI; known by the allies as the Mark VI) tank, in the opinion of many military and engineering experts, was not the greatest tank in World War II, but it had the most fearsome reputation of any armored vehicle.[2] Yes, many tanks were easier to build, less expensive, more reliable in their operation, mounted bigger main guns, could fire faster, possessed greater cross country and road speed, were more mobile in rough terrain, could traverse the turret faster, and had greater operational range on a load of fuel.

These "deficiencies" provided no solace to the Russians over eleven hot and dusty days during July 1943, in an obscure area about which German Colonel General Heinz Guderian, one of the "fathers" of modern armored warfare, once dramatically chided the Führer, Adolf Hitler, with this acerbic question: "How many people do you think even know where Kursk is?"

Now, not only do military experts know where Kursk is, they know what happened there, especially concerning the Tiger tank. During the Kursk Offensive—the opening phase of the Battle of Kursk from July 5 to July 15, 1943—the 2nd SS Panzer Corps squared off in combat against five Soviet tank corps. From July 6 through July 9, the Waffen-SS unit ground the Soviet 31st Tank Corps into a fine red dust, reducing its tank strength from 184 to 54. Then the corps, led by its deadly complement of just three companies of Tiger tanks, turned its malevolent appetite to the 5th Guards "Stalingradskikh" Tank Corps, leaving it with only sixteen percent tank strength after the savage mauling was completed.

By the by, the 2nd SS Panzer Corps also rammed into the enemy 10th Tank Corps, and the only reason that it did not claw that Russian corps' tank strength to shreds was that the 10th Tank Corps' tanks had already departed the sector to face the German 48th Panzer Corps advancing to the west. No matter; the 2nd SS Panzer Corps then bounded through the Soviet 2nd Tank Corps. Only the Soviet 2nd Guards Tank Corps conserved its tank strength—finishing with seventy-five percent operational tanks—after it met the claws of the Tigers, leaving surviving Soviet tank commanders scratching their heads as shell after shell bounced off their foes.[3]

Bad news traveled fast, and from the deserts of North Africa, to the twisting mountain roads in Italy, to the deadly bocage in Normandy, when the Germans were known—or simply perceived—to have Tiger tanks in the vicinity, British, American, and Soviet troops from private to colonel started to sweat. They sweat in the African heat and they sweat in the freezing snow of the Ardennes. Combat veterans might be seen puking behind a tree before an attack when "Tiger fever" or "Tiger psychosis" started to spread. Rumors abounded that if the 88 mm main gun didn't get you, then the multiple machine guns surely would. And in the ultimate nightmare, veterans told "green" troops how Tigers would even drive over hapless enemy infantrymen, pivot steering to grind their bodies into so much red mush that even their own mothers would not recognize the remains.[4]

So much fear from so few machines; during the two-year production run, German engineers and factory workers built only 1,347 Tiger tanks, what today we refer to as the Tiger I. Back then it was just called the Tiger—the Roman numeral I was added in 1944, when the later Tiger II (*Königstiger*, known by the Allies as the "King Tiger") entered the force.[5]

That paltry sum is certain to amaze "World of Tanks" aficionados who daily refight battles from World War II, and other conflicts, between the steel giants that have captured the imaginations of so many. Perhaps in no other battle does this hold true than at Kursk, *Unternehmen Zitadelle*, in July 1943. "The Greatest Tank Battle in History" has been a phrase used to describe the major action that was over in about two weeks. "The Death Ride of the Fourth Panzer Army," a description of the southern half of the Kursk battle, evokes images of imaginary Teutonic mythic figures such as Wotan, Siegfried, the Valkyries, and Valhalla.

Immediately after the war, estimates concerning the scope of Kursk pegged the German Ninth Army and Fourth Panzer Army attacking with three thousand panzers, opposed by the "Big Red Machine" that countered with five thousand armored fighting vehicles. Modern writers Col. David Glantz, US Army (*Ret.*), and Jonathan House believed that the Germans suffered 323 panzers destroyed, while the Soviets lost about 1,600 tanks. And at the apex of the fight at Prokhorovka, north of Belgorod, in a tank battle between the 2nd SS Panzer Corps and the 5th Guards Tank Army—regarded for years as the greatest single-day tank battle in history—three hundred German *panzers* squared off against eight-hundred Soviet *танк*.

And what of the Tiger tanks at Kursk? Soviet daily battle summaries, obviously mistaking other types of panzers for dreaded Tigers, reported destroying more Tiger tanks at Kursk than were fielded there. Combining the German northern attack and southern attack against the Kursk salient—beginning in earnest on July 5, 1943—the vaunted German Wehrmacht (German Armed Forces) fielded a total of just one-hundred and twenty operational Tiger tanks; 120.[6] The highly touted 2nd SS Panzer Corps, of the dreaded Waffen-SS and the main effort during much of the southern attack crossed the line of departure early on July 5 with exactly thirty-five operational Tigers of the forty-two that they had on hand.

This book is not focused on those machines.

It is focused on men.

The men who fought in these Tigers were not ten feet tall, although the Russians may have believed that during the twelve days that they shook the earth. They were an enemy that was far more dangerous: they had no concept of defeat. Look again at the front cover of this book. The young man in the turret and commanding Tiger **S32** in the Third Platoon of the 8th (Heavy) Company of Tigers in *Das Reich* is a corporal. His company will have the highest personnel losses of the three SS Tiger companies at Kursk, losing ten killed and eighteen wounded over the next eleven days—equating to a forty percent chance that he will become a casualty during that time. Over the war, thirty-one percent of the men who crewed the Waffen-SS Tigers at Kursk will be killed in action. Look at his face. He does not care about those odds. Until the day of his death, he will be "like a wolf running wild amongst a herd of sheep."

Twenty-one year old Kurt Baral had been an infantryman and had received the Infantry Assault Badge in Silver and the Iron Cross Second Class in 1941 before transferring to the panzers. At Kharkov in February 1943, he is the commander of a Mark III panzer in the light platoon of the company. He knows every panzer tactic in the book and many others that aren't. At Kursk, he will write home and his letter—recorded in this book—will tell how his gunner and loader are wounded, and states that during the first three days of the offensive his tank knocked out thirteen enemy tanks.

Kurt will later be assigned to the 102nd SS Heavy Panzer Detachment, where as a platoon leader he commands Tiger 131 in the Third Platoon of the 1st Company fighting against the British 7th Hampshire Regiment of the 43rd Wessex Division in Normandy east of Hill 112 at the village of Maltot. He later commands King Tiger 121 as the First Platoon leader in the 1st Company of the 502nd SS Heavy Panzer Detachment at the end of the war on the Oder Front.

Shortly after becoming the acting commander of the 3rd Company of the detachment, in a wooded area near the village of Briesen, on April 19, 1945 he will be killed by a burst of enemy machinegun fire while climbing into his tank that had driven into a shell crater. Originally buried the following day by his comrades in a cemetery in Briesen, Kurt Baral's remains are now buried at the military section of the cemetery in Berkenbrück in an end grave in Row 3.

One day men and women may not fight wars, leaving that unpleasant task to robots and artificial intelligence. Until then every physical characteristic of every armored fighting vehicle can be measured in numbers. The muzzle velocity, caliber, and type of shell can be analyzed to determine how far that ammunition will penetrate into an enemy tank at varying distances. The ground pressure exerted by the treads of a tank will determine how mobile it will be when it travels across country. The capacity of a tank's fuel cells, combined with the efficiency of its engine, will tell us how far it can travel and how long it can operate until it needs to be refueled. And the composition and angle of its armor can give engineers a very good calculation of how well it will survive on the battlefield.

The underlying truth is that *a tank is only as good as its crew*. In the case of the Tiger, five men (tank commander, gunner, loader, radio operator, and driver) had to work in unison—not only to destroy enemy tanks and other weapons' systems, but also to simply survive on the battlefield. Kursk was a bloody battle, and during the offensive some 54,000 Germans and 178,000 Soviets became casualties.

But for every Tiger crewman these big numbers simply didn't matter. You either blew the enemy's ass out of the back of his tank or he would do the same to you.[7]

Acknowledgments

Just as the Tiger had five crewmen, all of whom contributed to its success, so this book has its own "Fabulous Five" without whom this work could not have been successfully completed. Any writer wishing to know the technicalities of the Tiger tank and the nature of the battle at Kursk must first read authors Egon Kleine, Volkmar Kühn, Patrick Agte, David Schranck, Thomas L. Jentz, Hilary L. Doyle, Walter J. Spielberger, Robert Forczyk, Waldemar Trojca, Col. David Glantz, and Jonathan House, who have tackled those two subjects and done so well. And a special thanks must go to John P. Moore, whom I would not call a "Tiger guy," but would characterize as the go to source for locating people who are. John not only tells you whom you need to contact, but goes the extra mile and facilitates that communication, so it happens quickly and smoothly. And a special note of thanks must go to Marc Romanych, who is not only an excellent author with wonderful books on heavy artillery and fortifications, but for this project was able to provide so many excellent photographs of Tiger tanks from the US National Archives in College Park, Maryland. Now for the "Fab Five" in alphabetical order because my thanks go to each equally.

Christopher A. Lawrence, author of *Kursk: The Battle of Prokhorovka* (Sheridan, Colorado: Aberdeen Books, 2015). This 1,650-page labor of love is one you can curl up with over one winter someday—and be glad that you did. This is the one book on Kursk that anyone interested in the battle must own, and if one must own only one book on the battle, this is that book. It is also oversized, so your bookshelf better be reinforced. It costs a whole lot and it is worth *every* penny. The internet will never have as much information on the subject, so you can either go through life not knowing many aspects of the battle or get the book and have it all at your fingertips. Fifty times in this book I found information for this study that I could locate nowhere else.

George M. Nipe, author of *Blood, Steel and Myth: The II. SS-Panzer-Korps and the road to Prochorowka, July 1943.* "Coach" Nipe started as a source and ended up a friend. His book is wonderful—wonderful maps, wonderful discussion of the chronology of the battle, and wonderful source notes. George was the "go to" source for determining what each Tiger company did each day. He is also an expert on photographs of the Waffen-SS at Kursk and an acknowledged expert on the Eastern Front.

Oberst a. D. Wolfgang Schneider is the author of *Totenkopf Tigers, Das Reich Tigers, Tigers in Combat, Tigers in Combat II, Tigers in Combat III, Tigers in Normandy, The King Tiger Volume I, King Tiger Volume II,* and the list goes on. If you were to place every book ever written on the Tiger tank, Colonel (*Ret*). Wolfgang Schneider probably would account for twenty-five percent of them; his books are published in at least three languages. While his skills as an author and historian are impressive, he brings two additional attributes to the table that may be equally as important. The colonel served as a panzer officer for many years in the *Bundeswehr* and in his early years personally knew many individuals who had served on Tigers during the war. And uniquely, he understands the crew duties in a tank, because he rode in the turret of a tank for a long, long time during his *Bundeswehr* career. And he patiently has answered all my questions for a long, long time!

Rüdiger Warnick, on the other hand, is a young man, the kind of author you feel the subject will be in good hands with over the years after the old guys (starting with yours truly) are long gone. His *Tiger! Von schwere Kompanie/SS-Pz.Rgt.2 bis s.SS-Panzerabteilung 102/502* (Bayeux, France: Editions Heimdal, 2008—which he co-authored with Stephan Cazenave) is everything you ever want to know about the 8th (Heavy) Company of Tigers in the *Das Reich*. He also has an added value (*Mehrwert*), as he truly loves his subject, especially because his grandfather, Heinrich, served as the driver for Tiger 813 at the battle for Kharkov and knew many of the men in this book. Thus, Rüdiger has been able to access original source material and meet combatants that perhaps no other author could ever reach; in addition, he contacted several of his acquaintances, such as Bodo Langer. In fact, it is Rüdiger Warnick who found source material showing that Paul Egger was back in Germany at a leadership school and not at the Kursk Offensive, the first historian—I believe—to have discovered this.

I lost count how many times I contacted **Ian Michael Wood**, author of *Tigers of the Death's Head* (Mechanicsburg, Pennsylvania: Stackpole Books, 2013), on everything from when the light panzer platoon was disbanded in each division to personnel information on soldiers in the 9th (Heavy) Company. If the question is about Tiger tanks in the *Totenkopf* Division Mike has the answer.

Col. Schneider, obviously you need to climb into the commander's cupola; Mike, Rüdi, George, and Chris, the other four crew positions are yours!

Dedication

Grandfathers are wonderful people. They allow you to do things that your parents would never, ever consider. When you walk through a store with your parents and you see something that looks interesting, your parents squeeze your hand and tell you to move along, as they have to get going. When you visit a store with your grandfather and you stop to look at something, he often asks you if you want it—and then goes ahead and buys it for you. No matter what time it is, when you ask your parents if you can get something to eat, they say "no" because it is too close to supper. When you and your grandfather are out and see an ice cream store you both get something really great—even if supper is already waiting on the table for you back home.

All grandfathers have stories about the old days. And most of them are very similar. You have heard a thousand times from Gramps, Granddad, Opa, Abuelo, Nonno, Dedushka, or Ojiichan how he had to walk to school every day—five miles there and five miles back, and all of it was uphill. And it usually was raining or snowing. Then there is the story about Christmas, when at age five his new bicycle next to the fireplace had a wheel catch on fire, or how he found a lump of coal in his Christmas stocking that morning instead of candy.

But what would happen one day, while you were reading a book, watching a movie, or texting a friend if your grandfather, sitting in a chair next to you, suddenly asks: "Did I ever tell you about the time I was a Tiger tank driver in Russia during the war?" You stop what you are doing; either grandpa has finally gone over the deep end or you are about to hear a story that maybe your parents have not even heard. And you think that maybe you will never be the same again after you hear it. And you would be correct.

Opa lowers his voice and begins. He was born the son of a laborer in the village of Roßtal, a few miles west of the famous city of Nürnberg in the Franconia region of Bavaria on December 21, 1921. He tells you that he had been an engine mechanic by trade, which made him a special asset to a panzer unit. He tells you that prior to that, he was a member of the Hitler Youth for three years and what that was like; and it sounds like they did a lot more exercise than just walk five miles to school. He says that he used to be six feet tall and weighed 163 pounds when he joined the Waffen-SS on August 20, 1940. Opa hasn't weighed 163 pounds for a long time.

He tells you about going to the big city of Berlin, as shortly after joining the Waffen-SS he was assigned to the 1st Motor Vehicle Replacement Company at Berlin-Lichterfelde; he tells you that his superiors rated his leadership and technical skills to be very good. In mid-November 1940, he transferred to the SS Division *Wiking*, where he was assigned to the 10th Large Motorized Column for Logistics. He tells you about *Operation Barbarossa*, fighting at Tarnopol, Zhitomir, Rostov, and the Mius, sometimes in temperatures under zero, until March 1942, when he was transferred to the panzer detachment in the *Das Reich*. You have read bits and pieces about the *Wiking* and the *Das Reich*—they were hard units and they had hard soldiers—but grandpa has never been tough; in fact, he is always easy going. He tells you that he was lucky in Russia when the division sent him back to Germany to attend a motor vehicle repair course at the Daimler-Benz factory in Stuttgart from May 14 to June 21, 1942, and how he managed to visit his home then.

Then the story really gets interesting. Opa tells you that he was promoted to lance corporal and then corporal on January 1, 1943, as a member of the 8th (Heavy) Company of the *Das Reich*. At the battle for Kharkov he drove Tiger number 812, and the crew nicknamed the big tank "Tiki." He then was posted to the 3rd Company of the 3rd SS Panzer Regiment in the division and went to France to train on a new tank called a Panther and soon became a sergeant. And you find out that ten of his comrades in that Tiger company were killed in action in July 1943, at some place called Kursk—a place that you have never heard about, because your school never told you about those "former times."

He tells you about fighting in Russia and in Normandy, France. He tells you about not being able to move during the day or American fighter-bombers would attack you. He tells about fighting the Americans at the Battle of the Bulge and then how the division moved to Hungary and started fighting the Russians again, and how he had been a "half-platoon" leader in charge of two Panther tanks. Finally he tells you how in April 1945 he took a damaged Tiger I from the Vienna Arsenal and drove west towards the picturesque Melk Abbey, overlooking the Danube River, where he was supposed to join some battle group. Opa says they had a little problem, though. The Tiger had a malfunction and could not turn left when driving forward, so the old engine mechanic, whenever he wanted to go left, would first back up to the right and then go forward to achieve the desired left turn.

He also tells you about marrying Oma on September 30, 1944, but only after both of them had to submit a whole lot of paperwork to Berlin to get Waffen-SS permission. He reminds you that there were no computers or the internet back then and it took a really long time to find all that required information. He tells you that the war ended for him on May 11, 1945, when he went into captivity.

Finally he shows you a little box. Inside you see three small items: an Iron Cross Second Class, a Panzer Battle Badge in Silver, and a Wound Badge in Black. Then it really, really gets interesting. Opa tells you that several of his old tank buddies are still alive and that every so often they get together—and would you like to meet any of them? And from that moment to Opa's death in June 2008, your view of him and history changes forever.

The stories of these predominantly enlisted men is what really happened; not memoirs by officers who wanted to portray themselves in the most favorable light possible. Most of these junior ranks were never regarded as heroes, and even searches on the powerful internet for their names reveals nothing. German schools avoided talking about them in particular, or the war in general, for decades, and even in other countries interest in any type of national history seems to be waning. For those who revel in knowing very little the joke is on them. While they stare at their palms all day into a piece of plastic, you hear and read things that changed world events.

So you tell Opa, whom others know as Heinrich Warnick, that you would love to meet his friends, and sensing an opportunity, ask him if the two of you can go grab an ice cream first.[1]

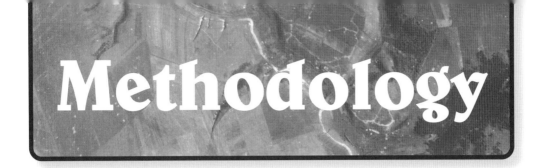

Methodology

This study initially began with the assumption that the most difficult research task for the book would prove to be identifying as many crewmen as possible who fought in the 13th (Heavy) Company, the 8th (Heavy) Company, and the 9th (Heavy) Company in the 2nd SS Panzer Corps during the Kursk Offensive in July 1943. And that has certainly been tough. However, determining what their duty positions were, and in which Tigers they served, was also like trying to find a needle in a haystack.

Part of the difficulty was that the study had to initially rely on secondary sources that were magnificent in describing what happened, but did not concentrate on too many of the crewmen other than selected Tiger commanders, such as Michael Wittmann, Paul Egger, and Franz Staudegger. When crewmen were named it was anecdotal evidence, sometimes derived from the memories of surviving crew. When a memory reveals that Johann Schmidt from East Prussia, an enlisted man with no known date of birth, was a driver for Tiger XX, that does nothing to help find the official personnel file for that soldier in the National Archives.

Additionally, secondary sources are sometimes at odds with each other on which man was at Kursk, his duty position, and his tank. In this case you have to make a judgement on the accuracy, which is doubly difficult when both authors are extremely reputable. Because these prominent authors are so sound, later authors get their facts directly from these previous secondary sources and any errors are perpetuated over and over again. While it may not matter in tactical histories which junior enlisted man was the radio operator for Tiger XX, it does in this book, because the Tiger experience at Kursk would repeat itself at Normandy, the Ardennes, and the 1945 Oder Front, as so many men that fought in Tigers at Kursk remained in Tigers until they were killed, or the war ended.

Then there is the single, short, primary source that overrides multiple secondary sources that are correct on almost everything else. My brother Dave, an excellent US Army armor officer in his own right, calls these events "black swans" because they are both unexpected and impactful. That happened when Rudi Warnick showed me a handwritten six-page letter that Gerhard Kaempf had written him years ago. In the letter the former Tiger gunner explained how he had been seriously wounded in the lung in 1943, and how he had remained in a hospital in the Black Forest until October 1944. In one stroke of his pen Kaempf invalidated every list of Tiger crewmen in the 102nd SS Heavy Panzer Detachment at Normandy that had shown that Gerhard was in the fighting there in summer 1944.

Once the study had names—and some additional ones kept creeping in until close to finishing the book—the next phase was to search through the microfilm of captured German records at the National Archives in College Park, Maryland (not the archives in downtown Washington!), because these are primary source, official Waffen-SS records from that exact period. While mistakes can certainly be made in an official record, normally the information is more accurate than someone's memory forty years later. Equally important, the SS personnel office had no expectation that these records would ever be made public, so there was no reason not to be accurate.

The three primary records groups, all on the fourth floor of the archives, are microfilm copies made in the 1950s and 1960s of captured German records, and there are millions of pages. The first group pertinent to this study is the *SS Officer Personnel Files*, Microfilm Publication A3343, Series SSO. There are more than 900 rolls of microfilm in this group, arranged alphabetically, and then for two people with the same names the oldest date of birth is first. Some 61,000 officers are covered, lieutenants through generals. Some files have dozens of pages; some have one, and unfortunately some officers have no file. There were not that many commissioned officers in the three companies at Kursk, but many enlisted men at Kursk were officer candidates and later were commissioned, and they may have a file. The problem in those cases is that the file has nothing before the time they received their commissions, so Kursk information can be sparse. In most officer files the researcher can verify date and place of birth and some assignments, and if the man was killed in the war. Obviously there is nothing in these files about after the conflict.

The second group of files is named *SS Enlisted Personnel Files*, Microfilm Publication A3343, Series SSEM. While most officers have a personnel file on microfilm, it appears that most enlisted men do not. There are quite a number available so they bear checking. These files are also organized alphabetically and then chronologically. While officer files are pretty standardized, the information for enlisted men is not; you'll find whatever is there—not as much as you'd like, but usually more than is in secondary sources.

Heinrich Himmler wanted control of a great amount of the lives of the people in the SS, both the Allgemeine-SS and Waffen-SS. One area concerned marriage, and an SS man had to send a voluminous amount of papers concerning the health and ancestry of both himself and his prospective bride. This paperwork will almost certainly have date and place of birth, as well as some information about the unit the soldier is in when he submits that request to be approved to marry. On more than one occasion the file would have the name of the company commander, with Michael Wittmann and Alois Kalss having more duties than just destroying enemy tanks. This group of files is known as the *Rasse-und-Siedlungs-Hauptamt (RuSHA) Files*, Microfilm Publication A3343, Series RS, and a valuable resource in many is a photograph of the SS man— sometimes in uniform.

The study created a database and attempted to obtain data for the following fields:

Last name
First name
Date of birth
Rank at Kursk
SS#
Date joined SS
Prior Luftwaffe (yes/no)
Height
Company
Platoon
Tiger Crew #1
Tiger Crew #2 (i.e., was on more than 1)
Wounded during Kursk Offensive
Awards during career (and dates)
Position on tank (at Kursk)
Duration at Kursk Offensive
Departed battle for
Highest rank in war

Officer (yes/no)
Cause of death
Place of birth
Married
Children
Killed or missing during the war
Survived the war
Date of death
Place of death
Later in 101st SS Heavy Panzer Detachment
Later in 102nd SS Heavy Panzer Detachment
Later in 103rd SS Heavy Panzer Detachment
Later in 501st SS Heavy Panzer Detachment
Later in 502nd SS Heavy Panzer Detachment
Burial location
Tank combat experience before Kursk
Tiger combat experience before Kursk
Infantry experience
Remarks
NARA Reel Number

Some of these categories will become clearer in the study. A few categories are just interesting facts, and others—such as whether the soldier had prior combat experience on a panzer or prior combat experience on a Tiger—can lead us to some interesting conclusions. The database was sortable, which helped immensely in research. More importantly the software was easy to use, so the experience remained concentrating on history and not software programming.

Then came the fun part: analyzing photographs of Waffen-SS Tiger tanks at Kursk. Many had turret numbers that told the company; with the database complete, intelligent conclusions could be made on the identity of some of the crewmen in the photographs. Knowing details about which Tigers were operational on each day narrowed the dates for some of the photographs, while shadows sometimes could help tell whether the photograph had been taken in the morning or afternoon. Hopefully future historians can use this information to push our understanding of the Kursk Offensive even farther.

In the end, you can be the judge of how much and how important the information is and the extent in which it is complete. It was my decision, and no one else's, to follow the dictum: "Don't let perfect be the enemy of good enough." That is especially true when you are a senior author. Far better to see your work in print and appreciated by some than to never finish it at all because there must be one more fact out there to be found.

The Tiger Tank

Genesis

The date was May 26, 1941, when two very accomplished men in Germany engaged in a duel of gigantic proportions. They were not armed with pistols or sabers, but with slide rules, as it was not a fight to the death, but a competition of how to turn forty-five tons of tough Krupp steel into a *Durchbruchswagen* (breakthrough vehicle) for the German Army. It was to be a radical new type of panzer, because it would carry a radical new type of cannon based on the superb 88 mm gun. A ground breaking task in more ways than one: they had to be ready by June 1942.

The decision to move forward with this breakthrough vehicle was made at the Berghof, Hitler's famous Eagle's Nest at Berchtesgaden.[1] The war was going well for Germany. France, Belgium, the Netherlands, and Norway had been crushed a year before. German forces in Africa had launched Operation Scorpion and advanced to Halfaya Pass. The German airborne invasion of Crete was nearing a successful conclusion—albeit with horrendous losses to the paratroopers—within just a few days. On the border of the German empire and the Soviet Union, Operation Barbarossa—the invasion of Stalin's Communist empire—was only four weeks away. Hitler was on a roll; only in the Atlantic was there bad news. Although the super battleship *Bismarck* had recently sunk the HMS *Hood* and heavily damaged the HMS *Prince of Wales*, May 26, 1941, was the last day the pride of the Third Reich would remain afloat, sinking the next day after a furious fight with superior British forces.

The two combatants for the tank prize were Dr. Erwin Aders, chief designer at the firm of Henschel and Son in Kassel, Germany; and Dr. Ferdinand Porsche, leader of his own company Dr. Ing. h. c. F. Porsche AG in Stuttgart. The "mad scientist" Porsche and Dr. Aders—a dour, balding man replete with a small white moustache and who looked like he sharpened pencils for entertainment—went to work.

The field of honor to determine the winning design would be not all that far from the Wolf's Lair—the headquarters of the Führer—outside of Rastenburg in East Prussia. The date would be April 20, 1942—easily remembered by all, as it was the Führer's birthday. The men designed; the engineers measured; and the steel makers, machine operators, and welders put together their prototypes. The German invasion of the Soviet Union on June 22, 1941, added an impetus to not exceed the deadline, as Germany was now faced with dangerous heavy tanks fielded by the Red Army—tanks that caused surprise and shock among the German Army panzer crews.[2]

Henschel and Son was a venerable German industrial giant; if the task was to bend large pieces of steel, the boys at Henschel could do it. Established in the early 1800s, Henschel made a name for itself building railroad locomotives, some of the best in the world. Seeing a new market for their talents, Henschel began manufacturing various armaments in the Great War. In 1918, those weapons became *verboten* under the Versailles Treaty so Henschel went back to big trains. Then came *Herr* Hitler in the 1930s, and the cash registers at Henschel & Sohn, and many other armaments related firms, began "ka-chinging" again.[3]

But Henschel did not have the capacity to weld massive armor plates and thus received tank hulls from two firms—Dortmund-Hörder Hüttenverein, in Dortmund; and Friedrich Krupp AG in Essen. Henschel received turrets from Wegmann and Company right there in Kassel.[4]

The clock ticked and the time came, and Henschel almost didn't make it. Part of the reason was interference by the Führer on the details. For example, in July 1941, Hitler directed that a tapered bore main gun would not be used in the vehicle, causing ramifications in the turret design.[5] Krupp sent the first hull by train on January 3, 1942, but the first turret did not arrive at Henschel until April 11, 1942. The engineers were finally able to mate together both major components on April 15, 1942. Forty minutes before the special train at Werk III was scheduled to depart for the test ground, racing technicians finished the Henschel prototype and loaded it on a flatcar.[6] The prototype Tigers arrived on April 19; a seventy-five-ton steam crane unloaded the heavy tanks from their railroad flatcars.[7]

Both prototypes had flaws; Henschel had problems with the clutch, radiator, and brake, while the Porsche model had a troubled gasoline electric hybrid power unit. The Army wanted a mechanical transmission for the Tiger, but Ferdinand Porsche was having serious doubts about the practicability of using such a mechanical unit. So he designed an electric motor similar to the diesel electric drives in powerful railroad locomotives. The power would be supplied by gasoline engines connected to electrical generators.[8]

Hitler looked and relooked, watched the two vehicles be put through a driving course—in which the Porsche model reached a speed of 50 kilometers per hour (31 mph) and the Henschel hit 45 kilometers per hour (28 mph)—and despite the fact that he leaned toward the Porsche design, the leader of Greater Germany . . . could not make up his mind.[9]

It would not be the last time that Adolf Hitler was indecisive with respect to an aspect of the battle of Kursk. He turned to Albert Speer, Reich Minister of Armaments and War Production; Speer would not only decide which firm should produce the vehicle, but also to go ahead with the anticipated series production. Speer, in turn, turned to Colonel Wolfgang Thomale, recently the commander of the 27th Panzer Regiment in the 19th Panzer Division on the Eastern Front and a winner of the prestigious Knight's Cross of the Iron Cross. Thomale was intimately familiar with not only German panzers but also the lethal Soviet tanks, primarily the T-34 and the KV-1. He directed that the two prototypes, Tiger (P) and Tiger (H), be sent to the Berka Training Area (near Eisenach) for the period November 8–14, 1942; he assembled a team, tested the vehicles—that included Albert Speer actually test driving them—and made the recommendation to Hitler to produce the Henschel version, which the Führer accepted.[10] The Tigers were also tested at the automotive proving grounds near Kummersdorf (*Kraftfahrversuchstelle Kummersdorf*), south of Berlin.[11] Ironically, the Tigers took many of their first steps at Kummersdorff in May 1942, and at Kummersdorff the last Tigers to die for the Third Reich fell at the beginning of May 1945.

The Weapon

Each finished Tiger cost a quarter million Reichsmarks—two and one-half times the cost of a Mark IV tank and just more than twice the cost of a Mark V Panther tank—weighed about sixty tons, was just over twenty feet long (over twenty-seven feet long with the main gun facing forward), was a few inches over eleven feet wide, and was nine feet ten inches tall.[12] The turret by itself weighed eleven tons, more than the overall weight of many light tanks on the battlefield. The six-hundred-ninety horsepower Maybach engine could propel the tank to a sustained speed of twenty-five miles per hour on roads and up to sixteen miles per hour cross country, all while slurping so much fuel that the operational range of the vehicle was only one hundred and twenty-one miles on the road and a miniscule sixty-eight miles over hill and dale. After the go ahead, by the end of 1942, Henschel & Son had produced eighty-three vehicles.[13]

During this period one could not think of the central German city of Kassel without thinking of the three huge Henschel works in and near there. They were busy places; during the war production was round the clock, conducted by two twelve-hour shifts. Noise was incessant, and workers were constantly moving: to work; at work; and going home. Werk I, in Kassel, produced locomotives and guns; Werk II, a large foundry at Rothenditmold (in the northern section of the city), made boilers and other large locomotive components. But it was Werk III in Mittlefeld (just north of Rothenditmold) where most Tigers were born.[14]

The 8,000 workers at Werk III scurried about two main shops within which the tanks were assembled. They bustled about the sheds that held Tiger turrets and hulls. And they raced to put finished Tigers on railroad cars and take parts made elsewhere out of arriving railcars coming in on dozens of spur lines. There was a method to the madness. Production managers developed a nine-step manufacturing system to create a Tiger from scratch.[15] Even so, supply could not keep up with requirements.

Armor plates were mostly flat (not sloped as on many tanks), almost four inches thick on the front hull and front turret, about two and a half inches thick on the hull side plates, and just over three inches thick on the side of the turret. Bottom armor was only one inch thick; enemy gunners were taught that their only chance was to attack from the rear and hope they scored a mobility hit. Like most items on the Tiger, the armor plating was over-engineered. Armor joints were not riveted, as was done on many tanks, but were interlocking and welded of a special class of low carbon, ultra-high-strength steel called maraging steel. Overall, the Tiger had sufficient armor to stop most shots of the Soviet 76 mm guns, except at very close range. One part of the Tiger was weak: the commander's cupola. This projection from the top of the turret was capped by the commander's hatch and served as the point of entrance through which the commander entered and exited the turret. There were several vision slits around its round circumference. Although it had some armor it was not welded solid to the turret, and enemy antitank rounds could often cause the cupola to shear off, killing the tank commander if he was inside.[16]

The vaunted 88 mm main gun (8,8 cm Kampfwagenkanone 36 L/56), which should not be confused with the antiaircraft gun of the same caliber, could destroy any enemy tank on the battlefield in July 1943, often at great ranges. The weapon had a maximum elevation of fifteen degrees and a maximum depression of minus eight degrees.[17] Soviet engineers, using a captured Tiger I in field trials, measured that the Tiger's main gun round could penetrate the front armor—the thickest on the vehicle—of the superb T-34 tank at a range of up to 1,500 meters.

The gun could fire several types of projectile and the Tiger could carry ninety-two rounds, although in certain command Tigers this was reduced to sixty-six because of extra equipment onboard. These projectiles usually consisted of high explosive fragmentation shells (*Sprenggranaten*) and armor piercing, capped, ballistic cap with explosive filler and tracer (*Panzergrenate 39*) shells that could penetrate four inches of armor at 1,000 meters with a hit probability of ninety-three percent. When they were available, the Tiger could carry *Panzergrenate 40* rounds—armor piercing, composite rigid with a sub-caliber tungsten core that could penetrate five and a half inches of armor at 1,000 meters with a hit probability of eighty percent. The #40 was not as lethal after penetration as the #39 because it did not explode inside as the former round did.[18] So the commander and gunner would develop "what if" situations based on the type of enemy tank and range. Another type of round that was produced in lesser lumbers was the high explosive antitank (HEAT) round *Panzergrenate 39 HL*, with a shaped charge that could penetrate three and a half inches of armor at 1,000 meters with a hit probability of sixty-two percent. That was less than the other two antitank rounds, but the #39 HL was dual purpose and could also be used against soft targets.[19] Determining the ninety-two shells to carry in the Tiger became as much an art as a science.

Made by the renowned optical firm of Ernst Leitz G.m.b.H. in Wetzlar, the main gun sight (T.Z.F.9b) on the Tiger was two-and-one-half power strength (2.5×); it did not have an advanced range finder, but used some adjustable range scales. This placed a premium on the gunner and tank commander being able to accurately estimate the correct range to the target. The process went as follows: the tank commander ordered the target selection, type of ammunition, and estimated the range. The gunner laid the gun on the target, fired the weapon, observed the strike of the round, and reported his observations to the tank commander. The tank commander ordered corrections if he wanted another round fired at the target or searched for a new target and repeated the process.[20]

Crews were taught that they could open fire immediately and attempt to obtain a first round hit at enemy tanks at ranges of 1,200 meters or less. At greater ranges than 1,200 meters the crew was instructed to use bracketing fire with jumps of 200 or 400 meters and switching to fire for effect when the strike of the last round was within 100 meters of the target. The expected performance of a good crew was that the gunner would hit the target by the fourth round at ranges from 1,200 to 2,000 meters. In exceptional cases an individual tank could fire at a stationary enemy tank at 2,000 to 2,500 meters. When firing at moving enemy tanks crews were instructed not to fire at ranges greater than 2,000 meters.[21]

When a platoon was firing together at stationary enemy tanks, they were permitted to engage out to 3,000 meters.[22] As the combination of tank commander gunner became more experienced together the process got quicker and quicker. Knowing what the expected target would be and the most likely range allowed for the loader to "pre-load" a round before the tank commander gave the command concerning type of ammunition, which could cut a few seconds off the engagement time. Crews that had already proven to be excellent shots were often permitted to shoot at the enemy at almost any range that the tank commander decided was prudent. *SS-Rottenführer* Balthasar "Bobby" Woll, a Tiger gunner discussed in this study, always set his range finder to 800 meters and then adjusted should a second round be necessary.[23]

Combat against enemy tanks was treated as an art form, with some of the brush strokes described here:[24]

> Independent, swift handling by the company commander and strict control of the company with short, clear orders are the basis for success. Immediately attacking is usually the best solution. The enemy is to be repeatedly fooled and confused by constant changes in the methods of attack . . . Open fire from ambush out of favorable positions (hull down or positions along edges of forest, towns, etc). at effective ranges and from unexpected directions. During counterattacks by enemy tanks, build a fire front and send elements to engage them with flanking fire. Let the enemy tanks close range. Shut down the engine in order to hear better. Destroy the enemy with a counterstrike. Envelop or bypass through difficult terrain. Go into action against the flanks and rear by exploiting the sun's position, the wind direction and the ground cover. If a strong defensive front is unexpectedly encountered, along with tank obstacles, immediately withdraw from the enemy fire and renew the attack from an unexpected position.

The Tiger I also carried two 7.92 mm Model 1934 machine guns: one mounted in the hull and the other in the turret coaxially with the main gun. These were used to keep enemy infantrymen at bay and in some cases to suppress nearby antitank guns. Neither was much use against enemy aircraft. Some ingenious crews used the turret machine gun as a range finder for the 88 mm cannon. The gunner would traverse the turret and begin firing the machine gun, whose ammunition belts contained tracer rounds. Once the tracers were observed hitting the target—a fortified village perhaps—the gunner would read the range and use that information to fire the main gun high explosive rounds to hit the same point of impact. The company commander's Tiger had no turret machine gun; in its place was an additional radio set. This modification would result in the death of one company commander at Kursk.[25]

Other aspects of mobility helped determine where a Tiger could go and where it could not go. A Tiger could cross a trench that was no wider than 2.5 meters. Since the Soviets had previously captured a Tiger they knew this. Concerning crossing streams, if the bottom of the stream consisted of gravel or small rocks the Tiger could ford the stream up to a depth of 1.6 meters. If the streambed was muddy or had boulders the tank could not ford, and if the water was deeper than 1.6 meters, regardless of streambed condition, the Tiger could not cross. The Tiger could climb a gradient of up to 35 degrees. Finally, the Tiger had a ground clearance of 0.47 meters (18.5 inches). Obstacles higher than that could cause the Tiger to become immobile if it drove over them. This included large, blown down tree trunks that could not only cause a Tiger to have problems driving over them between the tracks, but if the trunk was partially under one of the two tracks it could cause that track to be thrown off the drive sprocket, stopping the Tiger and causing a disaster for the crew.[26]

Doctrine

To understand how the Tiger tanks in the 2nd SS Panzer Corps were used during the Kursk Offensive, we must first understand how the German Army wanted them to be employed on the battlefield, and to do that we must first review the doctrine for their use. After several months of reviewing Tigers in combat in late 1942–early 1943, the army determined that it must publish doctrine to maximize the strengths of the vehicles and eliminate mistakes that had already been made in combat. By May 20, 1943, doctrine writers had published two documents: the heavy tank company and the heavy tank battalion.[27]

To begin, the manual on the heavy tank company established four underlying principles for their use. These were:[28]

1. Destroy heavy enemy tanks and other armored targets at long ranges
2. Attack in the first wave against strong defenses
3. Use to decisively defeat the enemy defenses
4. Break through positions reinforced by defensive works

The manual devoted its first segment to the organization of the heavy tank company. More important to this study, the second half outlined basic tactical guidance, followed by a discussion on formations that would best achieve those tactical goals. "The most important task of the heavy tank company is the engagement of enemy tanks. It always has priority over every other assignment." Offense at the decisive point was paramount to force a decision.[29]

To accomplish their tasks, especially in tank-versus-tank combat, platoons were instructed to employ one of the following four formations:[30]

1. **Column**: all four tanks following one another. While this did not place overwhelming firepower to the front, if a platoon was negotiating an enemy minefield in a hasty fashion, driving in the same path as the tank in front could minimize mine strikes. It was also the obvious formation for road movement.
2. **Line**: all four tanks online, left to right. This formation allowed every tank to fire forward and presented simultaneous multiple targets to an enemy antitank gun, which might cause confusion for enemy gunners and thus slow their fires.
3. **Double column**: this looked like a box, with two Tigers forward and two following roughly behind them. The advantage was that in addition to moving forward, it could respond well to the right or left against an unanticipated threat.
4. **Wedge**: this looked like an upside down V, with one tank in front, two tanks slightly to the rear and flanks, and the last tank either on the far left or far right, depending on terrain and anticipated direction of enemy threats. The manual stated that the wedge was the preferred formation for the attack.

The company also had formations from which to choose based on the mission, threat, and terrain:[31]

1. **Column**: with the three platoons each in their own column abreast of each other
2. **Double column**: with the platoons in two columns
3. **Wedge**: one platoon in front with the other two platoons behind; looked like an upside-down V; the platoons themselves were also in wedges
4. **Broad Wedge**: two platoons forward and one platoon behind; looked like a V. The manual stated that the broad wedge was the most useful formation in the attack. To be able to better see all his vehicles the Tiger company commander's tank was usually toward the center of this formation

During the Kursk Offensive Colonel General Hermann Hoth, the commander of the 4th Panzer Army, would follow these doctrinal recommendations closely, placing the Tigers in the lead, with Mark III and Mark IV panzers following.[32] This would form the notable *Panzerkeil* (tank wedge) offensive armored formation that would be used numerous times on the southern attack axis at Kursk.[33]

Concerning distances between individual tanks, a company broad wedge occupied an area 700 meters wide by 400 meters deep. Given that the February 28, 1943, memorandum—signed by Adolf Hitler—concerning the assignment of duties of the Inspector General of Panzer Troops entitled Colonel General Heinz Guderian to direct the panzer troops in the Waffen-SS and Luftwaffe in matters of organization and training, it is logical to believe that the Tiger crews in the 2nd SS Panzer Corps would have received this doctrinal maneuver, fire, and general combat information before the offensive began.[34]

As with every other model panzer, units receiving Tiger tanks sent their crews to a panzer school. The Panzer School at Paderborn was designated to train Tiger crews. During the period that the Waffen-SS crews received their Tigers Captain Hannibal von Lüttichau was the commander of this school. Von Lüttichau was a highly respected panzer officer that would later command the 509th Heavy Panzer Battalion of Tiger tanks and receive the Knight's' Cross of the Iron Cross.[35]

Co-located at Paderborn was the head of training for the Inspectorate of Armored Troops Lieutenant Colonel Hans Christern, who had served in the panzers since 1938 and had been a tactics instructor at the Panzer School in Wünsdorf. Christern, who had already received the Knight's' Cross of the Iron Cross for his actions during the 1940 French Campaign and would later command the 7th Panzer Division at the end of the war, recognized that he had a significant challenge.[36] While the crews for units receiving Tigers for the first time would return to Paderborn, later replacements to Tiger units might not. What the German Army needed were manuals to assist units to train themselves in the field, but the traditional manuals were so difficult to wade through that forty-three-year-old Christern probably doubted that many soldiers ever attempted to read them.

So he turned to a younger officer who might better understand the learning patterns of the young soldiers that would crew the Tigers. Twenty-eight-year-old Lieutenant Josef von Glatter-Götz, who was born in Jägerndorf, Austria, took the task to heart and conceived a manual that not only would be read by the young troops, but also ensured that these soldiers would retain what they read and learned. Von Glatter-Götz used limericks; he used puns; he used risqué illustrations of young women—especially a blond named Elvira; and he used slang that the young troops understood. And most importantly, he got the attention of the young men training on the Tiger. Titled *Tigerfibel*, which means "Tiger primer," it was different in another respect: it had no swastikas or other Nazi Party symbols.

The entire aura of *Tigerfibel* was unique in one other key aspect. Josef von Glatter-Götz was not a career military officer. He was not a panzer expert, nor was he a weapon's engineer. Josef was an artist, and he built some of the greatest European church organs the world had ever heard played. Established by Franz Rieger about 1845, in Schwarzach, Austria, not far from Lake Constance, Franz Rieger & Sons ascended to the pinnacle of organ making by winning a gold medal at the Viennese World Exhibition in 1873. In 1924, Austrian Lieutenant Colonel Josef von Glatter-Götz, a former member of the General Staff of the Imperial Army of Austria-Hungary, purchased the firm after having assumed the position of General Manager after the Great War. Progress went smoothly until 1938, when the company turned from organ making to building war supplies.[37]

It was natural, then, for the son of this general staff officer, young Josef von Glatter-Götz, to enter the family business, which he did about 1930, advancing to an organ builder apprenticeship before continuing his studies in Breslau and Berlin, where in 1936 he earned an engineering degree in the field.[38] In 1938, his services not needed to build ammunition crates and other wooden military items, he entered the Germany Army. He would return to Rieger Orgelbau after the war in 1946 and lead the company, but now his main mission was to assist the crews in the Tiger tank to play beautiful music with their special machine.[39] Thanks to Josef's manual they did. There was only one problem with *Tigerfibel*: it was not published until August 1, 1943—over two weeks after the Kursk Offensive ended.

Tiger Killers

Tiger tanks at Kursk were not invulnerable, although many a Russian soldier probably thought otherwise. Tiger tank crews had a healthy respect for several types of enemy heavy antitank guns, IL-2 *Sturmovik* ground attack aircraft, SU-152 assault guns, and the rarely seen KV-2 tank, but also understood that additional types of enemy weapons could cause a mobility kill to their panzer. The following Soviet weapons and combat multipliers present at the Kursk Offensive could damage and sometimes even destroy a Tiger tank.

Antitank Rifles

One would assume that the ubiquitous Russian 14.5 mm antitank rifle could do little against a Tiger, and one would be correct. Rounds from the weapon could splinter viewing periscopes and vision blocks, but do little more.[40] As there were some 15,259 antitank rifles deployed against the southern German attack pincer at Kursk, there may have been several thousand of these weapons in the attack zone of the 2nd SS Panzer Corps at Kursk, and in every case but one they had little effect on a Tiger.[41] The only exception occurred when a Tiger commander had his head blown off by an antitank rifle when he was exposed in the cupola.

Flamethrowers

Flamethrowers could certainly destroy any tank on the battlefield, but the weapon had an extremely short range, and also had a signature that made it highly visible to the enemy. Soviet man portable flamethrowers at the battle carried 2.4 gallons of fuel and had an effective range of twenty-five meters. The Soviets deployed a special flamethrower battalion along the 2nd SS Panzer Corps route of advance at the village of Yakhontov but the Tigers avoided it.[42] Flamethrowers were a ferocious weapon and had a psychological effect on tank crews if thought to be in the area—being burned to death inside a tank was a fearsome thought.

Antitank Guns

The Soviets at Kursk deployed several types of antitank guns: the 45 mm (M-42), the 57 mm (ZiS-2), the 76.2 mm (ZiS-3), the 85 mm (1939), and the 122 mm gun. The 45 mm was pretty helpless against a Tiger; a lucky hit on a track or drive sprocket could cause damage though. The 57 mm could penetrate the side of the body of the Tiger at 900 meters and the rear of the hull at 500 meters; shooting at the turret seems to have been a waste of ammunition. But the rounds had limited explosive effect; there were only a limited number of these weapons at Kursk. The 76.2 mm had more explosive power but really needed to engage a Tiger at no more than five hundred meters.

The 85 mm Model 1939 could penetrate the side hull of a Tiger at 1,450 meters and could do serious damage from the front at 1,000 meters; there were some 225 85 mm antiaircraft cannon in the area of the southern attack pincer at Kursk. The 122 mm howitzer, with 480 deployed against the southern attack pincer, and the 152 mm howitzer, with 144 deployed against the Fourth Panzer Army at Kursk, could also destroy a Tiger.[43] Direct hits on the turret from antitank guns, while not penetrating the armor, could cause sufficient interior concussion to produce nosebleeds and ringing in the ears of the tank commander, loader, and gunner.

As the 2nd SS Panzer Corps attacked it penetrated units of the Sixth Guards Army, most specifically the 375th Rifle Division, the 51st Guards Rifle Division, and the 52nd Guards Rifle Division. Altogether, on July 4, 1943, these units fielded ninety-nine 45 mm guns, ninety-three 76.2 mm guns, and twenty-two 122 mm howitzers. The Sixth Guards Army additionally had 132 45 mm guns, 205 76.2 mm guns, thirty-six 122 mm guns, and thirty-six 152 mm guns in separate units that could be moved about the battlefield.[44] The closest mobile antitank reserve that could respond to the 2nd SS Panzer Corps attack was the 1440th Self-Propelled Artillery Regiment, with nine SU-76 assault guns (open topped) and twelve SU-122 assault guns.[45] Both used the same model howitzer as that in the towed artillery.

Tiger crews had several options after realizing that an enemy antitank gun was firing at them—the key was picking an option quickly and executing it before the enemy could fire a second shot. The commander could decide to fire smoke dischargers to partially obscure the Tiger. The driver could drive the vehicle to orient the front of the Tiger—where the armor was thickest—toward the antitank weapon, so if the enemy did fire a second shot it would have less effect. Third, the radio operator and the gunner could immediately fire long bursts of machine gun fire (hull machine gun and coaxial machine gun) at the antitank crew to cause the enemy crew to take cover, which would delay their follow-on shot. Another option occurred before the engagement began, if the commander and crew made an assessment that based on the terrain and information about the enemy the most likely threat would come from an antitank gun. In that case, the loader would load a high explosive round in the breach of the 88 mm, which was far more effective against an antitank gun than an armor piercing round would be.

However, the Soviets were not dumb. They assumed that Tigers would lead the attack in many sectors, so they formed antitank fronts composed of ten antitank guns. Knowing that the Germans would destroy many of the guns, Soviet officers believed that with ten weapons some would survive and be able to shoot the German vehicles in the flank or rear, or failing that, engage lesser armored German vehicles following the Tigers.

Tanks and Assault Guns

The T-70 light tank appeared all over the battlefield at Kursk; fortunately for the Tiger crews the T-70 mounted the 45 mm gun. The most capable Russian tank at Kursk was the famous T-34/76 armed with the 76.2 mm tank gun M1940 F-34, which could be effective at less than five hundred meters. At Kursk the T-34 had one other vulnerability: a two-man turret. Thus the tank commander was also the gunner, which presented all types of efficiency problems; one of the most crucial was a slower rate of fire. The KV-1 heavy tank, also with a 76.2 mm tank gun, was nearing the end of its operational life, as was the KV-2 heavy tank that packed the short barrel 152.4 mm M1938 (M-10) howitzer. Such a projectile could heavily damage a Tiger, but both the muzzle velocity and the rate of fire were very slow. One source indicates that the Voronezh Front opposite the Fourth Panzer Army had 105 KV-1s.[46]

The closest Sixth Guards Army mobile tank reserves that could respond to the 2nd SS Panzer Corps attack were the 230th Tank Regiment to the west, with twelve Lend-Lease US M3 Grant tanks and twenty-seven M-3 Stuart tanks; the 245th Tank Regiment, which was similarly equipped; and the 96th Tank Brigade with five T-70s and forty-six T-34 tanks.[47] As the Fifth Guards Tank Army began to arrive near Prokhorovka, Soviet armor strength skyrocketed with the addition of 208 T-70 tanks, 389 T-34 tanks, eighteen Lend Lease British Churchill tanks, one KV-1 tank, seventeen SU-76 assault guns, and twenty-four SU-122 assault guns. Opposing the 2nd SS Panzer Corps north of the Psel River, meanwhile, were elements of the First Tank Army. In addition to the tanks and assault guns mentioned above, this organization possessed a dozen SU-152 assault guns, nicknamed *Zveroboy* ("Beast Slayer").[48] The nickname came from the ability of the SU-152 to defeat the German Panther and Tiger tanks, deadly beasts in the eyes of Russian soldiers.

The SU-122 was a vicious little vehicle; based on a T-34 chassis and standing only 7'7" tall, it could hide undetected in the numerous folds of the battlefield. Armed with a 122 mm howitzer M1938 (M-30), the weapon fired a high explosive shell that could cause significant damage to the track and suspension system of a Tiger. The gun had no muzzle brake, and therefore was harder to detect when it fired (guns with muzzle brakes frequently redirected the muzzle blast toward the ground, where it often raised a cloud of dust on dry ground in the summer that could be seen from hundreds of yards away).

Aircraft

Soviet ground attack aircraft, especially the IL-2 *Sturmovik* "the Flying Tank," could destroy a Tiger with bombs and 20 mm cannon, as the armor on the top of the tank was only about one inch thick. Although the 1st Assault Aviation Corps—with some 288 *Sturmoviks*—flew over the sector of the 2nd SS Panzer Corps at Kursk, it does not appear that any Waffen-SS Tiger was destroyed or even damaged by an enemy air attack during the July 5 to July 15 period.

Armored Trains

It may sound counterintuitive, but armored railroad trains played an active role on the Eastern Front for much of the war. In mid-1943, the Soviets fielded many categories of trains, one of the best being a Type BP-43, built around an armored PR-43 locomotive. The armored train additionally often pulled four artillery cars and two antiaircraft cars. Most antiaircraft cars each mounted two 37 mm antiaircraft guns, while the armored artillery cars each had up to four 76.2 mm guns, often mounted in T-34 turrets. Despite its weight—some cars had up to 45 mm of side armor—an armored train could approach speeds of thirty miles per hour; a somewhat difficult target to hit from the ground, but easier picking if the Luftwaffe was in the area.[49] Sixteen 76.2 mm tank guns firing simultaneously could do some damage, not to mention a potential pair of 107 mm cannon, as the Tigers found out on July 7, 1943.

Mines

Soviet antitank mines would not kill a Tiger tank, but they could immobilize it by blowing off a tread, damaging the suspension system, or harming the tank's transmission, such as breaking a reduction gear; this was a precarious situation, as Gerhard Kaempf, gunner in Tiger **S31** and Tiger **S22** of the 8th (Heavy Company) of the *Das Reich* later said: "A panzer that could not move was soon a candidate for death."[50] These mines caused damage by their blast effect; the TM-35 mine, for example, had an explosive content of 6.17 pounds of TNT.

An antitank mine could also wound the driver or radio operator, who sat in the hull of the tank (e.g. not the turret) that was lower to the ground and thus closer to the blast. The Soviets understood this and sited antitank guns, dug-in tanks, artillery concentration points, and even flamethrowers to cover every minefield, both to impede German pioneers from clearing a path through the field and to inflict more damage on a tank already immobilized from a mine. To add misery to the German pioneers' task, the Soviets also emplaced large numbers of antipersonnel mines in every minefield to kill or maim these specialized counter mine troops.[51]

The attack zone of the 2nd SS Panzer Corps had the objective of penetrating two defensive belts of the Soviet Sixth Guards Army, each generously protected by both types of mine. In the first echelon of defenses the 52nd Guards Infantry Division stood ready, occupying a frontage of 13.5 kilometers (8.38 miles). Soviet engineers had been busy that spring, and anticipating where the Germans would attack, had laid 1,220 antitank and 1,051 antipersonnel mines per kilometer of this frontage. Several miles north of the 52nd Guards Rifle Division stood the Soviet second echelon of defenses, and in the 2nd SS Panzer Corps attack zone this meant the 51st Guards Rifle Division. The second echelon did not have as many mines, but it was still formidable. With a frontage of 14.4 kilometers, there were 242 antitank and thirty-three antipersonnel mines per kilometer. Not included in these totals for the Sixth Guards Army were special munitions buried a few feet underground at mobility chokepoints. Constructed of artillery shells, these 21,000 "improvised explosive devices" were deadly, especially when wired to a 152 mm howitzer shell.[52]

To negotiate enemy minefields unit commanders and tank commanders had three options, any of which had advantages and disadvantages. First, they could press forward and hope that they would not run over a mine, or if they did, that it would cause little damage. If you did move straight forward and take a direct route through a minefield you had to ensure that you stayed in the exact same track marks that the Tiger front of you made. Second, you could stop and let attached dismounted pioneers clear safe lanes through the minefield—which took time—and then go through these safe lanes. Another danger of this option was that the enemy often wanted you to temporarily halt, because it made it easier for their nearby antitank weapons to hit your stationary vehicle. Or third, you could search for the edge of the minefield and drive around it on safe ground.

Antitank Ditches

Typical Soviet antitank ditches at Kursk came in many sizes, including twenty feet wide and seven to ten feet deep and twenty-seven feet wide and sixteen feet deep.[53] Antitank ditches would not damage a Tiger unless the driver drove over the edge of the trench, causing the tank to fall into it and probably injuring some of the crew members. The idea of an antitank trench was to funnel enemy tanks around the trench and into a pre-planned kill zone of mines, antitank guns, and other weapons. At Kursk several Russian soldiers reported seeing a few Tigers deliberately enter antitank ditches and then drive toward the far side of the trench at an angle so that the treads of the tank would begin to claw down the side, permitting the panzer to eventually climb up the ramp of soil formed by the maneuver.[54]

Timber obstacles, sometimes called *abatis*, could also slow down an enemy attack, although high explosive shells or demolitions emplaced by pioneers could sometimes neutralize them. Barbed wire obstacles are not generally thought of as tank immobilizers, but in some cases, if the wire is dense enough, it can wrap around the front drive sprockets and cause mobility problems, such as causing a thrown track. Generally, though, the Tigers avoided the patches of woods they encountered moving forward.

A thrown track can be pure hell for the crew and can be the result of poor maintenance; bad driving technique; poor "tank terrain" such as deep sand, large rocks, thick mud, and downed trees; poor tank commander instructions to the driver; and the effects of enemy weapons and obstacles. The thrown track can either be to the outside or even to the inside—where it is partially under the tank—which is even worse. It may take hours to get the track back on the tank and in working order; sometimes the crew can accomplish this by themselves, but often it requires mechanics from the recovery section to come forward and assist them. During the entire procedure to repair a thrown track the crew is extremely vulnerable to enemy fire.

In the first echelon 52nd Guards Rifle Division the Soviets constructed 17.8 kilometers of antitank trenches, one kilometer of timber obstacles, and thirty-six kilometers of barbed wire obstacles. At the second echelon defensive positions there were 600 meters of antitank ditches, 3.1 kilometers of timber obstacles, and 27.5 kilometers of barbed wire obstacles in the sector of the 51st Guards Rifle Division.[55]

Part of the confusion surrounding tank losses at Kursk is based on whether or not a tank was considered totally destroyed or damaged to some lesser degree. Clearly a tank that was hit by a powerful antitank shell that then caused a massive internal secondary explosion, which for instance then caused the turret to fly off, would be a total write-off. Lesser damage took a Tiger out of action, making it non-operational. If the enemy captured a non-operational tank that vehicle was a total write-off. Some immobilized tanks could be fixed right on the battlefield if damage was minimal. Others could be made operational by the next morning through the efforts of mechanics working all night at repair facilities. Still others would require from two to four days before reaching operational status.[56]

The Crew

The crew on any tank had to operate as a team; if the team had a weak link combat could swiftly expose that, resulting in damage to the tank, injury to the crew, or quickly replacing the crewman that could not measure up. Each of the five crew members of a Tiger had specific tasks related to his military skill and some general tasks that were specialty independent.

Commander: often the senior soldier in the vehicle, the commander was responsible for everything the vehicle did or failed to do. The commander directed the movement of the vehicle, giving general driving instructions on speed, direction of movement, and perhaps the next halting position. Additionally, the commander would provide orders for engaging the enemy—directing the gunner's attention to a specific target, often the most immediate danger to the Tiger. The commander often directed what type of ammunition to fire. The commander would also provide guidance on tactics, especially if he also served as the platoon leader or company commander. Concerning communication, the Tiger commander would give his superior (platoon leader in most cases) updates, such as how much ammunition and fuel remained and the status of the crew.

The commander had his own hatch on the top of the Tiger; he operated inside the turret on the left side and was to the rear and above the gunner. To increase their own vision and battlefield awareness, German tank commanders were encouraged to stand in the hatch with at least the top third of their bodies exposed. While it did increase situational awareness, as they could see farther, it also led to increased casualties among panzer commanders. The commander was responsible for firing smoke dischargers by means of three push buttons on each side of his seat. As the official manual summarized the role of the commander: "Only your clarity of thought, your assured order will give life to the Panzer, direction to speed and decisive impact to the projectile. You hold a hand full of trump cards; now learn to play the game."[57]

Postwar literature has concentrated on the achievements of a few Tiger commanders at Kursk. According to Colonel (Retired) Wolfgang Schneider, who has produced a wealth of books on Tigers during the war, the key individual was not the commander, but instead: "The two key crew members in the tank were the driver and the gunner."[58]

Gunner: the role of the gunner often depended on his familiarity with the commander. In some tanks, the commander would pick the target and the gunner would aim and fire the main gun, and also might provide an estimate of the distance to the target and how fast the target was moving. When the gunner was experienced, he might have an agreement with the commander to handle all or most of that himself so the commander could look "one step out" and see the next engagement. The gunner also had a very useful device to his left front inside the turret: a large azimuth indicator. Looking like a clock face, the indicator showed the direction in which the main gun was facing: for example, 3 o'clock (the gun facing to the right), 6 o'clock (indicating the gun and turret were facing directly to the rear), and 12 o'clock (in which the gun and turret were facing directly forward.)[59]

While in assembly areas before combat, the gunner was responsible for checking and performing some maintenance on the gun, as well as organizing the crew to clean the main gun. The gunner operated in the turret on the left side; he was almost always inside the turret except when the tank was in column—especially on a road march—during which he looked out of a hatch to provide an extra set of eyes to warn of enemy aircraft attacks. As the manual said of the role of the gunner: "Aiming a shot into dead center is a matter of art, but not black magic. In order to shoot better than your opponent, you have been given the sharper weapon and the sharper mind. Using the 88 gun you can shoot off a mosquito's right canine tooth."[60]

The gunner was also responsible for firing the 7.92 mm Model 1934 coaxial machine gun. This weapon fired in the exact same direction and elevation as the main gun, although the trajectory dropped off quicker and it was not effective much past 800 meters. The gunner fired the machine gun mechanically by means of a pedal near his right foot.[61]

Loader: although often a junior member of the crew, the loader's job was to load the correct type of ammunition—determined by the commander, or sometimes the gunner—and then reload as fast as possible. Not every main gun round found its mark, and the tank that could fire faster was often the one that survived. So no matter how junior the loader was, he held the lives of the other crewmen in his hands, as he had just seconds to load each round. During rearming operations the loader had the mission of taking more of the heavy main gun rounds on board until the maximum load, ninety-two rounds, was attained. He would also place them in the ammunition ready racks inside the turret. The loader had to continuously inspect all the ammunition for serviceability, ensure the gun tube had no residue inside, and take the muzzle cover off the main gun before combat. The manual had an admonition for the loader as well: "60 tons of steel and 700 horsepower serve only one purpose, to set in motion and protect the weaponry you operate. If you fail, all of that will be in vain. If you prove yourself competent, a multitude of enemy tonnage and horsepower will be destroyed with your aid."[62]

In sequence, the loader located the correct round, loaded it into the breach of the gun, and then pressed a push button switch that completed the firing circuit and lit up a signal light in front of the gunner, telling the gunner the cannon was loaded and prepared to fire.[63] The loader also provided updates to the commander on the type and number of main gun rounds remaining onboard. On night marches, moving from assembly areas to new positions and not in contact with the enemy, the loader often had an additional duty. He would come out of his hatch and sit on the forward outer corner of the left track guard. In this position he could assist the driver in viewing what was in the vehicle's path and yell instructions through the open driver's hatch.

Radio Operator: World War II German tactical vehicle radios needed frequent adjustment, especially when the vehicle changed position, or was coming to the outer communications' range, which for many panzer radios was painfully short. Weather and magnetic anomalies also had an effect, most often negative. This requirement for adjustment was the main reason that German tanks had a fifth crew member in charge of communications. Tigers generally had one radio set, the Fu 5 10-watt transmitter with ultra short wavelength receiver; it had a usable range of four to six kilometers (2.5 to 3.75 miles). The entire company would be on that frequency, allowing all of them to talk and listen to one another. The two company headquarters' Tigers, and each of the platoon leader Tigers, also had a second radio receiver to be able to listen to non-company radio nets and even the regimental panzer commander on a different frequency; this radio was the Fu 2 ultra short wavelength receiver. The Fu 2 was never used on its own. So the radio operator in the company command Tiger or on a platoon leader's Tiger sometimes had to monitor two different communications simultaneously—a challenge in heavy combat.[64] Concerning the duties of the radio operator, as the manual stated: "Your set reaches farther than the voice, the ear, the eye. It travels over distances faster than a tank or a projectile. The responsibility of whether it turns into a powerful and dangerous weapon or into a mean traitor is in your hands."[65]

The radio operator had two major responsibilities: maintain and operate the radio to communicate with other elements outside the Tiger and operating and maintaining the intercom set by which the crewmen, minus the loader, could talk to one another. As mentioned, the company commander's radio operator had to be especially capable, as he had to keep communications open not only inside the company, but ensure that he could hear the panzer regimental headquarters—often some distance away.

A secondary, but sometimes crucial mission for the radio operator was to fire the 7.92 mm Model 1934 machine gun ball mounted in the hull directly in front of him. While the weapon had a high rate of fire that could suppress infantry, antitank riflemen, and antitank crews, it had a narrow field of fire—basically just to the front. In tactical situations, the radio operator also scanned the area immediately in front of the vehicle for antitank mines and immediately alerted the driver so he could stop before running over one.

Many times during Kursk the company commander's tank would sustain severe damage, or have a significant maintenance problem. In those instances the commander would have to leave that vehicle and take command of another Tiger. The commander often took his gunner and radio operator with him, although the radios were not portable, and another Tiger would have a less capable radio system unless the commander took a platoon leader's Tiger. The maintenance platoon could often do wonders overnight installing new radios and corresponding antenna, but not while shooting was hot and heavy during daylight.

Driver: the driver was a busy man, but in many respects he was responsible for the survival of the crew. As the manual stated: "You drive a tank which has few opponents worthy of note, but also very few brothers. It is up to you whether the Tiger is transformed into a predator waiting to pounce or into a heap of scrap metal."[66]

So the good news was that there were not many apex predators out there that could kill them; the bad news was that there would never be that many other Tigers close by if they needed help. The driver was in charge of operating and maintaining the engine. He had to keep it fueled and lubricated, and periodically inspect it for signs of unusual wear. He had to keep the radiator system full and know when to add some antifreeze and when not to. The driver had to inspect the drive train and keep it operational. He had to keep the suspension, road wheels, and track in proper working condition.

If the Tiger threw a track through damage or driving where it shouldn't, the driver led the effort to put the track back on—a herculean task under the best of conditions. In combat, the driver had to know where to drive to avoid getting stuck; he also had to observe the terrain in front of the vehicle for tell tale signs of buried antitank mines. And when coming to a short halt, he had to try to create an oblique angle between the front of his Tiger—which had the thickest armor—and the enemy, which would actually increase the effective thickness of the armor.

The crew also had joint duties irrespective of their military specialties. At night, four members of the Tiger crew would sleep under the vehicle—as protection against enemy artillery fire or a nighttime air attack—while a fifth crewman would be inside manning the radio; each shift on radio duty might last a few hours. Replacing the track often took most of the crew to accomplish. In crowded assembly areas the driver would need one or more ground guides to ensure that he did not run over anyone or anything valuable. Rearming the main gun ammunition resulted in at least a three-man chain to pass the ammunition from a truck or loading dock to the tank and then inside the turret to its proper storage rack. If a Tiger had to be towed by a recovery vehicle, several crewmen were required to handle the tow cables and hook them up correctly.

Finally—and this applied to any tank in any army—a tank crew had to learn to get along. Conditions were cramped and stress could get high. Every crewman had to learn to not only carry out his proscribed duties, but to offer to help everyone else in the Tiger, so as to turn panzer and crew into a synchronized killing machine. As such initiative was encouraged. Just before the Kursk Offensive, for example, a soldier—probably a loader—in the 13th (Heavy) Company discovered that by slightly altering the individual containers for the 88 mm main gun rounds and the ammunition racks inside the turret the basic load on the Tiger could be increased from 92 rounds to 120 rounds.[67]

Vehicle Recovery and Maintenance

The unsung soldiers in a Tiger company were the vehicle recovery specialists and maintenance personnel, and nowhere were these men more important than at the Kursk Offensive. As with many issues in the Third Reich, the problems started at the top. Inspector-General of Armored Troops (*Generalinspekteur der Panzertruppe*) Colonel General Heinz Guderian repeatedly urged that German factories must give priority to manufacturing spare parts for tanks, especially for Tigers, as an adequate supply of spares would increase the panzer arm's combat strength far quicker and cheaper than simply building new tanks. Hitler gagged when told that this spare parts strategy would reduce actual armored vehicle production by twenty percent, and thus there were frequently shortages of crucial spare parts.[68]

Other problems were caused by the design of the vehicle; while the Tiger certainly would keep its crew alive in situations where other tanks could not, the large panzer was not "mechanic friendly." Here is an example of a design flaw: "Take the Tiger's wheels for example. Each suspension arm held an axle with three wheels on either side. These combined to form two interleaved courses, known as a *Schachtellaufwerk*, supporting each track. If one of the inner wheels became damaged, mechanics had to remove as many as nine wheels from the outer course (undoing fifty-four bolts in the process) before they could access the damaged inner wheel. Furthermore, not all the wheels were the same, so service personnel had to carefully label each one as they removed it to make sure it was reattached in the correct position."[69]

This problem was exacerbated by a failure of the German command to anticipate the high level of damage that would be caused by enemy antitank mines. As a result, they did not stockpile enough spare road wheel arm assemblies and the road wheels themselves.[70]

Then came crew error. If the Tiger threw a track and became immobile when the crew drove where they shouldn't, and if the driver could not get the track back on the sprocket and road wheels, a recovery crew had to come assist them—often in an area that was still dangerous.

This crew would arrive in a heavy halftrack, the Sd.Kfz.9 (*Sonderkraftfahrzeug* 9 [Special Motorized Vehicle 9]), a twenty-ton towing vehicle originally designed to pull heavy artillery. Now it pulled heavy tanks. One heavy halftrack had no problem recovering any German panzer up through the Mark IV, but a Tiger was far different. It could easily take one hour to get a thrown track back on.[71]

Even though it had a big 12-cylinder engine, a winch, and a unique steering system that would apply the brakes to the tracks when severe turns were required, one FAMO, named after the manufacturer Fahrzeug-und Motorenbau GmbH in Breslau, needed one to three of his brother vehicles to drag a Tiger to safety—the number depending on the terrain and extent of the Tiger's damage. The workshop platoon's recovery section in the Tiger company had just six FAMO; a lift section had an additional FAMO with a crane (six-ton capacity) and a heavy truck with a crane (3-ton capacity). With a powerful crane and the mechanical advantage of the correct pulley system, mechanics could remove the turret in about an hour for more detailed repairs.[72]

Fortunately for the 2nd SS Panzer Corps during the Kursk Offensive, as long as the frontline advanced, additional recovery vehicles at echelons above the company moved into the area and could be used to assist in recovery.[73] For example, at the panzer regiment in both *Leibstandarte* and *Das Reich* there was a workshop company that had six more FAMO and one FAMO with a crane, although they also had to support the tank battalion in each division.

When units were withdrawing they were instructed to blow up severely damaged tanks that could not be evacuated to prevent their falling intact into enemy hands.

Battle of Kursk Overview

Except perhaps in military schools around the world, Kursk has never captured the imagination as a pivotal battle of World War II in Europe in the way that the Battle of Britain, Stalingrad, Normandy, and the Battle of the Bulge have over the years since the end of the war. However, if size does indeed matter in some things in life—and main battle tanks may be one of these—then Kursk should stand in the front tier of battles of that conflict.

The Leaders

For starters, military battles are often judged by the previous accomplishments of the major commanders of the combatants, and in the case of both the Germans and the Soviets, the leaders at Kursk were certainly no shrinking violets. Field Marshal Erich von Manstein, commander of Army Group South, that would conduct the southern pincer of the German attack against the Soviet salient at Kursk, was regarded by many military historians and military officers who actually were practitioners of the art of war as the finest operational mind in the Wehrmacht.

His counterpart leading the northern pincer was Field Marshal Günther von Kluge, commander of Army Group Center. He held vital commands in Germany's blitzkrieg victories in Poland 1939 and France 1940, and later helped stabilize Army Group Center in late 1941, when the Soviets showed that they were indeed not finished in front of Moscow. It may be that a reason why von Kluge's name does not carry more weight today is that he wrote no postwar memoirs—having bit into a vial of cyanide on August 17, 1944, after being recalled to Berlin from France during the investigation into the plotters who had attempted to blow up the Führer on July 20, 1944, at Rastenburg.

On the Soviet side, Marshal Georgy Zhukov served as the *Stavka* (Ставка)—the high command of the armed forces—coordinator. While the position is somewhat difficult to compare to Western armies in World War II, one should remember that in the eyes of Winston Churchill and Franklin D. Roosevelt, Zhukhov was Russia's equivalent of Bernard Montgomery and Dwight D. Eisenhower rolled into one. He was also a field general. He commanded the First Soviet Mongolian Army Group and defeated the Japanese in 1939, at the Battle of Khalkhin Gol. Two years later he commanded the Western Front and stopped the German offensive in front of Moscow in 1941. As Deputy Commander-in-Chief he helped coordinate the defense of Stalingrad in 1942. And so it went; wherever Zhukov appeared a successful major Soviet offensive followed, culminating when his First Belorussian Front played a major role in the Vistula-Oder Offensive and capture of Berlin in 1945.[1]

Opposite Field Marshal von Kluge was Marshal Konstantin Rokossovsky, commander of the Central Front. No novice to battle, Rokossovsky had commanded the Don Front at Stalingrad. Rokossovsky was one of a kind. During Stalin's purge of his generals in 1937–38, security police arrested him on the basis of a false accusation of treason. In the ensuing interrogations they knocked out eight of his teeth and broke three of his ribs before hauling him before the Supreme Military Court. When records bore out Rokossovsky's defense, it appears that he became the only defendant acquitted in the purge. Stalin still wanted his pound of flesh and despite the acquittal, Rokossovsky was subsequently incarcerated in the dreaded Siberian gulag camp of Vorkuta before being "rehabilitated" and returned to duty.[2]

In the south at Kursk, opposite Field Marshal von Manstein, the Soviets fielded another capable officer, General of the Army Nikolai Vatutin, commander of the Voronezh Front. Born in Belgorod and capable and talented, he was also unique. Later commanding the First Ukrainian Front, on February 28, 1944, Ukrainian Insurgent Army guerillas ambushed his vehicle behind the front lines near the village of Mylyatyn in the Rivne Oblast of northwest Ukraine. Rushed to a hospital in Kiev, he reportedly died of sepsis six weeks later.

Since this work deals with the 2nd SS Panzer Corps Tiger tanks in one sector of the southern pincer, a few other commanders should be addressed on the German side. Colonel General Hermann Hoth would serve as the commander of the Fourth Panzer Army, the superior headquarters of the SS corps. Nicknamed "Papa Hoth," Hermann had served in combat as an infantryman in the Great War. In 1929 he became the commander of the First Battalion of the 4th Infantry Regiment in the *Reichswehr* (the name for the armed forces during the Weimar Republic); two years later he assumed command of the 17th Infantry Regiment.[3]

As a brigadier general Hoth commanded the 18th Infantry Division beginning in 1935, and assumed command of the XVth Motorized Corps in 1938 as a lieutenant general. During the battle against France in 1940, his corps blew through the Ardennes Forest with the 5th Panzer and the 7th Panzer Divisions (the 7th led by the later famous Erwin Rommel). After receiving what would be his final promotion, Colonel General Hoth commanded Panzer Group 3 as part of Army Group North during *Operation Barbarossa*, the invasion of Russia. Hoth then briefly commanded the Seventeenth Army. In June 1942, he assumed command of the Fourth Panzer Army. In February and March 1943, his command dealt the Soviets a harsh setback at Kharkov, when the Russians over-extended their line of attack.[4]

SS-Obergruppenführer Paul Hausser was widely considered to be the best organizer and operational leader in the Waffen-SS. Born in 1880 in Brandenburg, he served in the German Army from 1899 to 1932. During the Great War, as a captain he won numerous decorations serving as a general staff officer on the western front; he also served as a company commander there in 1915 with the 28th Infantry Regiment *von Goeben*. After that conflict Hausser remained in the new *Reichswehr*, commanding an infantry battalion and subsequently the 10th Infantry Regiment. Reaching mandatory retirement age in 1932, Paul Hausser departed the service as a major general.

Two years later the fledgling SS-Special Purpose Troops (*SS-Verfügungstruppe* [SS-VT]) knocked on Hausser's door. The organization belonged neither to the police nor the Armed Forces, but was composed of military trained men for use by the Führer in peace or war—in effect combat troops for the Nazi Party. Paul Hausser did not need the SS-VT, but the SS-VT needed Paul Hausser, as the organization was seeking legitimacy in the eyes of the German Army. Now an *SS-Standartenführer*, Hausser initially served as the inspector of the SS leadership school system, then became the inspector for the entire SS-Special Purpose Troops organization.

Hausser then became the commander of the just-formed SS-Special Purpose Troops Division, which would soon be better known as *SS-Division Deutschland* that in turn became *SS-Division Reich*. A lead-from-the-front division commander, Paul Hausser suffered a grave wound to his upper jaw and right eye socket in October 1941, when shrapnel from an enemy antitank shell struck him. The wound cost him his right eye and he spent the next several months undergoing various medical procedures. He became the commanding general of the SS Panzer Corps on September 14, 1942.[5] The corps was renamed the 2nd SS Panzer Corps in June 1943, just before the start of Operation Zitadelle.[6]

Order, Reorder, Chaos

While the senior commanders may have been distinguished, the thought process that launched the offensive was certainly not. As the German Sixth Army was in its final death throes in its encirclement at Stalingrad, the Soviet Southwest Front commenced *Operation Gallop* to seize the Donbass region in the eastern Ukraine on January 29, 1943. Three days later the Voronezh Front began *Operation Star*, the objectives of which were the liberation of the major cities of Kharkov and Kursk. The Germans quickly responded; the new Tiger tank company for the SS Panzer Grenadier Division *Leibstandarte Adolf Hitler* loaded trains at Fallingbostel on February 1, and arrived at Kharkov on February 9. However, Soviet tanks had already rolled into Kursk on February 8, and would do the same at Kharkov on February 16.[7]

About noon the following day, February 17, Adolf Hitler, Lieutenant General Alfred Jodl—the Chief of Operations Staff of the High Command of the Armed Forces (*Oberkommando der* Wehrmacht [OKW])—and Lieutenant General Kurt Zeitzler—Chief of the German Army High Command (*Oberkommando des Heeres* [OKH]) General Staff—arrived in Zaporozhye (Запоріжжя), the location of Army Group South headquarters. Field Marshal von Manstein greeted them skeptically; he would later hear that Hitler had intended to put some "backbone" into the Army Group South staff, while at least one other source indicated that the Führer intended to relieve von Manstein of his position. On February 18, 1943, "Papa" Hoth arrived, and one day later Field Marshal Ewald von Kleist, commander of Army Group A, joined the session.

It is worth a moment to explain some command relationships, because in World War II Germany *Miles' Law*—"where you stand depends on where you sit"—was in full force every day. Before the calamitous German defeat in front of Moscow in December 1941, in which not only was the Soviet capital not taken, but advance elements of Army Group Center were thrown back some 150 kilometers in places, the *Oberkommando des Heeres* was the most important element within the German war planning system. After the debacle at Moscow, not only did the Führer sack some forty general officers—including the Supreme Commander of the German Army Field Marshal Walter von Brauchitsch—he also ordered that the *Oberkommando der* Wehrmacht would assume war planning for all theaters of war *except* the Eastern Front, which would remain in the portfolio of the OKH. This was an extremely clever move, as Hitler could then claim that only he had complete awareness of Germany's total strategic situation should any commander request a transfer of resources between the theaters of operations.

According to a later account by Field Marshal von Manstein, at Zaporozhye he laid out in general terms that even in the best situation the correlation of enemy forces facing Army Group South was, and would continue to be, highly unfavorable to the German Army. Von Manstein's second point was that every spring the ground would thaw and a muddy season (known as the *Rasputitsa*) would follow, often lasting many weeks; during this period the enemy would prepare to attack and could pierce his army group's front at any place. Finally, the wily field marshal explained that to remain in its current positions—a prerequisite that the Führer always insisted in his "not one step backward" strategy—the OKH must launch a well-timed offensive stroke just as the ground finally dried. Von Manstein later added that his purpose was to persuade the Führer to consider operations on a long term basis.[8] Hitler did not commit, but Jodl and Zeitzler had heard von Manstein's thoughts on an upcoming offensive and almost certainly informed their subordinate planners in Berlin to begin conducting terrain and feasibility studies.

Meanwhile, von Manstein launched his "Backhand Blow" at the overextended Voronezh Front on February 19, chewing up enemy armor units as the SS Panzer Grenadier Division *Leibstandarte Adolf Hitler* deployed between Poltava and Baranovka, while the *Das Reich* and *Totenkopf* divisions shot up fleeing enemy units pushed in their direction by the German Army's 48th Panzer Corps. *Das Reich* reached the western outskirts of Kharkov on March 9. Hoth's intent was for the SS Panzer Corps to circle around Kharkov to the west, swing north, and then head east to the Donets River, isolating Soviet troops in Kharkov and depriving them of resupply.[9]

Paul Hausser was having none of it and violated his superior's orders according to acclaimed expert on the *Totenkopf* Dr. Charles W. Sydnor. Instead of encircling Kharkov as Hoth had ordered, the SS commander ordered his corps to take the city in a direct assault. The street fighting lasted three days and cost the SS Panzer Corps some 11,500 casualties. The Germans recaptured Kharkov on March 14 and Belgorod on March 18.[10] The result of these Soviet operations was a one-hundred mile wide salient gouging the German front line, the center point in the salient being the city of Kursk; part of the Soviet penetration was in the sector of Army Group Center, with a smaller portion belonging to Army Group South. During the next several weeks after the German recapture of Kharkov the spring thaws shut down any actual large-scale combat maneuvers, but this *Rasputitsa* did not shut down military planners on both sides from thinking how they might take advantage of this bulge. Although the Soviets would have the advantage of interior lines, for the Germans, one look at the map hinted at what might be feasible.[11]

More importantly, the February and March successes in the Ukraine provided Hitler with a shot of adrenalin—actually several shots.[12] The victories were really the first to be achieved in winter conditions since *Operation Barbarossa* had commenced. Second, the concentration of Waffen-SS divisions—the first of the war, as the Waffen-SS had played no vital role in the early blitzkriegs—had led to success on the battlefield; the Waffen-SS was ramping up in size and the best might be yet to come. And finally, the relatively new Tiger tanks had performed well at Kharkov; more were being produced every day and the new Mark V Panther, to counter the Soviet T-34 tank and to replace the Mark III panzer and the Mark IV panzer, was already in its third month of production. Von Manstein later wrote: "His [Hitler's] faith in the penetrating power of the newly established SS Panzer Corps was apparently unbounded."[13]

In fact, those German examinations of the Kursk salient appear to have commenced not long after Jodl and Zeitzler returned to Berlin, for on March 5, 1943, Hitler discussed the Eastern Front with Zeitzler, agreeing that after the muddy period was over, and if the panzer groups could be reinforced, Germany could launch an attack with them.[14] On March 13, 1943, the OKH issued "Operations Order Number 5," outlining a spring offensive. The directive ordered Army Group A and Army Group North, on the southern and northern flanks respectively, to defend in sector, while Army Group Center and Army Group South in the middle would form strong tank armies on the north and south side of the Kursk salient, respectively.[15] With both pincers attacking and meeting at Kursk, the resulting victory would achieve an operational level success not only to annihilate significant enemy troops and material inside the bulge, but also to shorten the front by 240 kilometers, which would provide the Germans with a strategic reserve force to counter any Soviet threats in other areas—or use on other fronts if necessary. The salient points concerning the offensive for Army Group South included:[16] "Behind the northern wing of the army group, the construction of a strong panzer army will be begun immediately, and must be completed by the middle of April, in order to begin operations before the Russian offensive at the end of the mud period can get underway. The object of this offensive is the destruction of the enemy forces facing Second Army through a northward attack from the Kharkov area, in conjunction with another assault group attacking out of the Second Panzer Army [northern pincer] zone."

Both Army Group South and Army Group Center were instructed to report their intentions by March 25 for how they would accomplish this mission. Major General Dr. Hans Speidel, chief of staff of Army Detachment Kempf—a subordinate element of Army Group South—appears to have been the "operational mind" in Army Group South for outlining the salient points for what was at the time called "Operation K." On April 1, Speidel outlined the following points important for the SS Panzer Corps: "Assault Forces: 57th Panzer Corps with Infantry Division (motorized) *Großdeutschland*, 11th Panzer Division and one panzer division from First Panzer Army . . . SS

Panzer Corps with *Leibstandarte Adolf Hitler, Das Reich*, and *Totenkopf* . . . One panzer corps from First Panzer Army with two panzer divisions from First Panzer Army. Execution of the Operation: Forcing of the Donets crossings for the right-hand panzer group will be the goal of Corps Raus. After the bridgeheads are secured, the SS panzer group will cross and immediately begin a deep penetration. The intermediate objective of the SS Panzer Corps will be the occupation of the intersection at Korocha [Короча] and the high ground at Skorodnoye [Скородное] and to the northwest of there."[17]

The forces and intermediate objectives would change before the final draft, as Korocha and Skorodnoye were too far to the northeast, but Colonel General Hermann Hoth and the Fourth Panzer Army signed off on the proposal on April 3.[18] Further details would follow; this occurred on April 11, when the OKH published its first draft of the order for *Operation Citadel*, along with a warning order which set required long lead logistical requirements in motion. Four days later, on April 15, the OKH issued "Operations Order Number 6" for the offensive.[19] Salient points of the order that would affect the 2nd SS Panzer Corps included: "I have resolved to proceed with the first of this year's offensive operations, the *Citadel* offensive, as soon as the weather permits . . . The best units, the best weapons, the best officers and great stocks of munitions must be positioned at the attack points. Success depends upon: preserving the element of surprise for as long as possible . . . Uniting the two attacking armies in one swift movement, through tight concentration and narrow attack frontages, and using local superiorities in all attack arms (tanks, assault guns, artillery, rockets, etc). to smash enemy opposition. Prosecute the offensive so rapidly that the enemy has no time to withdraw. The earliest possible date for the attack is May 3. The movement to the jumping off points will be conducted only via night marches."[20]

On April 23, 1943, Fourth Panzer Army published the schedule for the approach marches. The next day, head of the SS Heinrich Himmler visited the Tiger company of the *Das Reich* and rode on one of the giants, standing in the commander's hatch of Tiger 823. Not to be outdone by Colonel General Guderian, who had visited the *Leibstandarte* Tigers three weeks before, Himmler had the gunner fire a few main gun rounds.[21] Plus, the experience would be a good one to tell the Führer when the "*Reichsheine*" (a derogatory nickname used behind Himmler's back) next saw him. Army Group South appears to have been ready to attack on May 2. Heinz Guderian, whom we will soon meet, was convinced that the offensive plan was the brainchild of Lieutenant General Zeitzler, who in turn believed that the new Panther and Tiger tanks could achieve decisive success.[22]

Originally *Operation Citadel* was timed to begin in the first half of May, when the ground would be sufficiently dry from the spring thaws and when—according to von Manstein—the Soviets would still not have finished refitting their armor units. Seeing numerous problems, on April 26, the OKH agreed to postpone the start of the operation until May 5. Weather conditions did not help matters, and due to heavy rains in the area, on April 30, the OKH further postponed the start date until May 9, 1943. That afternoon, sensing confusion at all levels of command, the OKH ordered that all directives stating a particular start date should be cancelled and destroyed, indicating that a new date would be established after Hitler met with appropriate field commanders.[23]

On May 4, 1943, the OKH hosted a planning conference at the Berghof at Berchtesgaden. The officers who had met in February were in attendance: Colonel General Walter Model, commander of the Ninth Army, that would make the northern attack, might have been present; he had already informed Army Group Center that the Ninth Army could not attack before May 15, so Field Marshal von Kluge knew his views. Hitler began the conference by summarizing the situation in Russia and outlined the OKH plan. He then acknowledged that Colonel General Model had strong concerns against the planned offensive based on aerial photography that showed massive enemy fortifications on the lines of the German attack and also a paucity of Soviet armor in the salient—indicative that the enemy would concentrate his armor only after he saw where the Germans had attacked, and thus the Russians would maintain the initiative. Hitler seemed impressed by Model's logic.[24] Model was a master of details; on April 5, 1943, he had visited the Tiger company of the *Leibstandarte* at Kharkov so he could get the latest information from the troops that had just used it in combat.[25]

Von Manstein spoke next, offering that had the offensive commenced in April it would have had a good chance at succeeding, but now success would be doubtful unless Army Group South received an additional two full strength infantry divisions. Hitler told the field marshal that these reinforcements were not possible and asked again for von Manstein's opinion. It was not von Manstein's finest hour, and his response seems to have been tepid. Von Kluge spoke next and unambiguously supported Zeitzler's plan.[26] At some point Lieutenant General Alfred Jodl piped up and asked Hitler to cancel the offensive, saying the forces should be transferred to the Balkans and Mediterranean.

One more voice was now heard: Colonel General Heinz "*Schnelle Heinz* (Quick Heinz)" Guderian, one of Germany's premier panzer proponents, but a man who rubbed many other senior military leaders the wrong way. Guderian, who had commanded significant armor formations earlier in the war, said that he had been relieved of command of the Second Panzer Group in December 1941 in part—according to Guderian—because his direct superior von Kluge had not stood up to Hitler to save Guderian's job.[27]

Now Guderian, as Inspector-General of Armored Troops, declared that the attack was pointless for several reasons: first, Germany would suffer significant panzer losses that could not be replaced by new production that year; second, Germany would need to devote much of that new production of tanks in the near future to create a mobile reserve in the west against the Allied landings that were sure to occur within the next twelve months; and finally Guderian pointed out that the new Panther tanks, which would have a critical role in the upcoming fight, still had some serious teething problems.[28]

These were not just his opinions based on reports and third party observations; on his March 31, 1943, visit to the SS Tiger company in Kharkov he found out from the crews exactly what the Tiger could and could not do in combat. Albert Speer, the man who earlier had to select the final prototype for the new Tiger tank and had hands on experience with it, was present and seconded Guderian's opinion concerning the Panthers.[29]

Like a terrier chasing a rat, the Inspector-General of Armored Troops would not let go of the issue, reminding everyone that while the Tiger was indeed a marvelous weapon, there were simply not enough of them to go around. The Tiger had its first taste of combat near Leningrad on September 22, 1942. Part of an army unit, the vehicles experienced numerous breakdowns and mechanical problems, in part because of the rushed development. And it had done well at Kharkov, but was still not out of the woods yet with respect to mechanical problems.

Guderian recorded in his notes that as of May 3, 1943, Army Group South had fifty-three Tiger tanks, while Army Group Center had twenty. By May 9, sixteen more Tigers were en route to Army Group South. By June 10, a further twenty-eight Tiger tanks were on trains headed to von Manstein, while thirty-one Tigers were en route to Army Group Center. Therefore, according to Guderian's calculations, by the start of the offensive Army Group South would have ninety-seven Tiger tanks on hand while Army Group Center would have just fifty-one.[30]

Hitler remained undecided. On May 6, Hitler delayed the start of *Operation Citadel* until June 12, 1943, the rationale being that this would give more time for the panzer units involved to receive the new Panther and Tiger tanks.[31] On May 10, Colonel General Guderian was in Berlin to attend a conference with the Führer concerning Mark V Panther production. After the meeting the panzer expert asked to speak with the German leader. Reiterating his previous arguments, Guderian finally asked the Führer: "Why do you want to attack in the East at all this year?" Field Marshal Wilhelm Keitel, standing on the fringe of the conversation as he often did, offered his opinion that the offensive must be conducted for political reasons.

Perhaps for once in the war Wilhelm Keitel was correct, at least from the point of Hitler's logic. Nicknamed "the nodding ass," "Yes-Keitel," and "Toady," chief of the OKW Keitel was belittled by most in the military and hated by the rest. Often denigrated behind his back, the unkindest cut of all came from Luftwaffe Colonel Werner Baumbach, commander of several bomber wings, who said: ". . . You cannot win wars with a Field Marshal Keitel."[32] But as Keitel said, the offensive was for political reasons.[33]

Adolf Hitler's primary motive for the Kursk Offensive was to weaken Soviet military strength so much that with the Red Army unable to mount a major attack in 1943, he could move forces from Russia to Italy. The Führer believed—correctly, as it would be proven—that with Britain and the United States now victorious in North Africa, their next move would be to invade his political ally Italy. Hitler needed to keep Italy in the war on Germany's side. In fact, he needed to retain all Germany's allies, and at the moment several were on shaky ground. The Soviet victory at Stalingrad had not only destroyed the German Sixth Army, it had killed tens of thousands of Italian, Hungarian, and Rumanian (today Romanian) troops on the flanks of Field Marshal Friedrich von Paulus' doomed command. None of these three political allies were on terra firma in Hitler's mind. Threats to any of their territory could cause a political upheaval, an overthrow of their pro-German governments, and their leaving the war effort. If deposed, Benito Mussolini could be the first domino to fall.

Hitler's secondary objective was not achievable. After moving a significant part of the German military west, he believed that he would throw the Western allies into the sea, leave a skeleton defensive force in France, and then take the bulk of the Wehrmacht back east, where he would destroy the Soviet Union once and for all. Those options, though, were long gone.

Guderian pressed the issue, looking at the Führer: "How many people do you think even know where Kursk is? It is a matter of profound indifference to the world whether we hold Kursk or not. I repeat my question: Why do we want to attack in the East at all this year?" Hitler, perhaps shocked at the openness of the general, replied: "You're quite right. Whenever I think of this attack my stomach turns over." Guderian pressed the issue for all it was worth. "In that case, your reaction to the problem is the correct one. Leave it alone!" Hitler finally terminated the conversation, but told Guderian that he was by no means committed to the operation.[34]

There were still several remaining acts of this pathetic play. On June 5, 1943, Luftwaffe Colonel General Hans Jeschonnek, the chief of the Luftwaffe general staff, weighed in. Considered by many to be the most impressive of all the Chiefs of the General Staff, Jeschonnek stated to Hitler that Luftwaffe strength for the operation would not be sufficient to guarantee air control, or to provide adequate ground protection against enemy ground attack aircraft in all sectors simultaneously.[35]

On June 18, the operations staff of the OKW submitted an appraisal to the Führer to cancel the planned Kursk Offensive until an assessment could be completed concerning potential allied operations in Italy and/or the Balkans. On June 19, obviously unconcerned with what transpired in the Mediterranean, Army Group Center notified Berlin that a Soviet offensive against them was expected and the only way to disrupt this unfortunate situation was to launch Operation Citadel soonest. This last missive seems to have finally stirred Hitler to make a solid decision, and on June 21, he set July 3, 1943, as the start date for the offensive. Apparently this date was not quite set in concrete, as on June 25, after speaking with Model, von Manstein, and von Kluge, Hitler declared that July 5, 1943, would be the absolute certain date that the offensive would commence.[36]

2nd SS Panzer Corps

Fortunately for Hitler and his generals, the average German Army, Luftwaffe, or Waffen-SS soldier was unaware of the friction, confusion, and enmity at the top concerning the upcoming offensive. While some of these soldiers might have been appalled with the vacillation of the Führer and his senior military leaders, not many of these critics would have come from the 2nd SS Panzer Corps.

Formerly known as the SS Panzer Corps, it could boast of never having lost a battle. Big, highly disciplined, and well-equipped, it was convinced—at least in the leadership—that it could show the *Untermensch* (racially inferior, sub-human) Russians just who were the *Herrenvolk* (supermen, master race). With 71,446 soldiers, 601 armored fighting vehicles, 560 guns and rocket launchers, and 256 mortars, it was actually smaller than the 48th Panzer Corps and the 3rd Panzer Corps on its flanks, although if the Waffen-SS soldiers actually believed in their own doctrine, they would have considered themselves to be inferior to no one.[37]

The corps had three subordinate divisions: the SS Panzer Grenadier Division *Leibstandarte Adolf Hitler* (LSSAH), the SS Panzer Grenadier Division *Das Reich* (DR), and the SS Panzer Grenadier Division *Totenkopf* (T). While at this point in the war they were termed panzer grenadier divisions, they truly were panzer divisions. With 20,928 soldiers, the *Leibstandarte* held the distinction as the oldest division in the Waffen-SS, commanded for several years by one of the closest associates of Adolf Hitler, *SS-Obergruppenführer* Josef "Sepp" Dietrich. Dietrich had only recently been elevated to command what would soon become the 1st SS Panzer Corps—*SS-Standartenführer* Theodor "Teddy" Wisch replaced him; highly decorated, Wisch was an infantryman; he had attended the Panzer Troops School at Wünsdorf in January 1943.[38]

The division was composed of two panzer grenadier regiments (each with three battalions: two motorized in trucks and one in halftracks), one artillery regiment, one assault gun detachment, one antiaircraft (*flak*) detachment, one combat engineer (*pioneer*) battalion, one reconnaissance detachment, one antitank detachment, one panzer regiment (two battalions), and a wide variety of critical logistical troops who would play a very key role at the battle.

As tanks are the focus of this study, a closer examination of armored vehicles is in order. The panzer regimental commander was *SS-Obersturmbannführer* Georg Schönberger; originally an infantryman who subsequently served in the assault guns. The day before the Kursk Offensive began, the LSSAH reported the following strength: three Mark I panzers, four Mark II panzers, two Mark III (short-barrel) panzers, nine Mark III (long-barrel) panzers, seventy-nine Mark IV (long-barrel) panzers, nine Mark III command panzers, eight Mark III observation panzers, and twelve operational Mark VI Tigers—a total of 126 panzers—and a further thirty-four Mark III assault guns. The Tiger tanks, of which there were thirteen on hand, were all in the 13th (Heavy) Company of the panzer regiment.[39] The company had received its first five Tigers in December 1942, four more arrived in January 1943, and a final five reached the company in April 1943; the company had one Tiger a total loss in March 1943.[40]

In addition to the Tigers, the 13th (Heavy) Company also fielded a light platoon, under command of *SS-Unterscharführer* Gustav Swiezy. It consisted of five Mark III (long-barrel) panzers with turret numbers 1341, 1342, 1343, 1344, and 1345.[41] The platoon was subordinated directly to the 2nd Panzer Regiment.[42] The 13th (Heavy) Company had Field Post Number 48 165.

SS Panzer Grenadier Division *Das Reich* was another big outfit with 19,804 soldiers. *SS-Gruppenführer* Walter Krüger had commanded the unit since April; he was an infantry officer. *Das Reich* was organized very similarly to the *Leibstandarte*. The day before the offensive *Das Reich* fielded: one Mark I panzer, one Mark III (short-barrel) panzer, fifty-two Mark III (long-barrel) panzers, thirty Mark IV (long-barrel) panzers, nine Mark III command panzers, nine Mark III observation panzers, eighteen captured T-34 tanks, and twelve operational Mark VI Tigers—a total of 132 panzers—and forty-one Mark III assault guns. All Tiger tanks, of which there were fourteen on hand, were assigned to the 8th (Heavy) Company of the panzer regiment, which was commanded by *SS-Obersturmbannführer* Hans-Albin von Reitzenstein.[43]

The company had received its first Tiger in December 1942; nine more arrived in January 1943, five reached the company in April 1943, and a final Tiger arrived in May 1943. Meanwhile, the company reported two Tigers a total loss—one in February and one in March 1943.[44] Von Reitzenstein was also an infantryman, who later served in armored reconnaissance. The 8th (Heavy) Company was authorized four officers, fifty-six non-commissioned officers, and eighty-seven junior enlisted men; this strength included not only the Tiger crews, but also medics, supply, and maintenance personnel (which alone had twenty-six personnel).[45] The 8th (Heavy) Company had a designated Field Post Number of 58 505.

The third SS division in the corps was the SS Panzer Grenadier Division *Totenkopf*, commanded by *SS-Oberführer* Hermann Priess, who had previously commanded the unit's artillery regiment. The division had 19,176 soldiers assigned for the offensive. On July 4, 1943, *Totenkopf* reported the following tank strength: fifty-nine Mark III (long-barrel) panzers, seven Mark IV (short-barrel) panzers, forty Mark IV (long-barrel) panzers, eight Mark III command panzers, five Mark III observation panzers, and twelve operational Mark VI Tigers—a total of 131 panzers—and twenty-eight Mark III assault guns.[46]

The 9th (Heavy) Company had received its first nine Tigers in January 1943; five reached the company in April 1943 and a final Tiger arrived in May 1943.[47] All Tigers, of which there were fifteen on hand, were in this company of the panzer regiment; the regiment was commanded by *SS-Sturmbannführer* Eugen Kunstmann. Like the other two panzer regimental commanders, Kunstmann began his military career in the infantry, but then became a General Staff officer, holding several key staff positions before joining the panzers. The 9th (Heavy) Company was formerly designated the 4th (Heavy) Company until May 9, 1943, when the name was changed when the company was transferred to the control of the panzer regiment's Second Battalion.[48] The 9th (Heavy) Company had Field Post Number 48 786.

All three SS divisions had the same problem, and it was significant: less than sufficiently trained and experienced soldiers. During the fighting around Kharkov and Krasnograd between January 30, 1943, and March 20, 1943, SS Panzer Grenadier Division *Leibstandarte Adolf Hitler* had lost 167 officers and 4,373 sergeants and junior enlisted men killed in action, missing in action, or seriously wounded. Additionally, the crews of an entire panzer battalion of the *Leibstandarte Adolf Hitler* panzer regiment had returned to Erlangen, Germany (outside Nürnberg), in early June 1943, to receive and train with the new Panther tank; they would not return until after the Kursk Offensive. Although this battalions' Mark IV tanks remained with the division the veteran crews did not.[49] Finally, numerous LSSAH veterans had been reassigned to build the new SS Panzer Grenadier Division *Hitlerjugend* (Hitler Youth).

During the same period SS Panzer Grenadier Division *Das Reich* suffered 102 officers and 4,396 sergeants and junior enlisted men killed in action, missing in action, or seriously wounded. Unlike the *Leibstandarte*, which was at one hundred percent authorized strength at the start of the offensive, the *Das Reich* was filled at only eighty-nine percent authorized. As in the *Leibstandarte*, the crews of the entire first battalion of the *Das Reich* panzer regiment travelled to Mayon-le-Caen, France, in early June 1943 to receive and train with the new Mark V Panther tank and would not return until after the offensive.[50]

Conditions in SS Panzer Grenadier Division *Totenkopf* were slightly better, in that the panzer regiment had both battalions on hand. At Kharkov at the beginning of the year, *Totenkopf* suffered 693 men killed in action, seventy-two men missing in action, and 1,944 men wounded in action. *Totenkopf* was in a similar predicament as *Das Reich*, having an actual strength of only ninety-two percent of authorized levels.[51]

The corps had an Achilles heel, although it was not recognized at the time: bridging equipment. Field Marshal von Manstein knew that if his offensive was successful, he would have to cross the Psel River and then farther north cross the Sejm River. Both had somewhat soft banks, making fording operations problematic. German tanks needed bridges and the Soviets knew it. Correctly assessing that capturing an intact bridge would be dicey, von Manstein assigned army engineer assets to *SS-Obergruppenführer* Paul Hausser to include the 680th Engineer Regiment Staff, the 929th Bridge Column Staff, and the 8th Construction Troop Command. The last unit brought the 26th Bridge Construction Battalion to the offensive; the engineer staffs oversaw six Type B bridge columns and one Type I. The Type B assets could construct bridges that would support every vehicle in the corps except one: the Tiger. Another unit present, the 840th Bridge Column (Type I), could span a river with a bridge strong enough to support the Tiger, but there would be no redundancy if something happened to the 840th.

On May 14, 1943, Colonel General Heinz Guderian, in his position of Inspector General of Panzer Troops, finished reading an after action report submitted by the 13th Company (Tiger) in the German Army *Großdeutschland* Panzer Grenadier Division concerning their use of the vehicle in March near Belgorod. Guderian wrote in reply: "The Tiger unit is the most valuable and strongest weapon in a Panzer unit. If it is used as the point unit, it will quickly bring localized success because of its high combat power. However, they will have insufficient force at the start of a decisive battle that could mean destruction of the opponent in the depths of his position, because the Tigers will suffer heavy breakdowns due to mines, hits, and terrain obstacles. Therefore, they will enter the decisive phase of the battle already greatly depleted. Fundamentally, point units have increased fuel consumption. Because the Tiger already has a limited radius of action, when it is used as a lead vehicle it will sometimes be short of fuel at the start of the decisive phase of the battle . . . Fundamentally we should strive to employ the Tigers concentrated in a Panzer detachment with three companies [rather than provide a second Tiger company to the *Großdeutschland* Panzer Grenadier Division."[52]

With those thoughts in mind from the senior panzer leader in the Wehrmacht, in the next chapter we will see how the Tigers were used in the 2nd SS Panzer Corps and to what extent that unit took Heinz Guderian's thoughts to heart.

Terrain

But first, one final point should be entered into evidence concerning the upcoming use of the Tiger at the Kursk Offensive. *The terrain in the Kursk area of operations favored the defender.*

Obstacles

Improved roadways were scarce, which could delay resupply efforts the farther the Germans advanced. In the south several major rivers ran east to west; since the attack would generally run south to north, the Germans would have to cross those waterways, while the Soviets could defend behind them. Smaller feeder streams were swollen by recent rains and the ground near each was muddy and treacherous. One of the larger rivers was the Psel, running 446 miles from Russia southwest to its mouth on the Dnieper River. The Psel's northern riverbank was generally higher and steeper than its southern bank, which was generally lower. Fording sites over the Psel existed, but ones that facilitated crossing by heavy tanks were predictable. Other rivers included the Vorskla River, the Siverskyi Donets River, and the Solotinka River. The major impact of these three waterways was to divide the attack zones of the 48th Panzer Corps in the west and the 2nd SS Panzer Corps in the east, making cross boundary operations that much more difficult. The Lipovyy Donets River in the east served initially as the *de facto* eastern boundary of the corps. It proved to be no obstacle to attacking Soviet armor from the east before the 3rd Panzer Corps got there.

An additional obstacle was the Belgorod–Prokhorovka railway, or rather the tall embankment on which it ran in many locations. Tanks could not go over this obstacle and crews had to find level crossing sites in the same way as they would to cross a river. Especially difficult going was the stretch of embankment from Kalinin north to Prokhorovka.

Several dozen small villages dotted the landscape between Belgorod and the Psel River, each village being a potential trap for mounted movement. Along the southern bank of the Psel were a series of seven villages that would have to be negotiated before reaching the river, the banks of which were boggy. They included west to east: Krasnyy Oktyabr', Kozlovka, Vasil'yevka, Andreyevka, Mikhaylovka, Prelestnoye, and Petrovka. These were sometimes termed "ribbon villages" because they were very narrow north to south and wide west to east, as evident in aerial reconnaissance photographs. The village of Prokhorovka would be considered a large urban area, and as such it was a major obstacle; at the time of the offensive it was about 2.8 kilometers west to east and 1.5 kilometers south to north at its widest point. The northern edge of Prokhorovka was only five kilometers southeast of the Psel River.

Key Terrain

Prokhorovka was also key terrain, as the possession of it would give an enormous advantage to whomever controlled it. The village had a road heading due east, a second road heading northeast, a road heading northwest (toward Oboyan), and a road west that would bend south toward Belgorod. As long as the Soviets occupied the city they could bring supplies in from the east on the improved roads, and possibly the railroad. The same advantages of supply and transportation would accrue to the Germans if they controlled Prokhorovka. Clearly the major city of Kursk to the north was key terrain; its loss would force the Soviets to attempt to withdraw as many units from the western edge of the salient as possible—which could turn into a deadly rout reminiscent of the summer of 1941.

Observation and Fields of Fire

Over the entire corps sector, observation and ensuing fields of fire were generally very good, if not excellent. Terrain was rolling, open farmland. Wheat and grass would not restrict vehicle observation. While some reports indicate that some of the area was comprised of cornfields (although this study found no photographs supporting this), corn in early July would not have been more than waist high. Observation from hilltops was for several miles; there were about fifteen hilltops ranging in height from about 216 meters in the south to 252 meters in the north from the line of departure of the 2nd SS Panzer Corps to Prokhorovka that allowed observation of most of the battlefield. There was one three-kilometer-long ridge above 250 meters high just northeast of Teterevino (North) village; it had a commanding view northeast for five kilometers to the last defensible terrain in front of Prokhorovka at Hill 252.2 and the small village of Oktiabrskii Sovkhoz.

Cover and Concealment

Cover and concealment (cover being protection from enemy fire and concealment being hidden from enemy detection) were generally limited in the 2nd SS Panzer Corps sector. The two exceptions would be the fair number of deep *balkas* and several areas of woods. Photographs of *balkas* at Kursk show them large enough for an entire Tiger company to drive into and not be seen from nearby flat ground, although from the air the tanks could easily be observed. These *balkas* seem to have few trees in them, different from ravines and gullies in other countries. Extending through the middle of the sector, oriented south to north, were a series of wooded areas. In the south the Zhuravlinyi Woods (just southwest of the village of the same name) concealed a large number of Soviet artillery pieces at the start of the battle. The largest woods in the area were just north of the village of Smorodino. Approaching Prokhorovka to the east of the railroad embankment, the Sloyevoye District Forest guarded the southwestern approach to the village and could conceal infantry very well. Tree types included oak, elm, lime, and birch.[53]

Avenues of Approach

The 2nd SS Panzer Corps was a motorized/armored force. It had to make rapid time advancing north, not only to trap Soviet forces in the Kursk salient, but to keep up initially with the 48th Panzer Corps to its west and subsequently the 3rd Panzer Corps to its east. Dawdling was not in the concept of operation. Given the mission and the terrain already described, the corps had one feasible attack avenue of approach: right up the middle. The best road net ran from Belgorod initially to the village of Bykovka and subsequently to Yakovlevo, and that is exactly the route the *Leibstandarte* would initially follow.

From there the road network turned northeast past the villages of Luchki (North), Teterevino (North), and Komsomol'skiy (Комсомольский)—from there it was only a skip and a jump to Prokhorovka. A second major road headed north from Belgorod to the east of the Lipovyy Donets River, but that avenue was in the attack zone of the 3rd Panzer Corps and would not support both corps.

The problem for Paul Hausser was that the Soviets could read a map as well as he could.

Daily Battle
Actions

The Battle of Kursk was not just one gigantic tapestry of the ebb and flow of battle. Kursk, like most other modern battles, was actually an accumulation of thousands of vicious little engagements; the outcome of each would influence future events, but that influence could not be measured nor projected at the time the skirmish occurred. The results could be measured, to be sure, in terms of casualties and ground lost or won, but—like gravity—the pull of each engagement toward a final outcome might be felt but not seen right away.

The following summaries describe the actions of each Tiger company for every day of the offensive. Keeping track of time is especially difficult for Kursk, as the Germans referenced many actions in "Berlin time," while the Soviets used "Moscow time," which was one hour ahead of Berlin. All times are expressed in the military version: 2359 is one minute before midnight; 2400 is midnight; 0001 is one minute after midnight; and the count toward 2400 starts over. Therefore 1500 would be 3:00 p.m., 2245 would be 10:45 p.m., and so forth. Sunrise and sunset are local time. Most Tiger combat at Kursk did not occur in darkness, although road marches to new assembly areas and attack positions often occurred at night, when there was little danger of an enemy air attack on moving columns of large vehicles.

General histories of the battle sometimes bracket the German offensive as July 5 to July 16 and the Soviet counteroffensive as July 12 to August 23. This study has chosen to limit the end point at July 15, as after this date the three Tiger tank companies were not on the offensive. Some crew members are mentioned in the daily battle actions by name; much more information about each soldier will be presented later.

July 5, 1943[1]

Weather: over the previous several weeks rain had been above average; heavy rain the night before, sunny, partly cloudy, and light wind; 68° to 75°F
Terrain conditions: rolling grasslands, bare ground, often muddy; roads outside of ravines muddy, but becoming better and then dusty; terrain near the Vorskla River was soft, mushy, and hazardous
Sunrise: 0427 hours   **Sunset:** 2048 hours
Moon Phase: Waxing crescent, 8% illumination

The 2nd SS Panzer Corps attack plan called for its three divisions to advance northeast online, with SS Panzer Grenadier Division *Leibstandarte Adolf Hitler* on the left (west), SS Panzer Grenadier Division *Das Reich* in the center, and SS Panzer Grenadier Division *Totenkopf* on the right (east), starting slightly south of the other two divisions. Artillery preparation would begin at 0300 hours, with air support from the Luftwaffe's 8th Air Corps joining the fray at dawn. German fire support for the corps would total 24,464 artillery rounds and 9,270 mortar rounds.[2] To the west of the corps stood the 48th Panzer Corps; to the east was the 3rd Panzer Corps. Opposing the corps were elements of the Soviet 23rd Guards Rifle Corps of the Sixth

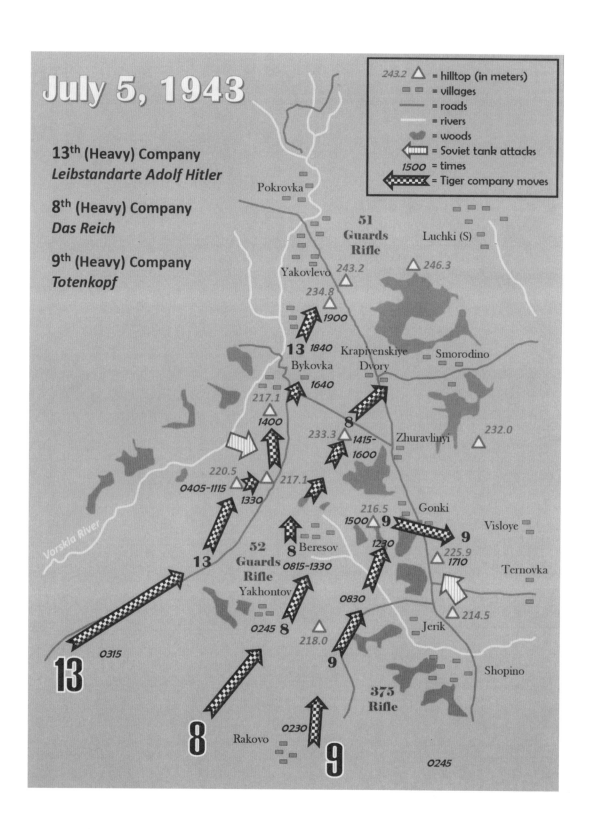

July 5, 1943

13th (Heavy) Company
Leibstandarte Adolf Hitler

8th (Heavy) Company
Das Reich

9th (Heavy) Company
Totenkopf

243.2 △ = hilltop (in meters)
▭ ▭ = villages
= roads
= rivers
= woods
= Soviet tank attacks
1500 = times
= Tiger company moves

Pokrovka

51 Guards Rifle

Luchki (S)

Yakovlevo   *243.2* △

△ *246.3*

234.8 △

1900

13 *1840*   Krapivenskiye Dvory   Smorodino

Bykovka

1640

217.1 △
1400

8

233.3 △ *1415-1600*   Zhuravlinyi   △ *232.0*

220.5 △ △ *217.1*
0405-1115

1330

216.5 △ **9**   Gonki   Visloye

1500

13   **52 Guards Rifle**   **8** Beresov   *1230*   **9**   △ *225.9* *1710*   Ternovka

0815-1330

Yakhontov

0830

△ *214.5*

0245 **8**   △ *218.0*   Jerik

13 0315   **9**   Shopino

375 Rifle

0230

8   Rakovo   **9**   0245

Vorskla River

Guards Army, specifically the 52nd Guards Rifle Division in the west and the 375th Rifle Division in the east; the corps' 51st Guards Rifle Division manned the second line of defense to the north. The 2nd SS Panzer Corps was most likely in possession of forty-two Tiger tanks, although only thirty-five were operational.[3]

Operational 2nd SS Panzer Corps Tiger strength at the beginning of the day: **35**

> 13th (Heavy) Company, 1st Panzer Regiment: **12**
> 8th (Heavy) Company, 2nd Panzer Regiment: **12**
> 9th (Heavy) Company, 3rd Panzer Regiment: **11**

13th (Heavy) Company, 1st Panzer Regiment,[4]
SS Panzer Grenadier Division *Leibstandarte Adolf Hitler*

Augmented by the attachment of the army's 315th Infantry Regiment and the Second Battalion of the 238th Artillery Regiment, the mission of the SS Panzer Grenadier Division *Leibstandarte Adolf Hitler* was to advance northward with the two panzer grenadier regiments online: the 2nd Panzer Grenadier Regiment *Leibstandarte Adolf Hitler* on the left (west) and the 1st Panzer Grenadier Regiment *Leibstandarte Adolf Hitler* on the right (east). Behind the two regiments was termed the panzer group, composed of the 1st Panzer Regiment (minus the 13th (Heavy) Company) reinforced with the Third Battalion of the 2nd Panzer Grenadier Regiment *Leibstandarte Adolf Hitler* equipped with halftracks and an antitank company.[5]

The 2nd Panzer Grenadier Regiment *Leibstandarte Adolf Hitler* made the main effort; the panzer group would dash forward if either regiment created a breakthrough of the forward enemy defensive line. Serving as the division reserve in case a situation good or bad developed was a battle group with the SS Reconnaissance Detachment and several antitank companies. The 1st Panzer Grenadier Regiment *Leibstandarte Adolf Hitler* made the supporting attack; its objective for the day was the capture of the village of Yakovlevo (Яковлево.)[6]

The day's mission for the 13th (Heavy) Company, which began the operation near Tomarovka (Томаровка) with between eleven and thirteen serviceable Tigers, was to support the 2nd Panzer Grenadier Regiment in an attack along both sides of the Tomarovka road toward the village of Bykovka (Быковка), clear a line of villages along the Vorskla River, eliminate flanking threats from the west bank of the Vorskla, and seize Bykovka, the objective for the day. The regiment was also augmented with the division assault gun detachment and one company of the division engineer detachment. Shortly after 0130 hours, the 2nd Panzer Grenadier Regiment advanced along the Tomarovka–Bykovka road in a sector defended by the 52nd Guards Rifle Division, arriving at attack positions at 0315 hours. In front of Hill 220.5, defended by the 151st Guards Rifle Regiment, enemy antitank ditches, barbed wire, antitank guns, and pillbox flamethrowers awaited the Germans. Several of the antitank guns were so well-camouflaged that if they held their fire they would not be observed by the Tigers until the Germans were just twenty meters away.[7]

The 13th (Heavy) Company began moving forward in the rain at 0315 hours to Hill 228.6, so as to pass through the lines of 2nd Panzer Grenadier Regiment at 0405 hours as artillery began to pound enemy positions. Tiger **1321**, commanded by *SS-Untersturmführer* Helmut "Bubi" Wendorff, was struck by an antitank round almost immediately and came to a halt with a damaged track; the vehicle had just received a new engine the day before. Wendorff was wounded in the encounter. Another Tiger was struck in the side by an antitank round and its crew temporarily dismounted. The Tigers and infantry broke through the first enemy defensive line in time to run into antitank fire from supplemental defensive positions.[8]

Leibstandarte Adolf Hitler reported heavy trench fighting at 1045 hours. Several enemy bunkers had large static flamethrowers—possibly FOG-1 models—and company commander Heinrich Kling in **1301** immediately began attacking those dangerous weapons; over the course of the day his crew would destroy ten of the monster flamethrowers.[9] The fierce fight for Hill 220.5 ended at 1115 hours. **1321** returned to action. The company then supported the attack on Hill 217.1, just one-half kilometer northeast of Hill 220.5. In this assault, the loader in **1331**, *SS-Panzerschütze* Walter Koch, was wounded in the head by an antitank shell that struck the tank from the rear; *SS-Panzerschütze* Max Gaube replaced him. Hill 217.1 fell by 1330 hours. Within the hour, some thirty enemy tanks from the 230th Tank Regiment began to attack from west of the Vorskla River just south of Bykovka. Tiger **1331** had to be towed to the rear with mine damage but apparently was quickly repaired. The next defensive position, guarded by the Soviet 1008th Antitank Regiment, was a second Hill 217.1, one-half kilometer south of Bykovka. That fight lasted until about 1400 hours. Division commander *SS-Standartenführer* Theodor Wisch visited the company to observe its progress.

Bykovka was subsequently assaulted, assisted by fire support from the 13th (Heavy) Company; the Germans captured the southern portion of the village about 1640 hours. During this fighting Tiger **1321** ran over mines and was immobilized; in **1331**, Tiger commander *SS-Untersturmführer* Michael Wittmann—who had to take his Tiger three times to the rear to replenish ammunition during the day—opened the commander's hatch and began spraying nearby Soviet infantrymen with submachine gun fire. Bykovka fell before 1840 hours, as at this time the division began attacking the Soviet second defensive line in the hills northeast of Bykovka. By 1900 hours, with the 13th (Heavy) Company still in the lead, both panzer grenadier regiments were approaching Hill 234.8. At that moment the Soviet 28th Antitank Brigade opened up from ambush positions, forcing the Germans to withdraw south.[10]

Sometime during the day, in **1311** tank commander *SS-Obersturmführer* Waldemar Schütz was wounded, as was loader *SS-Panzerschütze* Klaus Bürvenich, when an enemy antitank round struck the vehicle, probably from the rear. *SS-Sturmmann* Gustav Kirschner, driver in **1331**, was wounded when a shell from a T-34 hit a track; *SS-Unterscharführer* Möller, a second platoon driver of a Tiger undergoing repairs, became the driver of **1331**. *SS-Sturmmann* Heinz Owczarek was killed. In addition to **1331** and **1321**, the division reported that four other Tigers had been immobilized by antitank mines during the day; it appears that one of them was likely **1301**. Although he was not injured, overall during the day *SS-Hauptsturmführer* Heinrich Kling, the company commander, changed tanks four times due to damage to each; he began the fight in Tiger **1301**.[11]

Overall, the SS Panzer Grenadier Division *Leibstandarte Adolf Hitler* suffered 110 killed in action, 617 wounded in action, and twenty missing in action during the day-long attack north through Hill 220.5, the village of Bykovka, and to Hill 234.8. Meanwhile the defending Soviet 151st Guards Rifle Regiment, the 28th Antitank Brigade, the 1008th Antitank Regiment, and the 230th Tank Regiment lost 315 killed in action, 681 wounded in action, and 688 missing in action.[12]

8th (Heavy) Company, 2nd Panzer Regiment[13]
SS Panzer Grenadier Division *Das Reich*

Early morning on July 5 was a mess in the SS Panzer Grenadier Division *Das Reich*. While the SS Panzer Grenadier Regiment *Deutschland* stood ready online to the left (west) and the SS Panzer Grenadier Regiment *Der Führer* was ready on the right (east), the division's panzer group was delayed by muddy roads and snarling traffic jams in the division rear area; in fact, the assault gun detachment did not make it into the fight until after the first objective was taken. The panzer grenadiers would have to go in alone. To make matters worse for the staff officers, corps commander *SS-Obergruppenführer* Paul Hausser was at the command post of *Deutschland* and could see any delays in real time.[14] At 0300 hours German artillery began to bombard the enemy front lines, with eighty-eight Luftwaffe Stukas and other ground attack aircraft arriving at 0350 hours. But when the Stukas departed after their attack on Beresov—the first objective and the lynch pin in the division sector—attacking infantry and pioneers were still four hundred meters short of the village, instead of on its outskirts.[15]

The 8th (Heavy) Company, with eleven or twelve operational Tigers, advanced from rear assembly areas to Rakovo (Раково) just before 0200 hours, where all the Tigers were refueled—a lengthy process. They then began advancing about 0400 hours. They crossed the southernmost antitank ditch a mile north of Rakovo, but may not have arrived near Beresov until after 0515 hours in support of *Deutschland*, whose attack had already stalled at the village at 0510 hours, in part because of a second antitank ditch to the front of Beresov. Twenty-seven feet wide and sixteen feet deep, the trench had terraced edges and the steep walls had bunkers constructed into them. Along the route the company avoided the village of Yakhontov and a special flamethrower battalion defending it; infantry took that village at 0245 hours. Tiger **S01** soon struck an antitank mine and was disabled. The driver, *SS-Rottenführer* Georg Gallinat, was wounded, as was the gunner, *SS-Rottenführer* Kurt Meyer. Company commander *SS-Hauptsturmführer* Herbert Zimmermann dismounted the stricken vehicle and transferred to another Tiger, probably **S02**; *SS-Rottenführer* Julius Hinrichsen, the gunner, remained on **S01**. About this time Stuka ace Captain Hans-Ulrich Rudel of the 1st Squadron in the 2nd Stuka Wing *Immelmann* engaged enemy antitank guns firing at the stationary Tiger.[16]

The *Das Reich* had man pack flamethrowers and the Third Battalion of SS Panzer Grenadier Regiment *Der Führer* finally flanked the enemy defenses west of Beresov at 0815 hours; they then hooked back south and attacked the village from its most vulnerable northern side. *Das Reich* commander *SS-Gruppenführer* Walter Krüger moved to Hill 218 and observed that the northern portion of Beresov had been taken at 0947 hours; the entire village fell by 1330 hours. The 8th (Heavy) Company then led the division attack against Hill 233.3—six kilometers north of Beresov—at 1415 hours. Resistance was strong; *Das Reich* captured Hill 233.3 at 1600 hours and the Zhuravlinyi Woods about the same time. An enemy thirty-three tank counterattack failed with the Tigers destroying seven enemy tanks at a range starting at 1,000 meters.[17]

SS-Rottenführer Max Bläsing was wounded in action as the driver of Tiger **S02** when it later struck a mine. *SS-Panzerschütze* Wilfried Frenzel was seriously injured in an accident and was evacuated. Both *SS-Untersturmführer* Alois Kalss, the Third Platoon leader and commander of Tiger **S31**, and *SS-Obersturmführer* Walter Reininghaus, the Second Platoon leader and the commander of Tiger **S21**, were wounded in action but remained with the unit.

The company reportedly destroyed twenty-three enemy tanks in the vicinity of Beresov and Hill 233.3. Between two and five Tigers in the 8th (Heavy) Company struck enemy antitank mines and were immobilized.[18] That evening recovery teams towed **S01** to the rear and a repair facility. The verdict was not good; the transmission was completely broken and would require six days to replace.[19] Additionally *SS-Panzerschütze* Werner Märker was mortally wounded on July 5; he was evacuated from the battlefield but died later in the day at an SS medical facility at Streletskoye (Стрелецкое), on the outskirts of Belgorod.[20]

Overall, the SS Panzer Grenadier Division *Das Reich* had lost seventy-five killed in action and 246 wounded in action during the attack on the village of Beresov and Hill 233.3. Meanwhile, the defending 155th Guards Rifle Regiment and supporting elements from the 27th Antitank Brigade lost sixty-four killed in action, 181 wounded in action, and 133 missing in action.[21] As with the large numbers of Soviets missing in action against the *Leibstandarte*, these missing in action against *Das Reich* indicate that large numbers of Russian soldiers were, in fact, surrendering.

9th (Heavy) Company, 3rd Panzer Regiment[22]
SS Panzer Grenadier Division *Totenkopf*
The 9th (Heavy) Company occupied initial attack positions near Rakovo on July 3, 1943. Attached to the First Battalion of the 3rd Panzer Regiment, the 9th (Heavy) Company departed Rakovo

beginning at 0230 hours in support of the First Battalion of SS Panzer Grenadier Regiment 1 *Totenkopf*. Encountering an enemy antitank ditch southeast of Beresov, the company provided covering fire for divisional engineers who conducted a breach of the obstacle at 0830 hours. Leading the attack, the company moved across the obstacle, overcame a second antitank barrier at 0915 hours, blasted through another antitank ditch at 1230 hours, and advanced northeast of Beresov. At this encounter Tigers may have met their first Soviet SU-152 assault gun on the battlefield.

Hill 216.5 fell to the *Totenkopf* at 1500 hours. Then, turning to the east, the six remaining operational Tigers advanced to the Gonki–Belgorod *Rollbahn*[23] at 1545 hours and took Hill 225.9 about 1710 hours.[24] Five tanks sustained damage by antitank mines that damaged or knocked off tracks; Tiger **901**, minus a track, sat immobile in a minefield while the company commander and crew tried to repair the damage. By late that afternoon only six Tigers were operational, although a few more appear to have been repaired to the extent so as to be of limited value.[25] Tiger gunner *SS-Panzerschütze* Georg Schäfer was wounded in action.[26]

Overall SS Panzer Grenadier Division *Totenkopf* lost thirty-one killed in action, 119 wounded in action, and two missing in action during the advance to the Gonki–Belgorod *Rollbahn*. Meanwhile, the defending 375th Rifle Division and supporting elements lost 52 killed in action, 167 wounded in action, and 113 missing in action.[27]

According to the US Army Concepts Analysis Agency and the Dupuy Institute Kursk Database project, the 2nd SS Panzer Corps suffered **54** panzers put out of action, while the Soviets had **30** tanks put out of action on July 5, 1943; it is not possible to know how many of these were totally destroyed, versus those that could be brought back to operational status after repairs.[28] Several sources believe that Wittmann alone knocked out eight enemy tanks and seven enemy antitank guns on this first day of the offensive.

Day's advance (in kilometers) by each Tiger Company in 2nd SS Panzer Corps:
      13th (Heavy) Company, 1st Panzer Regiment: **19**
      8th (Heavy) Company, 2nd Panzer Regiment: **12**
      9th (Heavy) Company, 3rd Panzer Regiment: **11**
Operational 2nd SS Panzer Corps Tiger strength reported at the end of the day: **28**
      13th (Heavy) Company, 1st Panzer Regiment: **7** (1800 hours)
      8th (Heavy) Company, 2nd Panzer Regiment: **11** (1940 hours)
      9th (Heavy) Company, 3rd Panzer Regiment: **10** (1710 hours)

July 6, 1943[1]

Weather: light clouds, occasional rain showers in some areas, generally sunny and warm; 62° to 70°F
Terrain conditions: rolling, bare ground; roads passable for all vehicles, muddy fields
Sunrise: 0428 hours   **Sunset:** 2047 hours
Moon Phase: Waxing crescent, 14% illumination

13th (Heavy) Company, 1st Panzer Regiment
SS Panzer Grenadier Division *Leibstandarte Adolf Hitler*
The mission of the 13th (Heavy) Company was to seize the heavily fortified enemy position—protected by mines and barbed wire—on Hill 243.2. By early morning the Tigers had been rearmed and refueled. The attack began about 0930 hours, starting from southeast of Yakovlevo, and soon enemy antitank fire struck **1311**, causing minor damage. Tiger **1324** drove over an antitank mine that destroyed its right reduction gear, rendering the Tiger immobile; **1325** also drove over a mine that immobilized it by destroying a reduction gear. At 1145 hours, *Leibstandarte*

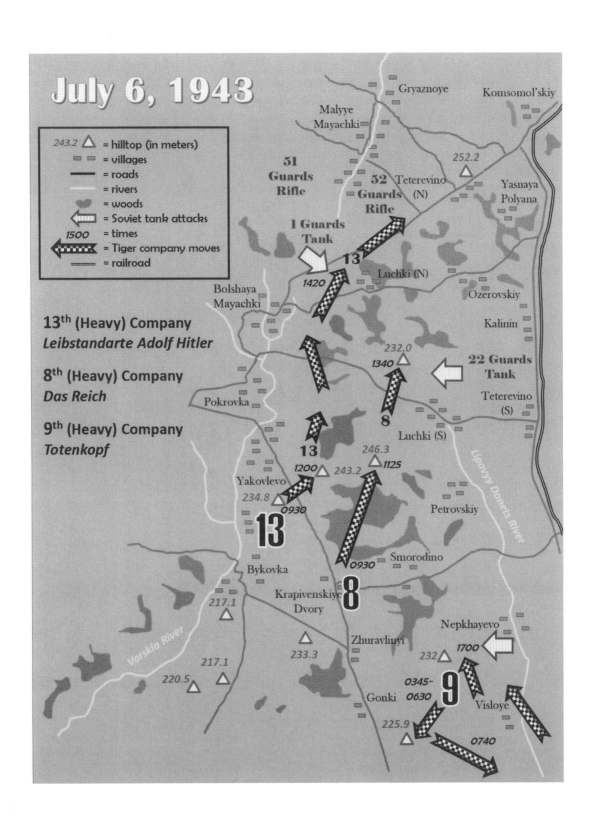

July 6, 1943

243.2 △ = hilltop (in meters)
⬚⬚ = villages
━━ = roads
━━ = rivers
🝙 = woods
⬅ = Soviet tank attacks
1500 = times
◄▨▨ = Tiger company moves
━━ = railroad

13ᵗʰ (Heavy) Company
Leibstandarte Adolf Hitler

8ᵗʰ (Heavy) Company
Das Reich

9ᵗʰ (Heavy) Company
Totenkopf

Gryaznoye
Komsomol'skiy
Malyye
Mayachki
252.2
51
Guards
Rifle
52
Guards
Rifle
Teterevino (N)
Yasnaya
Polyana
1 Guards
Tank
13
1420
Luchki (N)
Ozerovskiy
Bolshaya
Mayachki
Kalinin
232.0
1340
22 Guards
Tank
Pokrovka
8
Teterevino (S)
Luchki (S)
13
246.3
1125
Yakovlevo
1200 △ 243.2
234.8 △ *0930*
13
Petrovskiy
Bykovka
0930
Smorodino
217.1
8
Krapivenskiye
Dvory
Nepkhayevo
Zhuravlinyi
232 △ *1700*
233.3
217.1
0345–
Gonki 0630
9
220.5 △
Visloye
225.9 △ *0740*

Lipovyy Donets River
Vorskla River

Adolf Hitler received orders to swing northeast and assault Luchki [Лучки] (North). Hill 243.2 fell at noon, but by now only three Tigers of the company remained operational; *SS-Hauptsturmführer* Kling was in one of them, commanding the company. At 1315 hours thirty-eight enemy tanks, probably from the 1st Guards Tank Brigade of the 3rd Mechanized Corps, attacked, but were repulsed by the greatly reduced 13th (Heavy) Company.[2]

SS-Hauptsturmführer Heinz Kling continued to lead the company forward; during the day **1331** ran over an antitank mine that destroyed part of its right track.[3] Tank commander *SS-Unterscharführer* Jürgen Brandt, in **1334**, took the crippled **1331** under tow and pulled it to safety, which was strictly forbidden (as it took two Tigers out of action; when it did happen, the towing Tiger would only pull the disabled Tiger to the nearest covered position) but was often done, as it often took two or three traditional recovery vehicles to take a Tiger off the battlefield and to a repair facility.[4] Tiger commander Michael Wittmann moved from **1331** to another tank. According to one source the third platoon had five Tigers operational, that two dug-in Soviet KV-1 tanks, perhaps from the 203rd Tank Regiment, engaged the company near Luchki (North), and that a dug-in KV-1 destroyed one Tiger at a range of 600 meters, machine-gunning its fleeing crew.[5] This last assertion is not supported by other sources. At 1515 hours *Leibstandarte Adolf Hitler* received a preliminary order to continue the attack to seize the bridges over the Psel River at the village of Petrovka.

SS-Obergruppenführer Josef "Sepp" Dietrich visited the company that evening and authorized **1334** to be taken out of the line and to be stripped of parts so that other tanks could be made operational. That night four Tigers rushed northeast to intercept a tank column from the 5th Guards Tank Corps moving south to Teterevino (North). With Luftwaffe ground attack aircraft in support the company repulsed the attack. Over the first two days of the offensive, the 13th (Heavy) Company reportedly destroyed fifty-two enemy tanks, with *SS-Hauptsturmführer* Heinrich Kling accounting for nine of them.[6] That night the Tiger crewmen slept for the first time in forty-eight hours.[7]

Overall, SS Panzer Grenadier Division *Leibstandarte Adolf Hitler* suffered ninety killed in action, 415 wounded in action, and nineteen missing in action during the day-long attack northeast through the village of Yakovlevo, Hill 243.2, and past the village of Luchki (North). Meanwhile the defending elements of the Soviet 52nd Guards Rifle Division, the 1st Guards Tank Brigade, and the 203rd Tank Regiment lost 312 killed in action, 784 wounded in action, and 325 missing in action.[8]

8th (Heavy) Company, 2nd Panzer Regiment
SS Panzer Grenadier Division *Das Reich*

The division reported at 0500 hours that road conditions were difficult. *Das Reich* received the order to attack positions north of the village of Krapivenskiye Dvory (Крапивенские Дворы) and continue to push northeast, but because of these poor road conditions the division did not start until 0930 hours. Infantry from the SS Panzer Grenadier Regiment *Der Führer* attacked through broken terrain and heavy enemy resistance, finally seizing their objective (Hill 246.3) at 1125 hours. The 8th (Heavy) Company subsequently advanced via Hill 232 at 1340 hours and engaged T-34s of the 22nd Guards Tank Brigade in heavy fighting. SS Panzer Grenadier Regiment *Der Führer* cleared Luchki (South) of enemy forces by 1440 hours.[9] Although in the initial engagement near Luchki (South) the Tigers knocked out roughly a dozen enemy tanks, only seven Tigers remained operational by the end of the day.[10] At 1515 hours *Das Reich* received a preliminary order to continue the attack north to seize Prokhorovka (Прохоровка).

SS-Unterscharführer Kurt Baral, commander of Tiger **S32**, was lightly wounded in the head, but remained with his vehicle. His gunner, *SS-Panzeroberschütze* Jakob Kuster, was wounded in the same incident caused by an artillery round, as was his loader. Radio operator *SS-Funker*

Wilhelm Lotter was wounded in action, most likely when his Tiger ran over an antitank mine.

Overall the SS Panzer Grenadier Division *Das Reich* lost fifty-three killed in action, 205 wounded in action, and two missing in action during the attack on Hill 246.3, Luchki (South), and Hill 232. Meanwhile, the defending 158th Guards Rifle Regiment, the 5th Guards Tank Corps, and the 27th Antitank Brigade lost 254 killed in action, 402 wounded in action, and 481 missing in action.[11]

9th (Heavy) Company, 3rd Panzer Regiment
SS Panzer Grenadier Division *Totenkopf*

The 9th (Heavy) Company, supporting SS Panzer Grenadier Regiment 1 *Totenkopf*, led the assault about 0345 hours against Hill 225.9, and by 0600 hours had crossed a fork in the road on the objective, repelled an enemy attack from the woods south of the village of Yerik (Ерик), and then received antitank fire from Hill 214.5. The company subsequently moved toward Ternovka (Терновка), and by 0740 hours had reached a bridge west of Schopino (Шопино). Enemy ground attack aircraft made strafing runs on the company as the enemy brought up elements of the 2nd Guards Tank Corps.[12]

About noon, the company received a new mission to conduct a reconnaissance in the vicinity of Luchki (South) to make contact with the *Das Reich*. At 1700 hours thirty-three enemy tanks, including many British Churchills of the 26th Guards Tank Brigade, crossed the Lipovyy Donets River (река Липовый донец) a few miles to the north at Soschenkov. The company engaged the attackers, destroying most of the enemy tanks; during the fight **902** drove over an antitank mine and was damaged about 1930 hours. Tiger **911** knocked out a T-34 at the same time. Most of the company's operations during the day consisted of moving around terrain already seized to counterattack advancing enemy tank columns. As a result the company seized very little new terrain. The company received its mission—about 2245 hours—for the following day to throw the remaining enemy back across the river and to occupy the high ridges on the west of the Lipovyy Donets.[13] That would be a difficult task, given that night fell on just six operational *Totenkopf* Tigers.

Overall the SS Panzer Grenadier Division *Totenkopf* lost fifty-three killed in action and 234 wounded in action during the advance toward Yerik, Hill 214.5, Ternovka, and Soschenkov. Meanwhile, the defending 155th Guards Rifle Regiment, 375th Rifle Division, and elements of the 2nd Guards Tank Corps lost 257 killed in action, 604 wounded in action, and 240 missing in action.[14]

According to the US Army Concepts Analysis Agency and the Dupuy Institute Kursk Database project (completed in 1996), on July 6, 1943, the 2nd SS Panzer Corps suffered **79** panzers put out of action, while the Soviets had **149** tanks put out of action; it is not possible to know how many of these were totally destroyed versus those that could be brought back to operational status after repairs.[15]

Day's advance (in kilometers) by each Tiger Company in the 2nd SS Panzer Corps:
> 13th (Heavy) Company, 1st Panzer Regiment: **18**
> 8th (Heavy) Company, 2nd Panzer Regiment: **10**
> 9th (Heavy) Company, 3rd Panzer Regiment: **3**

Operational 2nd SS Panzer Corps Tiger strength reported at the end of the day: **17**
> 13th (Heavy) Company, 1st Panzer Regiment: **4** (derived; report not submitted)
> 8th (Heavy) Company, 2nd Panzer Regiment: **7** (0230 hours 7 July)
> 9th (Heavy) Company, 3rd Panzer Regiment: **6** (1915 hours)

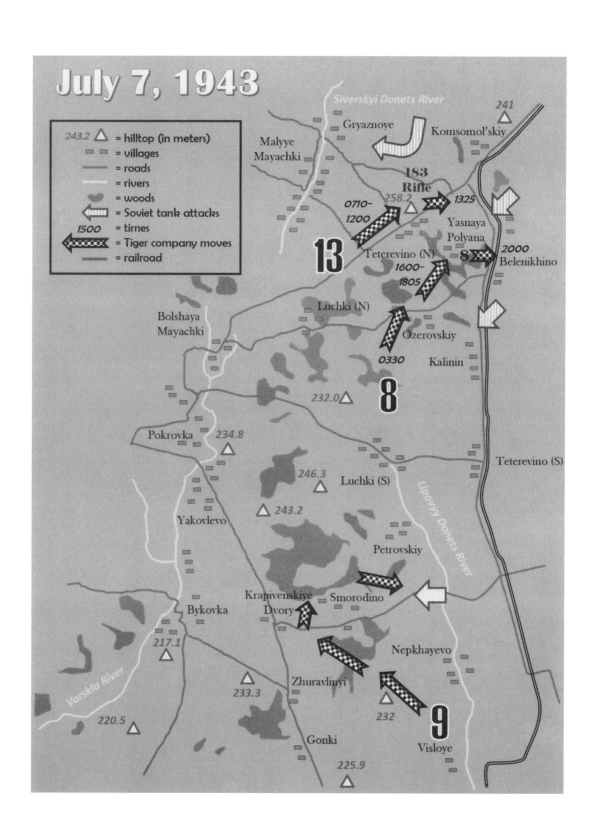

July 7, 1943

Siverskyi Donets River

Gryaznoye
Komsomol'skiy
241

Malyye Mayachki

183 Rifle

258.2

0710–1200

1325

13

Yasnaya Polyana

Teterevino (N)

1600–1805

8

2000 Belenikhino

Luchki (N)

Ozerovskiy

0330

Kalinin

Bolshaya Mayachki

232.0

8

Pokrovka

234.8

246.3

Luchki (S)

Teterevino (S)

243.2

Yakovlevo

Petrovskiy

Lipovyy Donets River

Krapivenskiye Dvory

Smorodino

Bykovka

217.1

Nepkhayevo

233.3

Zhuravlinyi

232

9

Vorskla River

220.5

Gonki

Visloye

225.9

243.2 △ = hilltop (in meters)
= villages
= roads
= rivers
= woods
= Soviet tank attacks
1500 = times
= Tiger company moves
= railroad

July 7, 1943[1]

Weather: clear, sunny, dry, and warm; later in the day cooler and overcast
Terrain conditions: rolling, mixed ground, hay fields; roads and farm tracks in good condition
Sunrise: 0429 hours   **Sunset:** 2047 hours
Moon Phase: Waxing crescent, 21% illumination

13th (Heavy) Company, 1st Panzer Regiment
SS Panzer Grenadier Division *Leibstandarte Adolf Hitler*

The division's mission for the day would stretch the unit to the breaking point. To the southwest, the 1st Panzer Grenadier Regiment *Leibstandarte Adolf Hitler*—for all practical purposes—defended in the Pokrovka–Bolshaya Mayachki area, oriented to the northwest to engage the Soviet 31st Tank Corps. To the east of the regiment were the assault gun detachment and the antitank detachment of the division in the vicinity of Luchki (North). They would also defend against attacks by the 242nd Tank Brigade and the 237th Tank Brigade. Finally, the 1st Panzer Grenadier Regiment and the 1st Panzer Regiment—including the 13th (Heavy) Company—would attack northeast.

Late at night, a company Tiger guarding the road at Teterevino (North) (Тетеревино) engaged and destroyed three enemy tanks carrying infantry—probably a continuation of the 5th Guards Tank Corps—and at dawn the enemy attacked the village again with about thirty tanks. Beginning at 0710 hours, the company began a five-hour tank battle against the 20th Guards Tank Brigade north of Teterevino (North), during which Stuka aircraft mistakenly attacked several Tigers but did not cause significant damage.

The company was now penetrating the third defensive line and fighting elements of the Soviet 31st Tank Corps. Two Tigers broke through enemy forces surrounding *SS-Sturmbannführer* Jochen Peiper's Third Battalion of the 2nd SS Panzer Grenadier Regiment. The fight for Hill 258.2 began about 0900 hours; the company encountered major antitank ditches, but seized the height when the defending 183rd Rifle Division abandoned it. By 1325 hours the *Leibstandarte Adolf Hitler* was slightly past Teterevino (North) and protecting the advancing *Das Reich* from threats coming from its north.[2] Tiger **1323**, commanded by *SS-Scharführer* Georg Lötzsch, suffered a transmission failure.[3] Tiger **1324** experienced additional mechanical problems. On **1331**, radio operator *SS-Panzerschütze* Paul Bender and driver *SS-Sturmmann* Walter Bingert were replaced due to exhaustion.

For the day, the SS Panzer Grenadier Division *Leibstandarte Adolf Hitler* suffered fifty-eight killed in action, 243 wounded in action, and three missing in action during operations at the village of Teterevino (North) and Hill 258.2 against elements of the 3rd Mechanized Corps and the 31st Tank Corps and the assault on Hill 258.2. Meanwhile, the 242nd Tank Brigade, the 237th Tank Brigade, the 20th Guards Tank Brigade, and the 183rd Rifle Division lost 106 killed in action, 212 wounded in action, and 106 missing in action.[4]

8th (Heavy) Company, 2nd Panzer Regiment
SS Panzer Grenadier Division *Das Reich*

At 0330 hours the company, with attached infantry, advanced toward Yasnaya Polyana (Ясная Поляна). The commander of the 2nd Panzer Regiment, *SS-Obersturmbannführer* Hans-Albin von Reitzenstein, directed that *SS-Hauptsturmführer* Karl-Heinz Lorenz, the regimental adjutant, proceed directly to the company when *SS-Hauptsturmführer* Zimmermann was wounded early in the morning. Meanwhile, at 1030 hours thirty enemy tanks attacked from the west but retreated to the north at about 1200 hours.

SS-Hauptsturmführer Lorenz, now in **S24**, brashly moved ahead of the company and crossed a railroad embankment east of Kalinin, ordering the other Tigers to follow him and continue the attack. Records show that about this time a Tiger commander reported that he was under fire from a Soviet armored train, possibly trains Number 737 and Number 746. These may have been type NKPS-42 trains with eight cars and a total of sixteen machine guns, six 37 mm antiaircraft guns, four 76 mm cannon, two 107 mm cannon, an armored car, and eight rifle squads. They were on the Belgorod–Kursk rail line and had probably deployed from Staryi Oskol. The 20th Guards Tank Brigade was also in the area of the fight.

It is likely that **S24** received two direct hits: one through the left side of the hull and the other through the right side of the hull, directly where the radio operator was located. Lorenz, in the commander's cupola, was killed in action, as was radio operator *SS-Panzeroberschütze* Ernst Schäfer, when he was killed by enemy infantry fire when he tried to escape the vehicle. *SS-Unterscharführer* Werner Schäfer, probably occupying the gunner's position, was gravely wounded.[5] The driver, *SS-Rottenführer* Franz Stemann, was wounded. *SS-Rottenführer* Heinz Wilken was seriously wounded and died of his wounds one day later.[6] Two other Tigers were also struck by fire from the train.

The other Tiger commanders, conscious that if they crossed the rail line embankment as their acting commander had just done it would expose their vulnerable tank underbelly to enemy fire, began seeking an alternative crossing point. Enemy antitank fire hit one of the Tigers on the main gun tube and it remained behind; only one operational Tiger reached Lorenz's position.[7]

Upon receiving the report, von Reitzenstein became enraged and accused the company of cowardice and dereliction of duty. As a result many award recommendations in the company for the battle appear to have been "short stopped." The company prepared to attack at 1600 hours against the 21st Guards Tank Brigade near Yasnaya Polyana. At 1805 hours the *Das Reich* drove the enemy out of Yasnaya Polyana. About 2000 hours the company helped seize the railroad station at Belenikhino (Беленихино).[8]

For July 7, the SS Panzer Grenadier Division *Das Reich* lost eighteen killed in action, 103 wounded in action, and one missing in action during the attack northeast to the village of Yasnaya Polyana and the village of Belenikhino. Meanwhile, elements of the defending 183rd Rifle Division, the 158th Guards Rifle Regiment, and the 21st Guards Tank Brigade lost 166 killed in action, 372 wounded in action, and 478 missing in action.[9]

9th (Heavy) Company, 3rd Panzer Regiment
SS Panzer Grenadier Division *Totenkopf*

The 9th (Heavy) Company advanced beginning 0430 hours near Soschenkov and swinging northwest to the village of Krapivenskiye Dvory before turning east. By 1030 hours, the Tigers had eliminated those enemy forces that had not retreated back across the Lipovyy Donets. At 1130 hours the division reported that the high ground west of the Lipovyy Donets was secure.[10] Tiger **914** in the First Platoon, commanded by *SS-Unterscharführer* Richard Müller, was hit by Soviet artillery rounds near Smorodino during the day and became a total loss; Müller was mortally wounded and died later. Two Tigers were reported damaged during the day. Once again, the 9th (Heavy) Company gained very little new ground; it was defeating penetrations but not advancing the attack forward.[11]

For the day, the SS Panzer Grenadier Division *Totenkopf* lost thirty-nine killed in action, 117 wounded in action, and one missing in action during the advance toward Smorodino. The defending 375th Rifle Division, 96th Tank Brigade, 1510th Antitank Regiment, 1076th Antitank Regiment, 649th Antitank Brigade, and other elements lost 191 killed in action, 562 wounded in action, and 155 missing in action.[12]

According to the Kursk Database project, the 2nd SS Panzer Corps suffered **55** panzers put out of action, while the Soviets had **86** tanks put out of action on July 7, 1943; we do not know how many of these were totally destroyed.[13]

Day's advance (in kilometers) by each Tiger Company in 2nd SS Panzer Corps:
      13th (Heavy) Company, 1st Panzer Regiment: **4**
      8th (Heavy) Company, 2nd Panzer Regiment: **7**
      9th (Heavy) Company, 3rd Panzer Regiment: **0**
Operational 2nd SS Panzer Corps Tiger strength reported at the end of the day: **16**
      13th (Heavy) Company, 1st Panzer Regiment: **4**
      8th (Heavy) Company, 2nd Panzer Regiment: **6**
      9th (Heavy) Company, 3rd Panzer Regiment: **6** (1900 hours)

At the end of the day Colonel General Hoth reported that the Fourth Panzer Army had lost only three Tigers; all other damaged Tigers could be repaired. [14]

July 8, 1943[1]

Weather: humid, partly cloudy and warm, overcast; 70°F
Terrain conditions: rolling terrain, deep ravines, dry roads and approaches in good condition
Sunrise: 0430 hours   **Sunset:** 2046 hours
Moon Phase: Waxing crescent, 30% illumination

The northern pincer, under Colonel General Walter Model, had gained a pathetic one mile on this day and the OKH staff in Berlin had a recommendation to make; their call was to continue the offensive in hope of improvement, especially from the attack in the south. As a result of the first three days of battle, Colonel General Hoth perceived an opportunity to encircle significant enemy armored forces in the form of the 31st Tank Corps, but the plan would force the 2nd SS Panzer Corps to turn west, away from Prokhorovka and its original axis of attack. The mission of the corps as a result, on July 8, was to pivot to the northwest and coordinate with their neighbor to the west, the 48th Panzer Corps, to encircle enemy forces south of the Psel River. Cognizant of the shift in direction, Hoth instructed Hausser to keep sufficient corps' combat power oriented to the northeast to prevent enemy attacks into the eastern flank of the planned encirclement.[2]

13th (Heavy) Company, 1st Panzer Regiment
SS Panzer Grenadier Division *Leibstandarte Adolf Hitler*

The 1st SS Panzer Grenadier Regiment seized Malyye Mayachki (Малые Маячки) at 0710 hours, which enabled the 13th (Heavy) Company and other armored elements to move northwest from Teterevino (North) at 0800 hours. After two Tigers suffered track damage, the company soon encountered enemy tanks of the 100th Tank Brigade southeast of Veselyy (Веселый) at 0920 hours. Fighting lasted until 1030 hours, when the company flanked a group of dug-in enemy assault guns, at which time the enemy veered south. The company advanced farther northwest, attacking by fire dug-in tanks at Hill 224.5.

    The company, now probably with four operational Tigers led by *SS-Hauptsturmführer* Kling, swung south, and at 1205 hours began engaging enemy tanks between Veselyy and Ryl'skiy (Рыльский). According to a report in his personnel file, Kling's company destroyed forty-two T-34 and three General Lee tanks in this action that lasted several hours. At 1700 hours the corps ordered the division to destroy enemy forces near Veselyy. About 1830 hours, Kling reported that two Tigers were damaged by antitank fire, causing track damage, from an undiscovered enemy antitank position near Veselyy; the report made it all the way to the corps headquarters. One source posits that Soviet SU-122 comprised this antitank position. *SS-Untersturmführer* Helmut Wendorff, the leader of the second platoon and commander of **1321**, was wounded in this action and evacuated to the main

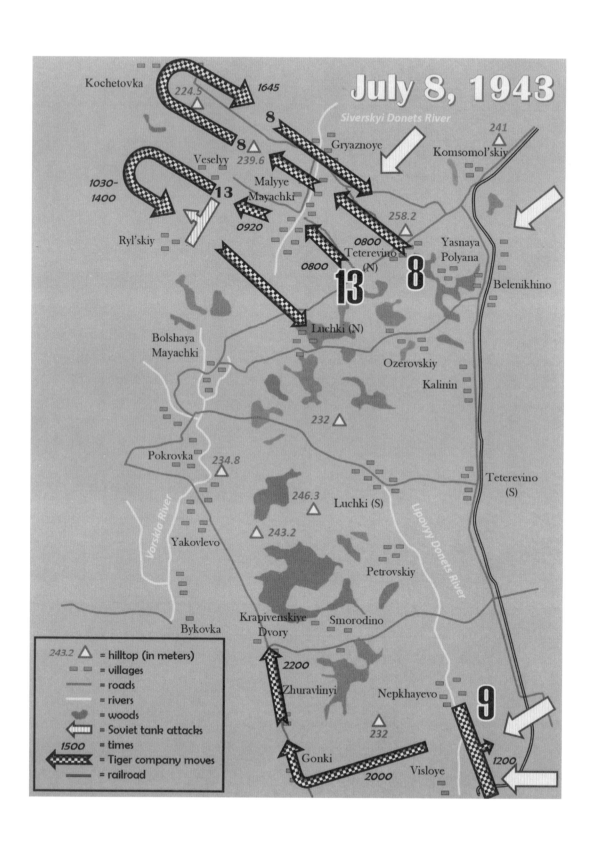

dressing station for treatment. *SS-Unterscharführer* Ewald Mölly in **1322** probably became the acting platoon leader. The other damaged Tiger remains unidentified. The 13th (Heavy) Company—which now had only one operational Tiger—and the rest of the regiment finished the day by returning east to Luchki (North).[3]

When the company departed that morning **1325**, commanded by *SS-Unterscharführer* Franz Staudegger, and **1324**, tank commander *SS-Sturmmann* Rolf Schamp, remained at the company forward maintenance area in Teterevino (North) due to vehicle mechanical problems; both Tigers could barely move due to track damage. In late morning German troops in the village received warning that fifty-plus enemy tanks, most likely from the 10th Tank Corps, were approaching; Staudegger fixed enough of the vehicle's track so that it would be mobile and headed toward the enemy, which was attempting to overrun the First Battalion of the SS Panzer Grenadier Regiment *Deutschland* of the *Das Reich*.

Staudegger picked a firing position on the northeast edge of Teterevino (North) next to an embankment that would partially protect the vehicle, while Schamp pulled his panzer slightly to the rear and west to protect Staudegger's flank. Over the next several hours **1325** was credited with destroying twenty-two enemy tanks, while the rest withdrew from the fight.[4] Schamp undoubtedly destroyed a few more, but his total is not known. At 2300 hours the division received the order for the next day's operation: attack with the two panzer grenadier regiments and clear enemy forces from a line Bolshaya Mayachki northward to protect the left flank of the *Totenkopf* division that was moving forward to attack across the Psel River.

For July 8, the SS Panzer Grenadier Division *Leibstandarte Adolf Hitler* suffered thirty-two killed in action, ninety-nine wounded in action, and six missing in action during the attack northwest through the villages of Malyye Mayachki and Veselyy against elements of the 31st Tank Corps. The 100th Tank Brigade, 192nd Tank Brigade, 29th Antitank Brigade, 1244th Antitank Regiment, and 210th Antitank Rifle Battalion lost ninety-eight killed in action, 273 wounded in action, and 148 missing in action.[5]

8th (Heavy) Company, 2nd Panzer Regiment
SS Panzer Grenadier Division *Das Reich*

Das Reich needed to concentrate combat power, so the corps issued an order that the reconnaissance detachment would be relieved of its sector by a blocking force of combat engineers. Meanwhile, the mission of the 8th (Heavy) Company, and the rest of the 2nd Panzer Regiment, was to advance along the following axis: Teterevino (North)–Gryaznoye (Грязное)–Hill 224.5–Kochetovka (Кочетовка)–Hill 235.9—and then just north of Novoselovka (Новоселовка). The reconnaissance detachment threw caution to the wind and by 0815 hours, *Das Reich* had pushed advance elements all the way to Hill 224.5.

8th (Heavy) Company began movement at 0800 hours to seize Gryaznoye; accompanying infantrymen seized an interim objective of Hill 239.6, west of the village, at 1100 hours. A large concentration of enemy tanks was spotted at 1230 hours east of Yasnaya Polyana. Luftwaffe aircraft largely destroyed the enemy at this location, freeing the Tigers to advance from Gryaznoye to Kochetovka, which they did. Another group of enemy tanks, possibly belonging to the 5th Guards Tank Corps, was spotted north of Teterevino (North) about 1630 hours. Such was the danger that the 8th Air Corps flew four Stuka groups, two ground attack groups, and several specialized tank busters against this target. Enemy pressure occurred at all points in the *Das Reich* sector and from 1300 hours to 1700 hours the fighting was fierce at Luchki (South) and Teterevino (South).[6] At 1645 hours the company pivoted from Kochetovka and slammed into the flank of this enemy advance.[7] The company returned to the Teterevino (North) area about 2100 hours.

At 2300 hours the division received the order for the next day's operation: halt and secure the eastern flank of the corps as the *Totenkopf* attacked north to establish a bridgehead over the Psel

River in the vicinity of Krasnyy Oktyabr'.

For July 8, the SS Panzer Grenadier Division *Das Reich* lost fifty-eight killed in action and 202 wounded in action during the attack northwest to the villages of Malyye Mayachki and Kochetovka against elements of the 5th Guards Tank Corps. Meanwhile, the opposing Soviet units lost 361 killed in action, 678 wounded in action, and 277 missing in action.[8]

9th (Heavy) Company, 3rd Panzer Regiment
SS Panzer Grenadier Division *Totenkopf*

Effective at 0215 hours, the 627th Pioneer Battalion (motorized) assumed responsibility for part of the *Totenkopf* sector, establishing a blocking force. At 0500 hours the 167th Infantry Division relieved the *Totenkopf* so it could begin to move north.[9] The 9th (Heavy) Company, with seven operational Tigers, advanced to the area of Hill 209.5. Tiger **911** then reported that the turret was jammed and moved back to repair facilities in the rear.

SS-Sturmbannführer Eugen Kunstmann, commander of the 3rd Panzer Regiment, was killed in action west of Visloye (Висло́е) at the Dolschik *balka* by Soviet antitank fire. *SS-Sturmbannführer* Georg Bochmann, commander of the Second Battalion, assumed command of the regiment, and *SS-Hauptsturmführer* Fritz Biermeier, commander of the 9th (Heavy) Company, assumed temporary command of the Second Battalion. Filling Biermeier's old position would be filled by company troop leader *SS-Obersturmführer* Wilhelm Schroeder. The promotion was short-lived, as in just a few hours a Soviet antitank rifle round struck him in the head as he was exposed in the cupola firing a submachine gun at advancing enemy infantry in a wheat field. Schroeder was probably in Tiger **901**; one source believes that **901** destroyed two T-34s while Schroeder was in command, but he had no coax turret machine gun to keep the infantry at bay.[10]

Although this was the official cause of death for Wilhelm Schroeder, the company may have been rocked by another report from the battlefield—that it was not enemy fire, but an errant round from a neighboring Sturmgeschütz III (Assault Gun Mark III) fired from close range that struck **901**, killing the commander. Given the close proximity and mass of the attacking armored columns, the surprise is not that perhaps fratricide (friendly fire) was the cause of the incident, but rather that more such incidents did not occur. In any event, time has obscured exactly what happened in that split second on July 8.[11]

SS-Untersturmführer Walter Köhler, first platoon leader, became the acting company commander; he transferred to **901**, as his own **911** was heading to maintenance with a jammed turret. The company repulsed an enemy tank attack by the 2nd Guards Tank Corps in ravines around Ternovka. Near Smorodino (Смороди́но) Soviet artillery rounds struck **912**, fatally wounding Tiger commander *SS-Unterscharführer* Josef Göckl and killing gunner *SS-Unterscharführer* Ludwig Zimmermann and loader *SS-Rottenführer* Ludwig Müller. Müller died later in the day at the Vasil'yevka casualty collection point for the *Totenkopf*. At 1645 hours the corps issued an order to *Totenkopf* to be prepared to begin moving northward. The company ended the day moving northwest to an assembly area near Krapivenskiye Dvory.[12]

At 2300 hours the division received the order for the next day's operation: attack north to establish a bridgehead over the Psel River in the vicinity of Krasnyy Oktyabr' and then push to the northwest to link up with the 11th Panzer Division of the 48th Panzer Corps.

For the day, the SS Panzer Grenadier Division *Totenkopf* lost twenty-eight killed in action and ninety-two wounded in action repelling Soviet attacks near the villages of Visloye and Nepkhayevo by the 2nd Guards Tank Corps. The 89th Guards Rifle Division, 93rd Guards Rifle Division, 96th Tank Brigade, and other elements lost 242 killed in action, 497 wounded in action, and 179 missing in action.[13]

On July 8, 1943, the 2nd SS Panzer Corps suffered **47** panzers put out of action, while the Soviets had **164** tanks put out of action.[14]

Day's advance (in kilometers) by each Tiger Company in 2nd SS Panzer Corps:

       13th (Heavy) Company, 1st Panzer Regiment: **7**

       8th (Heavy) Company, 2nd Panzer Regiment: **12**

       9th (Heavy) Company, 3rd Panzer Regiment: **0**

Operational 2nd SS Panzer Corps Tiger strength reported at the end of the day: **12**

       13th (Heavy) Company, 1st Panzer Regiment: **1** (1745 hours)

       8th (Heavy) Company, 2nd Panzer Regiment: **6**

       9th (Heavy) Company, 3rd Panzer Regiment: **5** (1715 hours)

July 9, 1943[1]

Weather: dry, partly cloudy, afternoon rain, some local thunderstorms that grew heavier during the night

Terrain conditions: roads deteriorated as the day wore on

Sunrise: 0431 hours   **Sunset:** 2046 hours

Moon Phase: First quarter, 39% illumination

13th (Heavy) Company, 1st Panzer Regiment
SS Panzer Grenadier Division *Leibstandarte Adolf Hitler*

The 13th (Heavy) Company concentrated on fixing non-operational Tigers in Teterevino (North). 2nd SS Panzer Grenadier Regiment, supported by a handful of Tigers, departed Luchki (North) and crossed the Bolshaya Mayachki road—their likely departure for the attack—at 1000 hours.

The regiment and company advanced to Ryl'skiy, clearing it by 1220 hours. However, it was reported at the same time that the crucial bridge at Sukhosolotino (Сухосолотино) had been destroyed by Soviet engineers. The unit continued the attack toward Sukhosolotino, reaching this objective at 1700 hours in the defense zone of the 51st Guards Rifle Division, but could not cross the Solotinka River (река Солотинка). At 2215 hours the division published the attack order for the next day. In Tiger **1315** tank commander *SS-Unterscharführer* Franz Enderl was killed in action. *SS-Untersturmführer* Michael Wittmann replaced *SS-Sturmmann* Rolf Schamp as tank commander of **1324** after Wittmann's **1331** experienced more mechanical problems and was not operational, remaining in Teterevino (North). *SS-Untersturmführer* Helmut Wendorff returned to duty and reported to the company combat trains.[2]

At 2200 hours the division received the order for the next day's operation: it was to attack northeast along the Belgorod–Prokhorovka highway and seize Prokhorovka. For the day, the SS Panzer Grenadier Division *Leibstandarte Adolf Hitler* suffered twelve killed in action, thirty-four wounded in action, and two missing in action during the attack northwest from the village of Bolshaya Mayachki to the village of Ryl'skiy toward Sukhosolotino and the Solotinka River. The defending 51st Guards Rifle Division, 242nd Tank Brigade, 29th Antitank Brigade, and 100th Tank Brigade suffered nine killed in action, fourteen wounded in action, and fourteen missing in action.[3]

8th (Heavy) Company, 2nd Panzer Regiment
SS Panzer Grenadier Division *Das Reich*

The night was quiet. The division received orders to hold to its existing forward limit of advance, but to withdraw key elements slightly so that required maintenance and repairs could be conducted. The panzer regiment, including the 8th (Heavy Company), withdrew to Ozerovskiy (Озерскийв) to accomplish these tasks.[4] During the afternoon, division troops observed about one hundred enemy tanks at 1500 hours; Stukas and bombers attacked this group at 1530 hours.

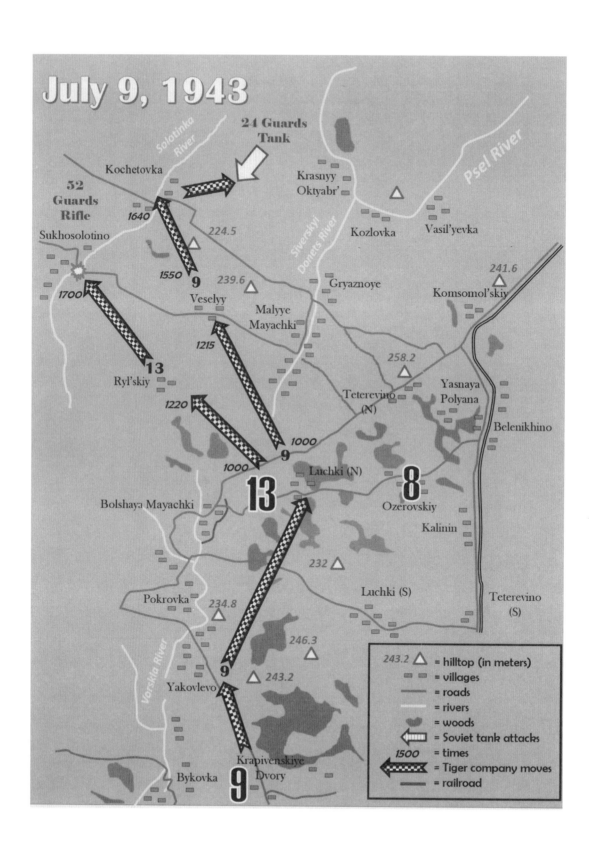

July 9, 1943

24 Guards Tank

52 Guards Rifle

Kochetovka

1640

224.5

Krasnyy Oktyabr'

Psel River

Sukhosolotino

1550   9

239.6

Kozlovka

Vasil'yevka

1700

Veselyy

Gryaznoye

241.6

Komsomol'skiy

1215

Malyye Mayachki

13

1220

Ryl'skiy

258.2

Teterevino (N)

Yasnaya Polyana

Belenikhino

1000

9

Bolshaya Mayachki

1000

13

Luchki (N)

8

Ozerovskiy

Kalinin

232

Pokrovka

234.8

Luchki (S)

Teterevino (S)

246.3

9

243.2

Yakovlevo

243.2 △ = hilltop (in meters)

⬜⬜ = villages

━━ = roads

━━ = rivers

🌳 = woods

⬅ = Soviet tank attacks

1500 = times

⬅ = Tiger company moves

━━ = railroad

Krapivenskiye Dvory

Bykovka   9

At 2200 hours the division received the order for the next day's operation: it was to protect the right (eastern) flank of the *Leibstandarte Adolf Hitler* as it attacked northeast along the Belgorod–Prokhorovka highway by attacking in echelon with the SS Panzer Grenadier Regiment *Deutschland*.

For July 9, the SS Panzer Grenadier Division *Das Reich* lost twenty-three killed in action, 149 wounded in action, and two missing in action defending near Kalinin against attacks by elements of the 5th Guards Tank Corps and the 2nd Tank Corps. For the day the opposing Soviet units, including the 99th Tank Brigade, the 169th Tank Brigade, 15th Guards Heavy Tank Regiment, and the 4th Guards Tank Brigade, lost 321 killed in action, 618 wounded in action, and 159 missing in action in the attacks across a frontage of sixteen miles.[5]

9th (Heavy) Company, 3rd Panzer Regiment
SS Panzer Grenadier Division *Totenkopf*

To better control the upcoming day's attack, the division headquarters moved north and set up on the point of a wood line northeast of Hill 232. The division reconnaissance detachment rolled early, and at 0730 hours reported that the village of Gryaznoye was defended by strong enemy forces.

The 9th (Heavy) Company began the day in an assembly area at Krapivenskiye Dvory. Battle Group Baum—from the SS Panzer Grenadier Regiment 1 *Totenkopf*—supported by the 9th (Heavy) Company, began rumbling up the road from Krapivenskiye Dvory toward Yakovlevo, but shortly before reaching the village veered off the road to the right and traveled cross country to the village of Luchki (North). The unit crossed the Bolshaya Mayachki road—their line of departure for the attack—at 1000 hours; their primary objective was the village of Kochetovka, on the Solotinka River.

The unit captured the village of Veselyy at about 1215 hours. The 9th (Heavy) Company continued the attack north at 1550 hours in the defensive zone of the 52nd Guards Rifle Division. By 1640 hours, the Tigers had gained the outskirts of Kochetovka and then repelled an enemy tank attack by the 24th Guards Tank Brigade racing in from the northeast; some of the combat occurred in a large *balka* that reduced firing ranges to only a few hundred meters. Now only two Tigers in the company were operational.[6] Tiger **911** spent the day undergoing repairs.[7]

Meanwhile, at 1150 hours reconnaissance patrols from the *Totenkopf* established contact with elements of the 11th Panzer Division one kilometer southwest of Sukhosolotino, the report of which undoubtedly raced to Army Group South headquarters. At 1230 hours Battle Group Becker, commanded by *SS-Standartenführer* Helmuth Becker, captured the village of Gryaznoye, the second time the Germans had seized this village during the offensive. At 1550 hours Battle Group Becker received the order to head to Krasnyy Oktyabr' and establish a bridgehead over the Psel River there. At 1850 hours the battle group reported it had seized the village of Kozlovka (Козловка) on the Psel River.

At 2200 hours the division received the order for the next day's operation: during the night establish a bridgehead over the Psel River and attack northeast down the Psel River valley to seize Beregovoye (Береговое) and the high ground to its northwest. For the day the company knocked out ten T-34s and a multiple rocket launcher.

For July 9, the SS Panzer Grenadier Division *Totenkopf* lost nineteen killed in action, sixty-nine wounded in action, and five missing in action advancing to Krapivenskiye Dvory, Yakovlevo, Luchki (North), Veselyy, and Kochetovka, toward the Psel River, against elements of the 52nd Guards Rifle Division and the 31st Tank Corps. The 52nd Guards Rifle Division, 11th Motorized Rifle Brigade, 178th Tank Brigade, 727th Antitank Regiment, and other elements lost seventy-eight killed in action, 124 wounded in action, and forty-two missing in action.[8]

The 2nd SS Panzer Corps suffered **34** panzers put out of action, while the Soviets had **135** tanks put out of action on July 9, 1943.[9]

Day's advance (in kilometers) by each Tiger Company in 2nd SS Panzer Corps:
> 13th (Heavy) Company, 1st Panzer Regiment: **7**
> 8th (Heavy) Company, 2nd Panzer Regiment: **0**
> 9th (Heavy) Company, 3rd Panzer Regiment: **13**

Operational 2nd SS Panzer Corps Tiger strength reported at the end of the day: **7**
> 13th (Heavy) Company, 1st Panzer Regiment: **4** (1735 hours)
> 8th (Heavy) Company, 2nd Panzer Regiment: **1** (1800 hours)
> 9th (Heavy) Company, 3rd Panzer Regiment: **2** (1745 hours)

July 10, 1943[1]

Weather: deep cloud cover, late morning showers, local afternoon thunderstorms; skies cleared at 1500 hours.
Terrain conditions: rolling mixed, bad roads; resupply difficult
Sunrise: 0432 hours   **Sunset:** 2045 hours
Moon Phase: First quarter, 49% illumination

The mission of the 2nd SS Panzer Corps was to attack north, seize Prokhorovka and Beregovoye, and clear the Psel River valley from Krasnyy Oktyabr' to Beregovoye to establish a line from just east of Kartaschevka in the west to Prokhorovka in the east while protecting the eastern flank of the corps' penetration. However, at 0215 hours *SS-Oberführer* Hermann Priess, commander of the *Totenkopf*, informed the corps commander that it would not be possible to establish the bridgehead over the Psel that night. Fifteen minutes later Priess transmitted an alternate plan that would establish a wider bridgehead by 1000 hours, with Battle Group Becker in the east at Kozlovka and Battle Group Baum, commanded by *SS-Obersturmbannführer* Otto Baum, in the west at Krasnyy Oktyabr'. At 0845 hours the 8th Air Corps reported that because of poor flying weather it would not be able to provide support for the operation on time. The corps transmitted this information to the three divisions at 0955 hours but said that "Nevertheless," the attack would go as scheduled.

13th (Heavy) Company, 1st Panzer Regiment
SS Panzer Grenadier Division *Leibstandarte Adolf Hitler*
The division objective for the day was Prokhorovka/East. The 13th (Heavy) Company, under the command of the 2nd SS Panzer Grenadier Regiment, received orders to penetrate enemy defenses northeast of Teterevino (North) and advance toward Prokhorovka. The plan called for the entire artillery regiment of *Leibstandarte Adolf Hitler* and the 55th Rocket (*Werfer*) Regiment to support the attack, as well as Luftwaffe ground attack aircraft.[1]

The company, with only four operational Tigers, began moving to an assembly area southwest of Teterevino (North) at 0001 hours, and by 0300 hours was prepared to attack. To make up for the lack of Tigers, the regiment received operational control of the division's assault gun detachment, with twenty vehicles. Artillery began hammering Soviet positions at dawn; the 13th (Heavy) Company—protected on its flanks by these assault guns—and the regiment began advancing at 1045 hours from Teterevino (North) on a narrow front between Komsomol'skiy to Ivanovskiy Vyselok (Ивановский Выселок), and by 1145 hours had reached the bend in the railway embankment of the Belgorod–Prokhorovka train tracks. The 1st Panzer Grenadier Regiment of *Leibstandarte* was being delayed in the west due to powerful flanking fire from the area near the Psel River. By 1350 hours the companies of the 2nd SS Panzer Grenadier Regiment were on both sides of the railway, while to the west several companies were in front of Hill 241.6. As the infantry penetrated the Sloyevoye District Forest the Tigers began firing on Hill

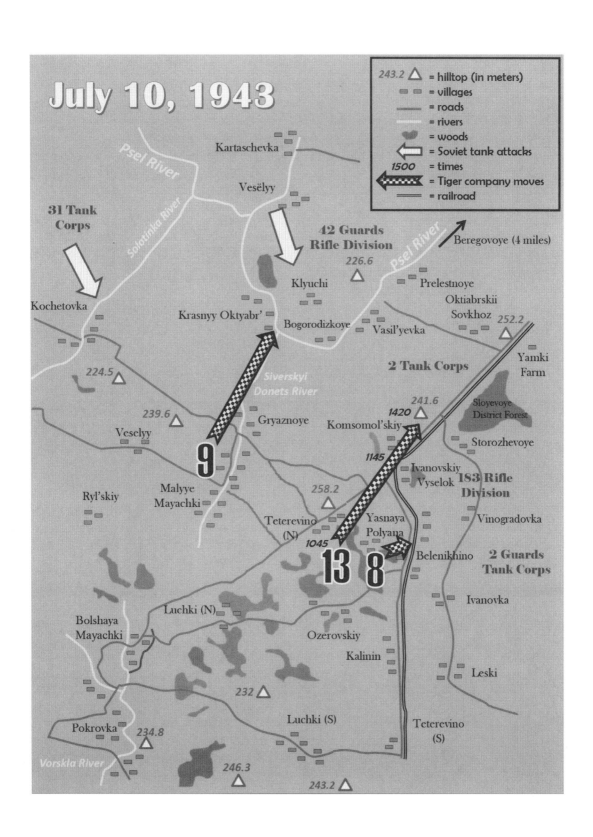

July 10, 1943

243.2 △ = hilltop (in meters)
⬜ ⬜ = villages
— = roads
— = rivers
🝖 = woods
⬅ = Soviet tank attacks
1500 = times
◄▦▦ = Tiger company moves
═ = railroad

Psel River

Kartaschevka

Vesëlyy

Solotinka River

31 Tank Corps

42 Guards Rifle Division

226.6

Psel River

Beregovoye (4 miles)

Klyuchi

Prelestnoye

Oktiabrskii Sovkhoz

252.2

Kochetovka

Krasnyy Oktyabr'

Bogorodizkoye

Vasil'yevka

Yamki Farm

Siverskyi Donets River

224.5

239.6

9

Gryaznoye

Komsomol'skiy

241.6

1420

1145

2 Tank Corps

Sloyevoye District Forest

Storozhevoye

Veselyy

Ryl'skiy

Malyye Mayachki

258.2

Teterevino (N)

1045

13

8

Ivanovskiy Vyselok

Yasnaya Polyana

Belenikhino

183 Rifle Division

Vinogradovka

2 Guards Tank Corps

Ivanovka

Bolshaya Mayachki

Luchki (N)

Ozerovskiy

Kalinin

Leski

232

Pokrovka

234.8

Luchki (S)

Teterevino (S)

246.3

243.2

Vorskla River

241.6, and by 1420 hours the Germans had taken the hill.[2] Two groups of Stukas finally arrived overhead at 1700 hours.

The operation was not without casualties, though. In **1311**, tank commander *SS-Obersturmführer* Waldemar Schütz was wounded outside of his tank by a shell fragment; *SS-Unterscharführer* Werner Wendt, the gunner, assumed command of the vehicle. At noon, in the company rear area, *SS-Oberführer* Theodor Wisch presented *SS-Unterscharführer* Franz Staudegger with the Knight's Cross of the Iron Cross; some twenty members of the company were present at the ceremony. Staudegger then departed to return to Germany to brief Adolf Hitler on the Tiger in battle.[3] During the day Tiger **1334**, which had been stripped of needed parts, began transportation to Germany for factory rebuild.[4]

For the day, the SS Panzer Grenadier Division *Leibstandarte Adolf Hitler* suffered eighteen killed in action, thirty-four wounded in action, and three missing in action during the attack northeast toward Hill 241.6. The defending 183rd Rifle Division, 169th Tank Brigade, and 26th Tank Brigade lost 188 killed in action, 373 wounded in action, and sixty-seven missing in action.[5]

8th (Heavy) Company, 2nd Panzer Regiment
SS Panzer Grenadier Division *Das Reich*
Mechanics and tank crews in the company worked throughout the night, and by morning nine Tigers were operational. The mission of the division was to protect the eastern (right) flank of *Leibstandarte Adolf Hitler* as it advanced toward Prokhorovka. To accomplish this task the SS Panzer Grenadier Regiment *Deutschland* advanced in right echelon; these attacks began first with company-size assaults at 1050 hours. It appears that the Tigers, in support of *Deutschland*, advanced from Yasnaya Polyana toward the northeast, but could not get across the railroad embankment, as at 1800 hours there were still heavy enemy antitank units all along the railroad line in the division's sector. At the end of the day only one Tiger was operational; company mechanics, supported by other maintenance personnel from the division, attempted to repair the non-operational Tigers at Ozerovskii.[6] One of them was **S32**, which was in repair for engine damage.

For July 10, the SS Panzer Grenadier Division *Das Reich* lost sixteen killed in action, ninety-four wounded in action, and two missing in action during the attack from Yasnaya Polyana toward Belenikhino against elements of the 2nd Tank Corps. The opposing Soviet units, including the 4th Guards Tank Brigade, 25th Guards Tank Brigade, 6th Guards Motorized Brigade, and the 158th Guards Rifle Regiment, lost eighty-eight killed in action, 182 wounded in action, and 158 missing in action.[7]

9th (Heavy) Company, 3rd Panzer Regiment
SS Panzer Grenadier Division *Totenkopf*
The mission for the *Totenkopf* was to build a bridgehead during the night in the assigned area and create a crossing for tanks over the Psel River (Псел), and to advance in the Psel valley to the northeast and capture Beregovoye and the heights north of the Psel River. The division was also to secure the left flank of the corps along the southeast bank of the Solotinka River–Psel River–Ol'shanka Stream. The company had twelve operational Tigers, but none of the crews got any rest during the night. **911** drove over a mine in the darkness. *Totenkopf* infantry crossed the Psel River; the division reported at 1100 hours that a bridgehead had been created south of Klyuchi (Ключи). A subsequent report at 1125 hours stated that: "The river has not been crossed." Finally, at 1515 hours, the division reported that the left flank of Battle Group Becker had managed to "cross the stream." By 1700 hours that afternoon the Luftwaffe had arrived and the Tigers began to roll toward Gryaznoye. **901** ran over an antitank mine and was disabled.[8] By 1800 hours Battle Group Becker had gained eight hundred meters of ground north of the Psel and was approaching Hill 226.6, while Battle Group Baum was over the Psel, hunkered down in a woods south of Klyuchi.

The Tigers were slated to cross the Psel River at this point—the Achilles heel of the 2nd SS Panzer Corps finally made itself known. Bridges large enough to support the Tigers were not in place. A pioneer bridge building unit assigned to the 680th Special Pioneer Staff, which had the mission of building two bridges across the Psel west of Bogorodizkoye (one being Tiger capable), was shelled by Soviet artillery and would be delayed from beginning work until July 11. Some sources state that the Tigers crossed the Psel River (probably near Krasnyy Oktyabr') on July 10, then captured the village of Klyuchi, but this is probably incorrect. Given that Klyuchi is only one thousand meters north of the south bank of the Psel, it is more likely that the company only supported by fire any attack on the village on July 10, and now with only two operational Tigers. At 1915 hours Hill 226.6 finally fell to the infantry of the *Totenkopf*. One Tiger was reported to be in short term repair, while two Tigers were in long term repair.

For July 10, the SS Panzer Grenadier Division *Totenkopf* lost seventy-seven killed in action, 292 wounded in action, and five missing in action advancing to Krapivenskiye Dvory, Yakovlevo, Luchki (North), Veselyy, and Kochetovka, toward the Psel River, against elements of the 52nd Guards Rifle Division and the 31st Tank Corps. The 52nd Guards Rifle Division, 11th Motorized Rifle Brigade, 178th Tank Brigade 727th Antitank Regiment, and other elements lost seventy-eight killed in action, 124 wounded in action, and forty-two missing in action.[9]

On July 10, 1943, the 2nd SS Panzer Corps suffered just **3** panzers put out of action, while the Soviets had **55** tanks put out of action; we do not know how many of these were totally destroyed, versus lesser damage that later could be brought back to operational status after repairs.[10]

Day's advance (in kilometers) by each Tiger Company in 2nd SS Panzer Corps:
>13th (Heavy) Company, 1st Panzer Regiment: **7**
>8th (Heavy) Company, 2nd Panzer Regiment: **1**
>9th (Heavy) Company, 3rd Panzer Regiment: **6**

Operational 2nd SS Panzer Corps Tiger strength reported at the end of the day: **7**
>13th (Heavy) Company, 1st Panzer Regiment: **4** (1750 hours)
>8th (Heavy) Company, 2nd Panzer Regiment: **1** (1900 hours)
>9th (Heavy) Company, 3rd Panzer Regiment: **2** (1710 hours)

July 11, 1943[1]

Weather: heavy rainfall clearing about noon; better weather later in the day, increasingly windy, unfavorable flying weather
Terrain conditions: rolling mixed, roads extremely muddy and deteriorating, barely passable for wheeled and tracked vehicles, causing delays
Sunrise: 0433 hours   **Sunset:** 2044 hours
Moon Phase: First quarter, 59% illumination

Because heavy thunderstorms during the night had soaked the roads throughout the corps' sector, the start time for the day's assault was postponed from 0600 hours to 1045 hours. Even with the delay artillery was still late being brought forward to new firing positions to be able to range enemy positions north of the Psel.[2]

13th (Heavy) Company, 1st Panzer Regiment
SS Panzer Grenadier Division *Leibstandarte Adolf Hitler*
Losses in *Leibstandarte* were piling up. Although the overall strength of the division for the day was reported as 22,104 soldiers, the battle strength (combat "trigger pullers") was only 11,257 men.[3] The 2nd SS Panzer Grenadier Regiment hunkered down in the Sloyevoye District Forest

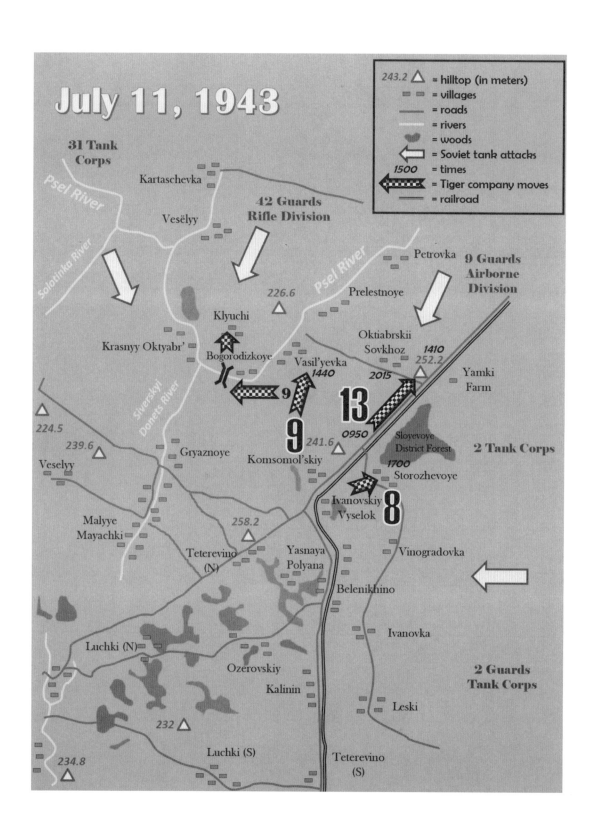

July 11, 1943

31 Tank Corps

Kartaschevka

Vesëlyy

42 Guards Rifle Division

Psel River

Salotinka River

226.6

Klyuchi

Krasnyy Oktyabr'

Bogorodizkoye

Vasil'yevka

1440

9

9

Gryaznoye

Komsomol'skiy

241.6

224.5

239.6

Veselyy

Malyye Mayachki

258.2

Teterevino (N)

Yasnaya Polyana

Belenikhino

Luchki (N)

Ozerovskiy

Kalinin

232

234.8

Luchki (S)

Teterevino (S)

Petrovka

9 Guards Airborne Division

Prelestnoye

Oktiabrskii Sovkhoz

1410

252.2

Yamki Farm

2015

13

0950

Sloyevoye District Forest

2 Tank Corps

1700

Storozhevoye

Ivanovskiy Vyselok

8

Vinogradovka

Ivanovka

2 Guards Tank Corps

Leski

243.2 △ = hilltop (in meters)
⬚ ⬚ = villages
—— = roads
= rivers
= woods
⬅ = Soviet tank attacks
1500 = times
⬅ = Tiger company moves
= railroad

southwest of Yamki (Ямки) farm. The division reported heavy enemy artillery fire coming from the Prelestnoye (Прелестное) and Petrovka (Петровка) areas and with counter-battery artillery being delayed, there was little to remedy the situation.

Stuka attacks against enemy troops forward of the division began at 0900 hours. At 0900 hours the First Company of the 1st SS Pioneer Battalion cleared lanes through enemy minefields and helped capture an antitank ditch, freeing the Tigers to attack toward Hill 252.2. At 1100 hours the division reported that the assault on Hill 252.2 was ongoing. The fighting was tough, and the division committed the Third Battalion of the 2nd SS Panzer Grenadier Regiment, mounted on halftracks, against Hill 252.2 at 1230 hours. At 1410 hours *Leibstandarte Adolf Hitler* was in possession of the elevation. The tiny state farm of Oktiabrskii Sovkhoz was a tougher nut to crack and protected by a well-positioned antitank trench; it did not fall until 2015 hours, when Tigers actually penetrated the hamlet.[4]

The attack, just one-and-a-half kilometers from Prokhorovka, destroyed twenty-eight enemy antitank guns, but company commander Heinz Kling was seriously wounded when his Tiger **1301** was hit by enemy antitank fire. *SS-Untersturmführer* Michael Wittmann assumed command of the company. **1331** was hit twice by enemy antitank fire, wounding radio operator *SS-Sturmmann* Kurt Pollmann in the upper arm. The large concentration of Soviet artillery north of Prelestnoye and the Psel River continued to be a thorn in the side of *Leibstandarte*, forcing the offensive, with only four Tigers now operational, to halt for the evening. The company then returned to Ozerovskii for repairs and resupply of fuel and ammunition.[5] For July 11–12, the company probably destroyed twenty-four T-34 tanks, twenty-eight antitank guns, and six howitzers.[6]

For July 11, the SS Panzer Grenadier Division *Leibstandarte Adolf Hitler* suffered thirty-three killed in action and 304 wounded in action during the attack northeast toward Hill 252.2. The defending 285th Rifle Regiment, 295th Rifle Regiment, and 26th Guards Airborne Regiment suffered 279 killed in action, 582 wounded in action, and 109 missing in action.[7]

At 2250 hours the division received orders for the next day: with the left flank hold in current positions; with the right flank advance toward Yamki farm. After the *Totenkopf* advanced northeast *Leibstandarte* would continue the attack toward Prokhorovka.

8th (Heavy) Company, 2nd Panzer Regiment
SS Panzer Grenadier Division *Das Reich*

Das Reich was also experiencing heavy losses. On this day the overall strength of the division was reported as 20,120 soldiers; the battle strength was just 9,443 men.[8] At 1130 hours the division reported that it had seized the high ground south and southeast of the village of Storozhevoye (Сторожевое).

Earlier, at 1000 hours, the severely understrength (with probably no more than five operational tanks) 8th (Heavy) Company was defending in the high ground southwest of the village when company commander *SS-Hauptsturmführer* Herbert Zimmermann was wounded in the arm while commanding Tiger **S01**, which had just returned to action with a new transmission.[9] During the day each Tiger received an order to report how much ammunition was remaining on board. In **S31** loader *SS-Panzerschütze* Heinz Schöneberg was given the mission to take that information to the command tank; en route he was likely hit by enemy artillery and was seriously wounded in action.[10] *SS-Obersturmführer* Philipp Theiss, commander of the first platoon, assumed command of the company; given the state of damage in **S02** Theiss probably commanded from **S01**. *SS-Untersturmführer* Heinz Tensfeld arrived later that afternoon from the First Battalion of the 2nd Panzer Regiment to become the new first platoon leader in **S11**, but by nightfall only one Tiger was operational.[11] One of the non-operational Tigers was **S32**, which was in repair for engine damage.

For July 11, the SS Panzer Grenadier Division *Das Reich* lost twenty-nine killed in action, 181 wounded in action, and one missing in action during the attack toward Storozhevoye against elements of the 2nd Tank Corps. The opposing Soviet units, including the 6th Guards Motorized Brigade, 1076th Antitank Regiment, 1510th Antitank Regiment, and 755th Antitank Battalion, lost fourteen killed in action, forty-five wounded in action, and seventeen missing in action.[12]

At 2250 hours *Das Reich* received orders for the next day: on the southern flank hold current positions; to the north seize the villages of Vinogradovka and Ivanovka. Advance the main line of battle to the high ground southwest of the village of Pravorot'.

9th (Heavy) Company, 3rd Panzer Regiment
SS Panzer Grenadier Division *Totenkopf*

Totenkopf seems to have been in the heaviest combat. The overall strength of the division for the day was reported as 20,694 soldiers; the battle strength (combat "trigger pullers") was only 9,203 men.[13]

Dead men remained dead, but "dead" Tigers frequently returned to life. After mechanics repaired nine non-operational vehicles all night, eleven Tigers were operational at the start of the day. Not enough praise can be given to the mechanics in each of the three companies. The Tiger was a complex piece of equipment and often did not appear to be designed for ease of maintenance.

At 0300 hours *Totenkopf* reported that a bridge could not be finished before 0700 hours. At 0500 hours *Totenkopf* reported company-size enemy attacks against the bridgehead; the enemy had closed to within hand grenade range by 0617 hours and the enemy was in regimental strength near Vesëlyy (Весёлый). *Totenkopf* reported at 0750 hours that construction of a bridge over the Psel River had not yet commenced. At 0830 the division reported an enemy infantry attack, supported by tanks, had ensued against the bridgehead. Problems for the *Totenkopf* continued, and at 1115 hours the division reported that it would have a bridge over the Psel River at the earliest in "late afternoon . . . (1800–1900 hours)."

At 1400 hours the first bridge across the Psel was in place; it appears this structure was capable of supporting Panzer Mark IVs. At 1452 hours the corps reported that two bridges had now been emplaced over the Psel west of Bogorodizkoye and that one of them was suitable for Tigers.

Meanwhile, the company repelled an enemy attack at the village of Vasil'yevka, with the fight lasting until 1440 hours, when the company disengaged and began moving toward the bridge. A few minutes later they had arrived, and the German engineers pushed wooden matting over the mud on the riverbanks to give the Tigers a solid bed on which to approach the bridge. More problems arose, and at 1615 hours *Totenkopf* reported: "Difficult road conditions make it impossible to advance from the bridgehead until the next day."

At the same time **911** experienced steering problems once again after it had been damaged by a mine and had to be towed to the rear for repairs.[14] Once it had crossed the river the company probably slowly advanced toward Klyuchi to get out of the dangerous area near the bridge, which would certainly be shelled throughout the night. With ten Tigers operational the unit would be in good shape for the following day. Two other Tigers were in short term repair and two were in long term repair.

For July 11, the SS Panzer Grenadier Division *Totenkopf* lost seventy-seven killed in action and 385 wounded in action advancing to the Psel River. On the other side, the 52nd Guards Rifle Division and the 11th Motorized Rifle Brigade suffered 123 killed in action, 338 wounded in action, and thirty-nine missing in action.[15]

The orders for the next day's attack came from corps headquarters at 2250 hours.[16] *Totenkopf* would attack to the Prokhorovka–Kartaschevka road and roll up the Psel River valley to the northeast.

On July 11, 1943, the 2nd SS Panzer Corps lost **16** panzers put out of action, while the Soviets had just **9** tanks put out of action; even if these were total losses, they seem at odds with just the number of Soviet tanks knocked out by the 13th (Heavy) Company.[17]

Day's advance (in kilometers) by each Tiger Company in 2nd SS Panzer Corps:

   13th (Heavy) Company, 1st Panzer Regiment: **3**
   8th (Heavy) Company, 2nd Panzer Regiment: **1**
   9th (Heavy) Company, 3rd Panzer Regiment: **7**

Operational 2nd SS Panzer Corps Tiger strength reported at the end of the day: **15**

   13th (Heavy) Company, 1st Panzer Regiment: **4** (1700 hours)
   8th (Heavy) Company, 2nd Panzer Regiment: **1** (1835 hours)
   9th (Heavy) Company, 3rd Panzer Regiment: **10** (1640 hours); two Tigers in short term repair and two Tigers in long term repair.

July 12, 1943[1]

Weather: cloudy, in places heavy rain showers
Terrain conditions: poor trafficable situations
Sunrise: 0434 hours   **Sunset:** 2044 hours
Moon Phase: Waxing gibbous, 69% illumination

The divisions formulated their own battle plans to support the mission of the corps received the night before. To the north and west, *Totenkopf* would advance to the Beregovoye–Kartashevka road to eliminate the flank threat of the enemy north of the Psel River, with one panzer grenadier regiment moving to Vasil'yevka to serve as an anchor point for the attack. In the center, *Leibstandarte Adolf Hitler* would hold its current position on its left at Oktiabrskii Sovkhoz and Hill 252.2, while it would push its right flank forward east of Yamki farm. The *Totenkopf* and *Leibstandarte Adolf Hitler* would then jointly attack toward Prokhorovka. *Das Reich* would attack along its left flank with the SS Panzer Grenadier Regiment *Deutschland* to seize the villages of Vinogradovka (Виноградовка) and Ivanovka (Ивановка), protecting the right flank of the *Leibstandarte*. *Das Reich* would then push northeast and seize Pravorot'.[2]

Colonel General Hermann Hoth understood the concept of *Schwerpunkt* and where the decisive point of battle would occur, and so traveled to the command post of the SS Panzer Grenadier Regiment *Der Führer* to watch the fight. He would not miss anything.[3]

13th (Heavy) Company, 1st Panzer Regiment
SS Panzer Grenadier Division *Leibstandarte Adolf Hitler*
The Soviets threw two tank corps against the division early in the morning. Fifty enemy tanks attacked the 2nd SS Panzer Grenadier Regiment in the Oktiabrskii Sovkhoz area at 0600 hours. At 0915 hours forty enemy tanks attacked the regiment from Petrovka, thirty-five enemy tanks attacked down the Prokhorovka–Teterevino (North) road, and forty enemy tanks attacked near Yamki farm against the 2nd SS Panzer Grenadier Regiment. The 13th (Heavy) Company, positioned behind the panzer grenadier regiments, had only four operational Tigers. Under the direction of *SS-Untersturmführer* Michael Wittmann, the four-Tiger company conducted a counterattack west of Oktiabrskii Sovkhoz against the 170th Tank Brigade, and finally the 181st Tank Brigade, which had commenced an attack from Andreyevka (Андреевка), aimed for the exposed western flank of the *Leibstandarte* to cut the unit's supply lines and overrun the German artillery positions; Wittmann's Tiger was hit twice by antitank rounds and the three other Tigers suffered mechanical problems.[4]

The enemy made a local penetration of the line at Hill 252.2 at 1130 hours; division elements counterattacked and restored the line at 1315 hours. That evening forward *Leibstandarte* elements at the Oktiabrskii Sovkhoz were ordered to withdraw to positions they had occupied that morning.[5]

Individual tank kill reports for the company are confusing. *SS-Untersturmführer* Wittmann and his new gunner *SS-Untersturmführer* Helmut Gräser, probably in **1331**, were credited with

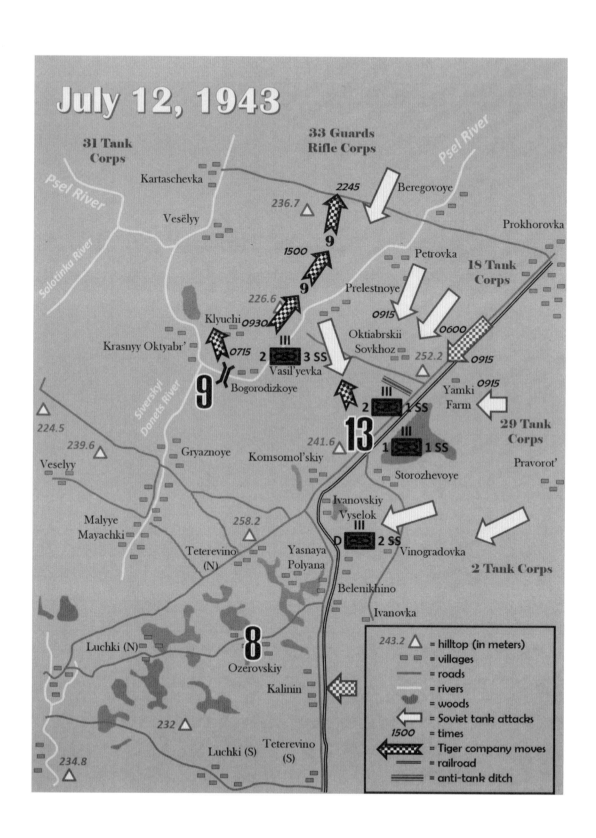

July 12, 1943

31 Tank Corps

Kartaschevka

Vesëlyy

Psel River

Solotinka River

33 Guards Rifle Corps

Psel River

2245

236.7 △

Beregovoye

Prokhorovka

1500

9

9

Petrovka

18 Tank Corps

226.6

9

Prelestnoye

0915

Klyuchi *0930*

III
2 🚂 3 SS
Vasil'yevka

Oktiabrskii Sovkhoz

0600

0915

Krasnyy Oktyabr'

0715

252.2 △

0915

9

Bogorodizkoye

III
2 🚂 1 SS

Yamki Farm

Siverskyi Donets River

13

241.6 △

III
1 🚂 1 SS

29 Tank Corps

Pravorot'

224.5 △

239.6 △

Gryaznoye

Komsomol'skiy

Storozhevoye

Veselyy

Malyye Mayachki

258.2 △

Ivanovskiy Vyselok

III
D 🚂 2 SS

Vinogradovka

Teterevino (N)

Yasnaya Polyana

Belenikhino

2 Tank Corps

Ivanovka

Luchki (N)

8

Ozerovskiy

Kalinin

243.2 △ = hilltop (in meters)
⬜⬜ = villages
── = roads
── = rivers
🌳 = woods
⬅ = Soviet tank attacks
1500 ⬅ = times
◀▨ = Tiger company moves
═══ = railroad
≣≣≣ = anti-tank ditch

232 △

Luchki (S)

Teterevino (S)

234.8 △

destroying twenty-eight T-34 tanks, while gunner *SS-Sturmmann* Karl-Heinz Warmbrunn, in Tiger **1301**, destroyed at least one. It appears that *SS-Unterscharführer* Kurt Quax Kleber commanded another Tiger in the attack, as did *SS-Scharführer* Georg Lötzsch, commanding **1323**. *SS-Unterscharführer* Arthur Bernhardt, commander of **1312**, was killed in action by tank fire on the forward slope of Hill 241.6 from the 181st Tank Brigade. 1312 would be immobilized and recovery crews were unable to evacuate the tank. Although company commander *SS-Hauptsturmführer* Heinz Kling had been wounded the day before and was not forward in a command tank, accounts show that he issued orders over the radio, perhaps from a command post farther rear. One Tiger appears to have been destroyed during the day.[6]

July 12—the defining day of the offensive—would prove to be a costly one. First **1312** was a total loss. The SS Panzer Grenadier Division *Leibstandarte Adolf Hitler* suffered forty-eight killed in action, 321 wounded in action, and five missing in action during the fighting at the Oktiabrskii Sovkhoz area and Hill 252.2. Soviet elements from the 29th Tank Corps and the 18th Tank Corps, including the 9th Guards Airborne Division, the 1529th Heavy Self-Propelled Artillery Regiment, the 31st Tank Brigade, the 32nd Tank Brigade, and the 53rd Motorized Rifle Brigade, lost 661 killed in action, 1,856 wounded in action, and 377 missing in action.[7]

8th (Heavy) Company, 2nd Panzer Regiment
SS Panzer Grenadier Division *Das Reich*

It appears that only one Tiger in the 8th (Heavy) Company was operational; it and the non-operational Tigers were at Ozerovskii at the maintenance facilities, which by that evening had repaired a second Tiger to operational status.[8] During the day forty enemy tanks attacked at Kalinin at 1205 hours—during which radio operator *SS-Sturmmann* Bruno Hofmann was wounded—and seventy tanks attacked at Yasnaya Polyana at 1430 hours. *SS-Rottenführer* Rudolf Zacharias served as a gunner in a Tiger until he was wounded in action on July 12, 1943, near Luchki (North). The division seized the village of Storozhevoye at 1700 hours.

For July 12, the SS Panzer Grenadier Division *Das Reich* also experienced significant casualties, losing forty-one killed in action, 190 wounded in action, and twelve missing in action during operations near Kalinin against elements of the 2nd Guards Tank Corps. Attacking Soviet units, including the 47th Guards Heavy Tank Regiment, the 16th Guards Mortar Regiment, the 26th Guards Tank Brigade, and the 25th Guards Tank Brigade, lost 495 killed in action, 900 wounded in action, and 164 missing in action.[9]

9th (Heavy) Company, 3rd Panzer Regiment
SS Panzer Grenadier Division *Totenkopf*

At 0400 hours the company began to advance on a group of barracks just west of the small village of Klyuchi. The location fell to the company, which was in support of the First Battalion of the 3rd Panzer Regiment, at 0715 hours.[10] During the combat around Klyuchi, acting company commander *SS-Untersturmführer* Walter Köhler was killed in action. *SS-Untersturmführer* Karl-Heinz Schüffler assumed temporary command of the company. After repelling an enemy attack and undergoing an enemy artillery barrage the company, now in support of the Second Battalion of the 3rd Panzer Regiment, which was under the command of *SS-Hauptsturmführer* Fritz Biermeier—former commander of the 9th (Heavy) Company—began moving at 0930 hours over Hill 226.6, reaching an area five kilometers northwest of Prelestnoye at 1500 hours; two Tigers had just been returned to operational status at 1430 hours.[11] At 1430 hours a maintenance report indicated that two Tigers were in short term repairs for less than six days and two other Tigers were in repairs estimated to take more than six days.[12]

The company continued the attack until it reached the Beregovoye—Kartashevka (Карташевка) road at about 2245 hours; it was a potent force with ten operational Tigers.[13] This would be the farthest advance to the north by any large German unit (not including small patrols and reconnaissance) of the Fourth Panzer Army during *Operation Citadel*. Loader *SS-Sturmmann* Ernst Vögler was killed when he suffered a fatal head wound. *SS-Untersturmführer* Willi Rathsack, the leader of the third platoon in **931**, was wounded in action. The company had two Tigers in repair with an estimated return time of ninety-six hours.

For July 12, the SS Panzer Grenadier Division *Totenkopf* lost sixty-nine killed in action, 235 wounded in action, and sixteen missing in action attacking along and north of the Psel River. On the other side, the 52nd Guards Rifle Division, the 95th Guards Rifle Division, the 11th Motorized Rifle Brigade, the 99th Tank Brigade, and the 181st Tank Brigade suffered 200 killed in action, 359 wounded in action, and thirty-nine missing in action.[14] Meanwhile, for the period July 5 to July 12, the Fourth Panzer Army lost 2,011 killed in action, 10,123 wounded in action, and 253 missing in action.[15]

Field Marshal von Manstein was informed of the progress made by the *Totenkopf* and the 2nd SS Panzer Corps. The commander-in-chief of Army Group South sent this reply: "My thanks and appreciation for your outstanding achievements and exemplary conduct in the fighting."[16]

The Tigers were close to a breakthrough now. They could smell blood.

Day's advance (in kilometers) by each Tiger Company in 2nd SS Panzer Corps:
> 13th (Heavy) Company, 1st Panzer Regiment: **2**
> 8th (Heavy) Company, 2nd Panzer Regiment: **0**
> 9th (Heavy) Company, 3rd Panzer Regiment: **6**

Operational 2nd SS Panzer Corps Tiger strength reported at the end of the day: **16**
> 13th (Heavy) Company, 1st Panzer Regiment: **4**
> 8th (Heavy) Company, 2nd Panzer Regiment: **2** (1835 hours)
> 9th (Heavy) Company, 3rd Panzer Regiment: **10** (1800 hours);
>   three Tigers in short term repair and one Tiger in long term repair.

July 13, 1943[1]

Weather: Cloudy, heavy rain showers in the afternoon
Terrain conditions: rolling, resupply operations of frontline troops adversely affected
Sunrise: 0425 hours   **Sunset:** 2043 hours
Moon Phase: Waxing gibbous, 79% illumination

Adolf Hitler discussed the progress of the operation with Field Marshal Erich von Manstein, commander of Army Group South, and Field Marshal Günther von Kluge, commander of Army Group Center, which was attacking towards Kursk from the north. Von Kluge recommended an end to the offensive, while von Manstein insisted that given certain conditions he desired to continue the attack, as he felt his forces were on the brink of success and were severely crippling enemy armored forces arrayed against them. The *Führer* duly suspended offensive operations for Army Group Center but allowed the Fourth Panzer Army of Army Group South to continue to destroy enemy forces in its zone of attack.[2]

13th (Heavy) Company, 1st Panzer Regiment
SS Panzer Grenadier Division *Leibstandarte Adolf Hitler*
The 13th (Heavy) Company attacked at 1000 hours toward Oktiabrskii Sovkhoz to regain terrain it had abandoned the evening before, reaching the foot of nearby hills by 1030 hours. There they found an antitank unit on the reverse slope of Hill 252.2 and could not advance farther, in part because of the muddy ground conditions of the roads. The four Tigers then

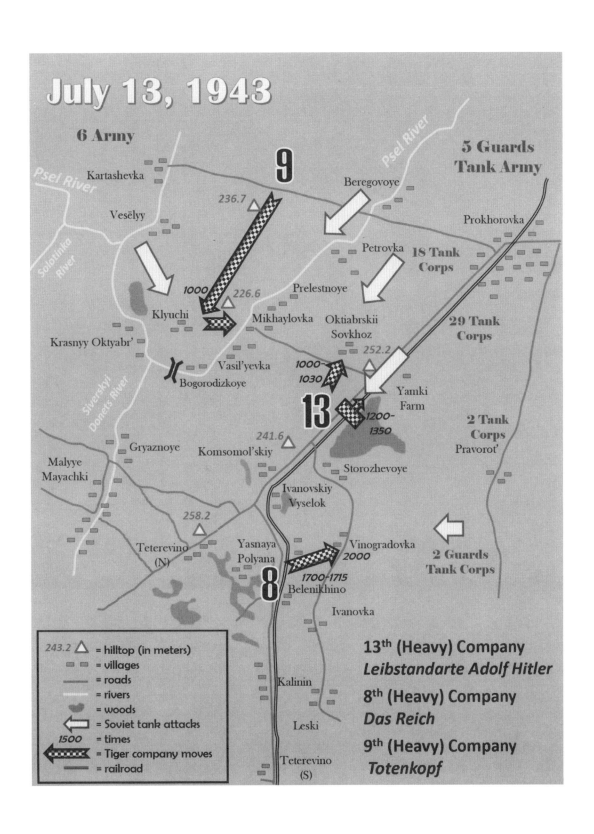

July 13, 1943

6 Army

5 Guards Tank Army

9

Psel River

Psel River

Kartashevka

Beregovoye

Prokhorovka

236.7 △

Vesëlyy

Petrovka

18 Tank Corps

1000

226.6 △

Prelestnoye

Klyuchi

Mikhaylovka

Oktiabrskii Sovkhoz

29 Tank Corps

Krasnyy Oktyabr'

252.2 △

Vasil'yevka

1000–1030

Bogorodizkoye

Yamki Farm

13

1200–1350

2 Tank Corps
Pravorot'

Gryaznoye

241.6 △

Komsomol'skiy

Storozhevoye

Malyye Mayachki

Ivanovskiy Vyselok

258.2 △

Teterevino (N)

Yasnaya Polyana

Vinogradovka

2000

2 Guards Tank Corps

8

1700–1715

Belenikhino

Ivanovka

Kalinin

Leski

Teterevino (S)

243.2 △ = hilltop (in meters)
▭ ▭ = villages
—— = roads
—— = rivers
◥ = woods
⬅ = Soviet tank attacks
1500 = times
⬅ = Tiger company moves
═══ = railroad

13th (Heavy) Company
Leibstandarte Adolf Hitler

8th (Heavy) Company
Das Reich

9th (Heavy) Company
Totenkopf

took up positions along the railroad to protect the right flank of the 2nd SS Panzer Grenadier Regiment.[3] From 1200 hours to 1350 hours two Soviet regiments, one on each side of the Belgorod–Prokhorovka highway, attacked southwest, but were repulsed. *SS-Panzerschütze* Walter Henke, loader on **1325**, was wounded by shrapnel in the left eye.

For July 13, the SS Panzer Grenadier Division *Leibstandarte Adolf Hitler* lost sixty-four killed in action, 260 wounded in action, and two missing in action during the fighting at the Oktiabrskii Sovkhoz area, Storozhevoye Woods, and Hill 252.2. Soviet elements from the 53rd Motorized Rifle Brigade, the 25th Tank Brigade, and the 26th Tank Brigade suffered 243 killed in action, 607 wounded in action, and fifty-one missing in action.[4]

8th (Heavy) Company, 2nd Panzer Regiment
SS Panzer Grenadier Division *Das Reich*

The 167th Infantry Division moved north and assumed the portion of the front held by *Das Reich* at Teterevino (South). At 0830 hours the enemy attacked in battalion strength near Yasnaya Polyana, making some local breakthroughs, but counterattacks by the *Das Reich* restored the lines.

Mechanics worked on every Tiger in the company the entire night to try to make some operational for the day's fight. The First Battalion of SS Panzer Grenadier Regiment *Der Führer* and the 13th (Heavy) Company attacked from positions near Yasnaya Polyana southeast to Vinogradovka, first seizing crossing sites at the by-now formidable railroad embankment at 1550 hours. The Germans broke through forward enemy defenses and reached the southern edge of the village by 2000 hours; during the way **S11** was hit and the new first platoon leader and tank commander, *SS-Untersturmführer* Heinz Tensfeld, abandoned the Tiger with the crew, but driver *SS-Rottenführer* Eduard Arzner remained with the damaged panzer. That night two volunteers crept forward into no man's land and helped the driver bring back the operational tank.[5] Meanwhile, *Das Reich* had advanced to a small woods one and one-half kilometers north of the village of Ivanovka.

For July 13, the SS Panzer Grenadier Division *Das Reich* suffered seventeen killed in action and forty-four wounded in action during defensive operations that also later included an attack toward the village Vinogradovka against elements of the 2nd Guards Tank Corps. Soviet units, including the 25th Guards Tank Brigade and the 1510th Antitank Regiment, lost 272 killed in action, 575 wounded in action, and 104 missing in action.[6]

9th (Heavy) Company, 3rd Panzer Regiment
SS Panzer Grenadier Division *Totenkopf*

The 9th (Heavy) Company, as well as the rest of the 3rd Panzer Regiment, withdrew from forward positions at the Beregovoye–Kartashevka road, the planned attack along the road now abandoned. By 1000 hours the company took up a position just behind Hill 226.6 to serve as a mobile reserve. The entire *Totenkopf* panzer force counterattacked advancing enemy forces east of the hill and fought against a Soviet armored attack from Vesëlyy against Hill 226.6 beginning at 1545 hours, but in the process all ten Tiger tanks in the fight suffered damage and had to be withdrawn for repairs.[7] *SS-Hauptsturmführer* Wilfried Richter, a former battery commander in the *Totenkopf* assault gun detachment and a Knight's Cross of the Iron Cross winner, probably assumed command of the company on this day. Without the Tigers the bridgehead was in a precarious situation. At 1725 hours *Totenkopf* sent this message to the corps: "The enemy attack has achieved local breakthroughs northwest of Hill 226.6. Urgently request help. Powerful enemy infantry."

By 1845 hours *Totenkopf* informed the corps that the enemy breakthroughs had been contained and that the old main battle line had been restored. For July 13, the SS Panzer Grenadier Division *Totenkopf* lost twenty-four killed in action and 136 wounded in action northeast up the Psel valley and north of the Psel toward the Beregovoye to Kartashevka road. On the Soviet side, the 95th Guards Rifle Division, the 11th Motorized Rifle Brigade, and the 24th Guards Tank Brigade suffered 558 killed in action, 1,132 wounded in action, and 317 missing in action.[8]

Day's advance (in kilometers) by each Tiger Company in 2nd SS Panzer Corps:
   13th (Heavy) Company, 1st Panzer Regiment: **1**
   8th (Heavy) Company, 2nd Panzer Regiment: **2**
   9th (Heavy) Company, 3rd Panzer Regiment: **0**
Operational 2nd SS Panzer Corps Tiger strength reported at the end of the day: **4**
   13th (Heavy) Company, 1st Panzer Regiment: **3** (1935 hours)
   8th (Heavy) Company, 2nd Panzer Regiment: **1** (1935 hours)
   9th (Heavy) Company, 3rd Panzer Regiment: **0** (1935 hours)

July 14, 1943[1]

Weather: hotter and dryer; later scattered showers
Terrain conditions: rolling and mixed; better traffic on roads and trails, although some places poor
Sunrise: 0426 hours   **Sunset:** 2042 hours
Moon Phase: Waxing gibbous, 8% illumination

13th (Heavy) Company, **1st Panzer Regiment**
SS Panzer Grenadier Division *Leibstandarte Adolf Hitler*
The mechanics were slowly losing the fight to fix all the damaged Tigers. The 13th (Heavy) Company now had five operational Tigers. The plan—part of *Operation Roland*, to envelope elements of the Soviet 69th Army—was for the division to wait northeast of Komsomol'skiy State Farm at Hill 241.6 until *Das Reich* had seized the village of Pravorot' (Правороть), then *Leibstandarte* would advance to Yamki farm.[2] To undertake a time-phased mission of this sort, the armored group of *Leibstandarte* was placed under the operational control of *Das Reich*. However, division reconnaissance forces detected that the Soviets were massing to attack near Yamki farm in the east and Mikhaylovka (Михайловка) in the west to cut off the salient held by the division and the 2nd SS Panzer Corps called off the attack of the *Leibstandarte*.[3]

For July 14, the SS Panzer Grenadier Division *Leibstandarte Adolf Hitler* lost twenty-one killed in action, 114 wounded in action, and sixteen missing in action during the fighting at the Oktiabrskii Sovkhoz area and Storozhevoye Woods. Soviet elements from the 53rd Motorized Rifle Brigade, the 31st Tank Brigade, the 25th Tank Brigade, and the 26th Tank Brigade suffered 144 killed in action, 467 wounded in action, and fifty missing in action.[4]

8th (Heavy) Company, **2nd Panzer Regiment**
SS Panzer Grenadier Division *Das Reich*
The division continued to execute its portion of *Operation Roland* and received orders to attack east from the line Vinogradovka–Ivanovka, take the enemy positions along this line, and to advance toward Pravorot' and then north to Prokhorovka. After an artillery and rocket bombardment of enemy positions, SS Panzer Grenadier Regiment *Der Führer* attacked about 0355 hours in house-to-house fighting against elements of the 2nd Guards Tank Corps in Belenikhino; by 0800 hours the infantry had penetrated deep into Belenikhino, destroying twelve enemy tanks in close combat. *Das Reich* reported at 0900 hours that the area was heavily mined and reported again at 1130 hours that Belenikhino had been captured.[5] As the right flank to the south of the division extended only to about two kilometers south of the village (with the 167th Infantry Division

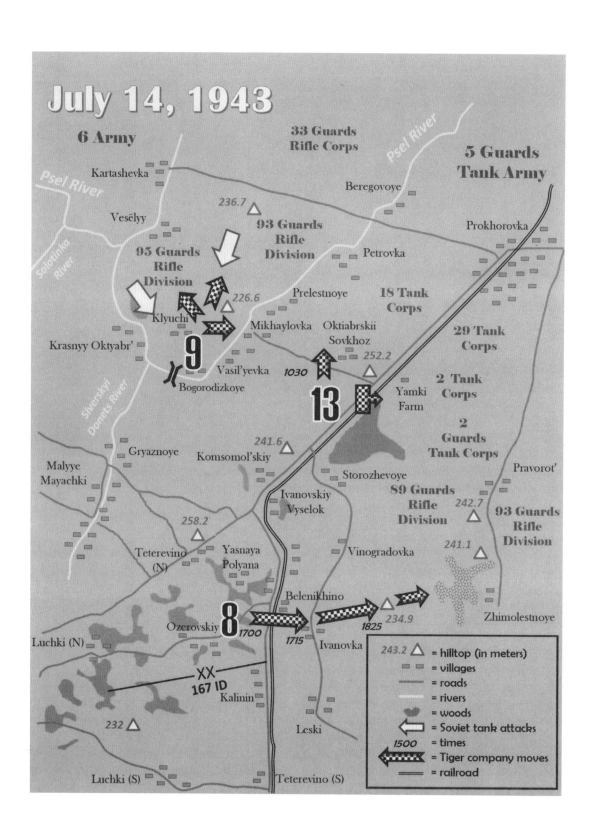

July 14, 1943

6 Army

33 Guards Rifle Corps

5 Guards Tank Army

Psel River

Kartashevka

Beregovoye

236.7

Psel River

Prokhorovka

Vesëlyy

93 Guards Rifle Division

Petrovka

Solotinka River

95 Guards Rifle Division

226.6

Prelestnoye

18 Tank Corps

Klyuchi

Mikhaylovka

Oktiabrskii Sovkhoz

29 Tank Corps

Krasnyy Oktyabr'

9

Vasil'yevka

1030

252.2

Bogorodizkoye

13

Yamki Farm

2 Tank Corps

Siverskyi Donets River

241.6

2 Guards Tank Corps

Gryaznoye

Komsomol'skiy

Storozhevoye

Pravorot'

Malyye Mayachki

Ivanovskiy Vyselok

89 Guards Rifle Division

242.7

93 Guards Rifle Division

258.2

241.1

Teterevino (N)

Yasnaya Polyana

Vinogradovka

Belenikhino

Ozerovskiy

8

1700

1715

1825

234.9

Zhimolestnoye

Luchki (N)

Ivanovka

243.2 △ = hilltop (in meters)

XX
167 ID

Kalinin

⬜⬜ = villages

= roads

= rivers

= woods

⬅ = Soviet tank attacks

232

Leski

1500 = times

= Tiger company moves

Luchki (S)

Teterevino (S)

= railroad

holding the line to the south), the division had enough concentrated combat power to continue the offensive; still farther south the 7th Panzer Division of the 3rd Panzer Corps made contact with the 167th Infantry Division, but Soviet forces fought their way out of the would-be trap and fled east.

The Tiger crewmen of *Das Reich* did not know any of that, and at 1700 hours the last four operational Tigers from the 8th (Heavy) Company commenced the attack with the rest of the 2nd Panzer Regiment, capturing Ivanovka by 1715 hours. By 1825 hours the infantry of *Das Reich* had seized Hill 234.9; the Tigers, which had been supporting by fire, reached the hill at 1850 hours and began engaging enemy armor at Hill 241.1, just north of the village of Zhimolestnoye (Жимолостное), using long range fire to inflict losses. The Tigers continued to attack well into the night.[6] West of Zhimolestnoye a huge ravine effectively blocked the German armored advance.

For July 14, the SS Panzer Grenadier Division *Das Reich* suffered fifty-eight killed in action and 229 wounded in action during the attack on Pravorot' against elements of the 2nd Guards Tank Corps. Soviet units, including the 25th Guards Tank Brigade, the 183rd Rifle Division, and the 1510th Antitank Regiment, lost 436 killed in action, 766 wounded in action, and ninety-six missing in action.[7]

9th (Heavy) Company, 3rd Panzer Regiment
SS Panzer Grenadier Division *Totenkopf*

By 0840 hours bridging engineers had emplaced a sixty-ton bridge over the Psel for the *Totenkopf*. The Soviets continued their attacks in the *Totenkopf* sector. By 1050 hours German aerial spotters had counted 138 enemy tanks in front of the division and *Totenkopf* requested Stuka support. The five operational Tigers were in constant action, attempting to destroy multiple enemy penetrations.[8] An enemy infantry attack in battalion strength, but without tanks, struck the abandoned barracks south of Klyuchi at 1230 hours, but was repulsed by 1445 hours. Meanwhile Heinkel He 111 bombers struck a concentration of enemy tanks northeast of Vesëlyy, while Stukas attacked the enemy in the *balkas* and woods east of that village.

For July 14, the SS Panzer Grenadier Division *Totenkopf* lost twenty killed in action, 144 wounded in action in action, and one missing in action defending its bridgehead north of the Psel River. The attacking Soviet forces, including the 95th Guards Rifle Division, the 97th Guards Rifle Division, the 24th Guards Tank Brigade, the 10th Guards Mechanized Brigade, and the 11th Motorized Rifle Brigade, suffered 497 killed in action, 1,141 wounded in action, and 304 missing in action.[9]

Day's advance (in kilometers) by each Tiger Company in 2nd SS Panzer Corps:
- 13th (Heavy) Company, 1st Panzer Regiment: **1**
- 8th (Heavy) Company, 2nd Panzer Regiment: **7**
- 9th (Heavy) Company, 3rd Panzer Regiment: **1**

Operational 2nd SS Panzer Corps Tiger strength reported at the end of the day: **17**
- 13th (Heavy) Company, 1st Panzer Regiment: **8** (1800 hours)
- 8th (Heavy) Company, 2nd Panzer Regiment: **4** (1800 hours)
- 9th (Heavy) Company, 3rd Panzer Regiment: **5** (1800 hours)

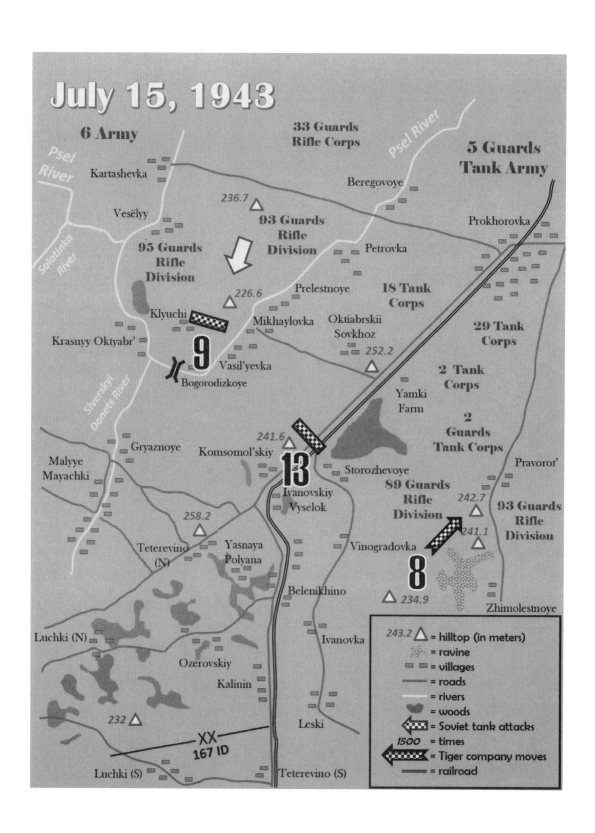

July 15, 1943

6 Army

33 Guards Rifle Corps

5 Guards Tank Army

Psel River

Psel River

Kartashevka

Veselyy

236.7 △

Beregovoye

Prokhorovka

Solotinka River

95 Guards Rifle Division

93 Guards Rifle Division

Petrovka

226.6 △

Prelestnoye

18 Tank Corps

Klyuchi

Mikhaylovka

Oktiabrskii Sovkhoz

29 Tank Corps

Krasnyy Oktyabr'

9

Vasil'yevka

252.2 △

Siverskyi Donets River

Bogorodizkoye

Yamki Farm

2 Tank Corps

2 Guards Tank Corps

Gryaznoye

241.6 △

Komsomol'skiy

13

Storozhevoye

Pravorot'

Malyye Mayachki

Ivanovskiy Vyselok

89 Guards Rifle Division

242.7 △

93 Guards Rifle Division

258.2 △

241.1 △

Teterevino (N)

Yasnaya Polyana

Vinogradovka

8

234.9 △

Belenikhino

Zhimolestnoye

Luchki (N)

Ivanovka

Ozerovskiy

Kalinin

243.2 △ = hilltop (in meters)

= ravine

= villages

= roads

= rivers

= woods

= Soviet tank attacks

1500 = times

= Tiger company moves

= railroad

232 △

Leski

XX
167 ID

Luchki (S)

Teterevino (S)

July 15, 1943[1]

Weather: mostly cloudy, heavy rain all morning in places
Terrain conditions: roads only partly navigable; difficult to haul supplies and ammunition; some roads sufficient for wheeled traffic only
Sunrise: 0427 hours **Sunset:** 2041 hours
Moon Phase: Waxing gibbous, 94% illumination

13th (Heavy) Company, 1st Panzer Regiment
SS Panzer Grenadier Division *Leibstandarte Adolf Hitler*

The planned attack by the *Leibstandarte* to seize Maloyablonovo (Малояблоново) was cancelled due to ground conditions and force ratios unfavorable for an offensive. The eight operational Tigers of the 13th (Heavy) Company assumed defensive positions along the Belgorod–Prokhorovka rail line.[2]

For July 15, the SS Panzer Grenadier Division *Leibstandarte Adolf Hitler* lost twenty-four killed in action, 103 wounded in action, and three missing in action during the fighting at the Oktiabrskii Sovkhoz area and Storozhevoye Woods. Soviet elements from the 53rd Motorized Rifle Brigade, the 31st Tank Brigade, the 25th Tank Brigade, and the 26th Tank Brigade suffered thirty-five killed in action and 123 wounded in action.[3]

8th (Heavy) Company, 2nd Panzer Regiment
SS Panzer Grenadier Division *Das Reich*

Das Reich reported at 0630 hours that it had still not seized Hill 242.7 and that in front of Pravorot' were deep minefields and a large antitank ditch. At 0840 hours the commander of the Fourth Panzer Army gave the order to *SS-Obergruppenführer* Paul Hausser to take the village of Pravorot' and the high ground to the north of it, and to subsequently seize the eastern half of Prokhorovka to the rail line splitting the town in two. At the same time the 3rd Panzer Corps on the right would continue its advance north three kilometers east of Pravorot' along the east flank of the 2nd SS Panzer Corps. At 1045 hours the corps "leaned on" *Das Reich* with another message: "The intent for the division is to take Pravorot' and the high ground north of it."

Das Reich answered at 1105 hours by stating that the defenses near Pravorot' and the high ground north of it were strongly occupied and that the enemy intended to hold the area. The 8th (Heavy) Company continued the attack to seize Hill 242.7, engaging enemy tanks on the hill. During the fight an antitank round hit the cupola of Tiger **S02** with company commander *SS-Obersturmführer* Philipp Theiss onboard, tearing his head off about 1300 hours. *SS-Obersturmführer* Walter Reininghaus assumed command of the company. Two other Tigers were hit and immobilized. The attack bogged down short of Pravorot' as difficult terrain, including a deep *balka*, echeloned enemy minefields and antitank, as well as antiaircraft guns in an antitank role, made the going slow for the last two operational tanks in the company.[4]

At 1230 hours *Das Reich* reported that the attack had halted, the situation at Vinogradovka was totally confusing, supply problems were overwhelming, Hill 242.7 was strongly defended by antitank and antiaircraft elements, and that an attack against the hill was only possible at night. Hausser exploded and sent the following reply to *Das Reich* within minutes: "*Höhe 242.7 muss unbedingt genommen werden* (Hill 242.7 must absolutely be taken)."

Das Reich did not reply for five hours until 1730 hours, when it radioed that the preparations to seize Hill 242.7 would be completed by 0200 hours the following morning. It would never occur.

For July 15, the SS Panzer Grenadier Division *Das Reich* suffered twenty-six killed in action and eighty-eight wounded in action during the final attempt to seize the village of Pravorot' against elements of the 2nd Guards Tank Corps. Soviet units, including the 25th Guards Tank Brigade, the 183rd Rifle Division, and the 1510th Antitank Regiment, lost sixty-two killed in action, 170 wounded in action, and sixteen missing in action.[5]

9th (Heavy) Company, 3rd Panzer Regiment
SS Panzer Grenadier Division *Totenkopf*
Rain lasted all morning. At 0910 hours *Totenkopf* reported that strong enemy reconnaissance efforts were being attempted along the entire front of the bridgehead and that the enemy was expanding its presence on Hill 236.7. *Totenkopf* began to evacuate the bridgehead north of the Psel River and move south. Nine of the company's Tigers were operational and remained in the bridgehead to provide a last-ditch defense should the enemy press too hard; it appears that two Tigers were damaged and declared non-operational.[6]

For July 15, the SS Panzer Grenadier Division *Totenkopf* lost nineteen killed in action and forty-six wounded in action defending its shrinking bridgehead north of the Psel River. The attacking Soviet forces, including the 95th Guards Rifle Division, the 97th Guards Rifle Division, the 24th Guards Tank Brigade, the 10th Guards Mechanized Brigade, and the 11th Motorized Rifle Brigade suffered 497 killed in action, 1,141 wounded in action, and 304 missing in action.[7]

The Tigers still had sharp claws.

Day's advance (in kilometers) by each Tiger Company in 2nd SS Panzer Corps:
      13th (Heavy) Company, 1st Panzer Regiment: **0**
      8th (Heavy) Company, 2nd Panzer Regiment: **2**
      9th (Heavy) Company, 3rd Panzer Regiment: **0**
Operational 2nd SS Panzer Corps Tiger strength reported at the end of the day: **17**
      13th (Heavy) Company, 1st Panzer Regiment: **8** (1840 hours)
      8th (Heavy) Company, 2nd Panzer Regiment: **2**
      9th (Heavy) Company, 3rd Panzer Regiment: **7** (1705 hours)

The fighting would continue, but the Kursk Offensive for the 13th (Heavy) Company, 8th (Heavy) Company, and the 9th (Heavy) Company was over. The numbers on both sides of destroyed vehicles have been argued passionately to this day. One source credits the 13th (Heavy) Company with destroying 151 enemy tanks and assault guns, and a further eighty-seven antitank guns from July 5 to July 15.[8]

There would be no additional attacks on Pravorot', no attacks on Prokhorovka, and no salvaging the bridgehead north of the Psel. The Tiger tanks had played their role, but could not obtain an operational level victory, no matter how many enemy tanks, assault guns, and antitank guns they destroyed each day.

Battle Rosters

Determining which crew members fought in which Tiger has proven difficult. Each of the three companies had more men assigned than were required to conduct operations because the Germans had enough combat experience since 1939 to know that many men would be wounded, and some would even be killed. The 8th (Heavy) Company, for example, appears to have had seventy Tiger crewmen assigned (five men for each of its fourteen Tigers), plus an additional five non-commissioned officers and eleven junior enlisted men.[1] These sixteen "spare" crewmen could perform other duties, such as driving light trucks, but primarily were a ready reserve of personnel when inevitable casualties started to mount.

Additionally, this study has found that some crewmen were reassigned from non-Tiger companies during the offensive. Finally, crewmen were sometimes directed to switch tanks during the battle, especially if a tank commander assumed the duties of a platoon leader or acting company commander.

The most accurate description of this section on battle rosters may be to say that some of the men remained on their Tiger for the entire duration of the offensive; some men served on one tank for part of the operation; and some men served on more than one Tiger during the offensive at Kursk from July 5–15. These battle rosters show which soldiers likely served in the following positions. They and other soldiers, who probably served on the Tigers, have biographical information in a subsequent chapter.

Legend: KIA = killed in action; WIA = wounded in action. Some men WIA could remain with the crew if their wounds were minor; others had to be evacuated for medical treatment.

13th (Heavy) Company, 1st Panzer Regiment
(Tank vehicle numbers 1301 to 1335)

Most sources state that the company began the offensive with fourteen Tigers and received several more probably just after it ended. This study shows seventeen Tigers, as a few sources indicate that may have been the count, and photographs show at least one of these additional turret numbers.

Company Headquarters

Company Commander: *SS-Hauptsturmführer* Heinrich (Heinz) Kling (July 5–10, WIA)
SS-Untersturmführer Michael Wittmann (July 11–15)

1301 (mobility kill by antitank mine on July 5)

Tank Commander: *SS-Hauptsturmführer* Heinrich (Heinz) Kling (July 5–10, WIA)
SS-Unterscharführer Jürgen "Captain" Brandt (July 10–15)
Gunner: *SS-Sturmmann* Karl-Heinz Warmbrunn
Radio Operator: *SS-Sturmmann* Wohlgemuth

Driver: *SS-Sturmmann* Heinrich "Hein" Reimers
Company Troop Leader:*SS-Obersturmführer* Waldemar Schütz

1302
First Platoon
Platoon Leader: *SS-Obersturmführer* Waldemar Schütz (July 10, WIA)

1311 (At the start of the Kursk Offensive the Tiger had ten kill rings on the gun tube)
Tank Commander: *SS-Obersturmführer* Waldemar Schütz (July 5–10, WIA)
                              SS-Unterscharführer Werner Wendt (July 10)
Gunner: *SS-Unterscharführer* Werner Wendt (July 5–10)
Loader: *SS-Panzerschütze* Klaus Bürvenich (July 5, WIA)
                              SS-Panzerschütze Walter Lau (July 5–13; relieved briefly once)
Driver: *SS-Panzerschütze* ewald Graf

1312 (Seriously damaged near Hill 241.6, July 12; vehicle abandoned in position and salvaged by the Soviets after the battle)
Tank Commander: *SS-Unterscharführer* Arthur Bernhardt (July 5–12, KIA)

1313
Tank Commander: *SS-Unterscharführer* Otto Augst
Gunner: *SS-Unterscharführer* Heinrich Knöss

1314
Tank Commander: *SS-Hauptscharführer* Fritz Hartel

1315
Tank Commander: *SS-Unterscharführer* Franz Enderl (to July 9, KIA)

Second Platoon
Platoon Leader: *SS-Untersturmführer* Helmut Wendorff (July 5–8, WIA)
                              SS-Untersturmführer Helmut Wendorff (July 9)

1321 (received a new engine July 4 at Tomarovka; mobility kill by antitank fire and antitank mine on July 5)
Tank Commander: *SS-Untersturmführer* Helmut Wendorff (July 5–8,WIA)

1322
Tank Commander: *SS-Unterscharführer* Ewald Mölly

1323 (transmission failure on July 7)
Tank Commander: *SS-Scharführer* Georg "Panzer General" Lötzsch

1324 (mobility kill destroying right reduction gear by antitank mine on July 6; mechanical problem on July 7; left drive wheel damaged on unknown date)
Tank Commander: *SS-Sturmmann* Rolf Schamp (July 5–9, replaced)
                              SS-Untersturmführer Michael Wittmann (July 9)
Gunner: *SS-Sturmmann* Siegfried Jung
Loader: *SS-Panzerschütze* Reinhart Wenzel

Radio Operator: *SS-Panzerschütze* Martin-Gerhard Iwanitz
Driver: *SS-Sturmmann* Franz Elmer

1325 (mobility kill destroying right reduction gear by antitank mine on July 6; mechanical problem on July 7; gun tube later had fifty kill rings painted on it)
Tank Commander: *SS-Unterscharführer* Franz Staudegger (July 5–10, began leave)
Gunner: *SS-Panzerschütze* Heinz Buchner
Loader: *SS-Panzerschütze* Walter Lau (July 5, moved to **1311**; July 13–15)
                           SS-Panzerschütze Walter Henke (July 5 to July 13, WIA)
Radio operator: *SS-Panzerschütze* Gerhard Waltersdorf
Driver: *SS-Sturmmann* Herbert Stellmacher

Third Platoon
Platoon Leader: *SS-Untersturmführer* Michael Wittmann (July 5–11, left to command company)

1331 (At the start of the Kursk Offensive the Tiger had ten kill rings on the gun tube; mobility kill by antitank mine on July 5; mobility kill by antitank mine on July 6; antitank shell destroyed hull machine gun on July 6 and evacuated; several mechanical problems on July 9)
Tank Commander: *SS-Untersturmführer* Michael Wittmann
                              (to company command July 11, but stayed in 1331)
Gunner: *SS-Rottenführer* Balthazar Woll (July 5–11)
                           SS-Untersturmführer Helmut Gräser (July 11–12)
Loader: *SS-Sturmmann* Kurt Berges (July 5, injured)
                           SS-Panzerschütze Walter Koch (July 5, WIA; July 6, WIA)
                           SS-Panzerschütze Max Gaube (July 7–15)
Radio operator: *SS-Panzerschütze* Paul Bender (July 5–7, replaced)
                           SS-Panzerschütze Karl Lieber (July 7–15, WIA)
                           SS-Sturmmann Kurt Pollmann (WIA July 11)
Driver: *SS-Sturmmann* Gustav Kirschner (July, WIA)
                           SS-Sturmmann Walter Bingert (July 7, replaced)
                           SS-Sturmmann Siegfried Fuss (July 7–15)

1332
Tank Commander: *SS-Oberscharführer* Max Marten

1333
Tank Commander: *SS-Unterscharführer* Hans Höld

1334 (Vehicle had track blocks bolted to the left side of the turret behind the turret number; designated July 6 to be stripped for parts; transported to Germany for factory rebuild on July 10, 1943)
Tank Commander: *SS-Unterscharführer* Jürgen "Captain" Brandt (July 5–6)
Radio Operator: *SS-Sturmmann* Peter Winkler (July 5–6)

1335
Tank Commander: *SS-Unterscharführer* Kurt Sowa

Unconfirmed tanks: *SS-Sturmmann* Leopold Aumüller, gunner
                           SS-Sturmmann Gunther Braubach, loader

SS-Sturmmann Georg Gentsch (July 5, KIA)
SS-Sturmmann Karl Heinz Grothum, radio operator
SS-Sturmmann Helmut Gruber
SS-Sturmmann Werner Hepe, driver
SS-Hauptscharführer Hans Höflinger, tank commander
SS-Sturmmann Gerhard Kaschlan
SS-Unterscharführer Kurt Kleber, tank commander
SS-Panzerschütze Ewald König, loader
SS-Sturmmann Helmut Lange
SS-Panzerschütze Alfred Lünser, gunner (beginning July 10)
SS-Rottenführer Karl Müller
SS-Sturmmann Heinz Owczarek (July 5, KIA)
SS-Rottenführer Willi Röpstorff, driver
SS-Panzeroberschütze Walter Rose
SS-Panzerschütze Heinz Schindhelm, gunner
SS-Panzerschütze Siegfried Schneider
SS-Panzeroberschütze Alfred Schumacher
SS-Sturmmann Roland Söffker
SS-Sturmmann Paul Sümnich, loader

8th (Heavy) Company, 2nd Panzer Regiment
(Tank vehicle numbers S01 to S34)

Company Headquarters
Company Commander: *SS-Hauptsturmführer* Herbert Zimmermann
      (July 5–7, WIA; July 8 to 1000 hrs. July 11, WIA)
      SS-Obersturmführer Philipp Theiss (1300 hours July 11, to July 15, KIA)
      SS-Obersturmführer Walter Reininghaus (from July 15)

S01 (disabled by antitank mine on July 5; out of action until July 11, severely damaged by antitank round at 1200 hours on July 11)
Tank Commander:	*SS-Hauptsturmführer* Herbert Zimmermann
	(July 5; WIA, 1000 hrs. July 11)
Gunner:	*SS-Rottenführer* Julius Hinrichsen (July 5; July 11)
Radio Operator:	*SS-Unterscharführer* Helmut Cantow (WIA, July 5)
Driver:	*SS-Rottenführer* Georg Gallinat (WIA, July 5)
	SS-Unterscharführer August Koppelkamp
Company Troop Leader:	*SS-Unterscharführer* Albert Ratter
	SS-Hauptsturmführer Karl Heinz Lorenz (KIA, 1200 hrs. July 7)

S02 (severe damage from antitank mine on July 6; in maintenance at least July 7–9)
Tank Commander:	*SS-Unterscharführer* Albert Ratter (July 5)
	SS-Hauptsturmführer Herbert Zimmermann (July 5–6)
	SS-Obersturmführer Philipp Theiss (July 7 to July 15)
	SS-Obersturmführer Walter Reininghaus (from July 15)
Gunner:	*SS-Rottenführer* Kurt Meyer (July 6)
	SS-Rottenführer Heinz Wilken (to 1200 hours July 7, WIA)
	SS-Rottenführer Julius Hinrichsen (July 11–15)

Loader:	*SS-Panzeroberschütze* Alfred Grupe
Radio Operator:	*SS-Rottenführer* Hans Haselböck
Driver:	*SS-Rottenführer* Max Bläsing (July 5, WIA)

Unconfirmed position:	*SS-Sturmmann* Karl Grupe
	SS-Rottenführer Günther Grupe

First Platoon

Platoon Leader:	*SS-Obersturmführer* Philipp Theiss (to company command July 11)
	SS-Untersturmführer Heinz Tensfeld (from 1300 hrs. July 11)

S11 (in maintenance on July 9; mobility kill by antitank fire on July 13)

Tank Commander:	*SS-Obersturmführer* Philipp Theiss (to company command July 11)
	SS-Untersturmführer Heinz Tensfeld (from 1300 hrs. July 11)
Gunner:	*SS-Rottenführer* Kurt Meyer (July 5–6)
Driver:	*SS-Rottenführer* Eduard Arzner
Loader	*SS-Unterscharführer* Gebhardt

S12 (in maintenance on July 9)

Tank Commander:	*SS-Unterscharführer* Konrad Schweigert
	SS-Unterscharführer Karl Skerbinz
Gunner:	*SS-Sturmmann* Hermann Jörg
Driver:	*SS-Sturmmann* Fritz Schmid

S13 (in maintenance on July 9)

Tank Commander:	*SS-Unterscharführer* Hans-Joachim Boehmer
	SS-Unterscharführer Franz Kraml

S14 (in maintenance on July 9)

Tank Commander:	*SS-Unterscharführer* Kurt Mohrbacher
	SS-Unterscharführer Horst Schleusner
Loader:	*SS-Panzerschütze* Johannes Esslinger
Driver:	*SS-Rottenführer* Eduard Woll (July 13-15)

Second Platoon

Platoon Leader:	*SS-Obersturmführer* Walter Reininghaus

S21 (in maintenance on July 9)

Tank Commander:	*SS-Obersturmführer* Walter Reininghaus
Gunner:	*SS-Unterscharführer* Artur Glagow
Loader:	*SS-Sturmmann* Ludwig Schnabel

S22 (in maintenance on July 9)

Tank Commander:	*SS-Unterscharführer* Walter Knecht
	SS-Untersturmführer Alois Kalss
Gunner:	*SS-Rottenführer* Gerhard Kaempf
Loader:	*SS-Sturmmann* Paul Jadzewski
Radio Operator:	*SS-Panzerfunker* Anton Mühldorfer
Driver:	*SS-Unterscharführer* Hagbert Hobohm

S23 (in maintenance on July 9)

Tank Commander:	*SS-Oberscharführer* Kurt Hellwig
	SS-Unterscharführer Walter Reibold

S24 (total kill by antitank fire on July 7)

Tank Commander:	*SS-Unterscharführer* Wilhelm Schmidt (to 1030 hours July 7)
	SS-Hauptsturmführer Karl Heinz Lorenz (KIA, 1200 hrs. July 7)
Gunner:	*SS-Unterscharführer* Werner Schäfer
Radio Operator:	*SS-Panzeroberschütze* Ernst Schäfer (to 1200 hours July 7, KIA)
Driver:	*SS-Rottenführer* Fritz Stemann (to 1200 hours July 7, WIA)

Third Platoon

Platoon Leader:	*SS-Untersturmführer* Alois Kalss

S31 (Vehicle had track blocks bolted to the front lower hull for additional protection; in maintenance July 9)

Tank Commander:	*SS-Untersturmführer* Alois Kalss
Gunner:	*SS-Rottenführer* Gerhard Kaempf
Loader:	*SS-Panzerschütze* Heinz Schöneberg (to July 11, WIA)
	SS-Sturmmann Werner Obenaus
Radio Operator:	*SS-Panzerfunker* Günter Skribelka
Driver:	*SS-Unterscharführer* Hagbert Hobohm

S32 (in maintenance on July 9, July 10, July 11 for engine damage)

Tank Commander:	*SS-Unterscharführer* Kurt Baral (WIA July 6, but remained with vehicle)
Gunner:	*SS-Panzeroberschütze* Jakob Kuster (to July 6, WIA)
	SS-Sturmmann Heinz Ramm

S33 (in maintenance on July 9)

Tank Commander:	*SS-Oberscharführer* Johann Reinhardt
Gunner:	*SS-Rottenführer* Hans Ross

S34 (in maintenance on July 9)

Tank Commander:	*SS-Unterscharführer* Artur Ulmer (to July 7, WIA)
Gunner:	*SS-Rottenführer* Wolfgang Birnbaum

Unconfirmed tanks:	*SS-Rottenführer* Gottlob Bittner, radio operator
	SS-Panzerschütze Egon Allwinn, gunner
	SS-Rottenführer Heinrich Asmussen, driver
	SS-Unterscharführer Max Apöck
	SS-Rottenführer Willi Börker, driver
	SS-Unterscharführer Ludwig Bullay, driver
	SS-Unterscharführer Berthold Fink, driver
	SS-Unterscharführer Heinz Freiberger, driver
	SS-Panzerschütze Wilfried Frenzel, radio operator (Injured July 5: DOW July 15)
	SS-Rottenführer Erich Gleissner, driver
	SS-Sturmmann Helmut Gnerlich, gunner

SS-Sturmmann Peter Hans, driver
SS-Sturmmann Bruno Hofmann, radio operator (WIA July 12)
SS-Panzerschütze Richard Hoffmann
SS-Panzeroberschütze Erich Holzer, loader
SS-Rottenführer Dieter Hurlbrink
SS-Junker Alfred Kendziora, commander
SS-Sturmmann Hans Klötzer, radio operator
SS-Unterscharführer Ferdinand Lasser, gunner
SS-Rottenführer Albert Laumbacher, gunner
SS-Obergrenadier Wilhelm Lotter, radio operator (WIA July 6)
SS-Panzeroberschütze Erwin Malsch, driver
SS-Sturmmann Arno Nienke, driver
SS-Rottenführer Ernst Pleger, driver
SS-Unterscharführer Herbert Reissmann, driver
SS-Panzeroberschütze Erwin Sandmeier
SS-Panzerschütze Gerhard Sauer
SS-Rottenführer Karl Schäfer, loader
SS-Sturmmann Georg Schmidt, gunner
SS-Panzeroberschütze Heinz Seidel
SS-Sturmmann Horst Stolzenberg, driver
Johann Stuttenecker
SS-Sturmmann Emil Theunis, gunner
SS-Unterscharführer Heinz Trautmann, loader
SS-Sturmmann Paul Ullrich
SS-Rottenführer Herbert Erich Walter
SS-Sturmmann Emil Weissfloch
SS-Rottenführer Anton Wilfling
SS-Rottenführer Rudolf Zacharias, gunner (WIA July 12)
SS-Rottenführer Joachim Zimbehl, gunner

9th (Heavy) Company, 3rd Panzer Regiment
(Tank vehicle numbers 900 to 934)

Company Headquarters
Company Commander: *SS-Hauptsturmführer* Fritz Biermeier
      to Second Battalion/3rd Panzer Regiment, July 8)
      SS-Obersturmführer Wilhelm Schroeder (KIA July 8)
      SS-Untersturmführer Walter Köhler (KIA July 12)
      SS-Untersturmführer Karl-Heinz Schüffler (July 12)
      SS-Hauptsturmführer Wilfried Richter (from July 12)

901 (mobility kill by antitank mine on July 5; commander killed by antitank rifle on July 8; and mobility kill by antitank mine on July 10)
Tank Commander: *SS-Hauptsturmführer* Fritz Biermeier
      (to Second Battalion/3rd Panzer Regiment, July 8)
      SS-Obersturmführer Wilhelm Schroeder (KIA July 8)
      SS-Untersturmführer Walter Köhler (July 12)
      SS-Hauptsturmführer Wilfried Richter (from July 12)

Gunner:	*SS-Rottenführer* Ludwig Lachner
Loader:	*SS-Sturmmann* Fritz Hitz
	SS-Sturmmann Karl Küster
Driver:	*SS-Unterscharführer* Willi Probst
Company Troop Leader:	*SS-Obersturmführer* Wilhelm Schroeder (became company commander, July 8)

902 (disabled by antitank mine 1930 hrs. July 6)

Tank Commander:	*SS-Obersturmführer* Schroeder (became company commander, July 8)
	SS-Oberscharführer Willy Biber

First Platoon

Platoon Leader:	*SS-Untersturmführer* Walter Köhler (became company commander, July 8)

911 (pre-Kursk; six kill rings on photo; jammed turret; tank to repair facilities July 8, remained July 9; mobility kill by antitank mine on July 10; steering problems 1445 hours July 11)

Tank Commander:	*SS-Untersturmführer* Walter Köhler (became company commander July 8, but may have remained in this tank and was KIA July 12); *SS-Unterscharführer* Hans-Joachim Hoffmann
Gunner:	*SS-Sturmmann* Hermann Mocnik
Loader:	*SS-Sturmmann* Fritz Hitz, *SS-Mann* Hans Rex
Radio Operator:	*SS-Sturmmann* Karl Küster
Driver:	*SS-Sturmmann* Walter Lucht
Unconfirmed position:	Herbert Kranz
	SS-Rottenführer Karl Schulze-Berge

912 (severely damaged by artillery round July 8)

Tank Commander:	*SS-Unterscharführer* Josef "Fritz" Göckl (KIA July 8)
Gunner:	*SS-Rottenführer* Friedrich Selonke
	SS-Unterscharführer Ludwig Zimmermann (KIA July 8)
Loader:	*SS-Rottenführer* Ludwig Müller (KIA July 8)
Driver:	*SS-Sturmmann* Karl Blattmann

913 (eighteen kill rings on photo)

Tank Commander:	*SS-Unterscharführer* Edmund Fein
Loader:	*SS-Panzerschütze* Franz Hofer
Driver:	*SS-Rottenführer* Otto Köppen
Unconfirmed position:	*SS-Oberscharführer* Willy Kronmüller
	SS-Unterscharführer Walter Münch

914 (pre-Kursk zero kill rings on photo; total kill by artillery fire on July 7)

Tank Commander:	*SS-Unterscharführer* Richard Müller (WIA July 7; DOW July 12)

Second Platoon

Platoon Leader:	*SS-Untersturmführer* Heinz Quade (WIA in eye AT rifle, stayed with unit)

921

Tank Commander:	*SS-Untersturmführer* Heinz Quade
Gunner:	*SS-Unterscharführer* Artur Privatzki
Loader:	*SS-Sturmmann* Franz Hilgert
Unknown Position:	*SS-Sturmmann* Frielau

922

Tank Commander:	*SS-Oberscharführer* Hans Frank

923

Tank Commander:	*SS-Unterscharführer* Hein Bode

924

Tank Commander:	*SS-Unterscharführer* Hans-Joachim Hoffmann
Loader:	*SS-Mann* Hans Rex

Third Platoon

Platoon Leader:	*SS-Untersturmführer* Willi Rathsack (WIA July 12)
	SS-Untersturmführer Heinz Karl Schüffler (from July 13)

931

Tank Commander:	*SS-Untersturmführer* Willi Rathsack (WIA July 12)
	SS-Untersturmführer Heinz Karl Schüffler (from July 13)
Driver:	*SS-Sturmmann* Hans Joachim Matthäi

932 (eighteen kill rings in photo)

Tank Commander:	*SS-Oberscharführer* Alois Tasler
Gunner:	*SS-Rottenführer* Fritz Lein
Loader:	*SS-Mann* Fritz Rudolph
Unconfirmed position:	*SS-Mann* Georg Zieten

933

Tank Commander:	*SS-Oberscharführer* Otto Ernst Baumann
Gunner:	*SS-Unterscharführer* Artur Privatzki
Radio Operator:	*SS-Panzerschütze* Hans-Georg van Kerkom
Driver:	*SS-Sturmmann* Hans-Ludwig Bachmann

934

Tank Commander:	*SS-Oberscharführer* Hans Lampert
Unconfirmed tanks:	*SS-Unterscharführer* Franz Böhm
	Josef "Jupp" Franz
	SS-Sturmmann Günther Grüner, radio operator
	SS-Funker Werner Hoberg, radio operator
	SS-Oberschütze Fritz Hock
	SS-Panzerschütze Norbert Kochesser, loader
	SS-Sturmmann Wolfgang Kühnke

Fritz Lasch

SS-Sturmmann Friedrich Johann "Fritz" Lau

SS-Sturmmann Alois Mücke, radio operator

SS-Sturmmann Fritz Osha, driver

SS-Rottenführer Karl Sandler, tank commander

SS-Panzerschütze Georg Schäfer, gunner

SS-Panzerschütze Gunther Schreyer

SS-Oberschütze Werner Schweitzer, radio operator

SS-Sturmmann Ernst Vögler, loader, (KIA July 12)

SS-Unterscharführer Erwin Wehr, driver

SS-Rottenführer Felix Werner

SS-Unterscharführer Georg Wimmer

Crew Member Biographies

13th (Heavy) Company, 1st Panzer Regiment, SS Panzer Grenadier Division *Leibstandarte Adolf Hitler*

Otto Augst. *SS-Unterscharführer* Otto Augst was born on September 24, 1920. Prior to Kursk, on April 20, 1943, he had received the Iron Cross Second Class for the fighting at Kharkov in February–March, serving as a driver. During the Kursk Offensive, he was assigned to the First Platoon as the commander of Tiger **1313**. On November 2, 1943, *SS-Oberscharführer* Augst was in command of Tiger S14 of the company.[1] He later served as a Tiger commander in the Second Company of the 101st SS Heavy Panzer Detachment in Normandy in 1944.

Leopold Aumüller. Born on May 25, 1923, Leopold Aumüller served as a Tiger gunner in the 13th (Heavy) Company during the battle. Previously he had fought at Kharkov in February–March 1943 as a gunner. *SS-Sturmmann* Aumüller later served in Tiger 331 in the 3rd Company of the 101st SS Heavy Panzer Detachment and fought in Normandy.[2] He is believed to have been an *SS-Junker* (officer candidate) in the 3rd Company of the 501st SS Heavy Panzer Detachment in the Ardennes. Leopold Aumüller survived the war.

Paul Bender. How did a weaver by trade, who had his feet frostbitten so severely as an infantryman on the Eastern Front that he lost a toe, end up in a Tiger tank? Paul Bender, who was born in Wuppertal-Elberfeld on December 25, 1924, may have wondered that. The weaver joined the Hitler Youth on March 1, 1935. Standing 5'11" tall, he joined the Waffen-SS on August 20, 1942; he had blood type O. During his early service as an infantryman Bender was frostbitten in his feet, resulting in the amputation of a left toe (which resulted in a Wound Badge in Silver); he then retrained as a radioman. Bender was assigned to the company on December 25, 1942, and fought around Kharkov in early 1943, receiving a Panzer Battle Badge in Silver.[3]

Assigned to the Third Platoon, *SS-Panzerschütze* Bender served as a radio operator in Tiger **1331** from July 5 to July 7, when an abscessed tooth and infection led to his being replaced. He was promoted to *SS-Sturmmann* on September 1, 1943. Continued combat earned him an Iron Cross Second Class on June 3, 1944; at that time he was serving as a radio operator in a Tiger in the 2nd Company of the 101st SS Heavy Panzer Detachment. Days later the unit was fighting in Normandy. Paul Bender was awarded a Panzer Battle Badge in Silver for 25 Assaults on December 1, 1944, and appears to have been a radio operator in a King Tiger in the 1st Company of the 501st SS Heavy Panzer Detachment during the Ardennes Offensive, which became known in the United States as the "Battle of the Bulge," beginning December 16, 1944.[4]

Kurt Berges. *SS-Sturmmann* Berges served in the Third Platoon in Tiger **1331** as a loader on July 5. Early on that first day of battle the tank swerved and tilted in such a way that a main gun round (about thirty pounds) fell on his hand, severely injuring it. Unable to fully function, he was replaced later that day.[5]

Arthur Bernhardt. When Arthur Bernhardt joined the Luftwaffe he had no idea that he would ever participate in one of the largest tank battles in World War II—from the ground—but that is exactly what happened. Born in Leipzig on August 18, 1918, Arthur had previously served in the Luftwaffe until March 1943; he had no previous combat experience in a tank prior to Kursk. *SS-Unterscharführer* Bernhardt was assigned to the First Platoon, serving as the commander of Tiger **1312** from July 5 to July 12. On the latter date in the late morning, on the forward slope of Hill 241.6, enemy tank fire from the 181st Tank Brigade struck the Tiger numerous times, including the cupola, killing Arthur Bernhardt instantly. His remains have never been found and identified.[6]

Walter Bingert. Born on April 20, 1922, at Niederwürzbach in the Saar, Walter Bingert fought at Kharkov in the company in February–March 1943 as a driver. During the Kursk Offensive *SS-Sturmmann* Bingert was assigned to the Third Platoon as the driver for Tiger **1331**. For his bravery in the battle Walter was awarded the Iron Cross Second Class on July 23, 1943. On January 6, 1944, he reported with a small group to the Sennelager training facility to receive six of the first King Tiger panzers to be sent from the factory to the field. Later promoted to *SS-Rottenführer*, Walter fought in the 1st Company of the 101st SS Heavy Panzer Detachment in Normandy in summer 1944 as a driver for Tiger 105. Walter married his fiancée in November 1944. With the unit re-designated the 501st SS Heavy Panzer Detachment, *SS-Rottenführer* Bingert fought in the Ardennes Offensive beginning December 16, 1944, as the driver for King Tiger 105—company commander *SS-Obersturmführer* Jürgen Wessel's vehicle—in the 1st Company of the detachment. On December 18, 1944, American antitank fire struck the vehicle on the Rue Haut Rivage in the village of Stavelot, Belgium. Bingert threw the transmission into reverse and the tank crashed into a house, immobilizing it. Walter Bingert died on February 7, 1996.[7]

Jürgen "Captain" Brandt. "Captain" Jürgen Brandt was an old timer in the company—even though he was only twenty-one years old—having been assigned at its formation. Jürgen hailed from Rendsburg in Holstein, where he was born on September 2, 1921. He served in the Hitler Youth from April 1932 to October 1938, and was able to speak English and French. One of the taller men in the company at 6'2", Brandt had served in the infantry from November 24, 1939, to February 15, 1940. He then became a tank radio operator for three months before spending sixteen months doing ordnance duties, for which he received the War Merit Cross Second Class. On September 2, 1941, he became a gunner in a *Leibstandarte* assault gun in Russia and received the Eastern Front Medal on May 1, 1942. Jürgen then transferred to the new Tiger unit—the 4th Company—in the *Leibstandarte* on October 2, 1942; he initially commanded a Mark III N panzer and later Tiger 436, fighting near Krasnograd. He received the Panzer Battle Badge in Silver on March 1, 1943, and the Iron Cross Second Class on April 20, 1943, for combat at Kharkov.[8]

By June 1943, assigned to the Third Platoon, *SS-Unterscharführer* Brandt commanded Tiger **1334**. The tank saw combat on July 5 and 6, but then was designated to serve as a source for parts to make other tanks in the company operational; he later commanded Tiger **1301**. For his actions at Kursk—especially on July 9–10—Brandt was awarded the Iron Cross First Class on July 23, 1943. On November 16, 1943, he and two other Tigers virtually annihilated an enemy rifle battalion near Brusilov, demonstrating that the Tiger could also be a deadly foe to dismounted infantry.[9]

Jürgen Brandt fought in the 2nd Company of the 101st SS Heavy Panzer Detachment in Normandy in the summer of 1944, commanding Tiger 223 at the Battle of Villers-Bocage and Hill 160, and later receiving a Panzer Battle Badge in Silver for 25 Assaults on December 1, 1944. About this time his chain of command submitted him for the German Cross in Gold, which Sepp Dietrich approved on December 12. *SS-Oberscharführer* Brandt then fought in the Ardennes Offensive with the 501st SS Heavy Panzer Detachment, commanding King Tiger 131 as the leader of the Third Platoon of the 1st Company until December 25, 1944, when he was killed in action at Petit-Spai, Belgium, by an American artillery shell. Posthumously awarded the German Cross in Gold, his remains are buried in the German War Cemetery at Lommel, Belgium, in the section for the unknowns. Brandt is believed by many sources to have destroyed forty-seven to fifty-seven enemy tanks in his career.[10]

Gunther Braubach. *SS-Sturmmann* Braubach served as a loader in a Tiger in the 13th (Heavy) Company. On August 23, 1944, he received an Iron Cross Second Class for actions with the 2nd Company of the 101st SS Heavy Panzer Detachment in Normandy.

Heinz Buchner. The *Abitur*—the entrance examination that qualified a German student to enter a university—was a significant event, and one filled with great consternation—perhaps an excellent preparation for later pressures found in a Tiger in combat. Born in Pforzheim on May 3, 1924, Heinz Buchner finished secondary school and passed the *Abitur*. He was a member of the Hitler Youth from June 1, 1933, to July 1, 1942, and joined the Waffen-SS on July 4. At Kharkov in February–March 1943 he served as a gunner.[11]

SS-Panzerschütze Buchner, who stood 5'11" tall, served as a gunner for *SS-Unterscharführer* Franz Staudegger in Tiger **1325** in the Second Platoon. During the battle on July 8 he is believed to have destroyed twenty-two enemy tanks. For this achievement he received the Iron Cross Second Class and the Iron Cross First Class on July 23, 1943. Buchner was promoted to *SS-Unterscharführer* on January 30, 1944, and attended an officer leadership course in Klagenfurt, Austria, later in the year. Promoted to *SS-Untersturmführer* on October 20, 1944, he fought in the Ardennes Offensive with the 501st SS Heavy Panzer Detachment, where he commanded King Tiger 121 in the Second Platoon of the 1st Company. During his combat career Buchner is often cited for the destruction of fifty-one enemy tanks. Heinz survived the war and died on November 24, 1999.[12]

Klaus Bürvenich. Born on July 4, 1925, in Ratingen, North Rhine-Westphalia, *SS-Panzerschütze* Klaus Bürvenich was assigned as a loader in Tiger **1311** in the First Platoon. On the first day of the offensive he was wounded by a Soviet antitank shell hit on his vision slit and was evacuated for treatment. Klaus had previous combat experience in tanks, receiving the Panzer Battle Badge in Silver for actions at Kharkov in which he was the loader in Tiger 411 under the command of Waldemar Schütz. On September 16, 1943, Klaus Bürvenich received an Iron Cross Second Class.[13]

Franz Elmer. Born February 25, 1923, in Niederalteich, near Deggendorf, Bavaria, "Fran" Elmer fought near Kharkov in February–March 1943, with the company as a driver. At the Kursk Offensive *SS-Sturmmann* Elmer drove Tiger **1324** in the Second Platoon. He received the Iron Cross Second Class on September 16, 1943.[14] *SS-Unterscharführer* Franz Elmer was later a driver in the 101st SS Heavy Panzer Detachment for Helmut Wendorff in Tiger 205 in the 2nd Company and was in the engagement where Wendorff was killed.[15]

Franz Enderl. Franz Enderl was born March 7, 1920, in Borngrund, Hesse. Prior to joining the Waffen-SS Enderl served in the Luftwaffe. An *SS-Unterscharführer*, he served as the tank commander for Tiger **1315** in the First Platoon. He was killed in action on July 9 near Sukhosolotino. Franz's remains have never been found; his name is memorialized at the German War Cemetery some two miles north of the village of Kursk–Besedino, that holds 47,740 German dead from World War II.[16]

Siegfried Fuss. Siegfried Fuss was born in Baden-Baden on May 16, 1924. He was a member of the Hitler Youth from June 1, 1933, to July 1, 1942, completed secondary school, and passed the

Abitur. He probably joined the SS soon thereafter; he served in the company as a driver during the Kharkov counteroffensive in February–March 1943 as a driver. Standing 5'11" tall, *SS-Sturmmann* Siegfried Fuss fought at Kursk as a driver of Tiger **1331** in the Third Platoon, probably after July 8. For this accomplishment he received the Iron Cross Second Class on July 23, 1943; during the war he was also awarded the Wound Badge in Black and the Panzer Battle Badge in Silver. He received a belated Iron Cross First Class while in officer training in 1944. Siegfried finished the war as an *SS-Untersturmführer*, to which he was promoted on October 10, 1944. His last assignment was with the 501st SS Heavy Panzer Detachment. Siegfried Fuss is believed to have survived the war.[17]

Max Gaube. Born in Riegersdorf, in Silesia, on November 16, 1924, *SS-Panzerschütze* Max Gaube served as the loader in Tiger **1331** in the Third Platoon, taking over midday on July 5, when the original loader was wounded. Later assigned to the 101st SS Heavy Panzer Detachment, he received the Iron Cross Second Class on June 3, 1944, then fought in Normandy. Max Gaube was killed in action at Hill 213 in Normandy on June 15, 1944. He is buried at the German War Cemetery at Cheux-St.-Manvieu, Normandy, in Block 11, Row F, Grave 9.[18]

Georg Gentsch. Born February 5, 1924, in Erfurt, *SS-Sturmmann* Gentsch briefly served in a Tiger in the 13th (Heavy) Company on July 5, but was killed in action that day. George's remains have never been found; his name is memorialized at the German War Cemetery some two miles north of the village of Kursk–Besedino.[19]

Ewald Graf. *SS-Panzerschütze* Graf served as the driver for Tiger **1311** in the First Platoon. He had served the company since it received the new tanks at the Troop Training Grounds Bergen at Fallingbostel, Lower Saxony, in January 1943, and had fought at Kharkov as a loader, winning a Panzer Battle Badge in Silver. Later in the war Ewald was seriously wounded on December 28, 1943, at Antopol–Bojarka. At least one source indicates that Graf subsequently served as a loader in Tiger 331 in the Third Platoon of the 3rd Company in the 101st SS Heavy Panzer Detachment in Normandy in June 1944, and that he received the Iron Cross Second Class on September 30, 1944, as an *SS-Sturmmann*.[20]

Helmut Gräser. Helmut Gräser, who was born on May 22, 1922, in Liegnitz, in Silesia, entered the SS on October 23, 1939; he was single. He was promoted to *SS-Rottenführer* on March 1, 1942. At Kharkov in February–March 1943 he served as a gunner. At Kursk *SS-Rottenführer* Gräser served as the gunner in Tiger **1331** in the Third Platoon on July 11–12. Helmut was promoted to *SS-Unterscharführer* on August 1, 1943, and awarded the Iron Cross Second Class on September 16, 1943.[21]

Karl-Heinz Grothum. For men whose heights are known, Karl-Heinz Grothum was one of the shortest at 5'6" tall, although that did not stop him from having an excellent career in the Waffen-SS. Born June 27, 1924, in Glogau, Lower Silesia, Karl-Heinz was the son of a police official. He began training as an electrician before enlisting in the Waffen-SS on July 15, 1941. Promoted to *SS-Sturmmann* on September 1, 1942, Grothum trained as a radio operator. Karl-Heinz joined the 13th (Heavy) Company at the Troop Training Grounds Bergen at Fallingbostel on December 11, 1942. At Kursk, *SS-Sturmmann* Grothum served in a Tiger in the company, probably as a radio operator. He received the Iron Cross Second Class on September 16, 1943; he also received the Panzer Battle Badge in Silver. Grothum was promoted to *SS-Rottenführer* on August 1, 1943, and to *SS-Unterscharführer* on November 1, 1943. Karl-Heinz was married. A form in his personnel file indicates that he served in the 1st Company of the 501st SS Heavy Panzer Detachment. It is believed that Karl-Heinz Grothum survived the war.[22]

Helmut Gruber. Born in Vienna, Austria, on April 28, 1925, Helmut—who was Catholic—finished high school and a National Political Institution of Teaching. He also joined the Hitler Youth in March 1938. Standing 5'8" tall, he joined the Waffen-SS on August 1, 1942. He was assigned to the SS Panzer Replacement Battalion at Weimer-Buchenwald on October 2, 1942. *SS-Sturmmann* Gruber served in a Tiger crew—possibly as a radio operator—in the 13th (Heavy) Company. Helmut received the Iron Cross Second Class on September 16, 1943; he also was awarded the Panzer Battle Badge in Silver about the same time. He attended the 4th SS Panzer Officer Candidate Course at Königsbrück (near Dresden, Saxony) from July 17, 1944, to November 7, 1944. Gruber was promoted to *SS-Junker* on July 1, 1944, and to *SS-Standartenjunker* on September 1, 1944. Helmut Gruber was commissioned an *SS-Untersturmführer* on January 30, 1945, and was then assigned to the reconnaissance detachment of the 5th SS Panzer Division *Wiking*.[23]

That unit, commanded by Knight's Cross with Oak Leaves winner *SS-Sturmbannführer* Fritz Vogt, fought in Hungary and Austria before surrendering to American forces at the end of the war. Helmut Gruber was not one of them; he was seriously wounded and died at a *Totenkopf* Division medical aid station at Iskaszentgyörgy, Hungary, on March 17, 1945. *SS-Untersturmführer* Gruber is buried at the German Military Cemetery at Veszprem, Hungary, in Block 3, Row 12, in Grave 912.[24]

Fritz Hartel. Born May 10, 1914, in Grünhagen, East Prussia, and a miller by trade, Fritz Hartel joined the SS on July 30, 1934, receiving SS number 265812. With brown hair and blue-green eyes, he stood 5'11" tall and weighed 189 pounds. Married on October 18, 1939, he and his wife had two children. During this period Hartel was assigned to the 9th Company of the *Leibstandarte SS Adolf Hitler* Regiment in Berlin. Fritz Hartel was promoted to *SS-Oberscharführer* on October 1, 1941. *SS-Oberscharführer* Hartel commanded the First Platoon of the company at Kharkov in February–March 1943, in Tiger 418. At the Kursk Offensive he was the commander of Tiger **1314** in the First Platoon. On November 9, 1943, Hartel was promoted to *SS-Untersturmführer*. Fritz Hartel was posted missing in action on December 30, 1943, near Berdychiv–Khazhyn, in the Ukraine. There is some confusion concerning the date, as the German War Grave Commission lists that he became missing in action on December 1, 1943. His remains have never been discovered.[25]

Walter Henke. Walter Henke had a lifelong reminder of the Kursk Offensive—he lost an eye because of the fight. Born April 28, 1923, in Augarten, near Konin, in what would become the Warthegau, Henke—who stood 5'11" tall—joined the SS in April 1941, and the Waffen-SS on June 20, 1942; he had blood type O. He joined the 1st Panzer Regiment on October 10, 1942, and received Tiger training two months later. As a result he had previous combat experience in the vehicle at Kharkov, for which he received the Panzer Battle Badge in Silver. At the Kursk Offensive *SS-Panzerschütze* Henke was a loader in Tiger **1325** until July 13, when near Oktiabrskii Sovkhoz he was wounded in the left eye. Evacuated to a reserve military hospital in Dresden, Walter's eye could not be saved, and surgeons removed it on August 16, 1943; this resulted in the bestowal of the Wound Badge in Silver. Walter had also received the Iron Cross Second Class on July 23, 1943 (for his role in Franz Staudegger's destruction of twenty-two enemy tanks), and was promoted to *SS-Sturmmann* on September 27, 1943. Henke could speak Polish and Ukrainian.[26]

Werner Hepe. Werner Hepe was born on February 2, 1925, in Dortmund. He entered the Waffen-SS on September 15, 1942. *SS-Sturmmann* Hepe served as a driver in a Tiger in the company during the Kursk Offensive. In February 1944, Hepe's Tiger was damaged by enemy fire and had to be destroyed during the Cherkassy relief operation. Werner received the Panzer Battle Badge in Silver. He served in the 2nd Company of the 101st SS Heavy Panzer Detachment in Normandy in summer 1944 and was promoted to *SS-Rottenführer* on September 1, 1944.[27]

Hans Höflinger. Hans Höflinger was born on April 22, 1918, in Kiefersfelden, in the extreme south of Bavaria on the Austrian border. A Catholic, he joined the Hitler Youth on April 1, 1933, and remained in the organization until November 11, 1934, when he joined the Allgemeine-SS; he was a metal smith by trade. He enlisted in the Waffen-SS on May 3, 1937. Prior to joining the company, he served in the SS Panzer Grenadier Division *Das Reich* as an infantryman in the *Deutschland* regiment, participating in the annexation of Austria and the Sudetenland. In September 1939 he took part in the invasion of Poland. Höflinger was promoted to *SS-Oberscharführer* on April 20, 1942. He was married. Hans was attending the *SS-Junkerschule* at Bad Tölz when on February 1, 1943, he became ill and was hospitalized for jaundice at a reserve hospital in Bad Tölz, Bavaria.[28]

At the Kursk Offensive, *SS-Oberscharführer* Höflinger served as a tank commander in the Third Platoon in the company; by October 1, 1943, he commanded Tiger **S23** in the Second Platoon of the company; he was listed in command of the same tank on November 2. Höflinger was promoted to *SS-Hauptscharführer* on April 1, 1944; he later commanded Tiger 213 in the 2nd Company of the 101st SS Heavy Panzer Detachment in Normandy, helped shoot down an enemy fighter-bomber on June 10, 1944, and fought at the Battle of Villers-Bocage. On August 8, 1944, near Saint-Aignan-de-Cramesnil, Normandy, Höflinger's Tiger was about two hundred and fifty meters behind Michael Wittmann and witnessed when Wittmann's Tiger was destroyed. Höflinger received the Iron Cross First Class on November 20, 1944. Hans Höflinger survived the war.[29]

Johann "Hans" Höld. *SS-Unterscharführer* "Hans" Höld was born in Defflingen, in the Black Forest on October 17, 1919. Prior to Kursk he had received a Panzer Battle Badge in Silver for armored actions around Kharkov the previous winter, where he commanded Tiger 433. He also received the Iron Cross Second Class on April 20, 1943. At Kursk, Hans served as a tank commander for Tiger **1333** in the Third Platoon. He became engaged on September 5, 1943. On September 16, 1943, he received the Iron Cross First Class. On November 2, 1943, he was in command of Tiger S12 of the company, but on November 22 he was killed in action near the village of Yastrebenka, in the Brusilov area of the Ukraine, when an enemy antitank round sheared off the cupola of his Tiger, fatally striking his forehead. Johann's remains rest at the German War Cemetery at Kiev in Block 8, Row 8, in Grave 655; the cemetery contains approximately 26,000 war dead.[30] Rolf Schamp, who served in the same crew as Hans Höld, later said that the two enjoyed serving together and got along well.[31]

Martin-Gerhard Iwanitz. *SS-Panzerschütze* Iwanitz came from Plauen in Saxony, where he was born on December 23, 1921. He served as a loader in the company during the fighting around Kharkov in February–March 1943. At Kursk he served in the Second Platoon as a radio operator in Tiger **1324**. Later promoted to *SS-Rottenführer*, Martin was killed in action at Lissowka on November 16, 1943. He had received the Panzer Battle Badge in Silver. His remains have never been found.[32]

Siegfried Jung. Born on May 23, 1925, in Dortmund, *SS-Sturmmann* Jung served as a gunner in Tiger **1334** in the Second Platoon. He received the Iron Cross Second Class on September 16, 1943. Previously he had served as a gunner in the Kharkov area in February–March 1943. Siegfried was also a gunner in the unit on October 1, 1943.[33]

Gerhard Kaschlun. *SS-Sturmmann* Kaschlun, who was born on March 14, 1925, in Bad Oldesloe, in Schleswig-Holstein, served in a Tiger in the company. He received the Iron Cross Second Class on September 16, 1943. In Normandy, Gerhard served as a gunner in the Second Company of the 101st SS Heavy Panzer Detachment; for his actions *SS-Rottenführer* Kaschlun received the Iron Cross First Class on September 30, 1944.[34]

Gustav Kirschner. "Gustl" Kirschner served as a driver in the Third Platoon. He was wounded on July 5 by the effects of an antitank shell. Previously, during training at the Ploërmel training area in Brittany, France, when the company was receiving its Tigers, Kirschner drove for Michael Wittmann.

Kurt "Quax" Kleber. "Quax" Kleber was known for his sense of humor. He was born on October 14, 1922, at Bütow, Lake Plateau, in Mecklenburg. Originally in the Luftwaffe, *SS-Unterscharführer* Kleber reported to the company in spring 1943, and was assigned to the Third Platoon for the Kursk Offensive. On November 2, 1943, Kleber was in command of Tiger S25 of the company. In Russia on February 19, 1944, his tank's steering system was seriously damaged and the Tiger had to be blown up with explosive charges to prevent it from falling into enemy hands. Receiving the Iron Cross Second Class on April 16, 1944, he was killed in action by an Allied fighter-bomber on June 9, 1944, near the village of Dreux in Normandy while commanding Tiger 232 in the 2nd Company of the 101st SS Heavy Panzer Detachment. Kurt is buried at the German War Cemetery at Solers, France, in Block 1, Row 20, in Grave 832; the cemetery holds 2,228 sets of remains.[35]

Heinrich Kling. One would think that a soldier who had been wounded eleven times during the war might ask for a desk job in the rear, but such was not the case with Heinrich Kling. In fact in 1944, his regimental commander, Jochen Peiper, had this to say in a recommendation for Kling's promotion: "Kling is a soldier proven in war and peace. Quite calm and balanced, he has a great deal of experience and, with good teaching ability, is able to train his officers. As the commander of the most successful Tiger Company of the Eastern Front, he has excelled by being a daredevil and is crisis-resistant."[36] At Kursk he needed to be "crisis resistant," as *SS-Hauptsturmführer* "Heinz" Kling was the commander of the 13th (Heavy) Company, and in this position was also the commander for Tiger **1301** in the Headquarters Platoon.

Born on September 10, 1913, in Kassel, in the state of Hesse, Germany, he joined the Nazi Party (NSDAP number 1254524) and the SS on the same day (August 1, 1932), receiving SS number 39402. He joined the Waffen-SS on August 28, 1935, and was assigned to the SS Regiment *Germania* in Arolsen; Kling graduated from the *SS-Junkerschule* (Officers' Candidate School) at Bad Tölz in Bavaria in November 1938, and was promoted on November 9 to *SS-Untersturmführer* in the Waffen-SS (he had already become an officer in the Allgemeine-SS). He then commanded the 9th Company of *Germania*.[37]

Kling was assigned to the 12th *Totenkopf Standarte* on November 14, 1939, initially commanding the 6th Company of infantry, winning the Iron Cross Second Class on August 20, 1940; the War Service Cross Second Class with Swords on January 30, 1941; and the Iron Cross First Class on July 16, 1941. He had been promoted to *SS-Obersturmführer* on June 1, 1940. Standing 5'8" tall, he was married on May 8, 1941, at Radolfzell and had one son, born on November 6, 1942; the family would later have two other children.[38] Part of the 12th *Totenkopf Standarte* was complicit in the murder of 1,100 mental patients in the fall of 1939 at a psychiatric hospital in Owińska, Poland; the study does not know if Kling was part of that operation.

His unit absorbed into the *Leibstandarte Adolf Hitler* in late 1941, Heinz Kling was promoted to *SS-Hauptsturmführer* on November 9, 1941, and received the Infantry Assault Badge in Bronze on March 23, 1942. Kling soon transferred to the panzer arm, attending the Panzer School at Wünsdorf, and became the commander of the 4th Company on December 24, 1942, which was renamed the 13th (Heavy) Company; in this role he rode in Tiger 405 on February 1, 1943. At Kursk, *SS-Hauptsturmführer* Kling is believed to have destroyed eighteen Soviet tanks in **1301** before he was wounded on July 11, when an antitank round struck the cupola. According to his later recommendation for the German Cross in Gold, Kling was forced to change tanks four times in the fighting due to battle damage. The recommendation also credited Kling's company with destroying fifty-two enemy tanks for the period July 5–6, forty-five enemy tanks on July 8, and twenty-four tanks for the period July 10–11.[39]

During the war Heinrich Kling was wounded eleven times and became a winner of the Wound Badge in Gold on August 26, 1943. He won the German Cross in Gold on December 30, 1943—turning the company over that day to Michael Wittmann. Heinrich Kling received the Knight's Cross of the Iron Cross on February 23, 1944. Kling was promoted to *SS-Sturmbannführer* on June 6, 1944.[40]

Heinz Kling became the commander of the Second Battalion of the 1st SS Panzer Regiment in August 1944, and was wounded in action on August 21, 1944. On January 1, 1945, Kling became the commander of the First Battalion of the 12th SS Panzer Regiment in the 12th Panzer Division *Hitlerjugend* (Hitler Youth) that was fighting in the Ardennes Offensive. He returned to the 501st SS Heavy Panzer Detachment and later deployed to Hungary, fighting around Budapest. On March 20, 1945, he assumed command of the detachment; Kling was wounded in an air attack on March 25, 1945. For his career Heinz Kling is believed to have been credited with fifty-one enemy tanks destroyed from his Tiger.

After the war Kling was interned by the British at Bad Nenndorf. On his release he became a textile representative for the Schiesser Company in Radolfzell, before becoming an independent textile merchant in 1950. He is also believed to have worked at the *Radolfzeller Schürzenfabrik*, living at Schützenstraße 21. Business was apparently good, as Heinz joined the Radolfzell Yacht Club. Heinz Kling accidentally drowned in the Zeller See on lower Lake Constance, near the town of Radolfzell, on September 30, 1951, when his boat capsized.[41]

Heinrich Knöss. Whomever thought that a legal clerk in the Reichs Finance Ministry could not be an excellent Tiger tank gunner never met Heinrich Knöss. Knöss was born in Opladen, in the Rhineland, on December 26, 1907. Standing 6' tall, in civilian life he served as a legal official in the Reichs Finance Ministry in their Revenue Office at Beckum, North Rhine-Westphalia, having previously passed the *Abitur* and attending a university for seven semesters. Heinrich also managed to win the Reichs Sports Badge in Silver. He entered the SS with SS number 133686. During Kursk *SS-Unterscharführer* Knöss served as a gunner for Tiger **1313** in the First Platoon. He received the Iron Cross Second Class on December 5, 1943, was promoted to *SS-Untersturmführer* on June 21, 1944, and transitioned into assault guns. Heinrich Knöss finished the war assigned to the 3rd SS Panzer Division *Totenkopf* in the antitank detachment.[42]

Walter Koch. *SS-Panzerschütze* Koch, who was born on July 18, 1925, in Rathenow, in Brandenburg, served as the loader for Tiger **1331** in the Third Platoon at the beginning of the Kursk Offensive. There are two versions of Koch's service at Kursk. One is that he was wounded in the head by fragments of an enemy antitank round that struck the tank from the rear on the first day of the offensive, July 5, and was replaced. A second version states that he was wounded on that date but remained with the tank. The next day **1331** ran over an antitank mine that destroyed its right track. Enemy antitank fire then blew off a hatch cover, wounding Koch for a second time, and he was finally replaced. Whatever the case, on September 16, 1943, he received the Iron Cross Second Class in addition to his Wound Badge in Black.[43] Walter Koch had blond hair and looked like a recruiting poster for the Waffen-SS.

Ewald König. Ewald König was not a professional soldier; he was a Nazi Party "ladder climber." In Germany for the beginning of the war, he held several positions in the Nazi Party; he joined the unit at Kharkov to take the "Iron Cross Course," the derogatory term for short term front line service. Having said that, he proved to be a competent Tiger crewman.

Ewald König was born in Wuppertal on June 20, 1908. At Kursk *SS-Rottenführer* König served as a loader in the company. He received an Iron Cross Second Class and the Panzer Battle Badge in Silver on September 16, 1943, and was promoted to *SS-Unterscharführer*. After leaving the front—his Iron Cross in hand—he worked with the "Strength through Joy" morale organization and was responsible for soldiers' hostels in France. He later went to Paris and operated a soldiers' hostel on the Avenue des Champs-Élysées, visiting several of his old Tiger comrades in Normandy in summer 1944.[44]

Helmut Lange. *SS-Sturmmann* Lange, who was born on April 2, 1924, in Bad Oldeslohe, Schleswig-Holstein, entered the Waffen-SS on October 1, 1942. During the Kursk Offensive he served in a Tiger in the company. He received an Iron Cross Second Class on September 16, 1943. Helmut Lange was single and was promoted to *SS-Rottenführer* on April 20, 1944.[45]

Walter Lau. Walter Lau was born in Pomerania on February 18, 1923. Until after the Battle of Kharkov Lau had served as a supply specialist in the division, but losses forced many men to transfer to the combat troops—whether they wanted to or not. *SS-Panzerschütze* Lau was assigned to the Second Platoon in Tiger **1323** as a loader and fought in the tank July 13–15; he was promoted to *SS-Sturmmann* at the end of July 1943 and received the Iron Cross second Class on January 30, 1944. A year later *SS-Rottenführer* Lau was assigned to the Second Company of the 101st SS Heavy Panzer Detachment in Normandy, where he served as the gunner for Helmut Wendorff in Tiger 214 and later Tiger 234. Walter was seriously wounded in the right eye on August 14, 1944, in the same action in which Wendorff was killed; British forces took Lau prisoner and transported him to the 99th Field Hospital for medical treatment. He survived the war, and his Iron Cross First Class was approved on August 23, 1944. During his career Walter Lau served in stints as a Tiger gunner for Michael Wittmann, Helmut Wendorff, and Heinrich Kling; he knocked out twenty-six enemy armored vehicles during the war, all at Normandy. He was a good friend of Paul Sümnich. Concerning Michael Wittmann, after the German ace's death Walter Lau came to the realization that "we would not be able to withstand the onslaught." He died on March 4, 2005.[46]

Rudi Lechner. *SS-Sturmmann* Rudi Lechner served as a loader in the company at Kursk. He had previously fought at Kharkov, where he won an Iron Cross Second Class on March 20, 1943. He later was an *SS-Rottenführer* in the 2nd Company of the 101st SS Heavy Panzer Detachment at Normandy, where he served as a gunner; he held the same position later in the 2nd Company of the 501st SS Heavy Panzer Detachment in the Ardennes.[47]

Karl Lieber. *SS-Panzerschütze* Lieber, born February 14, 1923, in Limburg, Hesse, served as a radio operator in Tiger **1331** in the Third Platoon. It appears that he was in the battle from July 7–15. Karl was awarded the Iron Cross Second Class on September 16, 1943; he also received the Wound Badge in Black.[48] Karl Lieber is believed to have returned to Limburg after the war and taken up farming.

Georg "Panzergeneral" Lötzsch. Perhaps the first thing that Georg probably had to do whenever he met a new person was to explain how he had received the nickname "Panzergeneral." It would appear that the reason for this unusual moniker was that he had been detached on December 20, 1942, to the Tiger production factories of Henschel and Wegmann in Kassel and knew almost everything inside and out about the new panzer. Also nicknamed "Schorsch," Georg had a flair for machines—he had been an auto mechanic.

Born April 23, 1914, in Dresden, *SS-Scharführer* Georg "Panzergeneral" Lötzsch joined the Nazi Party on April 8, 1933, and the Allgemeine-SS on June 1, 1933, with SS number 133856.

Georg joined the Waffen-SS on August 20, 1938. His file indicates that he served in the 14th Company of the 10th SS *Totenkopf* Infantry Regiment from November 1939, then transferred to the 18th (Heavy) Company of the *Leibstandarte* in June 1941. He was wounded in action on July 15, 1941, in Russia, and subsequently sent back to Germany to a reserve hospital; on February 1, 1942, he joined the 1st Company in the panzer detachment of the *Leibstandarte*. At Kharkov in February–March 1943 he commanded a Mark III N panzer. At Kursk Georg served in the Second Platoon, commanding Tiger **1323**. Receiving the Iron Cross Second Class on September 16, 1943, on November 2 Lötzsch was in command of Tiger **S33** of the company.[49]

Georg later commanded Tiger 233 in the Third Platoon of the 2nd Company in the 101st SS Heavy Panzer Detachment in Normandy and fought at the Battle of Villers-Bocage; by this date he had been promoted to *SS-Oberscharführer*. He was wounded in action on August 11, 1944, near Le Bû-sur-Rouvres, France.[50] Subsequently promoted to *SS-Hauptscharführer*, he commanded King Tiger 233 in the Ardennes Offensive with Third Platoon of the 2nd Company of the 501st SS Heavy Panzer Detachment, taking part in the attacks on the village of Stavelot, Belgium, on December 19, 1944.[51] He and his wife Ruth received a stipend of 250 *marks* on the birth of his daughter, Ingrid, on October 1, 1944.[52] Georg Lötzsch survived the war.

Alfred Lünser. Born on July 2, 1925, *SS-Panzerschütze* Lünser joined the *Leibstandarte SS Adolf Hitler* Regiment at Berlin-Lichterfelde on June 19, 1942, as an infantryman. In October 1942, at Evreux, France, he was transferred to the panzers as a machine gunner. At Kharkov, Alfred served as a gunner on a Mark III N panzer; he was struck by a passing friendly tank and received a serious leg injury. After recuperating, at Kursk he served as a gunner in the company and fought in a Tiger from July 10–15. He was the recipient of the Wound Badge in Black. In Normandy Alfred served as a gunner in Tiger 314 in the 3rd Company of the 101st SS Heavy Panzer Detachment. Alfred Lünser survived the war, remaining in a British prisoner of war camp through 1947.

Max Marten. *SS-Oberscharführer* Max Marten served as a tank commander in a Mark III N panzer (4 L2) at Kharkov, receiving the Iron Cross Second Class on April 20, 1943, and the Panzer Battle Badge in Silver. At Kursk he commanded Tiger **1332** in the Third Platoon.[53] He may have assumed command of the Third Platoon when Michael Wittmann became the company commander, unless the overall number of operational Tigers was so small that Wittmann could do both.

Heinz Möller. *SS-Unterscharführer* Heinz Möller was assigned as the driver of Tiger **1331** of the Third Platoon on July 5. He replaced a driver that had been wounded earlier in the day. Prior to this move Möller had been assigned to the Second Platoon and his Tiger there was undergoing repairs.

Ewald Mölly. *SS-Unterscharführer* Mölly commanded Tiger 413 in the Third Platoon of the company during the fighting at Kharkov in February–March 1943. At Kursk he served as the commander of Tiger **1322** in the Second Platoon. Mölly commanded Tiger **1332** in the Third Platoon in November 1943. He received the Iron Cross First Class on January 30, 1944. In June 1944, in Normandy, Mölly commanded Tiger 224 in the 2nd Company of the 101st SS Heavy Panzer Detachment. As an *SS-Oberscharführer*, he later fought in the Ardennes Offensive with the 501st SS Heavy Panzer Detachment, where he commanded Tiger 232 in the Third Platoon of the 2nd Company. Ewald Mölly was the recipient of the Panzer Battle Badge in Silver.[54]

Karl Müller. *SS-Rottenführer* Karl Müller hailed from Triebelwitz, Lower Silesia, where he was born on September 12, 1923. He served in the company during the Kursk Offensive. Karl received the Iron Cross Second Class on September 16, 1943; he also was awarded the Wound Badge in Black. In Normandy, Müller served in the 101st SS Heavy Panzer Detachment and received the Iron Cross First Class on June 20, 1944. Karl Müller later fought in the Ardennes Offensive with the 501st SS Heavy Panzer Detachment, where he commanded King Tiger 223 in the Second Platoon of the 2nd Company.[55]

Heinz Owczarek. Born in Hindenburg, Upper Silesia, on November 14, 1923, *SS-Sturmmann* Owczarek served in the company, but was killed on the first day of the offensive, July 5. The German War Graves Commission lists his place of death as the village of Pushkarnoye (Пушкарное), behind the front line, which indicates that *SS-Sturmmann* Owczarek probably was gravely wounded, evacuated, and subsequently died at a casualty collection point or other medical facility.[56]

Herbert Pollmann. *SS-Rottenführer* Herbert Pollmann served as a radio operator in Tiger **1331** in the Third Platoon of the company. On July 11 enemy antitank fire struck **1331**, wounding Herbert Pollmann in the upper arm.

Heinrich "Hein" Reimers. "Hein" Reimers is another soldier to go down in history as one of Michael Wittmann's "boys"—a twenty-two-year-old who perished with Wittmann on August 8, 1944, and who shares a group memorial at the German War Cemetery in La Cambe, Normandy.
   "Hein" hailed from Schnepke/Syke, in Lower Saxony, on May 11, 1924. Single and a farm worker, he joined the SS on September 8, 1941. He served as the driver in Tiger 411 in the First Platoon during the fighting near Kharkov in February–March 1943, receiving an Iron Cross Second Class and the Panzer Battle Badge in Silver. At Kursk, *SS-Sturmmann* Reimers served as the driver of Tiger **1301** in the Headquarters Platoon. Heinrich was promoted to *SS-Rottenführer* on September 1, 1943, and *SS-Unterscharführer* on April 20, 1944. He subsequently served as a driver in Tiger 205 in Normandy. He was killed in action on August 8, 1944, near Saint-Aignan-de-Cramesnil, Normandy, serving in the 2nd Company of the 101st SS Heavy Panzer Detachment as the driver for Michael Wittmann, when their Tiger 007 was engaged by Sherman Firefly tanks from Squadron A of the 1st Northamptonshire Yeomanry. Undiscovered for four decades, the German War Graves Commission disinterred the bodies of five men in the early 1980s and found Heinrich Reimers' identity disc with one of the corpses. His remains are at the German War Cemetery in La Cambe, Normandy, in Plot 47, Row 3, in Grave 120G, along with the rest of the crew.[57]

Wilhelm Röpstorff. "Willi" Röpstorff was born on November 26, 1921, in Kiel-Pries in Schleswig-Holstein. At Kharkov in February–March 1943, he fought as a driver in the company. An *SS-Rottenführer*, he received an Iron Cross Second Class on March 20, 1943. At Kursk he served as a driver in the company. He also earned the Panzer Battle Badge in Silver.[58] It is possible that Willi Röpstorff lived in Karlsruhe after the war and worked as a mechanic.

Walter Rose. *SS-Panzeroberschütze* Walter Rose was born in Stassfurt, in Saxony-Anhalt, on May 27, 1903. He was a gunner in a Tiger in the company and received the Iron Cross Second Class on September 16, 1943.[59]

Rolf Schamp. Born September 22, 1921, at Weilburg/Lahn in Hesse, Schamp finished secondary school and passed the *Abitur*. *SS-Sturmmann* Schamp stood 5'9" tall and he had SS number 490242. At Kursk, Rolf commanded Tiger **1324** in the Second Platoon until July 9. He received the Iron Cross Second Class on October 14, 1943, and the Panzer Battle Badge in Silver. He departed the 13th (Heavy) Company on December 17, 1943. Schamp subsequently attended a non-commissioned officer's course in Lauenburg. Becoming an officer with the grade of *SS-Untersturmführer* on June 21, 1944, he was assigned to the 17th SS Panzer Grenadier Division *Götz von Berlichingen* on November 1, 1944, serving in the panzer detachment. Rolf Schamp survived the war, possibly residing in Frankfurt and living later in Weilburg, in Hesse, until his death on July 14, 2007. After the war he once said: "My dream was always the German Cross in Gold."[60]

Heinz Schindhelm. *SS-Panzerschütze* Schindhelm was born in Coburg, in the Upper Franconia region of Bavaria, on March 30, 1925. During the fighting around Kharkov in February–March 1943 Schindhelm served as a gunner. With this experience he served as a gunner again in the company at Kursk, receiving the Iron Cross Second Class on July 23, 1943. Heinz Schindhelm also received the Panzer Battle Badge in Silver.[61]

Siegfried Schneider. *SS-Panzerschütze* Siegfried Schneider, born March 28, 1925, in Nonnewitz, Saxony-Anhalt, served in the company during the offensive. He received the Iron Cross Second Class on September 16, 1943.[62]

Alfred Schumacher. *SS-Panzeroberschütze* Schumacher, who was born in Gladbach on January 30, 1902, served as a gunner in the company at Kursk. He received the Iron Cross Second class on September 16, 1943.[63]

Waldemar Schütz. Waldemar Schütz had guts. According to one source Waldemar, as a civilian, attended a reception for Sepp Dietrich at the city of Bad Ems—not far from where Waldemar resided—on December 7, 1939. Brazenly approaching the SS leader, Schütz inquired if he could join the *Leibstandarte SS Adolf Hitler* Regiment in Berlin. Dietrich, a man who knew how to cut through red tape, was apparently impressed with the young man's moxie and acquiesced—the next day Waldemar Schutz was in the prestigious regiment, assigned to the 13th Company.

Waldemar Schütz was born on October 9, 1913, at Dausenau/Lahn, east of Koblenz. After attending secondary school at Bad Ems he became a journalist; he was also a member of the Hitler Youth, receiving the Golden Hitler Youth Badge. In March 1940, he attended the *SS-Junkerschule* at Bad Tölz; he was promoted to *SS-Untersturmführer* on November 9, 1940. Married to his fiancée Hedwig on September 22, 1940, he stood just over 5'8" tall, had brown hair, and had SS number 372395. He saw his first combat the following spring in the Balkans. In the infantry, he received the Infantry Assault Badge in Silver, the Iron Cross Second Class (July 12, 1941), and the Wound Badge in Silver, and was promoted to *SS-Obersturmführer* on April 20, 1942. On August 28, 1942, he received a formal reprimand for unsoldierly appearance and conduct. At Kharkov in February–March 1943 he was the First Platoon leader and commanded Tiger 411.[64]

Waldemar Schütz served as the platoon leader for the First Platoon and in this capacity was the commander of Tiger **1311**, although the company was so large that Schütz often fulfilled duties of the executive officer, and even as the acting commander. At Kursk, Schütz was wounded by an enemy antitank shell that hit the rear of the Tiger on July 5, but remained in combat. On July 10, still commanding Tiger **1311**, Schütz dismounted the vehicle to meet with other tank commanders at the same time an enemy shell exploded nearby and he was wounded for a second time. This wound proved more serious and he was replaced, and was out of the fight for the rest of the battle.

Schütz was subsequently assigned to the SS Panzer Training and Replacement Regiment at Bitsch, France, until November 26, 1943, when he was assigned to the 12th SS Panzer Division *Hitlerjugend*. He attended a panzer training course at Erlangen, near Nürnberg, from February 7–March 1, 1944. Waldemar Schutz was later promoted to *SS-Hauptsturmführer* on April 20, 1944, and served as the commander of the supply company in the First Battalion of the 12th SS Panzer Regiment in the 12th SS Panzer Division *Hitlerjugend*, working again for Heinz Kling.[65]

Throughout the war Waldemar Schütz was wounded five times; he was a prisoner of war from 1945–46. After the war he wrote, was a publisher, owned K. W. Schütz Verlag, and served in the Lower Saxony Parliament for seven years in the National Democratic Party of Germany and the German Reich Party. Because of his head wounds received at Kursk he would maintain in later years that he had no recollection of the battle. Waldemar Schütz died on September 9, 1999, in Raubling, near Rosenheim, in Bavaria.[66]

Roland Söffker. In a postwar interview at the American Consulate in Hamburg to determine eligibility to travel to the United States, Roland Söffker stated that he had joined the Waffen-SS because it was an elite organization and that he "wanted to be part of the best."[67] Permission for Roland to travel was denied, but nowhere is there evidence that Roland Söffker ever regretted volunteering for that organization.

Born in Celle, in Lower Saxony, Germany, on November 13, 1923, Roland Söffker served in the Hitler Youth from 1935 to 1940. He finished secondary school and passed the *Abitur* in June 1940. *SS-Sturmmann* Söffker joined the Waffen-SS on July 20, 1942, receiving SS number 449669. Roland went through basic training in Berlin for eight weeks and then traveled to Evreux, France, to receive panzer training for three months. He went to the Troop Training Grounds Bergen at Fallingbostel, Germany, in December 1942, to train on the Tiger. Standing 5'11.6" tall, he fought as a gunner in a tank around Kharkov in the company in February 1943, receiving the Panzer Battle Badge in Silver and the Iron Cross Second Class. At Kursk, he served as a gunner in the company. He was still in this position on October 1, 1943, having briefly served in Italy in September 1943.

Söffker fought at Zhitomir, in the Ukraine, in November 1943, then was assigned to the SS Panzer *Junkerschule* at Fallingbostel. Söffker was promoted to *SS-Untersturmführer* on June 21, 1944. He was then assigned to the 18th SS Volunteer Panzer Grenadier Division *Horst Wessel* and was in the Debrecen, Hungary, area through October 1944. Ending the war in East Prussia, he was captured by the Soviets on May 4, 1945, and held in the Sverdlovsk prisoner of war camp (near Yekaterinburg) until October 10, 1955, when he was repatriated to West Germany. Roland Söffker moved to the Hamburg area and in November 1987 requested to travel to the United States; the request was denied.[68]

Kurt Sowa. Kurt Sowa was born in Gelsenkirchen, in the Ruhr district, on May 9, 1921. He was in the Hitler Youth from February 1933 to April 1939. He soon joined the Waffen-SS, serving with the *Leibstandarte SS Adolf Hitler* Regiment beginning March 14, 1940. Standing 5'5" tall, he was promoted to *SS-Rottenführer* on October 1, 1941, and to *SS-Unterscharführer* on April 20, 1943. Sowa served as a tank driver in the company around Kharkov in February–March 1943. He then served as the commander of Tiger **1335** in the Third Platoon during the Kursk Offensive. He received the Iron Cross Second Class on December 5, 1943. In June 1944, Sowa fought in the 101st SS Heavy Panzer Detachment and commanded Tiger 222 in the 2nd Company at the Battle of Villers-Bocage; during the fighting in Normandy he was seriously wounded on August 15, 1944, and his right arm was later amputated.

Promoted to *SS-Oberscharführer* on September 1, 1944, he received the Iron Cross first Class on September 30, 1944. Despite the severity of the wound, Kurt later was assigned to the 501st SS Heavy Panzer Detachment. At the Ardennes he commanded King Tiger 222 in the Second Company until his tank was disabled by an American tank destroyer at the south end of Stavelot bridge on December 20, 1944. Kurt was married on March 8, 1944; his first child was born on March 23, 1944.[69] Kurt Sowa is believed to have worked as a night watchman and guard in Gelsenkirchen after the war, living at Auguststraβe 8.

Franz Staudegger. Born in Unterloibach/Kärnten in Austria on February 12, 1923, and the son of a innkeeper, Franz Staudegger finished school in 1940 at nearby Klagenfurt and subsequently graduated from the *Wiener Theresianum*, a secondary level boarding school. Joining the Waffen-SS, Staudegger first trained as an infantryman and was wounded in Russia on July 7, 1941; he stood almost 6'3" tall. He subsequently transferred to the panzers. At Kharkov in February–March 1943 he fought in a Mark III N panzer (4 L3) and then advanced to command a Tiger. He received the Iron Cross Second Class on March 20, 1943, then the Panzer Badge in Silver on April 1. *SS-Unterscharführer* Staudegger commanded Tiger **1325** in the Second Platoon from July 5–10, 1943, during the battle. He received the Iron Cross First Class on July 6, 1943, for destroying two enemy tanks on the night of July 5–6, when he threw hand grenades inside their open hatches. On July 8, 1943, he was credited with destroying twenty-two enemy tanks, and was recommended for the Knight's Cross of the Iron Cross. The award was approved and presented him on July 10, with some twenty members of the company at the ceremony.

Staudegger then departed the front to return to Germany to brief Adolf Hitler on the battle and the performance of the Tiger. He would not return to the front until after the offensive had ended. In 1944, Franz was assigned to the 1st Company of the 101st SS Heavy Panzer Detachment and fought in Normandy as the commander of Tiger 123; he also was assigned to the unit after it was re-designated the 501st SS Heavy Panzer Detachment on September 22, 1944, when it received the Tiger II (King Tiger) tank. *SS-Standartenjunker* Franz Staudegger commanded King Tiger 123 as a section leader in the Second Platoon in the 1st Company of the detachment during the Ardennes. Sources credit Staudegger with destroying thirty-five enemy tanks during the war. After the conflict Staudegger worked as a railway official and then as an insurance agent. Married, he had no children. Franz Staudegger died in Frankfurt on March 16, 1991.[70]

Herbert Stellmacher. Herbert Stellmacher was born on May 20, 1924, in Grünberg, Hesse. *SS-Sturmmann* Stellmacher served as the driver in Tiger **1325** in the Second Platoon during the Kursk Offensive and assisted Franz Staudegger the day he earned the Knight's Cross. He received the Iron Cross Second Class on July 23, 1943. Later promoted to *SS-Unterscharführer*, Herbert Stellmacher later was assigned to the 2nd Company of the 101st SS Heavy Panzer Detachment and fought in Normandy as a Tiger driver.[71]

Paul Sümnich. Paul Sümnich was born in Glogau, Lower Silesia, on March 30, 1924. He was assigned as a driver in the company during the Kursk Offensive and received an Iron Cross Second Class on September 16, 1943. In October 1943 he served as a loader in the company; he was wounded in November 1943. Later assigned to the 2nd Company of the 101st SS Heavy Panzer Detachment as a loader, Paul Sümnich lost both legs on August 8, 1944, at Grimbosq, in the Calvados department of Normandy, France, when an enemy artillery shell exploded next to him when he was outside his tank.[72]

Gerhard Waltersdorf. Born at Grünberg in Silesia on April 18, 1924, Gerhard Waltersdorf served in the Hitler Youth from August 1, 1933, to October 15, 1942. He was a trained tool and die maker. Gerhard then joined the Waffen-SS and joined the *Leibstandarte* on December 15, 1942, and was in the company on February 1, 1943, later fighting at Kharkov. *SS-Panzerschütze* Waltersdorf served as a radio operator in Tiger **1325** in the Second Platoon during the Kursk Offensive and was with Franz Staudegger the day he earned the Knight's Cross. Gerhard received the Iron Cross Second Class on July 23, 1943.[73] Later promoted to *SS-Rottenführer*, he served in the 2nd Company of the 101st SS Heavy Panzer Detachment as a radio operator in Normandy in summer 1944. Photographs show that Gerhard was one of the shortest men in the company.

Karl-Heinz Warmbrunn. Karl-Heinz Warmbrunn was born on October 15, 1924, in Nürnberg, in the Middle Franconia district of Bavaria. Standing 6'2" tall, he joined the Waffen-SS on October

20, 1941. He fought at the battles around Kharkov in February–March 1943 as a Tiger gunner, receiving a Panzer Battle Badge in Silver and an Iron Cross Second Class on March 20, 1943. During the Kursk Offensive he served as the gunner in Tiger **1301** in the Headquarters Platoon; he has been credited for destroying eighteen enemy tanks during this battle. In February 1944, he reportedly shot down a Soviet IL-2 *Sturmovik* ground attack aircraft with his Tiger's machine gun. Warmbrunn was promoted to *SS-Unterscharführer* on June 1, 1944.[74]

Assigned to the 2nd Company of the 101st SS Heavy Panzer Detachment, he commanded a Tiger (believed to be Tiger 214). Warmbrunn shot down another enemy fighter aircraft with his cupola machine gun on an external antiaircraft mounting on June 10, 1944. Three days later he fought at the Battle of Villers-Bocage and destroyed four Sherman tanks. His tank was knocked out by a Sherman, or by an antitank gun, on June 27, 1944, but he commanded another Tiger. After engaging a Sherman on July 18, Warmbrunn's Tiger was hit by enemy fire that seriously injured his right eye, effectively ending his career as a tank commander. Bobby is believed by many sources to have destroyed about fifty-seven enemy tanks during the war. He received the Panzer Battle Badge in Silver for 25 Assaults on December 1, 1944.[75]

Bobby survived the war and spent time in an American prisoner of war camp at Gmunden am Traunsee in Austria and Darmstadt, Hesse, in Germany; he and his wife had two sons. With the opportunity for work difficult in immediate postwar Germany, Karl-Heinz Warmbrunn assumed the fighting name Robert "Bobby" Warmbrunn and became a professional heavyweight boxer. He lost on points in his first bout against Heinz Seelisch on October 26, 1947, at the *Zirkus Apollo* in Düsseldorf. Over his sixteen-year career he had fourteen wins, forty-nine losses, and five draws. A club level fighter, he lost his last sixteen bouts before hanging up the gloves on October 5, 1963, after losing to Adolf Mensinger by knockout at the *Fellbacher Stadthalle* in Fellbach, a small village outside of Stuttgart.[76] Karl-Heinz Warmbrunn then lived in Munich at Leopoldstaße 109, near the Englischer Garten, becoming a sports instructor.

Helmut Max Wendorff. "Bubi" Wendorff was born on October 20, 1920, in Grauwinkel, near Schweidnitz in Silesia, the son of a farmer. His family moved to Damme, near Uckermark, in 1931. He was in the Hitler Youth from 1933 to 1939; he completed secondary school and passed the *Abitur* after graduating from the Naumburg National Political School. He joined the 11th Company of the *Leibstandarte SS Adolf Hitler* Regiment on September 4, 1939, receiving SS number 365017. Standing 5'11" tall, he was wounded in 1940 while a member of an assault gun battery and received the Wound Badge in Black and the Iron Cross Second Class (September 14, 1941). An *SS-Oberscharführer* on November 1, 1941, he was subsequently promoted to *SS-Untersturmführer* on June 21, 1942, after graduating from the *SS-Junkerschule* at Bad Tölz. Wendorff fought at Kharkov in February–March 1943, commanding Tiger 435. Wendorff experienced a near disaster on March 6, 1943, when his Tiger broke through the ice crossing the Msha River, but he survived and recovery crews salvaged the vehicle some days later.[77]

At the Kursk Offensive, Wendorff served as the leader of the Second Platoon and commanded Tiger **1321**; he was wounded on July 5, but remained with his tank and crew; he was wounded again on July 8. He subsequently returned to Germany, where he married Hannelore Michel on September 4, 1943; he received the Iron Cross First Class on September 16, 1943, and appears to have been awarded a Wound Badge in Black that day as well. On December 27, 1943, near Tschubarovka, Helmut destroyed eleven T-34 tanks. Wendorff was promoted to *SS-Obersturmführer* on January 30, 1944, and assumed temporary command of the company two days later. He received the Knight's Cross of the Iron Cross on February 12, 1944. Assigned to the 2nd Company of the 101st SS Heavy Panzer Detachment, he commanded a Tiger (believed to be Tiger 205) and fought at the Battle of Villers-Bocage. Tiger 205 was heavily damaged near Hill 112 on July 2, 1944, but was subsequently recovered. On July 14, 1944, Wendorff led a counterattack at the village of Maltot, southwest of Caen, knocking out three Cromwell tanks, while one Tiger was damaged.[78]

On the morning of August 14, 1944, two miles outside the village of Maizières, in the Calvados region of France, Wendorff and his Tiger were ambushed by two tanks of the Canadian 1st Hussar Regiment. Sources indicate that Wendorff knocked out one enemy tank, but the second one hit the Tiger and set it on fire. Wendorff was killed, as was his loader. His last words were reportedly: "Beside it, the second Sherman!" The remains of Helmut Wendorff have never been found and identified. Sources credited Bubi Wendorff with destroying eighty-four enemy tanks during the war.[79]

Werner Wendt. Werner Wendt was born in Naugard, in Pomerania, in 1921. He began his career in the Waffen-SS as an artilleryman—fighting in France in 1940 and Yugoslavia and Greece in 1941—but transferred to the panzer branch. He had fought at Kharkov in February–March 1943, as a gunner in Tiger 411 in the First Platoon, and was promoted to *SS-Unterscharführer* on April 20, 1943, in part because he had destroyed six enemy tanks during the seizure of Belgorod. At Kursk, Wendt served as the gunner in Tiger **1311** in the First Platoon from July 5 to July 10, when he became commander of **1311** after Waldemar Schütz was wounded. He served in the Third Platoon in the 1st Company of the 101st SS Heavy Panzer Detachment in Normandy, commanding Tiger 132, and in the Third Platoon of the 1st Company in the 501st SS Heavy Tank Detachment in the Ardennes.

In the latter battle *SS-Oberscharführer* Wendt commanded King Tiger 133. After American fire damaged the tank's transmission, the crew was forced to abandon it between Stavelot and Trois Ponts, Belgium, on December 25, 1944. An American P-38 Lightning then destroyed the Tiger with a bomb. Wendt destroyed about twenty-three enemy tanks during the war and received the Iron Cross Second Class, the Panzer Battle Badge in Silver, the Wound Badge in Black, and the Eastern Front Medal. He reportedly knocked out an American tank at the end of the war with a hand-held antitank *Panzerfaust*. Wendt was later captured by US forces.[80]

Later in life Werner Wendt finished a manuscript for his unit history of the 501st SS Heavy Panzer Detachment, but it appears that another author obtained a copy of it and published it under his own name instead of Wendt's. Werner Wendt died on February 26, 2005.

Reinhart Wenzel. Born on August 8, 1923, in Ilmenau in Thüringen, *SS-Panzerschütze* Reinhart Wenzel had fought at Kharkov in February–March 1943 as a loader. He served in the same position in Tiger **1324** in the Second Platoon during the Kursk Offensive. He also served as a radio operator during his career. *SS-Sturmmann* Wenzel later served in the 501st SS Heavy Tank Detachment in the Ardennes, where he was killed in action near Malmedy, Belgium, on December 24, 1944. Reinhart Wenzel is buried at the German War Cemetery in Lommel, Belgium, in Block 12 in Grave 362.[81]

Peter Winkler. Peter Winkler was born in Munich on August 31, 1924. He joined the Hitler Youth on October 1, 1933, and remained in the organization until March 1, 1942. He then served in the Reich Labor Service from April 8, 1942, to September 29, 1942. A salesman by trade, he joined the Waffen-SS and was assigned to the *Leibstandarte* on December 15, 1942. During the Kursk Offensive *SS-Sturmmann* Winkler was a radio operator in Tiger **1334** in the Third Platoon, but only on July 5–6, when the panzer was designated to be dismantled for parts to keep other Tigers operational. *SS-Rottenführer* Winkler was assigned in 1944 to the First Company of the 102nd SS Heavy Panzer Detachment as a radio operator. In 1945, he was assigned as a radio operator in the 1st Company of the 502nd SS Heavy Panzer Detachment. He appears to have been single during the war.[82]

Michael Wittmann. Considered by many to be the greatest German tank commander in World War II, Michael Wittmann was born on April 22, 1944, in the village of Vogelthal, in the Oberpfalz region of Bavaria, to Johann and Ulrike Wittmann.[83] He completed secondary school, remaining on his father's farm until February 1, 1934, when he joined the Reich Labor Service. He remained in this organization until July 31, 1934. On October 30, 1934, he joined the German Army as an infantryman and was assigned to the 10th Company of the 19th Infantry Regiment stationed at Freising, Bavaria. Rising to the rank of corporal, he left the service on September 30, 1936, upon the expiration of his military obligation. Wittmann applied to join the Allgemeine-SS at Ingolstadt on November 1, 1936. On April 5, 1937, he joined the 17th Company of the *Leibstandarte SS Adolf Hitler* Regiment in Berlin, serving as a *Staffel-Stürmmann*. He was measured at 5'9" tall and had SS number 311623. He was promoted to *SS-Sturmmann* on November 11, 1937.

Now an *SS-Unterscharführer*—he was promoted to this rank on April 20, 1939—Wittmann fought in a reconnaissance unit in Poland. He transferred to assault guns, in which he took part in the German invasion of Greece in 1941. Now in the 3rd Assault Gun Battery of the regiment, he won the Iron Cross Second Class near Zhitomir on July 12, 1941. In one engagement that summer Wittmann's assault gun knocked out eight enemy tanks; he was wounded and received the Wound Badge in Black on August 20, 1941, and the Iron Cross First Class on September 8, 1941. This was followed by a promotion to *SS-Oberscharführer* on November 9, 1941. Sensing that he had sufficient leadership qualities, the chain of command sent Wittmann to the *SS-Junkerschule* at Bad Tölz in June 1942. He graduated from Bad Tölz on December 21, 1942, and was commissioned an *SS-Untersturmführer*. He joined the 4th Company of the 1st Panzer Regiment, which was undergoing transition to the new Mark VI Tiger tank at the Troop Training Grounds Bergen at Fallingbostel. He was with the company when it traveled to Russia in early February 1943, although during the ensuing fight around Kharkov Wittmann was not in a Tiger, but rather commanded the Fourth (Light) Platoon composed of Mark III N panzers, which were armed with short-barrel 7.5 cm cannon; he commanded 4 L1.

During the Kursk Offensive *SS-Untersturmführer* Wittmann commanded the Third Platoon and Tiger **1331**. On the first day of the offensive he was reported to have destroyed eight enemy tanks. His tank was also immobilized by enemy antitank mines. The tank also experienced mechanical problems on July 9. On July 11 he became the acting commander of the company when Heinz Kling was wounded. At least one source credits Wittmann for destroying twenty-eight enemy tanks during the offensive, while others place the total at thirty-five. After the fight Wittmann—and much of the division—entrained for Italy to bolster the shaky régime of Benito Mussolini. He returned to Russia in November 1943. He subsequently fought near Brusilov, which was captured by the Germans on November 24. Wittmann assumed command of the company from Heinz Kling on December 30, 1943. Near the village of Sherepki on January 9, 1944, *SS-Untersturmführer* Wittmann destroyed ten enemy armored vehicles, which brought his total—according to the official Wehrmacht communiqués—to sixty-six enemy tanks destroyed during the war.

As a result Wittmann was recommended for the Knight's Cross of the Iron Cross, which would become a painful event, as on January 13 his head slammed into the turret wall which broke several of his teeth; he received a dental prosthesis to replace several of them. *SS-Brigadeführer* Theodor Wisch presented Wittmann with the award on January 16, 1944, near the front. By the end of the month Wittmann's total of destroyed enemy tanks reached the century mark, and on January 30, 1944, Adolf Hitler sent him a congratulatory telegram announcing the award of the Oak Leaves to the Knight's Cross of the Iron Cross. The same day he was promoted to *SS-Obersturmführer*. He left command of the company on February 1, 1944, and on February 2, 1944, hopped on a transport plane and flew to the "Wolf's Lair" headquarters at Rastenburg, in East Prussia, where the Führer presented him with the award.

Remaining in Germany the rest of the month, Wittmann married his nineteen-year-old fiancée Hildegard Burmester at Lüneburg on March 1, 1944. On March 20, 1944, the 13th (Heavy) Company was assigned to the 101st SS Heavy Panzer Detachment. Wittmann assumed command of the detachment's 2nd Company, which was then around Mons, Belgium. When the Allies invaded Normandy the 101st SS Heavy Panzer Detachment was in the Beauvais area of northern France, but it was rushed to the front, where it arrived on the night of June 12/13. On the day of June 13 Wittmann and his company, as well as elements of the 1st Company and elements of the *Panzer Lehr* Division, began what would later become famous as the Battle of Villers-Bocage. At one point he commanded Tiger 205. At Hill 213 and the village itself, Wittmann's 2nd Company engaged elements of the British 22nd Armored Brigade. When the fighting was done the next day, the British brigade had suffered some 217 casualties while losing twenty-three to twenty-seven tanks. Wittman's company lost one man killed and three wounded. The detachment as a whole lost six Tigers.

For the accomplishment, as well as his prior record, another award was deemed necessary. Sepp Dietrich decorated Wittmann with the Swords and Oak Leaves to the Knight's Cross on June 22, 1944, in the field in Normandy. The panzer ace was subsequently flown to the Obersalzberg, where Hitler made the official bestowal on June 26, 1944. During July 1944 Wittmann fought in the Battle for Caen. On July 13 he assumed command of the 101st SS Heavy Panzer Detachment, while *SS-Obersturmbannführer* Heinz von Westernhagen was sent home on leave. Von Westernhagen had been an assault gun battery commander on July 5 at Kursk—often fighting in close proximity to the 13th (Heavy) Company—but had received a near-fatal head wound that day and was never a well man the remainder of the war.[84]

Michael Wittman was killed in action on August 8, 1944, in Saint-Aignan-de-Cramesnil, when his Tiger 007 was engaged by Sherman Firefly tanks, firing 17-pound guns, from Squadron A of the 1st Northamptonshire Yeomanry—several sources naming Sergeant Douglas Gordon, commander, and Trooper Joe Ekins, gunner, in the Firefly named "Velikiye Luki" as the specific antagonists.[85] For many years accounts of his demise stated that enemy fighter-bombers had destroyed his Tiger, as many interested parties—in and outside of the Waffen-SS—wanted to believe that no Allied tank crew could have defeated the legendary "Black Baron." Shortly after the battle local French civilians hastily buried Wittmann and his crew.

The grave remained unmarked until the early 1980s, when researcher Jean Paul Pallud discovered it beside the main Caen–Falaise road (N 158). The German War Graves Commission disinterred the bodies of five men on March 25, 1983. The dental prosthesis, which was made after Wittmann's injury the previous January, led to Wittmann's identification. His remains are at the German War Cemetery in La Cambe, Normandy, in Plot 47, Row 3, in Grave 120G, along with the rest of his crew.[86]

Postwar armor experts, analyzing Michael Wittmann's performance, concluded that he was heavily influenced by his early experiences in assault guns. For example, he brought with him a scissors telescope that was installed in his panzer which he could raise in the cupola to observe the battlefield without exposing his head above the turret.[87] He also had a tendency as a Tiger commander to disregard enemy threats to his flanks, which the assault gun crews often did, although their missions were different from panzer operations.[88]

Wohlgemuth. *SS-Sturmmann* Wohlgemuth served as a radio operator in Tiger **1301** in the Headquarters Platoon. Photographs show he had received a Panzer Battle Badge in Silver as the radio operator of Tiger 411, commanded by Waldemar Schütz, during the fighting at Kharkov in February–March 1943. With blond hair, he appears to have survived Kursk and later, as an *SS-Unterscharführer*, served in the 2nd Company of the 101st SS Heavy Panzer Detachment in Normandy as a radio operator in summer 1944.[89]

Balthasar Woll. Balthasar "Bobby" Wohl was born on September 1, 1922, in Wemmetsweiler, in the Saarland; he was an electrician by trade. Joining the SS on August 15, 1941, he fought as a machine gunner in Russia in early 1942, in the Demjansk Pocket in the SS *Totenkopf* Division, in the 3rd Company of SS Grenadier Regiment 1 *Totenkopf*. Wounded in that fighting, he was evacuated to a hospital in Germany, where he received the Iron Cross Second Class and the Wound Badge in Black on July 23, 1942; he would later be awarded the Demjansk Shield. While in the *Totenkopf* he received assault gun training. Transferring to the *Leibstandarte*, he became a panzer soldier, training at Paderborn. At Kharkov in February–March 1943 he served as a tank gunner. At Kursk, *SS-Panzerschütze* Woll served as the gunner for Michael Wittmann in Tiger **1331** in the Third Platoon from July 5–9. Several sources credit him with destroying thirty-five Soviet tanks during the battle.

Balthasar Woll fought in the Ukraine with the company in October and November 1943. He was promoted to *SS-Rottenführer* on November 9, 1943. In 1944, Woll received the Knight's Cross of the Iron Cross on January 16, and was promoted to *SS-Unterscharführer* on January 30. He served as the best man at Michael Wittmann's wedding on March 1.

At this point his assignments during the war become murky. One source states that Balthasar Woll transferred to the Third Company of the 101st SS Heavy Panzer Detachment as the commander of Tiger 335.[90] Soon after the invasion in Normandy his panzer was involved in a fight near Bayeux, hitting three British Churchill tanks. However, Woll's days at the front were numbered, and an Allied fighter-bomber struck the tank with rockets, killing three of the crew and seriously wounding Woll, sending him back to Germany for further medical care. Another source adds that after recovering, Woll was promoted to *SS-Oberscharführer* and assigned to the 501st SS Heavy Panzer Detachment, and that he commanded a King Tiger at the Ardennes, but the vehicle broke down before firing a shot.

In 2004, author Gerd Nietrug, in his book about Knight's Cross winners from the Saarland, wrote that Woll's health had deteriorated so much by February–March 1944 that he was categorized as "not qualified for frontline duty" and was assigned to the 500th Panzer Training and Replacement Detachment at Paderborn. Thus he did not take part in the defense of Normandy in summer 1944.[91]

Later, in 1945 near Paderborn, Bobby received a Tiger I and fought for a few days in the Ruhr area before his tank was immobilized by an enemy antitank gun. The end of the war saw him commanding a Mark IV. After the conflict he became an electrician in West Germany. Bobby Woll died on March 18, 1996, at Bielefeld-Sennestadt in North Rhine-Westphalia.[92]

8th (Heavy) Company, 2nd Panzer Regiment, SS Panzer Grenadier Division Das Reich

Egon Allwinn. Egon Allwinn was born in Ludwigshafen, in the Rhineland-Palatinate, on February 19, 1924. He joined the Hitler Youth on May 1, 1934, at the age of ten. Allwinn subsequently worked in the Reich Labor Service from April 15, 1942, to September 13, 1942. A Catholic, he joined the Waffen-SS on September 15, 1942, receiving SS number 490213: he stood 5'8" tall. Allwinn immediately began panzer training. Trained as a gunner, he joined the 8th (Heavy) Company on December 6, 1942. After Kharkov he received a Panzer Battle Badge in Silver on March 27, 1943. He also earned the Iron Cross Second Class. During the Kursk Offensive *SS-Panzeroberschütze* Allwinn served as a gunner in the company; he was promoted to *SS-Unterscharführer* on November 1, 1943, and a week later returned to Germany to attend an SS Leader Candidate course for panzer troops at the Army Panzer Troops School at Putlos, Germany, along the Baltic coast.[1]

Egon Allwinn attended the officer candidate school from January 10, 1944, to April 5, 1944, and returned to the 2nd SS Panzer Regiment; on June 5, 1944, Allwinn received orders to report to the SS Panzer Training Detachment at Seelager, in western Latvia. According to one source Allwinn later served in the 102nd SS Heavy Panzer Detachment; he was promoted to *SS-Untersturmführer*. He received the following evaluation from his officer candidate course on October 7, 1944: "Allwinn is a good platoon leader but is also suited to be an adjutant or unit ordnance officer."[2]

Later in 1944 Egon married his fiancée Annemarie.[3] On January 14, 1945, Egon Allwinn was assigned to SS Panzer Detachment 11 in the 11th SS Volunteer Panzer Grenadier Division *Nordland* and took part in the Battle of Berlin in April 1945. Egon Allwinn survived the war and died in 2003. It is possible that he worked as an architect in Frankfurt after the war.

Eduard Arzner. Born in Tiengen, in Baden, on July 25, 1923, *SS-Rottenführer* Arzner served as the driver of Tiger **S11** in the First Platoon during the Kursk Offensive. He had previously served in the 2nd Company of the regiment until November 11, 1942. On that day he was detached to a special course for drivers at the Wegmann Company at Kassel. He was assigned to the Tiger company of the *Das Reich* effective November 15, 1942. On July 13, 1943, he showed great bravery when he remained with the tank after it had been immobilized while the rest of the crew abandoned it. Eduard was killed in action on July 31, 1943, near Brochorov (Hill 230.9), near the Mius River, by a direct hit from an antitank gun, bleeding to death from several wounds. His remains have never been identified.[4]

Heinrich Asmussen. Heinrich Asmussen was born on November 24, 1920, in Flensburg, in northern Germany. Protestant and a metal smith by trade, he joined the Luftwaffe at the start of the war. Asmussen transferred from the Luftwaffe to the 8th (Heavy) Company on April 9, 1943, and became an *SS-Rottenführer*. He probably served as a driver during the Kursk Offensive. Asmussen was wounded in action on September 9, 1943. In Normandy in 1944 he served as a gunner in the 1st Company of the 502nd SS Heavy Panzer Detachment. That November Heinrich became engaged. In spring 1945 *SS-Rottenführer* Asmussen served as a driver in the 1st Company of the 502nd SS Heavy Panzer Detachment on the Oder Front. During the war Heinrich received the Iron Cross Second Class, the Wound Badge in Black, the Panzer Battle Badge in Silver, and the Panzer Assault Badge in Silver for 25 Assaults.[5]

Max Aspöck. Max Aspöck was born on February 7, 1919, in Gaspoltshofen, in the Grieskirchen district of Austria; he was Catholic. *SS-Unterscharführer* Aspöck served in the 8th (Heavy) Company during the Kursk Offensive. He was assigned to the 101st SS Heavy Panzer Detachment from April 1944 to October 10, 1944, and was then assigned to the convalescence company in the SS Panzer Replacement Detachment at Sennelager, outside of Paderborn; at this location he submitted paperwork to the SS Race and Settlement Main Office as part of a request to marry, and it was approved; he married his fiancée Mitzi. Max Aspöck later served in the 502nd SS Heavy Panzer Detachment from that date through the end of the war, which he survived.[6]

Kurt Baral. A Waffen-SS efficiency report in 1944 on Kurt Baral said in part: "His command is clear and certain; his manner at the front is energetic; he understands how to prevail."[7] Kurt Baral prevailed in combat from his days as an infantryman in 1941 until just two weeks before the end of the war, when he was killed in action as the acting commander of the 3rd Company of the 502nd SS Heavy Panzer Detachment on April 19, 1945, near Berkenbrück, in the Fürstenwalde/Spree district on the Oder Front.

Kurt Baral hailed from Radelburg/Waldshut on the Swiss border, where he was born on February 19, 1922. Standing almost 5'8" tall when he joined the SS, he received SS number 490214. An electrician in civilian life, he had been an infantryman and had received the Infantry

Assault Badge in Silver (and the Iron Cross Second Class) on October 29, 1941, in the 3rd Company of the 2nd SS Police Regiment before transferring to the panzers. At Kharkov, he was the commander of a Mark III panzer (852) in the light platoon of the company. At Kursk, *SS-Unterscharführer* Baral commanded Tiger **S32** in the Third Platoon.

On July 11, 1943, he wrote the following letter to his parents back in Germany: "I want to take the opportunity to quickly write you a letter. Since yesterday I have been, in fact, at the maintenance area for two days so that minor damage to the engine could be repaired. This came at the right time as we have had some rain during which the offensive did not continue anyway. The operation has been quite successful, and Ivan has been severely shaken. In the first three days, our company has knocked out about sixty heavy tanks. If the Russians had come with more, they would have believed in it. My tank got thirteen I'm sure and I hope that more will come soon. However, Ivan already has a healthy respect for our Tigers, because their tanks try to make a big turn to get around us. Unfortunately, my gunner and loader were wounded. Naturally, they were not in our tank, but were sitting comfortably outside, when a shell hit. I myself was hit by a small fragment in the head, but it is not deep, so I can remain with our tank. I hope that you are still all healthy and greetings to you." (The wound in the head occurred on July 6; "Ivan" was the nickname that many German soldiers gave to Russian soldiers in general.)

The regimental commander signed the award for the Wound Badge in Silver for Kurt Baral on August 23, 1943. Kurt Baral was promoted to *SS-Oberscharführer* on October 1, 1943, and received the Iron Cross First Class on December 1, 1943. After a short leave at his parents' home, on January 10, 1944, he reported to a special panzer officer candidate course at the Troop Training Grounds Bergen at Fallingbostel, Germany. Upon graduating on April 5, 1944, he received an efficiency report that included the following evaluation: "Sound soldier with a serious attitude to life and an open, straight attitude. He has a clear view of the essentials. His strong will and ability to translate it to others demonstrate his leader qualities . . . Due to a wealth of experience at the front, he demonstrates above average leadership. His command is clear and certain; his manner at the front is energetic; he understands how to prevail. . . In his circle of comrades, as the experienced comrade, he is popular and respected. His appearance is without reproach."[8]

Kurt was later assigned to the 102nd SS Heavy Panzer Detachment, where he commanded Tiger 131 in the Third Platoon (for which he was the platoon leader) of the 1st Company; he fought against the British 7th Hampshire Regiment of the 43rd Wessex Division in Normandy east of Hill 112 at the village of Maltot as a platoon leader. Baral was commissioned an *SS-Untersturmführer* on June 21, 1944. He later commanded King Tiger 121 as the First Platoon leader in the 1st Company of the 502nd SS Heavy Panzer Detachment at the end of the war on the Oder Front.

Shortly after becoming the acting commander of the 3rd Company of the detachment, in a wooded area near the village of Briesen, on April 19, 1945, he was killed by a burst of enemy machine gun fire while climbing into his tank that had driven into a shell crater. Originally buried the following day by his comrades in a cemetery in Briesen, Kurt Baral's remains are now buried in the military section of the cemetery in Berkenbrück in an end grave in Row 3.[9]

Wolfgang Birnbaum. Born on January 24, 1922, in Ravensburg-Weingarten, Württemberg, Wolfgang Birnbaum joined the Waffen-SS on June 9, 1941, and first served as a motorcyclist. His brother Paul was also in the Waffen-SS. On November 15, 1942, Wolfgang joined the panzers and received training as a gunner. Promoted to *SS-Rottenführer* on July 1, 1943, at the Kursk Offensive he probably served as the gunner in **S11** in the First Platoon. Suffering a double hernia on October 30, 1943, Birnbaum spent several weeks in the SS Hospital in Prague, and in April 1944 he attended a two week course on the King Tiger at Paderborn.[10]

Wolfgang Birnbaum later served as the gunner in Tigers 111, 123, and 132 in the 1st Company of the 102nd SS Heavy Panzer Detachment. At the end of the war he served in the 1st Company of the 502nd SS Heavy Panzer Detachment as the gunner in King Tiger 132, King Tiger 121, and King Tiger 111; his commander in 132 was Walter Knecht. According to one source, in April 1945 Wolfgang Birnbaum knocked out eight Josef Stalin II Soviet tanks in a nine-minute span. He was in one of the last remaining Tigers to attempt to break out of the Halbe Pocket south of Berlin on April 28, 1945. During the war he received the Iron Cross Second Class, the Iron Cross First Class, Wound Badge in Black, Panzer Battle Badge in Silver, and the Panzer Battle Badge in Silver for 25 Assaults. The Soviets captured him and held Wolfgang Birnbaum in a prisoner of war camp until 1950.[11]

Gottlob Bittner. Gottlob Bittner was an ethnic German born on May 31, 1919, in Lelekowitz, Czechoslovakia. He passed the *Abitur* and planned to be an accountant. Able to speak Slovak and Czech, he stood 5'10" tall. Joining the Waffen-SS on July 4, 1940, Bittner served in SS Infantry Regiment 4 (motorized) *Langemarck* in the 2nd SS Infantry Brigade (motorized). On October 31, 1942, this regiment became the second detachment of the *Das Reich* panzer regiment, and he was assigned to the 8th (Heavy) Company effective November 15, 1942, becoming a radio operator in a Tiger—a position he also held at Kursk.[12]

Bittner was wounded by artillery shrapnel on October 30, 1943, and spent some weeks in a hospital before beginning various officer commissioning courses. During that time, on December 1, 1943, he became engaged. Gottlob was promoted to *SS-Untersturmführer* on November 9, 1944. After attending air defense courses he joined the *flak* detachment in the 16th SS Panzer Grenadier Division *Reichsführer-SS* and fought in Austria from March 14, 1945, to the end of the war. Bittner was awarded the Iron Cross Second Class. Gottlob Bittner is believed to have survived the war.[13]

Max Otto Wilhelm Bläsing. Max Bläsing was born at Oberallersdorf, near Sorau in Brandenburg, on January 29, 1922. As a youngster he served in the Hitler Youth from May 1933 to February 1940. He entered the SS on September 1, 1940, and began his service at the front in Russia on June 28, 1941, receiving the Eastern Front Medal on October 17, 1942. On November 11, 1942, he was detached to a special course for drivers at the Wegmann Company at Kassel. He was assigned to the Tiger company of the *Das Reich* effective November 15, 1942. After promotion to *SS-Rottenführer* on January 13, 1943, Max Bläsing was assigned as the driver of the company commander's Tiger at Kharkov in February–March 1943, and received the Panzer Battle Badge in Silver on April 9, 1943, for these actions.

At the Kursk Offensive he served as the driver in Tiger **S02** in the Headquarters Platoon and was wounded on the first day of the battle (he would receive the Wound Badge in Black for this on August 27). Still a driver, Max was wounded again near Kremenchuk, in the Ukraine, on September 11, 1943, and spent the next five weeks at a reserve hospital in Lublin, Poland, before being assigned to the SS Panzer Training and Replacement Regiment at Beneschau (Benešov) in Bohemia. *SS-Rottenführer* Bläsing would later serve as a driver in the 1st Company of the 102nd SS Heavy Panzer Detachment in 1944, and as a driver in the 1st Company of the 502nd SS Heavy Panzer Detachment at the Oder Front in 1945. Max Bläsing died in Backnang, Baden-Württemberg, on July 16, 1998; his wife, Luise, preceded him in death by four years. He is buried at the Backnang *Stadtfriedhof* (city cemetery) in Grave 2124.[14]

Hans-Joachim Boehmer. Hans-Joachim Boehmer, nicknamed "Chicken Fright," was born on September 2, 1920, in Elbing, East Prussia. Originally serving in the German Army as a lieutenant, he transferred to the Waffen-SS (SS number 468435) and became the commander of Tiger **S13**

in the First Platoon just before the Kursk Offensive. In August 1943 he switched platoons and commanded S21. An *SS-Untersturmführer*, later in the war he was assigned to the 35th SS Panzer Grenadier Regiment in the 16th SS Panzer Grenadier Division *Reichsführer-SS* and finished the war as an *SS-Obersturmführer*. Hans-Joachim Boehmer spent extensive time in a British prisoner of war camp after the war.[15]

Willi Börker. Willi Börker was born on July 16, 1921, at Förste, in Lower Saxony. He joined the Waffen-SS on February 28, 1941. Willi was promoted to *SS-Sturmmann* on March 1, 1942. Assigned to the new Tiger company in the *Das Reich* in February 1943, he became a driver, was promoted to *SS-Rottenführer* on April 1, 1943, and was in this position at Kursk. Willi was wounded in action on July 6, 1943; he later received the Wound Badge in Black. On September 29, 1943, Börker was placed on orders for a future assignment to the SS Panzer Training and Replacement Regiment at Beneschau, south of Prague. In April 1944 Willi Börker joined the 1st Company of the 102nd SS Heavy Panzer Detachment and was the driver of Tiger 121, fighting in Normandy. He received the Iron Cross Second Class on September 14, 1944. The unit was designated the 502nd SS Heavy Panzer Detachment in October 1944, and *SS-Rottenführer* Börker served in this unit on the Eastern Front. British soldiers later captured him and Börker was taken to a prisoner of war camp in England. Willi Börker survived the war but committed suicide in 1995.[16]

Ludwig Bullay. Ludwig Bullay was born on March 1, 1920, in Saarbrücken. As a youngster he joined the Hitler Youth in 1933, and remained in that organization until June 24, 1937. A salesman by trade, he joined the Waffen-SS on June 25, 1937. Promoted to *SS-Unterscharführer* on November 11, 1939, he initially served in the 6th Company of SS Infantry Regiment 4 (motorized) *Langemarck* until October 31, 1942, when the second battalion of the regiment became the second battalion of the *Das Reich* panzer regiment. During his time in the infantry he was wounded in action and awarded the Wound Badge in Black. On November 15, 1942, Ludwig joined the Tiger company of the *Das Reich*, as he had all three classes of driver's license. At Kursk, as an *SS-Unterscharführer*, he is believed to have been a driver; he later received the Panzer Battle Badge in Silver. On December 28, 1943, he was married. In 1944, Ludwig Bullay reported for assignment to the SS Panzer Training and Replacement Regiment at Paderborn.[17]

Helmut Karl Cantow. Hailing from Leopoldshagen in Mecklenburg, Helmut Cantow was born on September 30, 1920. He joined the Hitler Youth on October 1, 1932, remaining in that organization until 1938, when he joined the Reich Labor Service. A baker by trade, he later resided in Torgelow, twenty-five miles northwest of Stettin. Joining the Waffen-SS on April 1, 1939, he served as a communications specialist in the invasion of Poland and France; he was promoted to *SS-Sturmmann* on June 1, 1940. The following year he served at the front in the Balkans and was elevated to *SS-Rottenführer* on April 20, 1941. He participated in Operation Barbarossa in June 1941, remaining in Russia until October 9, 1941, when he attended the SS Non-commissioned Officer School at Lauenburg (Pomerania). Helmut was promoted to *SS-Unterscharführer* on April 1, 1942, and was assigned to the signals replacement and training detachment associated with the panzer troops at Weimar-Buchenwald on July 22, 1942.[18]

Helmut Cantow was assigned to the 8th (Heavy) Company on January 1, 1943. At Kursk he would have been the radio operator in Tiger **S01**, but was wounded on the first day of the offensive. On August 17, 1943, he was wounded in action at Hill 196, near Nikitovka, in the Ukraine. On September 29, 1943, he was placed on orders for a future assignment to the SS Panzer Training and Replacement Regiment at Beneschau. He received the Panzer Battle Badge in Silver on October 20, 1943, and the Wound Badge in Black on November 28, 1943. He subsequently had several assignments in various training and replacement units; during the war Helmut Cantow was single until October 1944, when the SS Race and Settlement Main Office approved his marriage request.[19]

Johannes Esslinger. *SS-Panzerschütze* Johannes Esslinger served as the loader in **S14** in the First Platoon. In Normandy, *SS-Panzeroberschütze* Esslinger was seriously wounded near Maltot, Normandy, by artillery fire serving as a loader in a Tiger I in the 1st Company of the 102nd SS Heavy Panzer Detachment. He was subsequently invalided out of the service due to the serious nature of his wounds.[20]

Berthold Gustav Otto Fink. Berthold "Percussion Cap" Fink hailed from Karlsruhe, where he was born on June 25, 1922, the son of Eduard and Kamülla Fink. He entered the Waffen-SS on October 1, 1940. Promoted to *SS-Rottenführer* on November 1, 1942, he was assigned to the Tiger company of the *Das Reich* effective November 15, 1942. Berthold Fink was promoted on *SS-Unterscharführer* on April 1, 1943. At Kursk he served as a driver in a Tiger. In early 1944, he was assigned to the 2nd Company in the 102nd SS Heavy Panzer Detachment as a driver and fought at Hill 112 at Normandy in July 1944. Berthold Fink received the Panzer Battle Badge in Silver for 25 Assaults on September 21, 1944. During the war Berthold also received the Panzer Battle Badge in Silver, the Iron Cross Second Class, and the Wound Badge in Silver.

Nicknamed "Percussion Cap," in 1945 Fink drove King Tiger 123 (commanded by Gerhard Kaempf) in the Second Platoon of the 1st Company in the 502nd SS Heavy Panzer Detachment on the Oder Front; he is also believed to have been a driver for King Tiger 111. On April 28, 1945, he was among the last handful of King Tigers in the detachment to attempt to break out from the near encirclement of what would become known as the Halbe Pocket. His Tiger made it to the village of Beelitz on May 1, 1945, before it ran out of fuel and the crew blew it up. American soldiers later captured him, and he remained in a prisoner of war camp in Regensburg until 1947.

After the war Berthold Fink lived in Karlsruhe, where it appears he was the general representative for *Leipziger Feuer* and *Alte Leipziger* insurance companies from 1952 to 1985; he lived on Adlerstraße 8. Fifty years after the war Berthold Fink made the following statement in reflection: "I should have forgotten by now, fifty years after I began serving in the war in 1940, everything about it, but three places will never leave my memory: Belgorod, Hill 112, and Halbe."[21]

Heinz Freiberger. Heinz Freiberger was born on January 25, 1921, in Münchwies/Ottweiler, in the Saar. He joined the SS on April 12, 1939, and served in the Thuringia Death's Head unit, a concentration camp guards organization—quite probably at Buchenwald. He was promoted to *SS-Unterscharführer* on April 1, 1942. He was assigned to the Tiger company of the *Das Reich* effective November 15, 1942. At Kharkov he served as the driver for the Mark III N panzer (851) commanded by Alois Kalss. Freiberger served as a Tiger driver at the Kursk Offensive. By 1944, he was assigned as a Tiger driver in the 1st Company and subsequently as driver in the 3rd Company of the 102nd SS Heavy Panzer Detachment. In 1945, he was assigned to the 1st Company of the 502nd SS Heavy Panzer Detachment, driving King Tiger 341—the company commander's tank. During the war he was awarded the Iron Cross Second Class and the Panzer Battle Badge in Silver. His wife Amalia, whom he married during the war, was from Carinthia, Austria. The Soviets captured Heinz Freiberger at the end of the war and held him in a prisoner of war camp until 1950.[22]

Wilfried Frenzel. Wilfried Frenzel was born in Stellrade on October 26, 1924. He had been assigned to the SS Panzer Training and Replacement Battalion in Prague and arrived at the company days before the Kursk Offensive. He had already been selected to begin the track to become an officer, but it was not to be. *SS-Panzerschütze* Frenzel, a radio operator in a tiger, was seriously injured in an accident on July 5, and was evacuated to the rear. He died of his injuries on July 15, 1943, at the SS Hospital in Kharkov. Wilfried Frenzel is probably buried among the unknowns at the German War Cemetery at Kharkov.[23]

Georg Wilhelm Gallinat. Born on July 25, 1923, in Goldauer, near Goldap in East Prussia, George Gallinat was a baker by trade. He served in the Hitler Youth from March 1, 1933, to September 7, 1941. Standing 5'10" tall, he joined the Waffen-SS the next day, but a problem developed. It appears from his personnel file that Georg also volunteered for the Luftwaffe. Both services went forward and backward, but he finally became a soldier in the Waffen-SS, and after basic training as a signalman in Nürnberg was assigned to the *Das Reich*. At Kursk, *SS-Rottenführer* Gallinat fought in Tiger **S01** of the Headquarters Platoon as the driver. He was wounded in action on the first day, when the vehicle struck an enemy antitank mine.[24] Georg Gallinat is believed to have later served in the 102nd SS Heavy Panzer Detachment in Normandy.

Gebhardt. *SS-Unterscharführer* Gebhardt served as a loader in Tiger **S11** in the First Platoon during the Kursk Offensive.

Artur Glagow. Artur Glagow was born in Tuchlin, in East Prussia, on January 18, 1920. He served in the Hitler Youth from April 1933 to February 1939, and joined the Waffen-SS on April 15, 1940. Promoted to *SS-Unterscharführer* on November 1, 1942, he was married on January 20, 1943, before going to Russia. *SS-Unterscharführer* Glagow served as the commander of Tiger 842 during the fighting at Kharkov in February–March 1943. Glagow was the gunner in Tiger **S21** in the Second Platoon in the Kursk Offensive and may also have temporarily commanded Tiger **S32** in the Third Platoon. He later commanded Tigers 122, 124, and 132 in the 1st Company of the 102nd SS Heavy Panzer Detachment in Normandy. He was listed as missing in action on August 19, 1944, but he actually was captured by the British. Artur Glagow survived the war, returned to Germany, and passed away in 1998.[25]

Erich Gleissner. Born on January 18, 1922, at Wimmelburg, near Eisleben in Saxony, Erich Gleissner first enlisted in the Luftwaffe on October 1, 1939, but was transferred to the Waffen-SS and 8th (Heavy) Company on April 9, 1943.[26] As an *SS-Rottenführer* he served as a driver in the company beginning the day he arrived and through the Kursk Offensive. In April 1944, Gleissner was assigned to the 1st Company of the 102nd SS Heavy Panzer Detachment; he was shot in the stomach on July 10, 1944, near Hill 112. When the unit was designated the 502nd SS Heavy Panzer Detachment, *SS-Rottenführer* Gleissner served in the 1st Company as a driver. He was promoted to *SS-Unterscharführer* on December 1, 1944. Erich survived the war. He likely resided in Munich later in life and died in 2003.[27]

Helmut Gnerlich. Helmut Gnerlich was born in Hamburg on May 2, 1924. A postal inspector by trade, he was Protestant and single, joining the Waffen-SS on April 1, 1942; he was 5'10" tall and could speak both English and Spanish.[28] *SS-Sturmmann* Gnerlich served at the 2nd SS Training and Replacement Battalion in Prague until June 25, 1943, when he transferred to the 8th (Heavy) Company. He served in a Tiger as a gunner during the Kursk Offensive. Helmut Gnerlich was transferred to the Second Battalion of the 2nd SS Panzer Regiment on July 24, 1943.[29]

Alfred Grupe. Alfred Grupe was born on January 6, 1925, at Negenborn, just north of Hannover, in Lower Saxony.[30] Killed in action on July 7, 1944, near Caen, France, he was buried in the British War Cemetery at Cheux-St.-Manvieu, Normandy.[31]

Günter Grupe. Günter Grupe was born in Marienhagen, near Hildesheim in Lower Saxony, on March 1, 1924. Single, he was a barber by trade. He joined the Waffen-SS on October 1, 1942. *SS-Rottenführer* Grupe was assigned to the company commander's panzer at Kharkov in February–March 1943 as a loader in Tiger **S02** in the Headquarters Platoon during the Kursk Offensive. He had previously won the Panzer Battle Badge in Silver. Technically after the offensive, he was wounded on the left forearm and right hand by shrapnel on July 18. After recuperating, he was assigned to the 5th Company of the 3rd *Totenkopf* Infantry Regiment on November 2, 1943, as a sniper. Günter Grupe was promoted to *SS-Unterscharführer* on April 1, 1944.[32]

Karl Grupe. Born March 16, 1922, in Marienhagen, near Hildesheim in Lower Saxony, Karl Grupe was a member of the Hitler Youth in 1939.[29] Standing 5'8" tall when he entered the Waffen-SS, he was married and had one child. He fought with the company around Kharkov in February–March 1943 and received the Panzer Battle Badge in Silver on March 27, 1943. At the Kursk Offensive *SS-Sturmmann* Grupe served in Tiger **S02** in the Headquarters Platoon. On September 29, 1943, he was placed on orders for a future assignment to the SS Panzer Training and Replacement Regiment at Beneschau. Karl later served in the 102nd SS Heavy Panzer Detachment in Normandy.[30]

Benno Hackbarth. Benno Hackbarth was born in Marienthal, in the district of Schlawe, Pomerania, Germany, on May 30, 1922. He joined the Waffen-SS on May 8, 1940, and was promoted to *SS-Rottenführer* on November 11, 1942. Hackbarth served in the 8th (Heavy) Company in the Kursk Offensive in an unknown crew position on a Tiger. *SS-Rottenführer* Benno Hackbarth received the Iron Cross Second Class on August 4, 1943. Benno Hackbarth died on April 4, 1945, the first day of the US First Army drive east to seize Leipzig. In one of the thousands of small skirmishes during the war, two King Tiger tanks took up defensive positions at the saltworks of the town of Bad Karlshafen. Under heavy machine gun fire a company of roughly seventeen American Sherman tanks assaulted the position, which was on the Weser River, setting several structures on fire and forcing the two King Tigers to attempt to withdraw east toward the village of Solling. It appears that Benno died during this fight. He is buried in the military section of a small cemetery at Bad Karlshafen, north of Kassel; the exact location is Grave 6, in Row 1, of Block E.[33]

Hans Xaver Haselböck. Hans Haselböck was born in Höchst, hear Frankfurt in Hesse, on September 6, 1923, the son of Xaver Haselböck. Standing 5'10" tall when he entered the Waffen-SS on June 15, 1941, he was single and had blood type A. Haselböck joined the first detachment of the *Das Reich* panzer regiment in early 1942. He joined the company on December 11, 1942, and fought at Kharkov in February–March 1943 as the radio operator of Tiger 801, winning a Panzer Badge in Silver on March 27, 1943. He was promoted to *SS-Sturmmann* on April 1, 1943. At Kursk, *SS-Sturmmann* Haselböck served as a radio operator in Tiger **S02** in the Headquarters Platoon until he was wounded on July 7. He subsequently spent three months in medical care at facilities in Aschersleben and Eichstätt, Germany. Because it was his third wound he was awarded the Wound Badge in Silver. On September 29, 1943, he was placed on orders for a future assignment to the SS Panzer Training and Replacement Regiment at Beneschau.

Haselböck is believed to have also served in the 102nd SS Heavy Panzer Detachment. On March 5, 1945, he was transferred to the 31st Waffen-SS Volunteer Grenadier Division, which was composed mainly of ethnic Germans living in Hungary. The division joined the German 17th Army in Silesia, where it was surrounded by the Red Army and surrendered near Hradec Králové in May 1945. Hans Haselböck survived the war.[34] He is believed to have been an electroplater in Frankfurt, residing at Schliephakeβtrasse 6. A Catholic, Hans and his wife Elisabeth had a stillborn child on August 10, 1955.[35] Surveying his personnel file reveals that Hans Haselböck had received the following injuries and wounds during the war: bruised feet, two shrapnel wounds in the right calf, and three bullet wounds.

Max Heering. The strange case of Max Heering began on July 23, 1921, when he was born in the village of Schwarzheide, west of Spremberg, in southern Brandenburg. *SS-Sturmmann* Heering fought in the 8th (Heavy) Company during the Kursk Offensive, for which he was awarded the Iron Cross Second Class on August 20, 1943. He was probably wounded later in August 1943 and spent four weeks in a hospital. On October 1, 1943, he was assigned to the SS Panzer Training and Replacement Regiment at Beneschau before an assignment to the First Company of the 102nd SS Heavy Panzer Detachment. When that unit was reformed, *SS-Rottenführer* Heering was assigned to the First Company of the 502nd SS Heavy Panzer Detachment. He quickly ran afoul of the authorities for some serious transgression. According to historian Rüdiger Warnick, the SS executed Max Heering in December 1944.[36]

Kurt Hellwig. Born in Berlin-Moabit on August 24, 1913, Kurt Hellwig finished grade school and then apprenticed as a miller, the trade of his father. On April 1, 1935, he joined the Reich Labor Service and stayed there half a year. Kurt Hellwig then joined the Waffen-SS on October 21, 1935, and reported to the *Leibstandarte SS Adolf Hitler* Regiment in Berlin with SS number 286971. Assigned to the 8th Company (Machine gun) in the regiment, he was promoted to *SS-Sturmmann* on October 1, 1937; to *SS-Rottenführer* on September 1, 1939; and to *SS-Unterscharführer* on August 1, 1939. On October 25, 1940, he transferred to the *Das Reich* (then called the *SS-Verfügungsdivision*). *SS-Oberscharführer* Hellwig fought at Kharkov with the company in February–March 1943, receiving a Panzer Battle Badge in Silver. At Kursk, he commanded Tiger **S23** in the Second Platoon. Commanding Tiger **S02** on July 31, 1943, he was lightly wounded at Hill 230.9, near Brochorow. He later served in the 2nd Company of the 102nd SS Heavy Panzer Detachment in Normandy as both a Tiger commander in the Second Platoon and in the recovery and maintenance section. At the end of the war on the Oder Front, Kurt Hellwig commanded King Tiger 222 in the 2nd Company of the 502nd SS Heavy Panzer Detachment.[37]

Julius Hinrichsen. Julius Hinrichsen was the same as millions of soldiers who served in World War II—or in any war for that matter—he liked pretty girls. However, the Waffen-SS had rules concerning what a soldier could do and not do in that arena, and one of the *verboten* actions was giving a female a ride in a Tiger. Despite knowing that restraint, at Kharkov in mid-May 1943, he gave a ride in his Tiger to a German female; unfortunately for Julius that indiscretion was observed by an officer. Julius was ordered to report to *SS-Oberführer* Werner Ostendorff, the chief of staff for the 2nd SS Panzer Corps. As Julius later wrote, he "came away without a court-martial."[38] We can assume that *SS-Oberführer* Ostendorff was not amused.

Born March 12, 1921, in Schafflund, in Schleswig-Holstein, Julius Hinrichsen joined the Waffen-SS on January 3, 1941, and first served in the assault gun detachment of the SS *Totenkopf* Division, fighting at the Demjansk Pocket, where he was wounded three times. He was promoted to *SS-Sturmmann* on October 1, 1941. After fifteen months at the front with the *Totenkopf* he went on recuperation leave, reporting to Weimar-Buchenwald on October 8, 1942, for panzer training. He then transferred to the Troop Training Grounds Bergen at Fallingbostel on December 8 for Tiger training, departing for Russia on January 24, 1943. While in Fallingbostel, on January 13, 1943, he received the Iron Cross Second Class for his time at Demjansk. Hinrichsen fought in Tiger 801/802 as the gunner in the 8th (Heavy) Company at Kharkov in February–March 1943, receiving the Panzer Battle Badge in Silver on March 27, 1943; he was promoted to *SS-Rottenführer* on April 1.[39]

At Kursk, Julius served as a gunner first in Tiger **S01**; the vehicle ran over an enemy antitank mine and was towed to the workshop repair company, where mechanics worked on the vehicle for six days. Hinrichsen then served in Tiger **S02** in the Headquarters Platoon. That fall a previous wound to the jaw gave him problems and Julius was shipped to the University Clinic in Göttingen, where he had surgery and recuperated for five months. Promoted to *SS-Unterscharführer*, he later fought in Normandy with the 102nd SS Heavy Panzer Detachment. During the war Hinrichsen received the Wound Badge in Gold and was credited in many sources as destroying a total of twenty-two enemy tanks in the conflict; he finished as an *SS-Standartenoberjunker*. Julius Hinrichsen survived the war and died in 1995.[40]

Hagbert Hobohm. Born in Hamburg on May 13, 1920, Hagbert Hobohm was a metal smith by trade before joining the Waffen-SS on September 3, 1939. He initially served in SS Regiment *Germania* and was promoted to *SS-Rottenführer* on August 1, 1941, before joining the 3rd Company of the *Das Reich* panzer detachment. On November 15, 1942, Hobohm joined the Tiger Company and became a driver, having just been detached to a special course for drivers at the Wegmann Company at Kassel. At the fighting near Kharkov in February–March 1943 he served as the driver in Tiger 831 and was promoted to *SS-Unterscharführer* on April 1, 1943. During the Kursk Offensive he drove **S31** in the Second Platoon; he also drove in **S22** for part of the fighting. A photograph of him in summer 1943 shows Hagbert wearing the Iron Cross Second Class, the Iron Cross First Class, the Infantry Assault Badge in Silver (for service in *Germania*), and the Wound Badge in Black.[41] Hobohm was seriously wounded in the head on October 30, 1943, when an enemy shell hit one of his vision blocks. He was promoted to *SS-Oberscharführer* on July 1, 1944. Hagbert Hobohm survived the war, appears to have been a laborer in Hamburg, and died in 1976, probably in Hamburg.[42]

Richard Hoffmann. Richard Hoffmann was born on July 29, 1902, in the town of Erkner, near Berlin. He attended technical school for the trade of construction. Hoffmann joined the Nazi Party on April 20, 1933, and the Allgemeine-SS with SS number 101091. By January 30, 1939, he was an *SS-Untersturmführer*. He had received the Olympia Medal Second Class for helping to host the Olympics in 1936. On June 8, 1940, Hoffmann ran into trouble and was reduced in rank for not taking care of a disabled SS comrade. He received a War Service Cross Second Class with Swords in 1942 but decided he needed to join the Waffen-SS, which he did on February 24, 1943. Married with one daughter, he stood 5'10" tall and was assigned to the Tiger company as an *SS-Panzerschütze*. It is not known in which Tiger he served, nor his position. On September 29, 1943, Hoffmann was placed on orders for a future assignment to the SS Panzer Training and Replacement Regiment at Beneschau. Later in 1943, Richard Hoffmann received the Iron Cross Second Class and the Panzer Battle Badge in Silver.[43]

Bruno Hofmann. Born on December 27, 1924, at Bürgstadt on the Main River in Lower Franconia, Bruno Hofmann was Catholic and an electrician by trade; he joined the Hitler Youth on May 1, 1934, at age nine. He entered the Waffen-SS on September 15, 1942, and attended radio operator training before joining the 8th (Heavy) Company. *SS-Sturmmann* Bruno Hofmann served as a radio operator in a Tiger during the Kursk Offensive until July 12, when he was wounded in the left thigh by shrapnel during a Soviet armored attack near Kalinin; he subsequently received the Wound Badge in Black. After spending a month in a hospital he returned to the company on August 26, 1943, and remained there until October 1, 1943, when he was assigned to the SS Panzer Training and Replacement Regiment at Beneschau. In early 1944 he attended panzer reconnaissance training. Bruno Hofmann was killed near Hatvan, Hungary, on November 18, 1944, likely assigned to the 31st Waffen-SS Volunteer Grenadier Division. His remains have never been located.[44]

Erich Holzer. Erich Holzer was born in Landshut, Bavaria, on August 8, 1925. A Catholic and single, when he enlisted in the Waffen-SS he stood 5'7" tall. He had previously worked for the

German Railway. Holzer was assigned to the 1st Company in the 2nd Panzer Regiment on December 8, 1942. He was hospitalized with jaundice on April 9, 1943; the next day he was awarded the Iron Cross Second Class on April 10, 1943, for fighting at Kharkov in February and March as a loader in a panzer Mark III N (851). Released from the 562nd Field Hospital on April 19, Erich came down with hepatitis on April 20; records indicate that he was released to his unit on June 4.

Eric Holzer was assigned to the 8th (Heavy) Company on June 7, 1943. During the Kursk Offensive *SS-Panzeroberschütze* Holzer served as a loader in a Tiger; he received the Panzer Battle Badge in Silver on August 27, 1943. But the soldier could not stay well and was diagnosed a second time with jaundice on November 26, 1943, and was treated at the 168th Field Hospital. He returned to the *Das Reich* and remained there until March 10, 1944.

Now assigned to the 1st Company of the 102nd SS Heavy Panzer Detachment as the loader in Tiger 111, Erich Holzer was killed in action near Caen, France, on June 27, 1944, during an air attack. He is buried at the German War Cemetery at Noyers-Pont-Maugis, France, in an end grave in Block 4 (Grave 1834) among 26,843 German war dead, of which 4,880 are from World War II.[45]

Dieter Hurlbrink. *SS-Rottenführer* Dieter Hurlbrink was born on December 27, 1920, in Dortmund, Westphalia. He joined the Waffen-SS on October 23, 1939. After serving on Heinrich Himmler's personal staff he joined the *Das Reich* panzer regiment and was assigned to the company in June. He was promoted to *SS-Rottenführer* on July 1, 1943, and served in an unknown position on a Tiger during the offensive. Hurlbrink was wounded on October 21, 1943, and spent more than four weeks in hospitals; he was assigned to the SS Panzer Training and Replacement Regiment in Beneschau, in Bohemia. Dieter Hurlbrink was promoted to *SS-Unterscharführer* on February 1, 1945.[46]

Paul Jadzewski. *SS-Sturmmann* Paul Jadzewski was born December 4, 1921, at Braunnitz, near Tuchel in West Prussia. A Catholic, he could speak Polish and joined the Waffen-SS on January 1, 1941, with SS number 386316; he stood just over 5'6" tall. He served in a tank at Kharkov in February–March 1943, receiving the Panzer Battle Badge in Silver on March 29, 1943. At Kursk, Paul served as a loader in **S22**. He won the Iron Cross Second Class on August 20, 1943. In spring 1944, *SS-Sturmmann* Jadzewski was assigned as a loader in the 1st Company of the 102nd SS Heavy Panzer Detachment. In 1945, he was assigned to the 1st Company of the 502nd SS Heavy Panzer Detachment as a loader in a King Tiger.[47] It is likely that Paul Jadzewski lived in Hamburg after the war.

Hermann Jörg. Hermann Jörg was born on October 12, 1924, in Forbach, Baden, the son of a salesman. He joined the Hitler Youth in 1934; he was a middle school student before joining the Waffen-SS on September 15, 1942. At Kursk *SS-Oberschütze* Jörg fought in Tiger **S12** in the First Platoon as a gunner. After serving in the company, he attended the 2nd SS Leader Candidate course at the Panzer Troops School at Putlos from January 1, 1944, to April 15, 1944, then appears to have been assigned to the 4th Company in the 2nd SS Panzer Regiment *Das Reich*, and subsequently to the 2nd Company of the 102nd SS Heavy Panzer Detachment on May 24, 1944; he subsequently fought in Normandy. Jörg was killed in action on August 28, 1944, in the Soissons-Laon area of France; his remains appear to have never been found. During the war Hermann Jörg received the Iron Cross Second Class and the Panzer Battle Badge in Silver.[48]

Gerhard Kaempf. *SS-Rottenführer* Gerhard Kaempf was born on July 20, 1924, in East Prussia. Early in his career he served in the first company of the motorcycle battalion of the *Das Reich* in

May 1941 and earned the Infantry Assault Badge in Bronze and the Eastern Front Medal; during the withdrawal from Moscow he was wounded in action on January 21, 1942; the temperature that day was -25°F. In late summer 1942 he was assigned to Fallingbostel, where he became a gunner in a Mark III panzer. Gerhard Kaempf received the Iron Cross Second Class on March 23, 1943, for bravery as a gunner in Mark III N (851) commanded by Alois Kalss.

At the Kursk Offensive Gerhard served as the gunner for Tiger **S31** in the Third Platoon and subsequently became the gunner in Tiger **S22**. On July 18, he was standing behind his Tiger when he was wounded in the left side by enemy infantry fire—he later thought it might have been friendly fire that struck him. Gerhard was promoted to *SS-Unterscharführer* and awarded the Iron Cross First Class on August 4, 1943 (at which time he had a total of thirty-six enemy tank kills); he was wounded again on November 27, 1943, when shrapnel from an exploding Stalin Organ rocket struck him in the thigh and shoulder blade, puncturing his lung. By this time Gerhard believed that he had destroyed forty-six enemy tanks.[49]

Gerhard Kaempf was evacuated to a hospital at Königsfeld, in the Black Forest, not far from Villingen-Schwenningen, where he remained until October 1944.[50] Despite some sources reporting that Kaempf commanded Tiger 124 in the 1st Company of the 102nd SS Heavy Panzer Detachment at Normandy, he did not.

Kaempf reported to the SS Panzer Replacement and Training Regiment Detmold. Although his wounds classified him as not fit for frontline service, his old comrade Alois Kalss made an exception. In the final month of the war on the Oder Front, *SS-Unterscharführer* Kaempf commanded King Tiger 123 in the Second Platoon of the 1st Company in the 502nd SS Heavy Panzer Detachment. Gerhard Kaempf was on one of the last remaining Tigers to attempt to break out of the Halbe Pocket south of Berlin on April 28, 1945. Sources credit him with destroying forty-six enemy tanks during the war. American soldiers later captured him, and he remained in a prisoner of war camp in Regensburg until 1947. Gerhard had high regards for his Tiger commander, Alois Kalss, saying about him: "About *SS-Untersturmführer* Kalss concerning his soldierly and humanistic qualities, I can only say the very best about him."[51]

Alois Kalss.[52] Born at St. Gilgen, Austria, on February 18, 1920, and the son of a forester, Alois "Lois" Kalss finished grade school, then attended business school in nearby Salzburg. His deeper passion seemed to be the military organization espoused by the illegal Austria Nazi Party and he drifted toward it. Alois was in the Hitler Youth in Austria from 1934 to 1936, entered the Austrian SS in 1936, and after the Austrian Annexation joined the Waffen-SS on April 1, 1938, receiving SS number 269184. Standing 5'10.5" tall and able to speak English, he first was assigned to SS Infantry Regiment *Deutschland*, then SS Division *Wiking* in 1940, where he served in SS Infantry Regiment 10 *Westland* from January 1941 to July 1942, when he transferred to the 2nd Company of the Reconnaissance Detachment in that division.

Alois Kalss received the Iron Cross Second Class on July 10, 1941, and the Iron Cross First Class on September 17, 1941. Alois then was selected for officer training and studied at the 6th *Kriegs Junkerlehrgang* at the *SS-Junkerschule* at Bad Tölz from February 1, 1942, to May 9, 1942. While at Bad Tölz other awards caught up to him, including a Wound Badge in Black (March 13, 1942), Wound Badge in Silver (April 13, 1942), and Infantry Assault Badge in Silver (May 12, 1942).

Promoted to *SS-Untersturmführer* on September 1, 1942, he finally was assigned to the 8th (Heavy) Company in November 1942. He commanded the Fifth Platoon in the company in February 1943 and the Fourth Platoon in March 1943 during the Kharkov fight, fighting from a Mark III panzer (851); he was wounded in the head by shrapnel on March 14, 1943, during the fighting but remained with the unit. When the company commander was relieved Kalss assumed temporary command on March 29, 1943, and held the position until April 8, 1943, when he reverted to command of the Third Platoon; he was sick and in hospital from June 13 to June 30.

At the Kursk Offensive Alois Kalss commanded Tiger **S31**. He was wounded on July 5, but remained with the unit. Awarded the Wound Badge in Gold on August 23, 1943, Kalss assumed temporary command of the 8th (Heavy) Company on September 18, 1943, and was awarded the German Cross in Gold on September 23, 1943, in part for his performance at Kursk. He also was in temporary command of the unit beginning November 16, 1943. He was promoted to *SS-Obersturmführer* on January 30, 1944. On May 5, 1944, he received orders to the 102nd SS Heavy Panzer Detachment—which formally became known by this designation on November 4, 1943— becoming the acting commander of the 1st Company and commanding Tiger 141.

During the Normandy fighting in June and July 1944, his company distinguished itself at Hill 112, to the extent that in the recommendation for the Knight's Cross of the Iron Cross by *SS-Gruppenführer* Wilhelm Bittrich, the 2nd SS Panzer Corps commander, he was credited with destroying forty-two enemy tanks to this point in the war. Alois Kalss received the Knight's Cross on September 23, 1944, and was promoted to *SS-Hauptsturmführer* on November 9, 1944. Equipped with new King Tiger tanks, the newly designated 502nd SS Heavy Panzer Detachment deployed to the Eastern Front, which was rapidly being pushed west to the Oder River.

During the final defensive battles for the Third Reich he fought at Dolgelin, near Seelow; Kalss, now in command of the 1st Company of the detachment, subsequently fought near Heinersdorf and Steinhöfel in the Halbe Pocket. The last days of the war were chaotic and there are two versions of his death. The first to emerge was that Alois Kalss was killed in action in the Kummersdorf Forest (Kummersdorf Estate) on April 29, 1945, when his King Tiger 101 received a direct hit from an enemy antitank gun. The second version is that he was seriously wounded in the head by a Soviet sniper on April 30, 1945, and that he succumbed to this wound on May 2, 1945.

In either case, Alois Kalss was officially listed as missing in action on May 2, 1945. His remains have never been identified. During the war *SS-Hauptsturmführer* Alois Kalss was credited with destroying fifty-four enemy tanks; among his awards are also two Tank Destruction Badges. He is also believed to have been awarded the Panzer Battle Badge in Silver for 75 Assaults and the Panzer Battle Badge in Silver for 100 Assaults.

Paul Egger, another Knight's Cross winner in the unit, had a favorable opinion of his fellow officer: "*SS-Obersturmführer* Kalss was Austrian, as was I, so we understood each other very well. He was one of the very best open-minded company commanders and comrade."

Other comrades recalled that Alois Kalss had a human side; during one fight his Tiger knocked out a Soviet T-34. As his gunner began to rotate the turret to machine gun the enemy crew, which had jumped off their tank and begun to run away, Kalss told him to let them go.

Alfred Ernst Kendziora. When the Federal Republic of Germany rearmed and formed the *Bundeswehr* (Federal defense unified armed forces of Germany) in 1955, the initial intention was not to admit any former Waffen-SS troops. Ultimately less than 1,000 men were admitted, but perhaps no one thought then that a former Waffen-SS officer would ever become a brigadier general in the *Bundeswehr*. They were wrong.

SS-Junker Alfred Kendziora was born on February 12, 1925, in Danzig. He enlisted in the assault gun detachment of the *Das Reich*. As his grandfather was of Russian origin, Alfred spoke fluent Russian and could monitor Soviet radio transmissions. At the Kursk Offensive his assault gun was damaged severely on the first day, and three days later Alfred was transferred to the 8th (Heavy) Company, where he was installed as a Tiger commander for the period July 8 to July 15. The assignment did not come without some *Sturm und Drang* (storm and stress). As he later said: "The crew did not at all agree with someone assuming command who had not previously fought in the unit. They accepted me only pursuant to expressed orders."[53]

Alfred was later promoted to *SS-Untersturmführer*. During the war he received the Iron Cross Second Class, the Panzer Battle Badge in Silver, and the Wound Badge in Black. Surviving the war, Alfred graduated from a mining program and decided to join the *Bundeswehr*; he commanded the Panzer Grenadier Battalion 43 in Göttingen and was the deputy commander of Panzer Brigade 8, as well as many other postings, and achieved the grade of brigadier general before retiring; postwar he received the Officer's Cross of the Order of Merit of the Federal Republic of Germany. Alfred died on August 27, 2011.[54]

Walter Knecht. *SS-Unterscharführer* Walter Knecht fought at the Kursk Offensive as a commander of Tiger **S22** in the Second Platoon. A photograph of him in summer 1943 shows Walter wearing the Iron Cross Second Class, the Infantry Assault Badge in Silver, and the Wound Badge in Silver.[55] He later served in the 1st Company of the 102nd SS Heavy Panzer Detachment, commanding Tiger 132, and subsequently in the 3rd Company in Normandy, commanding Tiger 323. On the Oder Front at the end of the war Walter, now an *SS-Oberscharführer*, served in the 1st Company of the 502nd SS Heavy Panzer Detachment commanding King Tiger 113 and Tiger 132; his gunners then included Wolfgang Birnbaum. Knecht was wounded in the eye on March 22, 1945, near Alt Tucheband, just west of Küstrin; he was wounded again four days later near Gorgast when an enemy artillery shell tore off both the loader's and commander's hatches, seriously injuring him, but medics took Knecht to an aid station and he survived. During the war Walter Knecht is believed to have destroyed at least twenty enemy tanks; he is also believed to have been wounded five times.[56]

August Koppelkamp. Born in Suderwich, near Recklinghausen, in North Rhine-Westphalia, on January 26, 1915, August Koppelkamp served in the Hitler Youth beginning in 1933, before he joined the Waffen-SS with SS number 276386 on September 28, 1935, and was assigned to the *Germania* infantry regiment. He was Catholic. Serving at the front beginning in September 1939, he was assigned to the Tiger company of the *Das Reich* effective November 15, 1942, after his promotion to *SS-Unterscharführer* on November 1, 1942. August served as the driver for Tiger **S01** during the Kursk Offensive. He received the Iron Cross Second Class. August served as the driver of Tiger 141 in the 1st Company of the 102nd SS Heavy Panzer Detachment in Normandy. Koppelkamp was promoted to *SS-Oberscharführer* on August 1, 1944. His wife had a son in September 1944. On the Oder Front in spring 1945, *SS-Oberscharführer* Koppelkamp served as a driver in the 1st Company of the 502nd SS Heavy Panzer Detachment.[57] After the war he was likely a machinist in Essen-Mülheim, residing on Thingstraße 5.[58]

Franz Kraml. Franz Kraml was born on December 1, 1917, in Winterberg, in the district of Prachatitz, then part of Austria (and later the Sudetenland). Entering the Waffen-SS on April 1, 1939, he was assigned to the *Deutschland* Regiment before transferring to the *Das Reich* panzer detachment's 1st Company. Promoted to *SS-Unterscharführer* on September 1, 1942, he remained in this unit until late February 1943. During the fighting at Kharkov in February–March 1943, *SS-Unterscharführer* Franz Kraml served as the gunner of Tiger 800, and later 802, in the Headquarters Platoon of the 8th (Heavy) Company.[59]

During the Kursk Offensive Franz was the commander of Tiger **S13** in the First Platoon. He transferred to the 1st Company of the 102nd SS Heavy Panzer Detachment on February 23, 1944, where he commanded Tiger 112 and subsequently fought in Normandy. In 1945, Kraml commanded King Tiger 112 in the First Platoon of the 1st Company in the 502nd SS Heavy Panzer Detachment. During the war he received the Panzer Battle Badge in Silver and the Wound Badge in Black. British soldiers later captured him and he was taken to a prisoner of war camp in England, where he was confined for almost three years. He and his wife later had a son. On May 11, 1991, Franz Kraml—who is seen holding his Luger as the commander in one of the most iconic photographs of Tigers at Kursk—died in Fallingbostel.[60]

Friedrich Robert Krichel. Fritz Krichel was born on October 14, 1910, in Mainz-Kastel, the son of Jakob Maximilian and Anna Margareta Krichel. A carpenter, he joined the Allgemeine-SS on March 15, 1933, receiving SS number 143754. Married in 1934, Fritz had two sons. After joining the Waffen-SS, he first was assigned to the 10th Company of SS Infantry Regiment 4 (motorized) *Langemarck* until October 1942, when the second battalion of the regiment became the second battalion of the *Das Reich* panzer regiment. He had been promoted to a reserve *SS-Rottenführer* on May 1, 1942. He then took driver training and finally reported to the company on November 15, 1942. During the Kursk Offensive *SS-Rottenführer* Krichel served as a Tiger driver, a position he later held in the 1st Company of the 102nd SS Heavy Panzer Detachment and in the 1st Company of the 502nd SS Heavy Panzer Detachment. A court at Sperenberg, in Brandenburg, East Germany, on April 4, 1946, declared that Friedrich Krichel had been killed in action on April 30, 1945, near the Kummersdorf gunnery range.[61]

Jakob Kuster. *SS-Panzeroberschütze* Jakob Kuster was the gunner in Tiger **S32** in the Third Platoon of the 8th (Heavy) Company. He was wounded outside the tank on July 6, 1943, when an enemy artillery round struck near him, also wounding the loader and tank commander.

Ferdinand Lasser. Born on May 3, 1911, at Graz, Austria, *SS-Unterscharführer* "Ferl" Lasser served as a gunner in the 8th (Heavy) Company during the Kursk Offensive. He had been promoted to that rank on October 1, 1942. At Normandy in 1944, Ferdinand served as the gunner of Tiger 112 in the First Platoon of the 102nd SS Heavy Panzer Detachment. In spring 1945, Lasser served as a gunner in King Tiger 121 and 112 in the 1st Company of the 502nd SS Heavy Panzer Detachment.[62] The German War Graves Commission lists a soldier with the exact same name and date of birth as missing in action in March 1945 near Küstrin, which is the exact location the 502nd SS Heavy Panzer Detachment fought. The soldier is registered in the memory book at the German Military Cemetery at Stare Czarnowo, Poland (forty miles north of Küstrin [Kostrzyn]). This study believes the two are the same man. Whether Ferdinand Lasser perished on the battlefield or was captured and subsequently died remains unknown.[63]

Albert Laumbacher. Son of a brewery worker, Albert Laumbacher was born on September 26, 1921, in Wangen, Württemberg; he graduated from grade school and trade school before becoming a baker's apprentice. Catholic and single, he stood 5'9" tall when he joined the Waffen-SS on April 1, 1939. Laumbacher was promoted to *SS-Sturmmann* on June 1, 1940, and to *SS-Rottenführer* on September 1, 1941. He served in the Fourth Battalion of the SS Infantry Regiment *Deutschland* in the *Das Reich* and then the staff company of the regiment, and finally the security company of the *Deutschland* before transferring to the 8th (Heavy) Company just before the offensive. At Kursk he served as a gunner. Albert remained in the *Das Reich* until April 28, 1944. Promoted to *SS-Unterscharführer* on April 1, 1944, Laumbacher later was assigned as a gunner in Tiger 134 in the Third Platoon in the 1st Company of the 102nd SS Heavy Panzer Detachment. He later was a Tiger gunner in the same company of the 502nd SS Heavy Panzer Detachment. He was married and had a son. During the war he received the Infantry Assault Badge on March 22, 1941, and the War Service Cross Second Class with Swords on August 22, 1942. Albert Laumbacher survived the war, spent several years in a Soviet prisoner of war camp, and after his return to Germany was a factory worker in Memmingen, Bavaria; he died in February 1998.[64]

Karl-Heinz Lorenz. Like father, like son did not seem to apply to Karl-Heinz Lorenz. His father was a music director in Hannover and enjoyed the classic sounds of the string sections, woodwinds, and brass. Karl-Heinz seemed far more at home with the deep rumble of a Tiger's six-hundred-ninety horsepower Maybach engine.

Karl-Heinz Lorenz was born on July 3, 1917, in Hannover. He was a member of the Hitler Youth for one year beginning July 1933, then finished high school. Joining the Allgemeine-SS on July 30, 1934, he received SS number 268839. Standing 5'11.6" tall, he joined the Waffen-SS on October 1, 1936, initially with the *Leibstandarte SS Adolf Hitler* Regiment, and served in the 16th Company that was equipped with heavy mortars. After attending the *SS-Junkerschule* at Braunschweig, he was promoted to *SS-Untersturmführer* on April 28, 1939. Later that year he was transferred to SS *Totenkopf* Infantry Regiment 3, where he was a platoon leader in the 13th Company, which provided short range fire support. In the French Campaign, he was wounded in action and received the Iron Cross Second Class on May 21, 1940, and the Wound Badge in Black on May 26, 1940, when he was seriously wounded that day near Le Cornet Malo, France.

Lorenz did not return to his unit until September 1940. Promoted to *SS-Obersturmführer* on April 20, 1941, during the invasion of Russia Karl-Heinz Lorenz received the Iron Cross First Class on July 10, 1941, the Wound Badge in Silver on October 7, 1941, and the Infantry Assault Badge on October 27, 1941, as the acting commander of a company. He was wounded again the next day near Dubrovka; his wounds, and illness, forced him into long term care in a hospital from November 1941 to March 15, 1942, when he was transferred to the *Das Reich* and the panzer regiment. During the Kharkov fighting he commanded the 2nd Company composed of Mark III and Mark IV panzers, distinguished himself, and was recommended for the German Cross in Gold; he appears to have been awarded the Panzer Battle Badge in Silver as well. Lorenz became the regimental adjutant on February 22, 1943, and received the German Cross in Gold on April 17, 1943; he was also promoted to *SS-Hauptsturmführer* on April 20, 1943.

At the Kursk Offensive on July 7, the 2nd Panzer Regiment commander dispatched Lorenz to the 8th (Heavy) Company to serve as the company troop leader (akin to the executive officer or second in command). Lorenz arrived, jumped in Tiger **S02**, and brashly moved ahead of the company, crossing a railroad embankment east of Kalinin and ordering the other Tigers to follow him and continue the attack. At 1200 hours the tank received a direct hit from an antitank gun that instantly killed Karl-Heinz Lorenz. Karl-Heinz left behind a wife, Christa; after his death, the Wehrmacht issued the family an Honor Roll Clasp on September 19, 1943, for his service. His remains were never transferred to a German War Cemetery.[65]

Wilhelm Lotter. Wilhelm Lotter was born in Berlin on March 7, 1924; he was a Protestant. He was a member of the Hitler Youth from March 14, 1934, to September 14, 1943. Wilhelm Lotter was training to be a businessman for forwarding and logistics. He joined the Waffen-SS on the latter date; he stood 5'7" tall; his first assignment was training to be a radio operator at the Waffen-SS communications school at Nürnberg. *SS-Funker* Lotter reported to the company on December 8, 1942. He began the Kursk Offensive as a radio operator in a Tiger in the 8th (Heavy) Company. On July 6, he received multiple wounds in his left and right thighs, buttocks, and hip; the nature of these wounds suggests that something exploded under him as he sat in his position in the right hull of the Tiger, indicative of an antitank mine. Medics evacuated Wilhelm to War Hospital 3/684 in Kiev the same day and he was promptly flown to a reserve hospital in Prague. He received the Iron Cross Second Class on July 22, 1943, for his accomplishments during the first two days of the fighting. After his release from the hospital on August 27, 1943, he reported to the 14th Company of the SS Signal Training and Replacement Regiment at Nürnberg.[66]

Werner Richard Heinrich Märker. Werner Märker was born in Schwieloch, Brandenburg, on May 11, 1924. His initial assignment in the Waffen-SS was with the 10th Company of SS Infantry Regiment 4 (motorized) *Langemarck*, when the second battalion of the regiment became the second battalion of the *Das Reich* panzer regiment. He transferred to the 6th Company of the panzer regiment. He was assigned to the Tiger company of the *Das Reich* effective November 15, 1942. *SS-Panzerschütze* Märker was mortally wounded on July 5, the first day of the offensive, and died later that day at a SS medical facility at Streletskoye.[67] Although his name is mentioned at the German War Cemetery at Kursk–Besedino, his remains have never been found and identified.

Erwin Malsch. Born on December 12, 1924, at Steinbach, Thuringia, Erwin Malsch—who was a trained machinist—joined the company as an *SS-Panzeroberschütze* in February 1943. During the offensive he served as a driver on a Tiger. He was later wounded in action near Hill 181.1, northeast of Murafa, Ukraine. After recovery, he was assigned to the SS Panzer Training and Replacement Regiment in Beneschau, in Bohemia. During the war he was single. Erwin Malsch died in 1999.[68]

Waldemar Menninger. Born in Karlsbad, Czechoslovakia (Sudetenland), on April 3, 1925, ethnic German Waldemar Menninger joined the Hitler Youth on April 1, 1933. He entered the Waffen-SS on September 15, 1942; he had finished high school and stood 6'0" tall. He joined the 8th (Heavy) Company in February 1943 and joined the Nazi Party on April 20, 1943, with party number 9522490. As an *SS-Sturmmann*, Menninger served in a Tiger at Kursk and stayed in the company until November 11, 1943, and later served in the 102nd SS Heavy Panzer Detachment. He received the Iron Cross Second Class on August 4, 1943. He was promoted to *SS-Unterscharführer* on November 11, 1943—and now in the officer candidate system—an *SS-Standartenoberjunker* on April 1, 1944. On June 5, 1944, Menninger received orders to report to the SS Panzer Training Detachment at Seelager, in western Latvia. Waldemar was commissioned an *SS-Untersturmführer* on June 21, 1944. He was assigned to Officer Candidate School 3 in Königsbrück, near Dresden, in January 1945, when he submitted required paperwork for marriage. His days were numbered, as Waldemar Menninger was killed on February 13, 1945, during the first day of the massive Allied combined air attack on Dresden, Germany.[69]

Kurt Meyer. *SS-Rottenführer* Kurt Meyer was born on February 18, 1922, in Uetersen, Pinneberg, in Schleswig-Holstein. Entering the Waffen-SS on September 30, 1940, he served as a sharpshooter in the 6th Company of SS Infantry Regiment *Germania* from 1940 to April 1942. He was promoted to *SS-Sturmmann* on August 1, 1941. He was admitted to the German military hospital in Lublin for undisclosed reasons in 1942, then transferred to the SS Panzer Replacement Regiment at Weimar, with a subsequent assignment to the 8th (Heavy) Company on November 15, 1942.[70]

It appears that Meyer served in the company during the Kharkov fighting in February–March 1943 and received a Panzer Battle Badge in Silver on March 29, 1943, serving as a gunner in Tiger 813; he was elevated to *SS-Rottenführer* on April 1, 1943. At Kursk, he was the gunner for Tiger **S11** in the First Platoon, but when the company commander switched from **S01** to **S02** on July 6, Meyer became his new gunner. He was decorated with the Iron Cross Second Class on August 4, 1943; he later received the Iron Cross First Class. Kurt was promoted to *SS-Unterscharführer* on October 1, 1943, when he was believed to have twelve enemy tank kills.[71] Meyer also served later in Normandy with the First Platoon in the 1st Company of the 102nd SS Heavy Panzer Detachment as the gunner for Tiger 111 and held the same position later on King Tiger 101 in the 1st Company of the 502nd SS Heavy Panzer Detachment. British soldiers later captured him and he was taken to a prisoner of war camp in England. Surviving his internment, Kurt Meyer died in December 2009.[72]

Kurt Mohrbacher. *SS-Unterscharführer* Kurt Mohrbacher was born on December 28, 1921, at Schmittweiler, near Bad Kreuznach. He commanded a Mark III N panzer (854) during the fighting around Kharkov in February–March 1943 and received a Panzer Battle Badge in Silver, as well as an Iron Cross Second Class on March 21, 1943. At Kursk Mohrbacher commanded Tiger **S14** in the First Platoon. Kurt Mohrbacher was killed in action on August 26, 1943, at the Korotych collective farm in the Ukraine while on Tiger S13.[73]

Anton Mühldorfer. Anton "Toni" Mühldorfer was born in Regensburg, Bavaria, on May 31, 1924. The son of a salesman, he was a member of the Hitler Youth from May 1, 1933, to July 1, 1942. After finishing trade school Toni also became a salesman. Joining the Waffen-SS on September 15, 1942, he was blond with blue eyes, Catholic, and stood 5'7" tall. Serving with the company at Kharkov, he received the Panzer Battle Badge in Silver on March 27, 1943. During the Kursk Offensive he served as the radio operator in **S22** in the Second Platoon. In spring 1944, Anton joined the Second Platoon in the 1st Company of the 102nd SS Heavy Panzer Detachment as a radio operator in Tiger 123; he later shortly served as the gunner in Tiger 121; he was injured on August 18, 1944, when Tiger 121 drove into a bomb crater. In 1945, he was assigned to the 1st Company of the 502nd SS Heavy Panzer Detachment as a radio operator in King Tiger 122, and later 123. He was in one of the last handful of remaining Tigers to attempt to break out of the Halbe Pocket south of Berlin on April 28, 1945. Married and the father of two boys and two girls, he died in Regensburg on November 18, 2018. His wife, Maria, his sons and daughters, and several grandchildren survived him. He was buried at the Catholic Cemetery in Regensburg on November 23, 2018.[74]

Arno Nienke. Born in Kiupeln, East Prussia, on June 28, 1924, Arno Nienke served in the 2nd Company of the *Das Reich* panzer regiment until November 15, 1942, when he transferred to the 8th (Heavy) Company. At Kursk *SS-Sturmmann* Nienke served as a driver in a Tiger. He later held the same position in the 3rd Company of the 102nd SS Heavy Panzer Detachment, and from October 1944, the 3rd Company of the 502nd SS Heavy Panzer Detachment. Now an *SS-Rottenführer*, he was killed in action on March 27, 1945, near Gorgast, Brandenburg, just west of Küstrin, as the driver for *SS-Untersturmführer* Willy Biber in King Tiger 311, when the vehicle was immobilized by an antitank mine that destroyed its left track. After Biber went for help the crew remained with the tank until they were attacked by Russian infantry. *SS-Rottenführer* Nienke was observed seeking cover in a shell crater about ten meters away. One account posits that a mortar round from the opposing Soviet 47th Guards Rifle Division subsequently struck him in the head, instantly killing Arno Nienke.[75]

Werner Obenaus. *SS-Sturmmann*—he was promoted to this rank on June 30, 1943—Werner Obenaus was born on November 27, 1924. At Kursk, he was the loader in Tiger **S31**, in the Second Platoon. He is believed to have been wounded on October 21, 1942, and left the company for a military hospital. On September 29, 1943, Werner Obenaus was placed on orders for a future assignment to the SS Panzer Training and Replacement Regiment at Beneschau.[76]

Ernst Pleger. Born on April 6, 1920, Ernst Pleger served in the 9th Company of SS Infantry Regiment 4 (motorized) *Langemarck* until late October 1942, when the second battalion of the regiment became the second battalion of the *Das Reich* panzer regiment. He was assigned to the Tiger company of the *Das Reich* effective November 15, 1942. As an *SS-Rottenführer* he served as a driver during the Kursk Offensive. In 1944, Pleger was assigned to the 1st Company of the 102nd SS Heavy Panzer Detachment, where he was the driver for Alois Kalss in Tiger 141. His personnel file has information that he was reported missing in action on August 19, 1944.[77]

Heinz Ramm. Heinz "Heiner" Ramm was born in Ruthe, in the Hildesheim district, on March 6, 1922. He joined the Hitler Youth in 1930, and later finished eighth grade of school, hoping to become an administrator. Ramm worked in the Reich Work Service from February 1 to September 27, 1941. Entering the Waffen-SS on October 1941, he stood 5'9" tall. Ramm first served in the 6th Company of SS Infantry Regiment 4 (motorized) *Langemarck* until fall 1942, when the second battalion of the regiment became the second battalion of the *Das Reich* panzer regiment. He was assigned to the Tiger company of the *Das Reich* effective November 15, 1942. *SS-Sturmmann* Ramm served in the company during the Kursk Offensive as a gunner in Tiger **S32** in the Third Platoon. He was the recipient of the Eastern Front Medal and the Panzer Battle Badge in Silver. In 1944, he was transferred to the 1st Company of the 102nd SS Heavy Panzer Detachment and served as the gunner for Alois Kalss in Tiger 141. Tabbed a future officer, Ramm was promoted to *SS-Rottenführer* on November 1, 1943; *SS-Unterscharführer* on April 22, 1944; *SS-Scharführer* on June 1, 1944; *SS-Oberscharführer* on July 1, 1944; and to *SS-Untersturmführer* on October 20, 1944. Heinz Ramm then was assigned to an SS panzer regiment.[78]

Albert Ratter. An ethnic German, Albert Ratter was born on June 5, 1909, in the Volhynia region of Russia; he left school after sixth grade. Moving to Germany at a young age and joining the Nazi Party on January 1, 1931, he served in the SA for one year. Married on September 28, 1937, and a land owner, he joined the SS early and received SS number 14736; he had blood type A. Albert spent three months in the German Army in early 1939. During this period he lived in Berlin-Köpenick. Standing 5'9" tall, *SS-Unterscharführer* Ratter fought at Kharkov as a commander of a Mark III N panzer (853) in the light platoon of the company, winning a Panzer Battle Badge in Silver on March 27, 1943. At Kursk, Ratter first served as the company troop leader, commanding Tiger **S02**. Early in the attack **S01** became non-operational and the company commander switched tanks, placing Albert in **S01** to supervise its repairs. Albert Ratter later was promoted to *SS-Untersturmführer* on October 20, 1944, and also received the Iron Cross Second Class.[79]

Walter Reibold. Germans who lived outside of Germany and Austria were termed *Volksdeutsch* ("Germans in regard to people or race"), provided they were not of Jewish origin. Although these ethnic Germans were sometimes the butt of jokes from Germans within the original boundaries of the Third Reich, they were considered a prime source of military manpower by the Waffen-SS and were encouraged to join.

An ethnic German, Protestant, and a farmer, Walter Reibold was born in the village of Schibach, in the Crimea, on January 10, 1919. Soviet authorities arrested his father on November 15, 1929, and sentenced him to five to ten years of hard labor; after 1937 the family never heard from him again. After the arrest Walter's mother took the rest of the family to Germany, arriving on December 6, 1929.[80]

Walter was in the Hitler Youth from December 1, 1934, to November 1, 1937. He joined the Waffen-SS on August 30, 1939, receiving SS number 363300, and was assigned to the 7th Company of the *Leibstandarte SS Adolf Hitler* Regiment. He fought in the Balkans and was promoted to *SS-Sturmmann* on May 1, 1941. Fighting in Russia, *SS-Sturmmann* Reibold was wounded in the face by a grenade splinter on July 28, 1941, and subsequently spent eight weeks in the hospital, during which time he was promoted to *SS-Rottenführer* on September 1, 1941; he received an Infantry Assault Badge in Bronze. His brother was wounded in Russia on October 17, 1941, and died of his injuries on February 1, 1942. After extensive time in training and replacement units Walter was assigned to the 8th (Heavy) Company in November 1942, and promoted to *SS-Unterscharführer* on December 1, 1942. At Kharkov he was the commander of a Mark III N panzer in the light platoon of the company.[81]

During Kursk, Walter served as a Tiger commander for **S23**. He was wounded during the offensive and returned to the unit on July 29, 1943, to be the commander once again of Tiger S23. In April 1944, he transferred to the 1st Company of the 102nd SS Heavy Panzer Detachment and commanded Tiger 123; he received an overdue Iron Cross Second Class about this time, previously winning the Panzer Battle Badge in Silver and the Wound Badge in Black. In October 1944, the unit was designated as the 1st Company of the 502nd SS Heavy Panzer Detachment and Walter commanded King Tiger 123. He remained in this unit until March 18, 1945. Walter Reibold married his fiancée Hedwig in May 1943; he survived the war and died in 1990.[82]

Johann Reinhardt. *SS-Oberscharführer* Johann Reinhardt was born on March 16, 1918, at St. Georgen, in the Steiermark region of Austria. He began his military service in the motorcycle battalion of the *Das Reich* in summer 1941, winning the Iron Cross Second Class on July 25, 1941. He subsequently served in the 8th Company of the SS Infantry Regiment 4 (motorized) *Langemarck*, when the second battalion of the regiment became the second battalion of the *Das Reich* panzer regiment. He was assigned to the Tiger company of the *Das Reich* effective November 15, 1942. He commanded Tiger 832 at Kharkov. At Kursk, he commanded Tiger **S33** in the Third Platoon for the duration of the offensive. Reinhardt was promoted to *SS-Hauptscharführer* on August 1, 1943; according to one source, the same day in the fighting, near the Mius River, he received his ninth wound of the war. Johann Reinhardt was killed in action on August 25, 1943, northwest of Korotych, Ukraine. He was posthumously awarded the German Cross in Gold on September 25, 1943. Johann Reinhardt's remains have never been identified, but may be buried among the unknowns at the German War Cemetery in Kiev.[83]

Walter Reininghaus. Born in Velbert, in North Rhine-Westphalia, on February 16, 1904, Walter Reininghaus attended high school, worked initially as a salesman, and then worked at the Hamburg Electric Works. He served in the 69th Infantry Regiment in the German Army from February 6 to May 6, 1939. Joining the SS on March 15, 1940, he stood 6' feet tall, weighed 195 pounds, and received SS number 393334. Walter immediately received training in the SS *Totenkopf* troops for three months. His rise in the organization was speedy: in May 1940, he attended the reserve leaders' course at the *SS-Junkerschule* Braunschweig, and he was promoted to *SS-Unterscharführer* on September 17, 1940, and to *SS-Oberscharführer* on November 1, 1940.[84]

Promoted to *SS-Untersturmführer* of Reserves on June 21, 1941, Walter Reininghaus served as a platoon leader in the 11th Company of SS Infantry Regiment 4 (motorized) *Langemarck* from that date until January 1942, before briefly being assigned to a replacement battalion. He had been wounded in the right shin by shrapnel on October 9, 1941, during fighting near Kaluga, Russia. He returned to the *Langemarck* on April 24, 1942, and remained there until October 24, 1942, when he became a staff officer in the 2nd Panzer Regiment. Walter was promoted to *SS-Obersturmführer* on November 9, 1942, and transferred to the Troop Training Grounds Bergen at Fallingbostel for Tiger training. He commanded Tiger 821 and the Second Platoon of the company at Kharkov in February–March 1943. His personnel file shows that he won the Iron Cross Second Class, the Iron Cross First Class, and the Wound Badge in Black.[85]

At the Kursk Offensive, Walter Reininghaus commanded Tiger **S21** as the Second Platoon leader. He was wounded on July 5, but remained with the unit; he was wounded again on July 7—by artillery shrapnel in his head and back—and again remained with the company. He took temporary command of the company on July 15, and may have commanded another Tiger at that point. On August 26, 1943, Reininghaus departed the company for an assignment on the division staff.[86]

He is believed to have commanded a Tiger I in the 102nd SS Heavy Panzer Detachment in Normandy. Reininghaus made his final rank of *SS-Hauptsturmführer* on November 9, 1944.

He was married on February 9, 1944, and was seconded to the SS Leader Staff Baltic on January 21, 1945. One source says that in February 1945, he became the supply officer (Ib) in the *Das Reich* and later served as the Ib in the 9th SS Panzer Division *Hohenstaufen* beginning in March 1945.[87] It appears that Walter Reininghaus may have returned to the Hamburg Electric Works after the war.

Herbert Reissmann. Born in Freiburg, in Breisgau in Baden, on April 3, 1921, auto mechanic Herbert Reissmann originally served in a Stuka unit in the Luftwaffe before transferring to the Waffen-SS on April 9, 1943, when he arrived at the 8th (Heavy) Company. Because of his previous experience he was made an *SS-Unterscharführer* immediately. During the Kursk Offensive Herbert Reissmann served as a driver in a Tiger.[88]

Hans-Joachim Ross. *SS-Rottenführer* Hans-Joachim Ross was born on July 19, 1924, in Priorei, near Hagen, in the Ruhr district. During the Kursk Offensive he served as the gunner of Tiger S33 in the Third Platoon. He received the Iron Cross Second Class on August 4, 1943.

Erwin Sandmeier. Born on April 6, 1923, Erwin Sandmaier was assigned to the 2nd Company of the *Das Reich* panzer detachment until November 15, 1942, when he was assigned to the 8th (Heavy) Company. On November 11, 1942, he started a special course for drivers at the Wegmann Company at Kassel. He fought with this unit as a driver in a tank, participating in the fighting around Kharkov in February–March 1943. *SS-Panzeroberschütze* Sandmeier then became the driver of a Tiger. During the Kursk Offensive Sandmeier was wounded in action on July 5, 1943, and subsequently spent four weeks in a military hospital. He returned to the company and was a driver in a Tiger until he transferred in 1944 to the 1st Company of the 102nd SS Heavy Panzer Detachment, where again he drove a Tiger. In 1945, Erwin Sandmaier was assigned to the 1st Company of the 502nd SS Heavy Panzer Detachment.[89]

Gerhard Sauer. Born on February 13, 1925, in Hamburg, Gerhard Sauer entered the Waffen-SS on September 15, 1942. He arrived at the company in February 1943, as an *SS-Panzerschütze*. He fought at Kursk and remained with the company until October 21, 1943, later serving in the SS Panzer Training and Replacement Regiment at Beneschau as an *SS-Sturmmann*. Gerhard Sauer was awarded the Iron Cross Second Class on August 4, 1943.[90]

Ernst Schäfer. Ernst Schäfer was born in Bochum, in North Rhine-Westphalia, on June 26, 1924. During the Kursk Offensive he served as a loader in Tiger **S24** in the Headquarters Platoon. *SS-Panzeroberschütze* Ernst Schäfer was killed in action about noon on July 7, 1943, when his Tiger was struck by enemy antitank fire from an armored train near a railroad embankment east of Kalinin; he was struck by enemy infantry fire when he tried to escape the vehicle. His remains have never been recovered.[91]

Karl Schäfer. Born on December 5, 1923, in Saarbrücken, and the son of a police officer, Karl Schäfer was a locksmith/metalworker by trade. He joined the Hitler Youth on June 1, 1932, and stayed until April 1, 1941. After graduating from grade school he found work at Krupp AG in Essen. He joined the Waffen-SS on April 1, 1941, and was assigned to the company on November 15, 1942, as an *SS-Sturmmann*; he stood 5'8" tall. On November 11, 1942, he was detached to a special course for drivers at the Wegmann Company at Kassel. Karl was assigned to the Tiger company of the *Das Reich* effective November 15, 1942. For the fighting at Kharkov he received the Panzer Battle Badge in Silver on March 29, 1943.[92]

Promoted to *SS-Rottenführer* on June 1, 1943, he served as a loader during the Kursk Offensive. He was wounded in the head by shell fragments in August 1943. Karl Schäfer transferred to the SS Panzer Training and Replacement Regiment at Dondagen on October 1, 1943. He was assigned to the SS Panzer Replacement Detachment at Sennelager when he submitted a request to marry his fiancée Lisa to the SS Race and Settlement Office on November 2, 1944. In January 1945, Karl Schäfer was stationed at the town of Augustdorf, probably with the SS Replacement Brigade *Westfalen*.[93]

Werner Karl Wilhelm Georg Schäfer. Werner Schäfer hailed from Eschwege, in Hesse, where he was born on June 15, 1922. *SS-Unterscharführer* Schäfer commanded Tiger **S24** in the Second Platoon at Kursk until Karl-Heinz Lorenz took temporary command. He was wounded on July 7, when an antitank round struck the vehicle. He appears to have died of these wounds eleven days later on July 18, at an aid station near Ssawodskoje. His remains have never been identified; it is possible that they rest in the German War Cemetery at Kharkov among the unknown.[94]

Horst Schleusner. Horst Schleusner was born on January 16, 1924. He served as a motorcycle driver on the staff of the First Battalion of the 2nd Panzer Regiment until December 1942, when he was assigned to the SS Replacement and Training Detachment at Weimar-Buchenwald. *SS-Unterscharführer* Schleusner served as the commander of Tiger **S12** in the First Platoon at Kursk. Horst Schleusner is believed to have served later at Normandy with the 102nd SS Heavy Panzer Detachment and is reported to have destroyed twenty-six enemy tanks in the war.

Fritz Schmid. Fritz Schmid was born on February 8, 1923, in Eschendorf, near Deggendorf, in Lower Bavaria. A locksmith by trade, Fritz grew up as a Catholic. He was assigned to the company in late fall 1942. *SS-Sturmmann* Schmid served as the driver for Tiger **S12** in the First Platoon during the Kursk Offensive. He was wounded about October 1, 1943. After recovering, he briefly returned to the company and then transferred to the 1st Company of the 102nd SS Heavy Panzer Detachment, and subsequently to the 1st Company of the 502nd SS Heavy Panzer Detachment; it appears that he served in the recovery and maintenance sections of both. He applied to be married to his fiancée Hildegard in November 1944. Promoted to *SS-Unterscharführer* on November 9, 1944, Fritz Schmid probably was killed in action during the Halbe breakout on April 30, 1945. During the war Fritz received the Iron Cross Second Class on August 20, 1943.[95]

Georg Schmidt. Georg Schmidt was born on April 13, 1925, in Zadel, Silesia; he attended technical school, then became an administrator in the land department of Frankenstein, in Lower Silesia. He also served in the Hitler Youth from March 1, 1933, to May 4, 1942. He joined the Waffen-SS that latter date, measuring 5'8" tall. After eleven months at the SS Panzer Replacement Detachment at Weimar-Buchenwald he joined the 8th (Heavy) Company in the Ukraine on April 15, 1943, and became a gunner in a Tiger. *SS-Sturmmann* Schmidt was a Tiger gunner in the company during the Kursk Offensive. He had an Iron Cross Second Class, a Panzer Battle Badge in Silver, and a Wound Badge in Black. Schmidt was promoted to *SS-Unterscharführer* on November 1, 1943, and assigned to the Panzer Troops School at Putlos on November 17. He was subsequently promoted to *SS-Junker* on June 1, 1944; to *SS-Oberjunker* on July 8, 1944; and to *SS-Untersturmführer* on October 20, 1944. Single, Georg Schmidt may have been assigned to the *Totenkopf* division after commissioning.[96]

Wilhelm Schmidt. Wilhelm Schmidt was born in Thiersheim, near Wunsiedel in Bavaria, on March 1, 1912. Promoted to the rank *SS-Unterscharführer* on July 1, 1941, he served in the 10th Company of SS Infantry Regiment 4 (motorized) *Langemarck* until October 1942, when the second battalion of the regiment became the second battalion of the *Das Reich* panzer regiment. He joined the Tiger company of the *Das Reich* effective November 15, 1942. Wilhelm Schmidt was assigned as the commander of Tiger **S24** in the Second Platoon during the Kursk Offensive. He was promoted to *SS-Oberscharführer* on August 1, 1943. Schmidt served later at Normandy with the First Platoon in the 1st Company of the 102nd SS Heavy Panzer Detachment, where he commanded Tiger 114, and later with the 1st Company of the 502nd Heavy Panzer Company, where he commanded King Tiger 112. He was badly wounded on April 25, 1945, in the Halbe Pocket. During the war he won the Iron Cross Second Class and the Panzer Battle Badge in Silver. After the war Wilhelm Schmidt ran a shoe store before he died in 1961.[97]

Ludwig Schnabel. *SS-Sturmmann* Schnabel served as a loader in the 8th (Heavy) Company at Kursk. As an *SS-Rottenführer*, he served as a gunner in the 1st Company of the 502nd SS Heavy Panzer Detachment at Normandy in 1944. As an *SS-Unterscharführer*, Ludwig Schnabel commanded King Tiger 114 in the First Platoon of the 1st Company in the 502nd SS Heavy Panzer Detachment on the Oder Front in 1945.[98]

Heinz Schöneberg. Heinz Schöneberg was born on August 12, 1924, at Hohendodeleben, near Magdeburg, in Saxony-Anhalt. *SS-Panzerschütze* Heinz Schöneberg was wounded on July 11, 1943, in Luchki (North) during the Kursk Offensive. He died of his wounds at the Luftwaffe District Hospital 2/VIII near Dnipro (called Dnipropetrovsk until May 2016) on July 13, 1943. Heinz Schöneberg's remains are probably buried among the unknowns at the German War Cemetery at Kharkov.[99]

Konrad Schweigert. Born in Großhaslach, near Ansbach in Bavaria, on March 24, 1920—the son of musician Michael Schweigert and Ludwina Katharina Hausmann—Konrad Schweigert attended elementary school and became a salesman. He joined the Waffen-SS on January 1, 1937, with SS number 285058 and was assigned to SS Infantry Regiment *Deutschland*. On September 6, 1939, he was seriously wounded in the left leg, resulting in two years of hospitalization and a leg that was four inches shorter than the other. After recuperating Konrad reported to Weimar-Buchenwald and panzer training. He was promoted to *SS-Unterscharführer* in December 1942, and was assigned to the *Das Reich* Tiger company.

Standing 5'10" tall, *SS-Unterscharführer* Schweigert commanded Tiger **S12** in the First Platoon during the Kursk Offensive. During the conflict Schweigert received the Iron Cross Second Class, the Iron Cross First Class (December 8, 1943), and the Panzer Battle Badge in Silver. He was promoted to *SS-Oberscharführer* on December 1, 1943, and to *SS-Untersturmführer* on January 1, 1945, after he finished the *SS-Junkerschule* at Bad Tölz. At the same time he joined the 502nd SS Heavy Panzer Detachment. He had previously served in the 1st Company of the 102nd SS Heavy Panzer Detachment.[100] Konrad Schweigert died in December 2005. He was regarded by many of the men in the 8th (Heavy) Company as being a friendly comrade.[101]

Heinz Seidel. Heinz Seidel was born on January 7, 1924, in Gelsenkirchen, the son of Felix Seidel, a dance instructor. Heinz joined the Hitler Youth in 1934 at age ten, later attended high school, then got a job in the German railway system. When he joined the Waffen-SS on September 15, 1942, he stood 5'8" tall. *SS-Panzeroberschütze* Seidel served in the company during the Kursk Offensive; during his career he received the Iron Cross Second Class and the Panzer Battle Badge in Silver. He was promoted to *SS-Unterscharführer* on November 1, 1943; on November 6, 1943, he returned to Germany to attend an SS Leader Candidate course for panzer soldiers at the Army Panzer Troops School at Putlos, Germany, along the Baltic coast. He subsequently was promoted to *SS-Junker* on March 1, 1944; to *SS-Oberjunker* on April 1, 1944; and to *SS-Untersturmführer* on June 21, 1944. Heinz Seidel was single.[102] After the war he returned to Gelsenkirchen, where he initially was a laborer. After the shock of the war subsided he followed in his father's footsteps and became a director of the *Dance Institute Seidel* in Gelsenkirchen. Heinz Seidel died on July 18, 2015, in the Buer suburb of Gelsenkirchen.[103]

Karl Skerbinz. *SS-Unterscharführer* Karl Skerbinz was born on April 7, 1922. At Kursk he commanded Tiger **S12** in the First Platoon for part of the offensive. He was later reduced in rank to *SS-Panzerschütze* for unmilitary conduct. After receiving the Panzer Battle Badge in Silver and the Wound Badge in Black, he joined the 1st Company of the 102nd SS Heavy Panzer Detachment on February 23, 1944, as a gunner. In 1945, he was assigned as a gunner to the 1st Company of the 502nd SS Heavy Panzer Detachment. Some sources state that he destroyed a total of twenty-six enemy tanks in the war.[104] It appears that Karl Skerbinz lived in Augsburg, Bavaria, after the war at Klinkertorstraße 1 and was a truck driver.[105]

Günter Skribelka. Günter Skribelka was born in Berlin on June 27, 1925. He joined the Hitler Youth on April 1, 1935, at the age of nine. After grade school Günter wanted to be a cartographer; he was Protestant. However, he had a small problem; his father had been a Communist and was imprisoned for a year. Times were tough, but Günter ran into an Allgemeine-SS officer and told him that he wanted to volunteer for service; Günter subsequently received the paperwork, and as he later said, he was fortunate that his parents did not have to sign the form.

When he joined the Waffen-SS on September 15, 1942, Günter stood 5'8" tall; he had blue eyes and blond hair. He reported to the 6th Company of the SS Signal Training and Replacement Regiment at SS Nürnberg for communications training. Joining the company on December 9, 1942, *SS-Funker* Günter Skribelka served as a radio operator and received a Panzer Battle Badge in Silver for fighting at Kharkov on March 27, 1943. For the Kursk Offensive Günter Skribelka served as the radio operator in Tiger **S31**, in the Third Platoon of the 8th (Heavy) Company.

Concerning the fighting at Kursk, Günter later recalled: "Sometimes it got up to 122°F in the turret; it was crazy hot, and we were thirsty. All we had left was a jerry can filled with water, from which I had drunk in my desperation. After a week I got a severe, scabby rash. The doctor told me that it was gas poisoning, kidney poisoning."

In September 1943, Skribelka fell ill and was taken to a field hospital, where he was diagnosed with jaundice (no doubt brought on by the water consumption episode at Kursk); he subsequently was transferred to a hospital at Poltava, but not before he left his home address with his fellow comrades in the company. He never received any letters from them and after the war found out the reason: his mother had destroyed all of them as they arrived. After subsequently staying at another medical facility at Altenburg in Thuringia, Günter Skribelka spent three weeks at home on convalescent leave. He then attended a non-commissioned officer's course at the SS Signal School in Metz, France, from November 15, 1943, to March 10, 1944. He subsequently was assigned to the 4th Company of the SS Signal Training and Replacement Detachment 5 at Sterzing, in the South Tyrol. While there he received the Iron Cross Second Class.

The British captured him near Sterzing at the end of the war and he spent time at a prisoner of war camp at Brindisi, Italy. He attempted to escape but was returned to the camp. After being discharged Skribelka returned to Berlin, where he worked as an auditor at a roofing felt company.

Günter Skribelka died of a heart attack at Brieselang, just west of Spandau near Berlin, on July 13, 2018—exactly seventy-five years after the high water mark of the offensive. A father, grandfather, and great-grandfather, Günter is buried there in the *Waldfriedhof*. His family quoted Victor Hugo in their announcement of his death: "You are no longer where you were, but you are everywhere that we are."[106]

Franz Stemann. Born on December 5, 1920, at Scheidingen, near Soest in North Rhine-Westphalia, *SS-Rottenführer* Franz Stemann served in the 3rd Company of the *Das Reich* panzer detachment before transferring to the 8th (Heavy) Company in November 1942. On November 11, 1942, he was detached to a special course for drivers at the Wegmann Company at Kassel. After Kharkov he received a Panzer Battle Badge in Silver. At Kursk, he served as the driver of Tiger **S02** in the Headquarters Platoon. Franz was seriously wounded in action at about 1200 hours on July 7, 1943, two kilometers east of Kalinin, when he was struck by six pieces of shrapnel caused by an antitank round. After recovering in a medical facility, Franz Stemann was assigned to an SS Panzer Training and Replacement Regiment before returning to the company in October. *SS-Unterscharführer* Stemann was reassigned to the 1st Company of the 102nd SS Heavy Panzer Detachment, where he was the driver of Tiger 111, and later Tiger 121; he was injured on August 18, 1944, when he drove Tiger 121 into a bomb crater. When the unit was reorganized as the 1st Company of the 502nd SS Heavy Panzer Detachment Franz Stemann remained with this unit until the end of the war, probably in the recovery and maintenance sections.[107]

Horst Stolzenberg. *SS-Sturmmann* Horst Stolzenberg was assigned to the 8th (Heavy) Company in February 1943. During the Kursk Offensive he served as a Tiger driver. In 1944, he was assigned to the 1st Company of the 102nd SS Heavy Panzer Detachment; when the unit reorganized he was assigned to the 1st Company of the 502nd SS Heavy Panzer Detachment until May 6, 1945, when he was killed.[108]

Johann Stuttenecker. Johann Stuttenecker was born on June 16, 1919, in the village of Perwald, in the Lower Danube region of Austria. He served in an unidentified capacity in the company but received an Iron Cross Second Class for his efforts.

Heinz Tensfeld. It was difficult for a twenty-year-old in the SS Regiment *Deutschland* in the Waffen-SS—if your father was already an *SS-Oberführer*. When you were commissioned an *SS-Untersturmführer* two years later, there were certain to be a few tongues wagging in the shadows that part of your rapid elevation was your father—who was now an *SS-Brigadeführer*. However, that was nothing compared to what you had to endure a few months after that when you were reduced in rank back to an enlisted man for unsoldierly conduct.

Heinz Tensfeld, the first son of *SS-Brigadeführer* and police general Willy Tensfeld, was born on May 11, 1919, in Kiel. He joined the SS Regiment *Deutschland* in the Waffen-SS on April 4, 1939, with SS number 400139. Standing almost 5'11" tall, he soon attended the *SS-Junkerschule* at Bad Tölz, and later the *SS-Junkerschule* at Braunschweig. Assigned to the 1st SS Brigade (Motorized), he became an *SS-Untersturmführer* on April 20, 1941, but received a severe reprimand for inappropriate severity toward his subordinates and was reduced in rank to *SS-Oberscharführer* on September 9, 1941. Tensfeld worked his way back to *SS-Untersturmführer* on January 30, 1942, and was assigned to SS Infantry Regiment 4 (motorized) *Langemarck*; by December 1942, he was assigned as the Third Platoon leader of the 4th Company in the 2nd Panzer Regiment. Heinz's younger brother Horst was killed in action as an *SS-Rottenführer* on November 6, 1942. Heinz married Lieselotte Wrede on January 1, 1943, and on January 15, 1943, the Waffen-SS assigned Heinz Tensfeld to the headquarters of the panzer regiment of the *Das Reich*; in this formation he was promoted to *SS-Obersturmführer* on April 20, 1943.[109]

The afternoon of July 11, 1943, during the Kursk Offensive, the commander of the 2nd Panzer Regiment ordered Tensfeld to depart the First Battalion of the regiment and report to the 8th (Heavy) Company to become the leader of the First Platoon—the incumbent platoon leader *SS-Obersturmführer* Philipp Theiss having been elevated to become the acting company commander when *SS-Hauptsturmführer* Herbert Zimmermann was wounded in the arm. Tensfeld did so, and also became the commander of Tiger **S11**. Two days later **S11** was struck by enemy antitank fire near Vinogradovka and Tensfeld abandoned the vehicle with the rest of the crew, except for the driver, who remained with the vehicle.

During his roller-coaster career, Heinz Tensfeld received the Iron Cross Second Class, the Iron Cross First Class (August 4, 1943), the Infantry Assault Badge in Silver, the Wound Badge in Silver, the Panzer Battle Badge, and the Honor Roll Clasp; the last for stopping, with just his own Tiger, an attack by seventeen enemy T-34s on August 8, 1943, during which he destroyed ten in the thirty-minute fight.[110] He was wounded in action on August 25, 1943, northwest of Korotych, Ukraine. Tensfeld later became the acting commander of the company and was killed in action on November 16, 1943, near Gralimki, Ukraine, south of Kiev. The previous day Heinz Tensfeld was announced as a winner of the Honor Roll Clasp for distinguishing himself in combat. He also received a posthumous promotion to *SS-Hauptsturmführer* on December 8, 1912.[111] The British captured *SS-Brigadeführer* Willy Tensfeld in May 1945, charged him with war crimes, and held him as a prisoner for two years. Willy Tensfeld was acquitted and died on September 2, 1982, in Hamburg.

Philipp August Eugen Theiss. Philipp Theiss was born in Neunkirchen, in the Saarland, on May 22, 1918, although he grew up in Frankfurt and often spoke with a Hessian dialect.[112] He joined the Waffen-SS on December 1, 1936, beginning his career in the signal troops; he subsequently took part in the march into Austria, the Sudetenland, and Poland. Promoted to *SS-Untersturmführer* on April 20, 1941, during the Balkan campaign, Philipp Theiss was assigned as a platoon leader in the 1st Company of SS Infantry Regiment *Der Führer* before being wounded through his right upper arm on October 9, 1941, near Ssamoty. Philipp had received an Iron Cross Second Class on July 29, 1941. After his recovery Theiss transferred to the SS Infantry Regiment 4 (motorized) *Langemarck* and remained with the unit until it was converted to a panzer detachment in the *Das Reich*. On November 9, 1942, he was promoted to *SS-Obersturmführer* on November 9, 1942, and assigned to an army panzer course at Wünsdorf. He had experience in Tiger 811 at Kharkov in February–March 1943, receiving the Panzer Battle Badge in Silver on March 27, 1943.

At the beginning of the Kursk Offensive, *SS-Obersturmführer* Theiss commanded Tiger **S11** as the leader of the First Platoon. He held this position until July 11, when he assumed command of the company when *SS-Hauptsturmführer* Herbert Zimmermann was wounded in the arm. He probably commanded from Tiger **S01**. On July 15, 1943, about 1300 hours the 8th (Heavy) Company was roughly two kilometers east of Vinogradovka-Luchki (North) when an enemy antitank round hit the cupola of probably **S02** (as **S01** was by then damaged), commanded by *SS-Obersturmführer* Philipp Theiss, decapitating him. He was temporarily buried nearby, but the location remains unknown. He posthumously received an Iron Cross First Class. *Das Reich* Tiger historian Rüdiger Warnick wrote this about the officer: "Theiss was a highly idealistic, extremely positive and sensitive leader who, through his correctness and camaraderie, quickly gained the full respect of his men."[113]

Hans Haselböck, who was assigned to the company, held similar views of *SS-Obersturmführer* Philipp Theiss: "My memories of Theiss are only the best, he was, as one would say today, a real buddy, in contrast to Kalss, Baral, or Egger."[114]

Emil Theunis. The Waffen-SS had an extremely large contingent of foreign-born soldiers and Emil Theunis was one of them. Theunis was born in Paal, Flanders, Belgium, on December 20, 1924. He was assigned to SS Infantry Regiment 4 (motorized) *Langemarck* until the regiment became the second detachment of the *Das Reich* panzer regiment. Promoted to *SS-Sturmmann* on July 7, 1943, Emil Theunis was a gunner.[115] He was later assigned to the First Company of the 102nd SS Heavy Panzer Detachment in 1944 as a gunner, and still later to the First Company of the 502nd SS Heavy Panzer Detachment as a gunner in a King Tiger.[116]

Heinz Trautmann. During the Kursk Offensive, *SS-Unterscharführer* Heinz "Heini" Trautmann served as a loader in a Tiger in the company. He later fought in Normandy as the radio operator, and later driver, in Tiger 134, in the Third Platoon of the 102nd SS Heavy Panzer Detachment; he received the Panzer Battle Badge in Silver on August 25, 1944; the Iron Cross First Class on September 1, 1944; and the Panzer Battle Badge in Silver for 25 Assaults on September 21, 1944; as well as two Tank Destruction Badges. Heinz Trautmann survived the war. He later returned to Hill 112 in Normandy, where he had fought during the war.[117]

Artur Ulmer. Born on June 15, 1914, at Argenau, Pomerania, *SS-Unterscharführer* Artur Ulmer served as the commander of Tiger **S34** in the Third Platoon of the 8th (Heavy) Company during the first few days of the Kursk Offensive. He was reported wounded in action on July 7, 1943; he died at Field Hospital 2/992 in Kharkov on July 15, 1943; a form in his personnel file indicates that he died on July 13. He was posthumously awarded an Iron Cross Second Class on July 22, 1943. His remains were never located nor identified after the war.[118]

Paul Ullrich. Paul Ullrich was born in Wernshausen, near Meiningen in Thuringia, on June 19, 1909. A Protestant, he graduated from trade school for small iron and steel and became a mechanic, but lost his job in 1931. He joined the Allgemeine-SS in 1933, with SS number 167098. In 1936, he found work in the BMW factory in Eisenach. Married, *SS-Sturmmann* Paul Ullrich served in the 8th (Heavy) Company during the Kursk Offensive, but we do not know what crew position or Tiger he was in. He later was assigned to the 102nd SS Heavy Panzer Detachment in Normandy and the 502nd SS Heavy Panzer Detachment on the Oder Front.[119]

Herbert Erich Walter. Herbert Walter was born in Hirschberg im Riesengebirge, in Lower Silesia (today Jelenia Góra, Poland), on August 8, 1922. He joined the Waffen-SS on October 15, 1940, and was promoted to *SS-Rottenführer* on November 1, 1942. He served on the crew of a Tiger in the 8th (Heavy) Company during the Kursk Offensive in an unknown capacity. He was single. Herbert Walter received the Iron Cross Second Class on September 14, 1944, as a member of the First Company of the 102nd SS Heavy Panzer Detachment.[120]

Emil Weissfloch. Born on November 10, 1924, in Langenau, Württemberg. He joined the Waffen-SS on April 15, 1942, and was assigned to the 8th (Heavy) Company in an unknown position in a Tiger. Emil was wounded in action during the offensive on July 8 and July 15, 1943. *SS-Gruppenführer* Walter Krüger approved and signed the certificate for his Iron Cross Second Class on August 4, 1943. Wounded a third time on April 12, 1944, he received the wound Badge in silver on June 6, 1944, at a reserve hospital in Füssen, Bavaria. That was it for his Tiger crew days, but *SS-Sturmmann* Weissfloch later served in the recovery and maintenance sections in the 1st Company of the 102nd SS Heavy Panzer Detachment in Normandy in 1944, and the same company of the 502nd SS Heavy Panzer Detachment on the Oder Front in 1945.[121]

Anton Wilfling. Anton Wilfling was born on December 20, 1922, in Pircha, Austria. He joined the Waffen-SS on January 31, 1941, and was assigned to the Third Company of the 2nd Panzer Regiment in the *Das Reich* on April 20, 1942. Promoted to *SS-Sturmmann* on July 1, 1942, he was assigned to the 8th (Heavy) Company in April 1943; on April 1, 1943, he was promoted to *SS-Rottenführer*.[122]

Heinz Wilken. Born at Warksow, Rügen Island, on November 20, 1922, *SS-Rottenführer* Wilken served as the gunner in Tiger **S24** July 5–7, but was seriously wounded in action on July 7. Medics evacuated him to the SS Medical Company 2/41 casualty collection point near Luchki (South). Heinz died the following day. His remains are not believed to have been interred after the war in any German military cemetery.[123]

Eduard Woll. Born December 14, 1918, in Düppenweiler, in the Saar, Eduard "Eddi" Woll first served in the Luftwaffe in the 5th Flight of *Jagdgeschwader* 52 until April 9, 1943, when he was transferred into the Waffen-SS; he stood 5'7" tall. At Kursk, *SS-Rottenführer* Woll served as the driver of Tiger **S14** in the First Platoon. In April 1944, he reported to the 1st Company of the 102nd SS Heavy Panzer Detachment, where he was the driver of Tiger 132. In October 1944, the unit was designated the 1st Company of the 502nd SS Heavy Panzer Detachment; in this unit he drove King Tigers 101, 102, and 121. Eduard married his fiancée Aneliese on February 23, 1945. Eduard Woll was in one of the last remaining Tigers to attempt to break out of the Halbe Pocket south of Berlin on April 28, 1945. During the war he earned the Panzer Battle Badge in Silver and the Wound Badge in Black.[124]

Rudolf Zacharias. Born on June 29, 1921, in East Prussia, Rudolf Zacharias entered the Waffen-SS on May 20, 1941. Promoted to *SS-Rottenführer* on July 1, 1943, Rudolf Zacharias served as a gunner in a Tiger in the 8th (Heavy) Company until he was wounded in action on July 12, 1943, near Luchki (North). He remained in the unit until October 1, 1943, when he was assigned to the SS Panzer Training and Replacement Regiment at Beneschau.[125]

Joachim Zimbehl. Joachim was born in Königsberg, East Prussia, on October 22, 1921. He entered the Waffen-SS on May 16, 1940. He was promoted to *SS-Rottenführer* on September 1, 1942. Single, he served as a gunner during the Kursk Offensive. At Normandy in 1944, Joachim Zimbehl served as a gunner in the 1st Company of the 102nd SS Heavy Panzer Detachment. Joachim was promoted to *SS-Unterscharführer* on September 1, 1944. At the end of the war *SS-Unterscharführer* Zimbehl served as a driver in the 1st Company of the 502nd SS Heavy Panzer Detachment southeast of Berlin.[126] During the war he earned the Iron Cross Second Class, the Panzer Battle Badge in Silver, and the Wound Badge in Silver. It appears that Joachim Zimbehl lived in Hannover after the war on Widemanstraße 10 and was a night watchman.[127]

Herbert Zimmermann. Born on May 31, 1916, at Eckartsberg, near Zittau in Saxony, Herbert Zimmermann was married with three children. He stood 5'10" tall and served in the Hitler Youth in 1933–34. Zimmermann entered the SS with SS number 242648 and initially served in the SS *Totenkopf* Regiment *Thüringen* before attending the *SS-Junkerschule* at Braunschweig in 1937. He was commissioned an *SS-Untersturmführer* on March 12, 1938. Herbert was promoted to *SS-Obersturmführer* on July 1, 1940; he won the Iron Cross Second Class and the Iron Cross First Class the same year as a platoon leader in an antitank detachment. From December 1940 to early 1942, Zimmermann served in the SS Division (Motorized) *Wiking* as the commander of the division's 1st Antitank Company, winning the General Assault Badge. Promoted to *SS-Hauptsturmführer* on January 30, 1942, he assumed command of the 8th (Heavy) Company on April 10, 1943, after commanding the 3rd Company of the panzer regiment.[128]

At Kursk, Zimmermann commanded the company beginning July 5 in Tiger **S01**, but when that vehicle was immobilized he likely transferred to **S02**, and remained with it while **S01** was in repairs. Zimmermann was wounded on July 7, and temporarily was evacuated for treatment. He was wounded in the arm, commanding **S01** when it returned to action on July 11, 1943. He received the German Cross in Gold on September 8, 1943. He served in the 102nd SS Heavy Panzer Detachment at Normandy in summer 1944. Herbert Zimmermann was killed in action on April 8, 1945, in the Ruhr Pocket; his remains are buried at the German War Cemetery at Breuna, Hesse, in Grave 209. At the time of his death *SS-Hauptsturmführer* Zimmermann was assigned to SS Panzer Brigade *Westfalen*, probably as the commander of the 1st SS Panzer Reconnaissance Training and Replacement Detachment in the SS Panzer Training and Replacement Detachment *Holzer*.[129]

Gerhard Kaempf of the 8th (Heavy) Company later recalled that Zimmermann was not particularly beloved and sometimes gave impossible commands to carry out, as if the driver could immediately turn the vehicle around. When that happened the driver would take his headset off and drive where he wanted to.[130]

9th (Heavy) Company, 3rd Panzer Regiment, SS Panzer Grenadier Division Totenkopf

Hans-Ludwig Bachmann. Hans-Ludwig Bachmann was born on November 29, 1923, in Frankfurt am Main. He received the Panzer Battle Badge in Silver in April 1943, presumably for combat in February and March around Kharkov. At Kursk, he drove Tiger **933** in the Third Platoon of the 9th (Heavy) Company. *SS-Sturmmann* Bachmann was killed in action at Hill 308, near Kolontaiv (Колонтаїв) in the Ukraine, on August 31, 1943. Driving Ludwig Lachner's Tiger, he survived a direct hit of artillery on the vehicle's rear deck, but noted that the strike had damaged the water cooler, and that the temperature of the coolant had risen to a precarious 248°F. The crew halted the vehicle and began inspecting the damage when another enemy artillery round struck, killing Hans-Ludwig. His remains are not in a German cemetery, but are reportedly buried near the village of Kubaschewka, near Poltava, Ukraine.[1]

Otto Ernst Baumann. Born on March 31, 1919, in Langenburg, in Württemberg, Otto Baumann joined the Waffen-SS on October 1, 1936. He was promoted to *SS-Unterscharführer* on October 1, 1938. Baumann served for several years in the SS Regiment *Deutschland*. Promoted to *SS-Scharführer* on February 1, 1942, he joined the *Totenkopf* panzer regiment on November 15, 1942, initially commanding a Mark IV panzer, then a Mark III in the 4th (Heavy) Company, and finally Tiger 443. He was awarded the Iron Cross Second Class and the Panzer Battle Badge in Silver on April 20, 1943, for his actions at Kharkov in February–March 1943.[2]

Promoted to *SS-Oberscharführer* on May 1, 1943, at Kursk he commanded Tiger **933** in the Third Platoon and was wounded in action at the end of July 1943. In September 1943, he transferred from the 9th (Heavy) Company of the *Totenkopf* to the 8th (Heavy) Company in *Das Reich*. On December 30, 1943, Otto Baumann joined the Second Platoon of the 1st Company of the 102nd SS Heavy Panzer Detachment, commanding Tiger 123, and remained in the unit until October 1, 1944, when he reported to the SS Panzer *Junker* Course at Königsbrück. Assigned to the SS Panzer Brigade *Westfalen*, Otto was promoted to *SS-Untersturmführer* on April 20, 1945, and was captured by US soldiers the following day.[3]

Willy Biber. Willy Biber was born in Thalwil, near Zürich, Switzerland, on June 8, 1915. His parents moved to Potsdam, Germany, when he was two years old; they later moved to Berlin. Before joining the SS he worked for the Edeka grocery company. During the fighting in the Ukraine in March 1943, Willy Biber commanded a Mark III M (long barrel) Panzer, turret number 423.[4] Standing 5'7" tall, *SS-Oberscharführer* Biber commanded Tiger **902** in the Headquarters Platoon during the Kursk Offensive. He received the Iron Cross Second Class on July 20, 1943, as well as the Panzer Battle Badge in Silver. That year he also received the Wound Badge in Black and on November 10, 1943, the Iron Cross First Class. He subsequently was promoted to *SS-Standartenjunker* on June 21, 1944; to *SS-Untersturmführer* on October 10, 1944; and was assigned to the 3rd Company of the 502nd SS Heavy Panzer Detachment at the end of the month, commanding the Second Platoon. Willy Biber was killed in action very early on the morning of March 23, 1945. Commanding King Tiger 321, the company was conducting a night attack from the village of Golzow toward the village of Gorgast, four miles west of the Oder River and Küstrin. There are two versions of what happened next. The first version was that King Tiger 321 bypassed the village of Alt Tucheband and was taken under fire by Soviet antitank guns; Willy Biber opened his hatch and was hit in the head by ricocheting shrapnel, tearing half of it off and killing him instantly. In the second version King Tiger 321 ran over a mine; Biber ordered the crew to remain inside while he dismounted to find another Tiger to assist them and he was never seen again.[5]

Fritz Biermeier. A great many soldiers in every army are brave. Many men in the Waffen-SS were brave, but only a few were declared to be so in writing by their division commander. Fritz Biermeier was one of those soldiers. In a 1944 recommendation for promotion, *SS-Brigadeführer* Hermann Priess, the *Totenkopf* commander, wrote this of Fritz Biermeier: "*SS-Hauptsturmführer* Biermeier is a brave and outstanding detachment leader, whose leadership is far above average. I endorse the recommendation for promotion to *SS-Sturmbannführer*."[6]

Fritz Biermeier was born on May 19, 1913, in Augsburg, in the state of Bavaria. He attended school through the tenth grade. An electrician by trade, he stood 5'8.5" tall when he joined the SS on November 1, 1933 (SS number 142869), and proceeded up the enlisted ranks. In his early enlisted days (1934–1936) he served in the guard detachment for the Dachau concentration camp. From April 1, 1937, to January 31, 1938, Biermeier attended the *SS-Junkerschule* at Braunschweig, and after some additional training was commissioned an *SS-Untersturmführer* on March 12, 1938. He returned to the 9th Guard Company at Dachau until September 1, 1939, at which time he joined the 1st SS *Totenkopf* Infantry Regiment and remained until July 27, 1941. He was promoted to *SS-Obersturmführer* on April 20, 1939. Biermeier received the Iron Cross Second Class on June 22, 1940, for his participation in the French Campaign as a platoon leader, and the Iron Cross First Class on October 7, 1941, for combat in Russia, during which he was seriously wounded near Luga on July 27, 1941. He also served as the adjutant for the Second Battalion of the regiment.[7]

Receiving the Wound Badge in Black on January 30, 1942, he then transferred to the panzer detachment of the *Das Reich* on February 7, 1942, remaining with the unit for two months at Wildflecken training area in northwest Bavaria, then returning to the *Totenkopf*. From June 5, 1942, to October 19, 1942, *SS-Obersturmführer* Biermeier served with SS Battlegroup Jeckeln (commanded by *SS-Obergruppenführer* Friedrich Jeckeln), a unit that conducted anti-partisan operations behind German lines in central Russia, but that also was later shown to have killed civilians. Promoted to *SS-Hauptsturmführer* on January 30, 1943, he received the Panzer Battle Badge in Silver on March 23, 1942, for combat near Kharkov the previous two months. Biermeier then returned to the *Totenkopf* in time to stand up a new heavy panzer company with the new Tiger tank.[8] At Kursk, he served as the commander of the 9th (Heavy) Company through July 8, 1943, and in this position also commanded Tiger **901** in the Headquarters Platoon. On July 8, he was elevated to command of the Second Battalion of the 3rd Panzer Regiment and he departed the company.

Fritz Biermeier was awarded the Knight's Cross of the Iron Cross on December 10, 1943, for actions near Myschelovka on November 14, 1943, when his small battle group of eleven panzers knocked out thirty-eight T-34 tanks; he was subsequently promoted to *SS-Sturmbannführer* on April 20, 1944.[9]

Still in command of the Second Battalion of the 3rd SS Panzer Regiment, Fritz Biermeier was killed in action near Modlin, Poland, on October 11, 1944. His remains were initially buried at a temporary German cemetery at Modlin in Field B in Grave Number 3. He was posthumously awarded the Oak Leaves to the Knight's Cross on December 26, 1944, for actions in August and September 1944 against large Soviet armored formations. Fritz Biermeier is buried in an end grave at the German War Cemetery at Nowy Dwór Mazowiecki, near Modlin, Poland. He was married at the time of his death.[10]

Karl Blattmann. Karl Blattmann was born in Furtwangen, in the Black Forest, on December 30, 1925. He holds a special distinction in this study: he was the youngest soldier of the three companies—at age seventeen years, six months—to fight in a Tiger during the Kursk Offensive; he is believed to have been the driver of Tiger **912** in the First Platoon. Heinz would go on to win the Iron Cross Second Class on November 10, 1943. On April 10, 1945, Blattmann was wounded during the fighting for Vienna. He was evacuated to a Waffen-SS medical facility in the city but was captured by Soviet troops; nevertheless, he survived the war. Karl Blattmann died on February 12, 2001.[11]

Hein Bode. *SS-Unterscharführer* Hein Bode commanded Tiger **923** in the Second Platoon of the 9th (Heavy) Company during the Kursk Offensive. He was also a former member of the *Führer* Escort Detachment. Later *SS-Oberscharführer* Bode commanded a Tiger in the 1st Company of the 101st SS Heavy Panzer Detachment. On January 6, 1944, he reported to the Sennelager training facility to receive six of the first King Tigers to be sent from the factory to the field. As of December 16, 1944, Hein Bode commanded King Tiger 112 in the First Platoon in the 1st Company of the 501st SS Heavy SS Panzer Detachment at the Battle of the Bulge.

Franz Böhm. Franz Böhm was born at Adelsdorf, near Erlangen in Bavaria, on September 9, 1921. *SS-Unterscharführer* Böhm was in a Tiger crew in the 9th (Heavy) Company at Kursk and received an Iron Cross Second Class on August 9, 1943. The sole document in his personnel file has the abbreviation "verst.," indicating that the soldier died during the war. This was most probably at a reserve hospital on September 19, 1943, at Troppau, Lower Silesia (today Opava, Czech Republic). His remains are not in a German military cemetery, but likely buried in the village of Adolfovice, Czech Republic.[12]

Edmund Fein. *SS-Unterscharführer* Edmund Fein was born on September 23, 1921, in Niderahr, in the Westerwald district of Rhineland-Palatinate. During the Kursk Offensive he commanded Tiger **913** in the First Platoon of the 9th (Heavy) Company; it appears that he remained in the position for the entire German attack. At about 1700 hours on August 12, 1943, he was killed in action by a Soviet heavy antitank gun (possibly a Lend-Lease 90 mm cannon from the US) near Pavlove (Павлове), in the Ukraine; his remains have never been found.[13]

Hans Frank. *SS-Oberscharführer* Hans Frank is believed to have commanded Tigers **922** and **921** in the 9th (Heavy) Company during the Kursk Offensive.

Josef "Jupp" Franz. Jupp Franz is believed to have served in a Tiger in the 9th (Heavy) Company during the Kursk Offensive.

Frielau. *Sturmmann* Frielau is believed to have served in Tiger **921** in the Second Platoon of the 9th (Heavy) Company.

Josef "Fritz" Göckl. Josef Göckl was born on July 14, 1910, in Gammertingen, near Sigmaringen. He joined the company on May 1, 1943.[14] An *SS-Unterscharführer*, he served as the commander of Tiger **912** in the First Platoon of the 9th (Heavy) Company during the Kursk Offensive from July 5 to July 8, when he was killed in action repulsing an enemy tank attack in a ravine near Visloye/Ternovka by an antitank round that struck the vehicle's cupola. His remains have never been found and identified after the war. The German War Graves Commission website has no information on Josef Göckl's death or burial.

Günther Grüner. Günther Grüner was born on July 4, 1923, in Saalburg, on the Saale River in Thuringia. *SS-Sturmmann* Grüner served as a radio operator in a 9th (Heavy) Company Tiger during the Kursk Offensive. Earlier, on March 15, 1943, he was admitted to a hospital for frostbite. A secondary source states that Grüner was killed in action at Hill 213.9, east of Stepanivka on the Mius front, in late July 1943. The German War Graves Commission website has no information on his death or burial and his personnel file indicates that Günther Grüner was promoted to *SS-Rottenführer* on June 1, 1944.[15]

Franz Hilgert. Franz Hilgert may not have thought of himself as a hero, but in one horrific moment in combat, the twenty-two-year-old Bavarian became one. Franz was born on March 20, 1921, in Kötsch, near Bamberg, Bavaria. At Kursk, *SS-Sturmmann* Hilgert served as the loader in Tiger **921** in the Second Platoon. On Hill 308 near Kolontaiv, in the Ukraine, on August 31, 1943, an enemy antitank round struck the cupola of the Tiger that Hilgert was driving, shearing the structure off, killing the commander, *SS-Untersturmführer* Heinz Quade, and wounding the other two crewmen in the turret. Franz took charge, restarted the engine, and drove the vehicle to safety. For this accomplishment under fire and other combat action Franz Hilgert received the Iron Cross Second Class on November 10, 1943.[16]

Friedrich "Fritz" Hitz. Friedrich Hitz was born on August 23, 1923, in Neustadt/Aisch, in Franconia. Hitz joined the Hitler Youth in 1933. A mechanic by trade, he stood 5'11" and joined the Waffen-SS on March 15, 1941, first studying communications; he had blood type O. On October 15, 1942, he joined the 2nd Company of the *Totenkopf* panzer detachment, winning the Iron Cross Second Class on March 28, 1943, for his service near Kharkov. At the Kursk Offensive, *SS-Sturmmann* Hitz served as a loader in Tiger **901** and Tiger **911** in the 9th (Heavy) Company. He was awarded the Panzer Battle Badge in Silver on July 29, 1943. Fritz was wounded in action about October 28, 1943, after which he spent several months in a reserve hospital. He was wounded again on August 13, 1944, probably while serving with the 102nd SS Heavy Panzer Detachment, which he had joined on May 15, 1944, in Normandy, and he again was treated for several months at a reserve hospital; one of his wounds was the fracture of his left foot by shrapnel. This wound may have led to an amputation, as Hitz received the Wound Badge in Silver at a later date. He was released from this hospital on March 10, 1945.[17] Fritz Hitz survived the war and died on October 2, 2000.

Werner Hoberg. Born on March 7, 1923, in Hornburg, near Wolfenbüttel, in the German state of Lower Saxony, Werner Hoberg was single and a member of the Hitler Youth from December 18, 1935, to September 1, 1941. Standing just over 5'6" tall, he could speak both English and French; he had blood type AB. After receiving communications training, he joined the *Leibstandarte* on June 12, 1942, but a week later began a twelve-day stay in a hospital at Klausenburg, Hungary (today Cluj-Napoca, Romania), after which he was reassigned to the *Totenkopf* and the 3rd Panzer Regiment.[18]

At Kursk, *SS-Funker* Hoberg served as a radio operator in a Tiger in the 9th (Heavy) Company. He survived the battle, and a document in his personnel file credits *SS-Oberschütze* Hoberg with later participating in three panzer assaults on Hill 213.9 east of Stepanivka, on the Mius front, on July 30, July 31, and August 1, 1943, as a Tiger radio operator, thus earning the Panzer Battle Badge in Silver. He was killed in action at Hill 308, near Kolontayev (sixty kilometers north of Poltava), on August 30, 1943. Werner Hoberg was posthumously awarded an Iron Cross Second Class on November 29, 1943.[19] The German War Graves Commission website has no information on his death or burial.

Fritz Hock. Born on July 18, 1924, in Kitzingen, in the Franconia region of Bavaria, Fritz Hock passed the *Abitur*, but not before he joined the Hitler Youth at age nine on August 31, 1933; he remained in that organization until August 20, 1942, when he entered the Waffen-SS. Hock was one of the taller members of the company, standing 6'2" tall. He received the Iron Cross Second Class and the Wound Badge in Black. He was promoted to *SS-Junker* on July 1, 1944, and to *SS-Standartenjunker* on September 1, 1944. Attending the 4th SS Panzer Officer Candidate Course at Königsbrück from July 17, 1944, to November 7, 1944. On January 30, 1945, Fritz Hock was promoted to *SS-Untersturmführer*.[20]

Franz Hofer. Franz Hofer was born in Agendorf, near Straubing, Bavaria, on February 23, 1913. *SS-Panzerschütze* Hofer served in Tiger **913** in the First Platoon of the 9th (Heavy) Company as a loader. On August 12, 1943, at about 1700 hours, as the loader in Edmund Fein's Tiger he was mortally wounded bailing out after the vehicle was hit by Soviet heavy antitank gun fire near Pavlove, in the Ukraine; he died of his wounds shortly afterward. His remains have never been found.[21]

Hans-Joachim Hoffmann. Hans-Joachim Hoffmann was born in Dresden on August 19, 1921. He had served in the company during the fighting around Kharkov, winning a Panzer Battle Badge in Silver. At Kursk, *SS-Unterscharführer* Hoffmann commanded Tiger **911** in the First Platoon and Tiger **924** in the Second Platoon during parts of the offensive. He received an Iron Cross Second Cass on November 10, 1943. Hans-Joachim Hoffmann survived the war and died on June 1, 1976.

Hans-Georg van Kerkom. The son of Hans van Kerkom and Hilde Remmel, and hailing from Gummersbach, east of Cologne in North Rhine-Westphalia, where he was born on March 25, 1924, *SS-Panzerschütze* Hans-Georg van Kerkom served as the radio operator in Tiger **933** of the Third Platoon of the 9th (Heavy) Company at Kursk. Van Kerkom received the Iron Cross Second Class on August 8, 1943. Assigned to the panzer regimental staff company, he was captured at the end of the war at Krems an der Donau. A Protestant, he survived the war, marrying Gertrud Ramsch in about 1945. She died in 2003; Hans-Georg van Kerkom died on July 3, 2004, in Gummersbach.[22]

Norbert Kochesser. Norbert Kochesser was born in the Austrian capital of Vienna on January 16, 1924; as a child he suffered from diphtheria. He was a member of the Hitler Youth from November 1936 to January 1941. He joined the SS on January 20, 1941, and the Waffen-SS on August 1, 1942, listing his profession as a student. At Kursk, *SS-Panzerschütze* Kochesser served as a loader in a Tiger in the 9th (Heavy) Company. He was killed in action on July 30–31, 1943, assaulting the fortified defenses at Hill 213.9 east of Stepanivka, on the Mius front. The company likely conducted a hasty burial of his remains on August 2. Norbert Kochesser is probably buried with the unknowns in the German War Cemetery at Kharkov in which rest the remains of 47,322 German soldiers.[23]

Walter Köhler. Walter Köhler was born in Vienna, Austria, on April 13, 1908. Joining the Waffen-SS, he received SS number 261430 and originally served in the *Leibstandarte*; promoted to *SS-Oberscharführer* by January 1941, he received the Iron Cross Second Class on April 16, 1941 (probably for action at the Battle of the Klidi Pass, during the invasion of Greece), and the Iron Cross First Class on December 3, 1941 (probably for action at the Battle of Rostov), as well as receiving a battlefield promotion to *SS-Untersturmführer* on April 20, 1942. He later commanded the Panzer Reconnaissance Platoon of the Second Battalion of the 3rd Panzer Regiment. Arriving at the company from that platoon on January 21, 1943, *SS-Untersturmführer* Köhler served in a Tiger in the fighting near Kharkov in February–March 1943. On March 8,

1943, Köhler's Tiger 421 broke through the ice crossing a river near Grijekovo. At Kursk, he first served as the leader of the First Platoon of the 9th (Heavy) Company and commanded Tiger **911**. On July 8, he assumed command of the company and probably transferred to Tiger **901** when *SS-Obersturmführer* Wilhelm Schroeder was killed in action. Walter Köhler was killed in action near Klyuchi on July 12, 1943, from a direct hit of an antitank round. His remains are probably buried among the unknowns at the German War Cemetery at Kursk–Besedino.[24]

Otto Köppen. *SS-Rottenführer* Otto Köppen (SS number 177789) served in Tiger **913** in the First Platoon of the 9th (Heavy) Company as a driver. He would go on to win the Iron Cross Second Class on November 19, 1943. Otto was killed in action near Jabłonna, Poland, on October 10, 1944. At the time of his death he carried a Czech CZ-27 pistol for personal protection.[25]

Herbert Kranz. Herbert Kranz served in the crew of Tiger **911** in the First Platoon of the 9th (Heavy) Company during the Kursk Offensive.[26]

Willy Kronmüller. It is an axiom in armored warfare to never take tanks into cities held by the enemy, but if it must be done, then do so only with substantial infantry support to keep tank killers at bay. The Germans violated this principle of combat during the 1944 Warsaw Uprising and it cost two soldiers dearly in this study: Willy Kronmüller and Walter Münch.

Willy Kronmüller was born on August 13, 1922, at Eutendorf, near Schwäbisch Hall in Baden-Württemberg. At the Kursk Offensive *SS-Oberscharführer* Kronmüller served in Tiger **913**. He received the Iron Cross First Class on July 20, 1943. On August 1, 1944, during the Warsaw Uprising, *SS-Oberscharführer* Kronmüller commanded a *Totenkopf* Tiger that advanced across the Vistula River on the Poniatowskiego Bridge into the city toward the main train station. Insurgents threw Molotov cocktails on the vehicle and the crew dismounted with portable fire extinguishers. A Polish Resistance sniper took aim and shot and killed Willy Kronmüller.[27]

Wolfgang Kühnke. Wolfgang Kühnke was born on August 24, 1924, at Freital, near Dresden in Saxony. *SS-Sturmmann* Kühnke served in a Tiger at Kursk in the 9th (Heavy) Company. He received an Iron Cross Second Class on August 9, 1943.

Karl Küster. Karl Küster was born in Berlin on July 14, 1925. Joining the Hitler Youth at age nine on April 20, 1934, he was a student before entering the SS. After signal training he joined the SS Panzer Replacement Battalion at Weimar on June 20, 1942; on December 27, 1942, Küster joined the Tiger company in the *Totenkopf*. He stood 5'10.5" tall. At Kursk, *SS-Sturmmann* Küster served as the radio operator in Tiger **911** in the First Platoon of the 9th (Heavy) Company. Küster would go on to win the Iron Cross Second Class on November 10, 1943, and the Panzer Battle Badge in Silver. Karl was wounded in action on February 9, 1944, and remained in a hospital until May 6, 1944. It appears he was captured in May 1945 at Enns, Austria. Karl Küster survived the war, spending ten years in Soviet captivity before being released in 1955.[28]

Ludwig Lachner. Ludwig Lachner was born in Liolein, Austria. Lachner was assigned to the SS Police Division before transferring to the Tigers. *SS-Rottenführer* Lachner received the Iron Cross Second Class on March 26, 1943, and the Panzer Battle Badge in Silver on April 20, 1943, for his contributions in the fighting near Kharkov in February–March 1943. At Kursk he was the gunner in Tiger **901** in the Headquarters Platoon. He later became a commander in August 1943. Wounded on April 10, 1945, in Vienna, Ludwig Lachner survived the war and died on February 22, 2001.[29]

Hans Jakob Lampert. Hans Lampert was born in Frankfurt am Main on March 19, 1914. He joined the SS in its early years, receiving SS number 92278. A good athlete, he won a Reichs Sports Badge and an SA Sports Badge. Lampert did his mandatory military duty from October 1935 to September 1937 in the German Army as a private. He submitted his required paperwork to be approved for marriage in 1940. Early in the war, as an *SS-Scharführer*, he served in the 3rd Company of the *Totenkopf* motorcycle battalion. As an *SS-Oberscharführer* he commanded Tiger **934** in the Third Platoon during the Kursk Offensive. Married, Hans Lampert was killed in action on July 30–31, 1943, in fierce combat at Hill 213.9 east of Stepanivka, on the Mius front, as he tried to evacuate his Tiger that was on fire and about to explode. The company conducted a hasty burial of his remains on August 2; the location of his remains are unknown, but they may be buried in the village of Pervomaiz'ke, Ukraine.[30]

Fritz Lasch. Fritz Lasch is believed to have served in a Tiger in the 9th (Heavy) Company during the Kursk Offensive.[31]

Friedrich Johann Lau. "Fritz" Lau was born on May 27, 1924, in Lengerich, in the district of Steinfurt in North Rhine-Westphalia. *SS-Sturmmann* Lau is believed to have served in a Tiger in the 9th (Heavy) Company at Kursk. He was reportedly beaten to death by Soviet soldiers after being captured on July 17, 1944, at Adamowicze, some five miles north of Grodno. Friedrich Johann Lau's remains have never been found.[32]

Fritz Lein. *SS-Rottenführer* Fritz Lein served as a gunner in Tiger **932** in the Third Platoon during the Kursk Offensive.[33]

Walter Lucht. *SS-Sturmmann* Walter Lucht served in Tiger **911** in the First Platoon during the Kursk Offensive. Lucht was later killed in action on September 16, 1944, near Hill 103, one mile west of Rembelszczyzna, Poland, and a dozen miles north of Warsaw, while driving a Tiger.[34]

Hans Joachim Matthäi. Hans Joachim Matthäi was born on August 4, 1923, at Steinach, in the Black Forest in Baden. As an *SS-Sturmmann*, he served as the driver of Tiger **931** in the Third Platoon of the 9th (Heavy) Company. Hans Matthäi was killed in action on July 30, 1943, at Hill 213.9 east of Stepanivka, on the Mius front—probably by enemy artillery fire, as he was working on the Tiger's drive train at the time of his death. His remains have never been found and identified.[35]

Hermann Mocnik. Hermann Mocnik was born in Tarvis, Austria (on the border with Italy west of Klagenfurt), on July 16, 1920. *SS-Sturmmann* Mocnik served as the gunner in Tiger **911** in the First Platoon during the Kursk Offensive. On August 9, 1943, he was awarded the Iron Cross Second Class; he had received the Panzer Battle Badge in Silver before Kursk. Hermann Mocnik was killed in action on March 26, 1944, north of Balta, in the Ukraine. His remains have never been found and identified. His name is listed in a memorial book at the German Military Cemetery at Kirovograd.[36]

Alois Mücke. Alois Mücke was born on August 1, 1923, in what was then termed Mährisch Ostrau, in Czechoslovakia (today Moravská Ostrava). Prior to the end of the Great War the area had been Austrian, and this is undoubtedly what Alois Mücke believed himself to be. After the incorporation of the area into the Third Reich in October 1938, Mücke joined the Hitler Youth on April 20, 1939, and remained in that organization until April 20, 1942. Single, he entered the Waffen-SS on July 15, 1942, and became a radio operator. During the Kursk Offensive it is believed that *SS-Sturmmann* Mücke served as a radio operator in a Tiger in the company. Alois Mücke was killed in action on July 31, 1943, assaulting Hill 213.9 east of Stepanivka, on the Mius front. An Iron Cross Second Class was posthumously awarded to him on November 10, 1943.[37]

Ludwig Müller. Ludwig Müller was born in the small town of Vohenstrauß, near Weiden in Bavaria, on October 23, 1922. *SS-Rottenführer* Müller served as the loader in Tiger **912** in the First Platoon until July 8, 1943, near Smorodino, when the Tiger was hit by Soviet artillery rounds, killing him. Ludwig Müller is buried at the German War Cemetery Kharkov in Block 10, Row 10 in Grave 1129.[38]

Richard Müller. Richard Müller was born in Neustadt on June 7, 1910. He received the Iron Cross Second Class on April 3, 1943. *SS-Unterscharführer* Müller was the commander of Tiger **912** in the First Platoon during the Kursk Offensive until July 7, when his Tiger was hit by Soviet artillery rounds near Smorodino. Mortally wounded, Richard was evacuated, but died on July 12 at an SS casualty collection point at Vasil'yevka. His remains may rest in the unknown section at the German War Cemetery two miles north of the village of Kursk–Besedino.[39]

Walter Münch. Walter Münch was born on November 2, 1918, in Apolda, a town in central Thuringia, Germany. He served with the company during the fighting near Kharkov in February–March 1943 and received a Panzer Battle Badge in Silver after the campaign. *SS-Unterscharführer* Münch served in Tiger 913 in the First Platoon during the Kursk Offensive. He received an Iron Cross Second Class on July 20, 1943. He also won an Iron Cross First Class during the war.[40]

On August 1, 1944, during the Warsaw Uprising, *SS-Unterscharführer* Walter Münch served as a driver of the *Totenkopf* Tiger commanded by Willy Kronmüller that advanced across the Vistula River on the Poniatowskiego Bridge into the city toward the main train station. Insurgents threw Molotov cocktails on top of the Tiger and Münch dismounted to fight the fire. A sniper shot and killed his commander Willy Kronmüller and seriously wounded Walter Münch.[41]

Fritz Osha. Fritz Osha was born in the small town of Dassel, near Holzminden in Lower Saxony, on September 23, 1909. An *SS-Sturmmann*, he drove a Tiger during the Kursk Offensive and received an Iron Cross Second Class on August 9, 1943. Fritz Osha died on March 15, 1986.[42]

Artur Privatzki. Artur Privatzki was born on September 7, 1921, in the small city of Weißwasser, Saxony. Before joining the company he fought in the Demjansk encirclement and received the Demjansk Shield. *SS-Unterscharführer* Privatzki fought with the company at Kharkov in February–March 1943, winning a Panzer Battle Badge in Silver. At Kursk he was the gunner in Tiger **921** in the Second Platoon; he may also have served as a gunner in Tiger **933**. Privatzki received the Iron Cross Second Class on October 31, 1943; he also possessed the Wound Badge in Black. *SS-Oberscharführer* Privatzki later commanded Tigers 933 and 934. Captured on May 25, 1945, Artur Privatzki is believed to have destroyed at least fourteen enemy tanks during the war.[43]

Willi Probst. *SS-Unterscharführer* Willi Probst joined the company on May 9, 1943, after his unit SS Motorcycle Regiment *Thule* disbanded. At Kursk, he was the driver of Tiger **901** in the Headquarters Platoon. As a Tiger commander Willi Probst was killed in action on September 13, 1944, at Hill 104 near Słupno, Poland.[44]

Heinz Quade. *SS-Untersturmführer* Heinz Quade was born on May 31, 1921, at Ueckermünde, in western Pomerania. A clerk by trade, he graduated from grade school and joined the SS at age seventeen on October 1, 1938, with SS number 423774. Quade initially served with *SS-Totenkopf Standarte Thüringen*. Standing 5'8" tall, he was wounded in 1940 and received a Wound Badge in Black. He also earned an Iron Cross Second Class. Quade attended the 7th *Kriegs Junkerlehrgang* at the *SS-Junkerschule* in Braunschweig and was promoted to *SS-Standartenoberjunker* on March

31, 1942. He was commissioned an *SS-Untersturmführer* on June 21, 1942. Briefly assigned to the *Leibstandarte* panzer regiment, he transferred to the *Totenkopf* panzer regiment on July 20, 1942. In October 1942, Quade was the platoon leader for the Panzer Reconnaissance Platoon in the First Battalion of the panzer regiment. Heinz was transferred to the heavy company on January 8, 1943.

At Kursk Heinz Quade commanded Tiger **921** as the leader of the Second Platoon for the duration of the offensive, even though he was wounded in the eye by enemy antitank rifle fire. He received the Iron Cross First Class on August 6, 1943. Heinz, now the acting company commander, was not so lucky on Hill 308 near Kolontaiv, in the Ukraine, on August 31, 1943. An enemy antitank round struck the Tiger's cupola, shearing the structure off and inflicting massive fatal effects to Heinz Quade. Another source states that the event happened about 0400 hours on September 1, 1943, at the same location. His remains are believed to be buried at the German War Cemetery in Kharkov.[45]

Willi Gustav Hugo Rathsack. In another life Willi Rathsack, a baker, would have made his *Berliner, Bienenstich,* and *Donauwelle* pastries, seen his children grow up, and played with his grandchildren in his twilight years—undoubtedly stuffing the youngsters whenever they came over to visit *Opa* (grandfather). And like so many other men in this study—and millions more men and women in World War II—those dreams were dashed by death.

Willi Rathsack was born on Strohkirchen, in Mecklenburg, on January 2, 1920, the son of a musician. A baker by trade, he attended middle school, was a member of the Hitler Youth from 1931 to 1938, and the Reich Labor Service in 1938–39; he joined the Waffen-SS on April 1, 1939, with SS number 423843. Willi also spoke Dutch and stood 5'10" tall. He served in Poland, Holland, Belgium, France, and Russia with the 2nd Company of SS Infantry Regiment *Germania*, where he won the Infantry Assault Badge in Silver and on October 30, 1941, the Iron Cross Second Class. He was wounded in action on July 25, 1941. Willi Rathsack was promoted to *SS-Sturmmann* on April 1, 1940; to *SS-Rottenführer* on July 1, 1940; and to *SS-Unterscharführer* on October 1, 1941.[46]

He then attended the 7th *SS-Kriegs Junkerlehrgang* at the *SS-Junkerschule* Braunschweig from November 1, 1941, to April 30, 1942; was commissioned an *SS-Untersturmführer* on June 21, 1942, then joined a panzer replacement battalion, the 3rd Company of the *Totenkopf* panzer detachment; and finally, on December 13, 1942, the 4th (Heavy) Company [which was later designated the 9th (Heavy) Company] after he had completed a course at the Panzer School at Wünsdorf. He received the Panzer Battle Badge in Silver after the fighting in March 1943, when he commanded Tiger 441.[47]

At Kursk, *SS-Untersturmführer* Rathsack commanded Tiger **931** and was the leader of the Third Platoon in the 9th (Heavy) Company through July 12, 1943, when he was wounded in action. He received the Wound Badge in Black. On July 30, 1943, he was wounded in the eye near Stepanivka, on the Mius front. Still recovering, he was wounded in the chest on August 12, 1943, near Pavlovo and was evacuated to a casualty collection point. Willi received the Wound Badge in Silver in September 1943.

Rathsack was subsequently assigned to the 2nd Company in the 102nd SS Heavy Panzer Detachment as the Third Platoon leader (in Tiger 231) early in 1944 and fought in Normandy. On July 13, 1944, he assumed command of the Second Platoon of the 1st Company. On August 18, 1944, near Trun/Chambois, France, *SS-Obersturmführer* Rathsack—who now was the detachment adjutant—was seriously wounded and was posted missing in action. In fact he had died. His remains are registered at the German War Cemetery at Champigny-St. André, France, but the exact location is probably with the unknowns in Block 13, Grave 1324.[48] According to historian Ian Michael Wood, contemporaries of Willi Rathsack found him to be unpopular and a difficult man with whom to get along.[49]

Hans Rex. Hans Rex was born at Boisheim, North Rhine-Westphalia, on June 20, 1924. A loader, he received the Panzer Battle Badge in Silver for combat near Kharkov in February–March 1943. During Kursk, *SS-Sturmmann* Hans Rex loaded in Tiger **911** and Tiger **924** and received the Iron Cross Second Class on November 19, 1943. Hans Rex survived the war and died on November 10, 2008.[50]

Wilfried Richter. Wilfried Richter was born on May 9, 1916, in Pforzheim. Trained as an auto mechanic, he attended high school and joined the SS and the Nazi Party on the same day, November 9, 1934. He received SS number 279192. Standing 5'9" tall, he would later marry and have a daughter born on December 26, 1940. Richter joined SS Regiment *Deutschland* on October 1, 1937, and graduated the *SS-Junkerschule* Bad Tölz soon thereafter. Joining the *Totenkopf* in October 1939 as an *SS-Untersturmführer*, he was assigned to the assault gun battery of the unit on August 10, 1940; he won the Iron Cross Second Class on September 19, 1941, and the Iron Cross First Class on October 22, 1941. Promoted to *SS-Obersturmführer* on January 30, 1942, he received the Knight's Cross of the Iron Cross on April 21, 1942, for bravery and achievement—including calling in friendly artillery fire on his own position, destroying enemy tanks, conducting a counterattack, and engaging in close combat fighting—in the Demjansk Pocket. Four days later Richter was promoted to *SS-Hauptsturmführer*. He commanded the battery from February 21, 1942, to October 22, 1942. The division transferred Richter to the panzer regiment and he initially commanded the 7th Company in the Second Battalion of the regiment.[51]

During the Kursk Offensive, *SS-Hauptsturmführer* Wilfried Richter assumed command of the 9th (Heavy) Company on July 12, 1943, when the acting company commander, Walter Köhler, was killed in action. In this position he probably commanded Tiger **901**. After the offensive, on July 30, 1943, at Hill 213.9, east of Stepanivka, on the Mius front, Richter was wounded in his lower body by artillery shrapnel when he was outside his tank after it had been immobilized by a mine and left command of the company. On March 1, 1945, he assumed command of the Second Battalion of the 95th SS Grenadier Regiment of the 38th SS Grenadier Division *Nibelungen*. Married before the war to his fiancée Ursel, Wilfried Richter survived the war; he died on April 18, 1981, in Engehausen, near Essel, in Lower Saxony.[52]

Fritz Rudolph. *SS-Sturmmann* Fritz Rudolph was the loader in Tiger **932** in the Third Platoon of the 9th (Heavy) Company at the Kursk Offensive.[53]

Karl Sandler. A weaver by trade, Karl Sandler was born on March 15, 1922, in Seidenhofen, near Kulmbach in Upper Franconia, Bavaria. He served in the Hitler Youth from May 1, 1933, to October 10, 1939, joining the Waffen-SS eleven days later as a communications specialist. With blond hair (which looks brown in his SS photograph) and gray-green eyes, he was listed as standing 5'9" tall, but was still growing and later measured just over 5'10". His first tactical assignment was with the 1st SS *Totenkopf* Infantry Regiment. He was wounded in action at the front in October 1941 and was still recovering from these wounds at the reserve hospital in Niederbries in December 1941.[54]

Sandler appears to have been a good soldier and was promoted to *SS-Rottenführer* on August 10, 1942; he was then transferred to the new Tiger company on December 10, 1942. During the war he would receive the Iron Cross Second Class, the Infantry Assault Badge in Silver, and the Panzer Battle Badge in Silver, as well as the Wound Badge in Black. At Kursk he commanded a Tiger in the 9th (Heavy) Company. Surviving that battle he remained with the company, and on August 1, 1944, became a platoon leader. He was married on December 30, 1944. Karl was promoted to *SS-Unterscharführer* on April 20, 1945, several days after he was wounded in action on April 10 in Vienna as part of an infantry battle group comprised of dismounted panzer crews whose vehicles had been destroyed earlier. Karl Sandler survived the war.[55]

Georg Schäfer. Georg Schäfer was born on November 9, 1924, in Richelsdorf, in northeast Hesse. Protestant, he joined the Hitler Youth in 1933; he later was a salesman. Standing 5'8" tall, he arrived in the 9th (Heavy) Company on December 26, 1942. *SS-Panzerschütze* Schäfer served as a gunner in a Tiger in the company at Kursk; he was wounded on July 5, 1943. Georg received an Iron Cross Second Class on August 9, 1943. He was single.[56]

Gunther Schreyer. *SS-Panzerschütze* Gunther Schreyer served as a loader in a Tiger in the company at Kursk. Gunther Schreyer was killed in action on August 1, 1943, at the heavily fortified Hill 213.9 east of Stepanivka, on the Mius front.[57]

Wilhelm Schroeder. At age forty-five, Wilhelm Schroeder was the oldest man in the crews in the three SS Tiger companies at Kursk, having been born on April 23, 1898, at Leipzig. That fact may be the reason that the men in the *Totenkopf* Tiger company nicknamed him "Papa." During the Great War he initially served in the 4th Hussar Regiment, but transferred to the flying service in 1918, with the rank of lieutenant. He subsequently was attached to a fighter unit (Jasta 7) as a flight commander, flying a Fokker D.VIII; he received the Pilot's Badge and won the Iron Cross Second Class and Iron Cross First Class.[58]

A landowner with university level schooling in agriculture, Schroeder was an early member of the Nazi Party, joining initially in 1923, but left after the failed "Beer Hall Putsch" on November 9, 1923—and after being jailed in 1924 for three months. Seeing the handwriting on the wall, Wilhelm rejoined the party on June 14, 1927, and received party number 63277, which qualified him for a Golden Party Badge. He was also a member of the *Reichstag*. Wilhelm—who was married in 1927 and would have five children—after first joining the *Sturmabteilung*, saw that after the 1934 "Night of the Long Knives" the SA would be stripped of power, so he transferred to the Allgemeine-SS on February 12, 1935 (SS number 261293), and immediately became an *SS-Standartenführer*. He would be promoted to *SS-Oberführer* on November 9, 1937. Prior to the war he would hold several Allgemeine-SS positions, the highest of which was the Chief of Staff of the Main District *Alpenland*, a position he assumed on June 1, 1939, and technically held until July 1943. When World War II began Schroeder joined the Luftwaffe as a lieutenant, completing sixty training flights, and was promoted to first lieutenant in 1940. He transferred to the Waffen-SS on August 15, 1942, first serving in an SS antitank replacement unit.[59]

Always the opportunist, *SS-Obersturmführer* of Reserves Wilhelm Schroder joined the panzer detachment of the *Totenkopf* on November 1, 1942, and after training at several panzer courses at Wünsdorf and completing leadership training he went to Russia and was assigned to the company on January 15, 1943. Schroeder received the Clasp to the Iron Cross Second Class on March 24, 1943. He began the Kursk Offensive as the Company Troop Leader (the second in command) for the 9th (Heavy) Company. In this position he commanded Tiger **902**, although this tank would be disabled by an enemy antitank mine at 1930 hours on July 6. On July 8, 1943, the company commander, Fritz Biermeier, was elevated to command the Second Battalion of the 3rd Panzer Regiment and Schroeder took command of the company—most likely in Tiger **901**. Within hours a Soviet antitank rifle round struck Schroeder in the head as he was firing a submachine gun at advancing enemy infantry and was partially exposed in the cupola; he died immediately. His crew buried him in a hasty grave under a tree.[60]

Although that was the official cause of death for Wilhelm Schroeder, *Totenkopf* Tiger historian Ian Michael Wood has unearthed interesting accounts of veterans that indicate that Schroeder was actually killed by friendly fire from a nearby Sturmgeschütz III (Assault Gun Mark III).[61] He had received a promotion to *SS-Hauptsturmführer* of Reserves on July 1, 1943.

Heinz Karl Schüffler. *SS-Untersturmführer* Heinz Schüffler was born on April 10, 1921, at Kranichfeld, near Weimar. He became a member of the Hitler Youth and won the Golden Hitler Youth Badge; he also took and passed the *Abitur*. Heinz joined the Nazi Party on September 1, 1939, and entered the Waffen-SS on March 27, 1940, receiving SS number 360293. Six months later he joined the 11th SS Infantry Regiment; from November 1, 1941, to January 30, 1942, he attended the *SS-Junkerschule* at Bad Tölz and was commissioned as an officer on April 20, 1942, in the *Das Reich*, serving in the reconnaissance detachment. *SS-Untersturmführer* Schüffler received the Panzer Battle Badge in Silver and the Iron Cross Second Class in spring 1943, after first attending a chemical warfare course in Germany until March 2, 1943, when he returned to the front to the 9th (Heavy) Company as a platoon leader.[62]

Heinz almost missed serving at Kursk, arriving on July 13; after *SS-Untersturmführer* Rathsack was wounded he served as the leader of the Third Platoon in command of Tiger **931**. He received the Iron Cross First Class on July 20, 1943, for his actions at the battle. On August 1, 1943, in heavy fighting at Hill 213.9 east of Stepanivka, in the Ukraine, Heinz received a serious wound to the head, blinding him. Heinz Karl Schüffler died the following day of these wounds at 4th Army Field Hospital of Army Medical Detachment 542 at Donetsk. The location of his remains is unknown to the German War Grave Commission.[63]

Karl Schulze-Berge. *SS-Rottenführer* Karl Schulze-Berge was born on August 28, 1924, at Fröndenberg, near Hamm in North Rhine-Westphalia. At Kursk, Schulze-Berge served in Tiger **911** in the First Platoon of the 9th (Heavy) Company. In 1944, he was ordered to a probationary platoon for breaches in discipline but then returned to his unit. He also served in the maintenance section for much of the war. Karl Schulze-Berge survived the war and died on May 25, 2004.[64]

Werner Schweitzer. Werner Schweitzer was born on October 28, 1924, in Waldhausen, east of Stuttgart in the state of Württemberg. He was single. During the Kursk Offensive Werner Schweitzer served as a radio operator in the 9th (Heavy) Company. An award document in Schweitzer's personnel file dated July 15, 1943, credited him for engaging in tank combat as a radio operator in a Tiger on July 6, 7, and 8. For this achievement he received the Panzer Battle Badge in Silver. On the morning of July 30, 1943, near Hill 213.9, east of Stepanivka, in the Ukraine, *SS-Panzeroberschütze* Werner Schweitzer was killed in action. He was hastily buried by the company near Pervomais'k on August 2, but his grave was never located after the war.[65]

Friedrich Wilhelm Selonke. Friedrich Selonke was born at Großwunneschin, near Krampkewitz, Pomerania, on November 2, 1905, to Wilhelm Selonke, a day laborer, and Auguste Lozz. He received the Iron Cross Second Class on April 3, 1943, for prior combat near Kharkov in February–March 1943. During the Kursk Offensive, *SS-Rottenführer* Selonke served as a gunner in Tiger **912** in the First Platoon. He later served in the 102nd SS Heavy Panzer Detachment in Normandy. Friedrich Selonke was wounded in action at Vienna on April 10, 1945.[66]

Alois Tasler. Alois Tasler was born on June 9, 1922. *SS-Oberscharführer* Tasler commanded Tiger **932** in the Third Platoon at Kursk. He was wounded on January 1, 1945, near Budapest. Captured on May 25, 1945, Alois Tasler survived the war.[67]

Ernst Vögler. *SS-Sturmmann* Ernst Vögler, from East Prussia, served as a loader in a Tiger during the Kursk Offensive until he was killed on July 12, 1943, when he was fatally wounded in the head.[68]

Erwin Wehr. *SS-Unterscharführer* Erwin Wehr was born at Goldbeck, in the district of Stendal in Saxony-Anhalt, on June 27, 1922. A bachelor, he joined the Waffen-SS on January 15, 1941, and was promoted to *SS-Rottenführer* on February 1, 1943. He received the Wound Badge in Black on April 13, 1943. He arrived in the company on July 1, 1943. During Kursk he served in the company as a driver of a Tiger. Later, on November 10, 1943, Erwin Wehr received the Panzer Battle Badge in Silver and the Iron Cross Second Class on March 1, 1945.[69]

Felix Werner. Felix Werner was born in Tampadel, in Lower Silesia, on November 20, 1921. At Kursk, *SS-Rottenführer* Felix Werner served in a Tiger in the company and received the Iron Cross Second Class on August 9, 1943.[70]

Georg Wimmer. George Wimmer was born in Geisberg, in the Alsace, on April 23, 1918. As an *SS-Unterscharführer*, he served in a Tiger in the company during the Kursk Offensive. He received the Iron Cross Second Class on August 9, 1943. George Wimmer died on April 10, 2002.[71]

Georg Hans Zieten. Georg Hans Zieten was born in Danzig on September 18, 1925, making him one of the youngest Tiger crewmen in the battle. He joined the Waffen-SS on October 15, 1942, having just turned seventeen. *SS-Sturmmann* Zieten served in Tiger **932** in the Third Platoon during the Kursk Offensive. Georg Zieten was promoted to *SS-Unterscharführer* on March 1, 1944.[72]

Ludwig Zimmermann. *SS-Unterscharführer* Ludwig Zimmermann served as gunner in Tiger **912** in the First Platoon until July 8, 1943, near Smorodino, when his Tiger was hit by Soviet artillery rounds. Ludwig Zimmermann was killed in the encounter.[73]

Analysis

The Kursk Offensive has been analyzed, dissected, and run through predictive software on powerful computers—often by large teams of highly regarded researchers, senior military experts, and award winning authors. In 1996, the US Army Concepts Analysis Agency and the Dupuy Institute created the Kursk Database (KDB), a 19,931 megabyte, 256 file behemoth that covered 1,065 Division Days of Combat; it includes seventeen German Divisions, thirty-seven Soviet Rifle Divisions, ten Soviet Tank and Mechanized Corps, and six Soviet Tank Brigades and attachments. It is in Dbase IV.

On the other hand, let us scale way down and just start our analysis with a look of what actually happened to the 13th (Heavy) Company, the 8th (Heavy) Company), and the 9th (Heavy) Company—and more importantly to their Tiger crews—during the battle.

Personnel Casualties

Tiger tanks had thick skins, but Tiger crewmen could be, and sometimes were, wounded or even killed behind their Krupp steel barricades. This study has identified a minimum of eleven crewmen who were killed in action (KIA) between July 5–15, 1943, including:

July 5	Georg Gentsch	13th (Heavy) Company		
July 6	Heinz Schönborn	8th (Heavy) Company		
July 7	Karl Heinz Lorenz	8th (Heavy) Company	Tiger **S24**	Antitank shell
July 7	Ernst Schäfer	8th (Heavy) Company	Tiger **S24**	Infantry fire
July 8	Ludwig Müller	9th (Heavy) Company	Tiger **912**	Artillery shell
July 8	Ludwig Zimmermann	9th (Heavy) Company	Tiger **912**	Artillery shell
July 8	Josef Göckl	9th (Heavy) Company	Tiger **912**	Antitank shell
July 9	Franz Enderl	13th (Heavy) Company	Tiger **1315**	
July 12	Arthur Bernhardt	13th (Heavy) Company	Tiger **1312**	Tank shell
July 12	Ernst Vögler	9th (Heavy) Company		Head wound
July 15	Philipp August Theiss	8th (Heavy) Company	Tiger **S02**	Antitank shell

A second category of casualty is often known as DOW (Died of Wounds)—one who dies of wounds or other injuries received in action after having reached a medical treatment facility. The eight Tiger crewmen in this study who received grievous wounds on the battlefield (between July 5–15) and expired at a casualty collection point or later in the medical treatment process included:

July 5	Wilfried Frenzel	8th (Heavy) Company	Died July 15 at Kharkov
July 5	Heinz Owczarek	13th (Heavy) Company	Died same day at Pushkarnoye
July 5	Werner Richard Märker	8th (Heavy) Company	Died same day at Streletskoye
July 7	Artur Ulmer	8th (Heavy) Company	Died July 15 at Kharkov
July 7	Heinz Wilken	8th (Heavy) Company	Died July 8 at Luchki (South)

July 7	Werner Schäfer	8th (Heavy) Company		Died July 18 at Ssawodskoje
July 8	Richard Müller	9th (Heavy) Company		Died July 12 at Vasil'yevka
July 11	Heinz Schöneberg	8th (Heavy) Company		Died July 13 Dnipropetrovsk

Finally, at least thirty-five Tiger crewmen received less-than-lethal wounds at Kursk during the offensive, including:

July 5	Waldemar Schütz	13th (Heavy) Company	Tiger **1311**	Antitank shell
July 5	Klaus Bürvenich	13th (Heavy) Company	Tiger **1311**	Antitank shell
July 5	Helmut Wendorff	13th (Heavy) Company	Tiger **1321**	Antitank shell
July 5	Gustav Kirschner	13th (Heavy) Company		Antitank shell
July 5	Herbert Zimmermann	8th (Heavy) Company	Tiger **S01**	
July 5	Georg Gallinat	8th (Heavy) Company	Tiger **S01**	Antitank mine
July 5	Helmut Cantow	8th (Heavy) Company	Tiger **S01**	Antitank mine
July 5	Max Bläsing	8th (Heavy) Company	Tiger **S02**	Antitank mine
July 5	Kurt Meyer	8th (Heavy) Company	Tiger **S11**	
July 5	Walter Reininghaus	8th (Heavy) Company	Tiger **S21**	
July 5	Erwin Sandmeier	8th (Heavy) Company		
July 5	Alois Kalss	8th (Heavy) Company	Tiger **S31**	
July 5	Georg Schäfer	9th (Heavy) Company		
July 6	Walter Koch	13th (Heavy) Company	Tiger **1331**	Antitank shell
July 6	Kurt Baral	8th (Heavy) Company	Tiger **S32**	Artillery shell
July 6	Willi Börker	8th (Heavy) Company		
July 6	Jakob Kuster	8th (Heavy) Company	Tiger **S32**	Artillery shell
July 6	Wilhelm Lotter	8th (Heavy) Company		Antitank mine
July 7	Hans Haselböck	8th (Heavy) Company	Tiger **S02**	
July 7	Franz Stemann	8th (Heavy) Company	Tiger **S02**	
July 7	Walter Reininghaus	8th (Heavy) Company	Tiger **S21**	Artillery shell
July 7	Herbert Zimmermann	8th (Heavy) Company	Tiger **S02**	
July 8	Helmut Wendorff	13th (Heavy) Company	Tiger **1321**	Antitank shell
July 8	Emil Weissfloch	8th (Heavy) Company		
July 10	Waldemar Schütz	13th (Heavy) Company	Tiger **1311**	Artillery shell
July 11	Heinrich Kling	13th (Heavy) Company	Tiger **1301**	Antitank shell
July 11	Kurt Pollmann	13th (Heavy) Company	Tiger **1331**	Antitank shell
July 11	Herbert Zimmermann	8th (Heavy) Company	Tiger **S01**	Arm wound
July 12	Bruno Hofmann	8th (Heavy) Company		
July 12	Rudolf Zacharias	8th (Heavy) Company		
July 12	Willi Rathsack	9th (Heavy) Company	Tiger **931**	
July 13	Walter Henke	13th (Heavy) Company	Tiger **1325**	Left eye
July 15	Karl Lieber	13th (Heavy) Company	Tiger **1331**	
July 15	Emil Weissfloch	8th (Heavy) Company		
July ?	Heinz Quade	9th (Heavy) Company	Tiger **921**	Antitank rifle

What is especially noteworthy is the number of crew members that became casualties who were riding in command tanks at the time of their wounds. Almost forty-two percent of the casualties—some twenty-two of the fifty-four men who were killed or wounded—were riding in a platoon leader's Tiger or a company commander's Tiger. Leadership had its price.[1]

Equipment Damage

Determining the cause of damage to Tigers was quite difficult for the study. It would not be a poor assumption that every Tiger that was operational was struck at least once per day by some enemy fire. Exploding antitank mines often immobilized a Tiger, but sometimes they did not. It is quite possible that in the din of fire what a crew thought was an antitank round was actually the same caliber round fired from an enemy tank instead. Equipment malfunctions infested the Tiger fleet, often sending the vehicles to the rear as non-operational. It should also be noted that a weapon hit on a Tiger that wounded or killed a crew member did not always result in serious damage to the vehicle. It could cause serious damage, but not always. The following information portrays significant damage inflicted by the enemy: a total kill indicates that the vehicle is out of action for good; a mobility kill indicates that the Tiger was evacuated to the rear for repairs to its transmission, suspension, or engine. Actual damage may have been quite more significant, but total losses were not—there were only three.

14.5 mm Antitank Rifle: killed commander of **901** on July 8 (per official sources; unofficial sources indicated cause was friendly fire from a German Mark III Assault Gun).
Flamethrower: no damage reported to any Tiger.
Antitank Gun: mobility kill of **1321** on July 5; two mobility kills in 13th (Heavy) Company on July 8 (possibly inflicted by SU-122 assault guns; mobility kill of **S11** on July 13; two mobility kills in 8th (Heavy) Company on July 15).
Tank: total kill on **1312** on July 12 near Hill 241.6.
Artillery: total kill of **914** on July 7; severe damage to **912** on July 7.
Assault Gun: possible that artillery kill of **914** on July 7 was caused by an assault gun.
Aircraft: no damage reported to any Tiger.
Armored Train: total kill of **S24** on July 7.
Antitank Mines: mobility kills of **1331, 1321, 1301** +1 (from 13th); **S01, S02** +3 (from 8th); **901** +4 (from 9th) all on July 5; mobility kills of **1324, 1325, 1331, 902** on July 6; mobility kills of **901, 911** on July 10.

Rates of Advance

Both the northern German pincer of Colonel General Walter Model's Ninth Army and the southern pincer of Colonel General Hermann Hoth's Fourth Panzer Army—as well as Lieutenant General Werner Kempf's Army Detachment Kempf that advanced to the right of the Fourth Panzer Army to protect its flank—failed to gain enough ground to encircle the six Soviet armies inside the Kursk salient. In fact, their advances were pathetic—especially the Ninth Army's—and they gained less than half the ground they needed for success.

Although success for the 2nd SS Panzer Corps was measured, in part, by terrain seized in the advance, the rates of advance of the three Tiger companies were not great. Here is a summary (in kilometers) of the daily advances for each unit:

	13th (Heavy) Company	8th (Heavy) Company	9th (Heavy) Company
July 5	19	12	11
July 6	18	10	3
July 7	4	7	0
July 8	7	12	0
July 9	7	0	13
July 10	7	1	6
July 11	3	1	7

July 12	2	0	6
July 13	1	2	0
July 14	1	7	1
July 15	0	2	0
Total	**69**	**54**	**47**

If we calculate this as a per day average, the 13th (Heavy) Company made a daily advance of 6.9 kilometers (4.28 miles); the 8th (Heavy) Company advanced an average of 5.4 kilometers (3.35 miles); and the 9th (Heavy) Company averaged a gain of 4.7 kilometers (2.92 miles) per day—all indicative of a slugfest, not a blitzkrieg. Given these paltry advance averages, coupled with successfully high numbers of kills the Tigers achieved against enemy tanks, one might ask the question: did the corps leadership want the Tigers to spearhead the gaining of ground north, pulling their divisions forward in their wakes, or did they envision the three companies to be mobile antitank killing units? Perhaps they gambled and wanted the Tiger crews to do both.

Professional Education and Advancement

Historian Gerald Reitlinger had this to say about training in the Waffen-SS: "The Waffen-SS was to develop the most efficient of all training systems of the Second World War, a cross between the Spartan Hoplites and the Guards Depot at Caterham."[2]

This training was divided into several segments. First was basic training that was conducted in Germany by a replacement unit. Upon graduation, the young SS man reported to a field unit. Training was difficult, with almost daily physical activities, such as long distance running and short distance sprinting, boxing, rowing, and obstacle courses; prior to 1939 the drills resembled more commando style training than that for regular infantry.[3]

By the end of 1938, the *Leibstandarte Adolf Hitler*, *Deutschland*, *Germania*, and *Der Führer* regiments had reached such a high level of combat training that Hitler granted the four units to use German Army training grounds *without* the restrictions of usual safety standards. Live ammunition was used in situations where it had not previously been a part and barrages of artillery were fired to hit within 50 to 70 meters of the troops. Training casualties rose; the Army said that such methods were unfortunate, but Himmler countered that such training would save casualties in wartime.[4]

In this study, it appears that at least ten soldiers in the 13th (Heavy) Company at Kursk first served in Waffen-SS infantry units. In the 8th (Heavy) Company at least twenty-four soldiers first served in the infantry; a further four initially served in motorcycle units. In the 9th (Heavy) Company, at least four troopers had first served in the infantry and at least another two were originally motorcycle troops.

The solution was to simply "baptize" regular infantry personnel "to become armor soldiers *without* corresponding training." [Author emphasis of information provided by Colonel (Retired) Wolfgang Schneider.] Sometimes this conversion was done at the individual level; the largest "baptism" appears to have occurred on October 31, 1942, when SS Infantry Regiment 4 (motorized) *Langemarck* in the 2nd SS Infantry Brigade (motorized) was reborn as the second detachment of the *Das Reich* panzer regiment.

The first of these conversions had already occurred from transfers to the panzers from the Waffen-SS assault gun units that supported the infantry, but assault guns did not fight like panzer, having different tactics and capabilities. At Kursk, this difference led some Tiger commanders with assault gun backgrounds to leave their flanks exposed; in Normandy a year later that discrepancy would lead to fatal results for many Tigers, including the one commanded by Michael

Wittmann. This discrepancy also manifested itself in training through the end of the war; the Waffen-SS did not have its own armor school, but rather sent non-commissioned officers and officers to German Army courses.[5]

After serving an initial tour with a field unit, troopers at the *SS-Sturmmann* level began to be identified as potential non-commissioned officers. These men were sent to the appropriate branch school, in the case of panzer troops the SS Panzer Replacement Detachment at Weimar-Buchenwald that later transferred to Bitsch/Alsace, and finally Augustdorf/North Rhine-Westphalia. Now at the grade of *SS-Rottenführer* (corporal), the soldier could then be promoted to *SS-Unterscharführer*. If further advancement was to be achieved the soldier would spend at least one year in this rank, with at least two months of that serving in a field unit, which made him eligible for advancement to *SS-Oberscharführer*.[6] There were, of course, some exceptions to these general requirements, especially if a soldier demonstrated extreme bravery and was in line for a high decoration, such as Walter Köhler in April 1943.

The study has identified eleven men from the three companies that were at the rank of *SS-Oberscharführer* at the time of the battle. All commanded Tigers. A further forty-five crewmen held the rank of *SS-Unterscharführer*. However, an interesting trend emerges. While twenty-nine *SS-Unterscharführer* commanded Tigers, not all did. The others were gunners and drivers, and even one appears to have been a radio operator—and this occurred across the board, not in one company. It would seem that the chain of command directed soldiers into crew positions based on skill level and not purely by rank, and also supports Colonel Schneider's conclusion concerning key crew positions.

Potential commissioned officers (lieutenants) in the Waffen-SS were often identified very early and identified as officer candidates. After recruit training and a minimum of two months of front line service a future officer could be promoted to *SS-Sturmmann*. Then the soldier faced four requirements. The first was completing non-commissioned officer training to the level of *SS-Junker*; the soldier then was required to complete the wartime *Junker* course to the level of *SS-Standartenoberjunker*. Next, the candidate completed weapons training courses, but after lengthy time at the front these were not that difficult. Finally, the officer candidate attended an *SS-Junkerschule* at Bad Tölz in Bavaria or Braunschweig, in Lower Saxony, and soon graduated to become an *SS-Untersturmführer*.[7]

Seven men in this study were *SS-Untersturmführer* at the time of the battle. All served as platoon leaders initially and included: Helmut Wendorff (Second Platoon) and Michael Wittmann (Third Platoon) of the 13th (Heavy) Company; Alois Kalss (Third Platoon) in the 8th (Heavy) Company; and Walter Köhler (First Platoon), Heinz Quade (Second Platoon), and Willi Rathsack and Heinz Karl Schüffler (both in Third Platoon) of the 9th (Heavy) Company. Nineteen enlisted men at Kursk among the Tiger crews were promoted to *SS-Untersturmführer* later in the war, primarily in the second half of 1944.

Service as a commissioned officer was a deadly business. None of the seven *SS-Untersturmführer* mentioned by name survived the war. Ten other men at Kursk were *SS-Obersturmführer* or *SS-Hauptsturmführer*. Of these twenty-nine men, who were officers at Kursk or became officers later, twelve of them were killed in action during the war.

Awards and Decorations

Napoleon Bonaparte is reported to have once stated: "A soldier will fight long and hard for a bit of colored ribbon." From the old days in Prussia through World War II, Germany instituted and maintained an easily recognizable system of awards and decorations throughout society—not just in the military services. The following awards and decorations were received by Tiger crewmen throughout the war and are shown as career award winners and not just for service during the Kursk Offensive, which was less than two weeks long.

Iron Cross Second Class. A venerable award that dated to 1813, the Iron Cross Second Class was awarded for bravery in battle, as well as other significant military contributions in a battlefield environment. Although somewhat difficult to understand in non-German eyes, a young soldier who was brave during several armored attacks under fire could receive the award, as could the captain at regimental headquarters who planned several successful attacks but did not fire a shot in anger in any of them. Some two and a half million (and maybe more) Iron Crosses Second Class were awarded during World War II; a soldier could be bestowed the award one time during the conflict.[8] Units were often given ceilings concerning how many of these awards could be bestowed after an operation, in an attempt to curb inflation. Some examples linked that one Iron Cross First Class could be awarded for every ten Iron Crosses Second Class awarded.

Intuitively one would think that almost every soldier in this study received the Iron Cross Second Class at some point during the war; sources—to include many personnel files—indicates that at least 133 did.

Iron Cross First Class. For repeated acts of valor or military achievement a recipient of the Iron Cross Second Class could be awarded the Iron Cross First Class, although the acts needed to be of greater magnitude and involve initiative. As the war progressed, commanders often tried to push through more Iron Cross First Class awards and had to be reminded that a ratio of one first class award for every eight second class awards was about the appropriate balance.[9] As with the Iron Cross Second Class, a soldier could receive only one Iron Cross First Class. Some three hundred thousand Iron Cross First Class decorations were presented during the war.[10]

A minimum of thirty-five Tiger crewmen that fought in the 2nd SS Panzer Corps during the Kursk Offensive received the Iron Cross First Class during their careers.

Knight's Cross of the Iron Cross. Instituted on September 1, 1939, the Knight's Cross was a new decoration. Criteria for the award varied by service and were adjusted as the war progressed. For U-boat commanders, for example, enemy warships sunk and the tonnage of merchant ships sunk were driving criteria. For a ground soldier in the German Army or Waffen-SS, the recipient must have proven himself by continuous acts of exceptional bravery. An awardee was required to have previously received the Iron Cross First Class. For ground commanders, generals, for example, could receive the award for formulating and/or executing a major battle resulting in significant gains. Adolf Hitler was the final approval authority for the decoration; a soldier could only win the award once. Overall the Association of Knight's Cross recipients believes that 7,321 presentations in total, of which 457 were Waffen-SS soldiers, during the war were valid presentations of the Knight's Cross.[11]

Eight Waffen-SS Tiger crewmen won the Knight's Cross of the Iron Cross in their careers. One soldier in this study, Wilfried Richter of the 9th (Heavy) Company, won the award for actions in another unit a year prior to Kursk. Franz Staudegger, of the 13th (Heavy Company), won the award for actions accomplished at Kursk—specifically destroying some twenty-two enemy tanks on July 8. Six other men in the study received the Knight's Cross between October 1943 and the end of the war, including: Heinrich Kling, Bobby Woll, Michael Wittmann, and Bubi Wendorff of the 13th (Heavy) Company; Alois Kalss of the 8th (Heavy) Company; and Fritz Biermeier of the 9th (Heavy) Company.

Knight's Cross of the Iron Cross with Oak Leaves. Seeing a need for a higher grade of Knight's Cross, Hitler instituted the Knight's Cross of the Iron Cross with Oak Leaves on June 3, 1940. The Führer was again the final approving authority of the award. An awardee was required to have previously received the Knight's Cross of the Iron Cross; for ground soldiers the recipient must have continued to displayed acts of exceptional bravery or significant achievement after the award of the Knight's Cross. A soldier could win the Oak Leaves one time. Some 882 personnel throughout the Wehrmacht received the Knight's Cross with Oak Leaves during the war; seventy-four went to Waffen-SS soldiers.[12]

In this study, none of the Tiger crewmen received the award for actions at Kursk. However, two men received the Oak Leaves in 1944: Michael Wittmann of the 13th (Heavy) Company on January 30, 1944, and Fritz Biermeier of the 9th (Heavy) Company on December 26, 1944 (posthumously.)

Knight's Cross of the Iron Cross with Oak Leaves and Swords. The war dragged on another year, and on June 21, 1941, Hitler instituted another higher grade of the Knight's Cross, the Knight's Cross of the Iron Cross with Oak Leaves and Swords. For ground troops, continued acts of exceptional bravery; again Adolf Hitler was the final approval authority. The Association of Knight's Cross Recipients believes that 160 presentations—of which twenty-four were Waffen-SS soldiers—during the war were made of the Knight's Cross with Oak Leaves and Swords.[13]

Only Michael Wittmann in this study of Tiger crewmen received the Swords; the award was presented to him on June 22, 1944.

War Order of the German Cross ("German Cross in Gold.") Instituted by Hitler in September 1941, the German Cross in Gold was intended to recognize a degree of bravery or combat related service above that warranted by the Iron Cross First Class but insufficient to earn the Knight's Cross. Some 24,204 presentations of the award were made during the war, of which 822 were to members of the Waffen-SS. The Commander in Chief of the Wehrmacht or the Commander in Chief of a service was the final approval of the award.[14]

Six Tiger crewmen that fought in the Kursk Offensive would receive the German Cross in Gold during the war: Karl Heinz Lorenz, 8th (Heavy) Company, received the award on April 17, 1943, before the Kursk Offensive. Herbert Zimmermann, 8th (Heavy) Company (September 8, 1943), Alois Kalss (September 23, 1943), and Johann Reinhardt, 8th (Heavy) Company (September 25, 1943), clearly received the award as a result of their performances at Kursk. Heinrich Kling received his award on December 30, 1943, and his leadership at Kursk played a role in the recommendation for the award. Jürgen Brandt of the 13th (Heavy) Company (January 13, 1945) received his award primarily for later-than-Kursk efforts.

Wound Badge in Black. First instituted by German Emperor Wilhelm II on March 3, 1918, to wounded or frostbitten soldiers of the Imperial German Army, it was awarded to members of all the military services in World War II who were wounded as a result of enemy hostile actions or for certain degrees of frostbite. After March 1943, it could also be awarded to civilian casualties during enemy bombing raids of Germany. To qualify for the award in black, the recipient must have been wounded once or twice by hostile action. Several million of these awards were issued during the war.[15]

At least seventy Tiger crewmen in this book received the Wound Badge in Black during the war.

Wound Badge in Silver. In the same family as the Wound Badge in Black, the Wound Badge in Silver could be awarded in two ways: first, for the accumulation of being wounded three or four times; or second, if a single wound resulted in the loss of a limb or the loss of eyesight in one eye, or the loss of hearing; some cases also included in the silver category were brain damage or severe facial disfiguration. In some instances a soldier initially received a Wound Badge in Black and several months later, if a limb had to be amputated, the soldier would receive the Wound Badge in Silver at the hospital. Tens of thousands of these badges were probably awarded, although no official count appears to have been ever recorded.[16]

At least twenty Tiger crewmen in this book received the Wound Badge in Silver during the war.

Wound Badge in Gold. The highest grade of wound badge was the Wound Badge in Gold. It could be awarded for an accumulation of five or more wounds and was also bestowed for very serious wounds, such as total blindness or total disability—for example, the loss of more than one limb.[17] At least seven Tiger crewmen in this book received the award and there may have been more.

Heinrich Kling, Kurt Sowa, Paul Sümnich, and Waldemar Schütz of the 13th (Heavy) Company and Walter Knecht and Alois Kalss, and Julius Hinrichsen of the 8th (Heavy) Company received the Wound Badge in Gold during the war.

Panzer Battle Badge in Silver. First awarded in the Great War, and again in the Spanish Civil War, the Panzer Battle Badge was reinstituted on December 20, 1939; the following year, on June 6, 1940, a separate class of the badge in bronze was instituted for crews of assault guns, halftracks, etc. For tank crews the award criteria included participation in three armored assaults on three different days; to have been wounded in the course of an armored assault; or to have earned a bravery decoration in the course of an armored assault. Tens of thousands, and maybe more, of these badges were probably awarded during the war.[18]

Company headquarters kept track of official armored assault days, as not all days of general combat qualified. For example, a support document in the personnel file of Werner Schweitzer, a radio operator in the 9th (Heavy) Company, credits him for official panzer assault days of July 6, 1943—*Attack at Ternovka*; July 7, 1943—*Attack at Nepkhayevo*; and July 8, 1943—*Defense against an enemy attack at the Dolschin Gulch*. The application for the award was sent from the company to the panzer regiment on July 15, 1943.[19] At this point in the war only tank crews could receive this award; later in the war combat support soldiers, such as tank recovery crews, could also receive the award, but only if they were in combat during their operations.[20] At least 103 crewmen in this study received the Panzer Battle Badge in Silver during the war.

Panzer Battle Badge in Silver for 25, 50, 75, 100, or 200 Assaults. By June 1943, German military leaders recognized that additional awards for additional assaults were deserved by panzer soldiers and thus developed numbered Panzer Battle Badges in Silver, as well as in bronze for assault gun crews, etc. It is not known how many were presented during the war.[21]

At least ten Tiger crewmen in this study received the Panzer Battle Badge for 25 Assaults: Paul Bender, Jürgen Brandt, and Karl-Heinz Warmbrunn, formerly of the 13th (Heavy) Company, received the award on December 1, 1944; Jürgen Brandt received the award on January 13, 1945 (posthumously). For men that had been in the 8th (Heavy) Company, Heinz Trautmann received the badge on September 21, 1944, while Wolfgang Birnbaum, Heinrich Asmussen, and Berthold Fink received it later in the war. Concerning former 9th (Heavy) Company Tiger crewmen, Fritz Biermeier received the award on October 1, 1944. Not only did Alois Kalss, formerly in the 8th (Heavy) Company, earn the Panzer Battle Badge in Silver for 25 Assaults, but several sources indicate that he would receive the Panzer Battle Badge in Silver for 100 Assaults.

Tank Destruction Badge. On March 9, 1942, the OKW published an order instituting the Special Badge for Single-Handed Destruction of a Tank. Given that an individual soldier, armed with a hand held weapon such as a hand grenade, antitank mine, satchel charge, or rocket grenade was always the awardee, panzer troops usually did not receive the award, but could if they were fighting dismounted using a weapon listed. There may have been thousands of awards bestowed, as it was locally approved. Reportedly the record for destroyed tanks by one man using the above criteria was twenty-one.[22]

This study concludes that Alois Kalss earned two Tank Destruction Badges during the war, as did Heinz Trautmann. Franz Staudegger could have received two Tank Destruction Badges at Kursk for destroying two enemy tanks on the night of July 5–6, but instead was awarded the Iron Cross First Class.

Infantry Assault Badge. Instituted on December 20, 1939, by the commander-in-chief of the German Army Colonel General Walther von Brauchitsch, the Infantry Assault Badge was a war badge awarded to Waffen-SS and German Army soldiers for "three assault attacks, on the front line, attacking with weapon in hand, on three different days of battle." When a counteroffensive led to fighting it could also be awarded; it was awarded in silver for regular infantry troops or in bronze for motorized or mechanized (panzer grenadier) troops. Medical personnel could receive the award for protecting wounded men in close combat situations on three different days of battle. Award of the badge was authorized at the regimental command level. Several hundred thousand were probably awarded.[23]

At least fourteen Tiger crewmen received one of the Infantry Assault Badges for their service in that branch before they joined the panzers. Some thirty-eight of the men were identified as serving in the infantry prior to joining the panzers.

General Assault Badge. Seeing that support troops were essential to the infantry, on June 1, 1940, Colonel General Walther von Brauchitsch instituted the General Assault Badge to personnel of the German Army, Waffen-SS, and Order Police who supported an infantry attack, such as soldiers in the combat engineers, artillery, antiaircraft and antitank who supported infantry units in combat, or to medical personnel attending to battlefield casualties, but were not part of specific infantry units and therefore did not qualify for the Infantry Assault Badge. Several hundred thousand of these badges were awarded during the war.[24]

Selection of Soldiers for Assignment

The headquarters of the Waffen-SS in Berlin published orders about October 14, 1942, for the creation of three heavy companies to be equipped with the Tiger: one in SS Panzer Grenadier Division *Leibstandarte Adolf Hitler*, one in SS Panzer Grenadier Division *Das Reich*, and one in SS Panzer Grenadier Division *Totenkopf*. A second order, signed by *SS-Gruppenführer* Hans Jüttner, chief of staff of the SS Leadership Main Office—which was responsible for the organizational and administrative leadership of the Waffen-SS—directed that the responsibility for the creation of the companies lay with each of these three divisions. The companies would officially be created on November 15, 1942. Each division would fill command positions (e.g., company commander) in the new companies. Each division would provide non-commissioned officers and enlisted men. The divisions were instructed to notify Berlin to backfill replacements in the units from which the transferred men originated.[25]

This appeared to be quite a different procedure than that used in the panzer forces of the German Army. According to historian Bob Carruthers, the army took many of its best panzer crews of other model tanks and sent them to form the cadre of the Tiger crews. This cadre, as well as other Tiger I instructors, were concentrated at the Panzer School at Paderborn, Germany.[26] The German Army panzer structure operated other schools as well. Panzer Troops School I in Munster, Lower Saxony, Germany, and Panzer Troops School II at Wünsdorf, south of Berlin, were the first two major schools established to train German panzer officers to operate and employ tanks. The army sent officer candidates here after twelve to sixteen weeks of basic training, plus successfully passing a two-month course at a war academy. Later they attended a sixteen-week course to familiarize themselves with the workings of a panzer and command field tactics; only then were they promoted to senior officer candidate and put on field probation. Instructors at these schools had been selected because they were skilled and been in combat and because they were well-decorated role models.

Between October and December the divisions began organizing. Kursk had not yet registered on anyone's mind. The German Sixth Army was surrounded at Stalingrad and fighting for its life. Within the *Totenkopf*, the responsibility for manning the bulk of the company fell to the 3rd Panzer Regiment, which received orders that the other panzer companies in the regiment were to release men for the initial cadre. Orders were orders, but the various company commanders within the regiment kept their best men and released surplus soldiers. The new cadre arrived; initial training on the Tiger was to be carried out under the supervision of the army's 502nd Heavy Panzer Detachment and would begin no later than December 26, 1942, at the German Army's Troop Training Grounds Bergen at Fallingbostel. On January 1, 1943, ten Panzer Mark IIIs were delivered for the *Totenkopf* to train with at Fallingbostel. Their first field exercise began on January 2, 1943.[27]

Many junior men came straight from their initial technical training—such as communications school for radio operators—to the three companies. Several men whose initial training had not been in any branch of the Waffen-SS arrived at their new homes in spring 1943. *SS-Reichsführer* Heinrich Himmler had reached an agreement early in 1943 with Luftwaffe chief Hermann Göring for a transfer of 2,500 airmen to the Waffen-SS to replace combat losses. Nowhere in the pact did it specify sending any of these men to panzer units. While the new Waffen-SS soldiers seemed to be well-received by their comrades and several were soon elevated to command of Tigers, they clearly had little in the way of previous panzer experience, not to mention rudimentary ground tactics. This begs the question of why these Luftwaffe men were sent to select Tiger units, rather than the infantry, or a branch of lesser technical requirements.[28] Seven former Luftwaffe airmen were transferred from that service to the units in this study: three to the 13th (Heavy) Company and four to the 8th (Heavy) Company.

The study has one other head-scratching question concerning Tiger personnel at Kursk. It is obvious that individual soldiers cannot swing the outcome of a major engagement. However, there are numerous instances throughout military history where professional education has been modified, and even shortened, to get young, capable soldiers out of the classroom and into front line units. The United States Military Academy (West Point) graduated the thirty-four-man class of 1862 a year early on June 24, 1861, so they could arrive in the Army now that the Civil War had commenced. Some eighty years later, during the height of World War II, Congress approved an accelerated program that scheduled the original West Point class of 1943 (normally graduating in June) for early graduation in January of that year.

One might think that the Waffen-SS, whose leaders knew of the upcoming Kursk Offensive several months before its start date, might have delayed the few Tiger crewmen scheduled to return to Germany for training so they could remain in their units until later that summer, but that does not appear to be the case. Historian Rüdiger Warnick has located a report dated July 1, 1943, that veteran Paul Egger and eight other Tiger crewmen from the 8th (Heavy) Company were back in Germany for Waffen-SS leadership training.[29] While training schedules were kept and attendance quotas filled, these men, and possibly others in the 13th (Heavy) Company and the 9th (Heavy) company, would be sorely missed in the fight.

Kursk: Training Ground for Normandy, the Ardennes, and the Battle of Berlin

Realizing that employing Tigers in separate companies was not the optimum solution for such a powerful weapon, the Waffen-SS, as well as the German Army, formed independent Tiger detachments, which in effect were battalions in size. Many fielded three companies; the intent was to use these companies together so as to achieve critical mass and shock value on the battlefield. Within the Waffen-SS, three heavy panzer detachments were created beginning in 1943: the 101st SS Heavy Panzer Detachment, the 102nd SS Heavy Panzer Detachment, and the 103rd SS Heavy Panzer Detachment. All fielded Tiger I tanks, as by now the initial Tiger II—King Tiger—versions were nearing production.

The 101st SS Heavy Panzer Detachment was created on July 19, 1943, to be part of the Ist SS Panzer Corps. The process involved incorporating the 13th (Heavy) Company of the *Leibstandarte* with two new heavy tank companies that also had Tigers; the new unit deployed to Verona, Italy, on August 23, 1943, to combat the anticipated Allied invasion of that country now that the island of Sicily had fallen. The unit remained in Italy until mid-October, when the unit sent some of its elements back to the Eastern Front.

Italy was invaded, but by early 1944, the threat to Germany in the west lay not in Italy, but the anticipated invasion from England to some part of the French—such as Pas-de-Calais—or even the Belgian coast. Elements of the unit were ordered to move west, which they did beginning in March 1944. It was stationed at various locations over the next three months, including Beauvais, northwest of Paris. With the Allied invasion of Normandy on June 6, 1944, the detachment received orders to move to Argentan, Normandy.

Over the next two months the detachment fought in significant battles, including the Battle of Villers-Bocage on June 13, 1944. On August 8, 1944, several detachment Tigers were destroyed near Saint-Aignan-de-Cramesnil, including renowned commander Michael Wittmann. By this time the detachment's surplus crews began outfitting with the new Tiger II tanks back in Germany. The 101st SS Heavy Panzer Detachment lost virtually all its remaining Tigers in the Falaise pocket and the subsequent German Seventh Army retreat from France. On September 9, 1944, the remains of the unit was ordered to rest and refit with the new Tiger IIs.

Thirty-one SS Tiger crewmen that fought in the Kursk Offensive later fought in the 101st SS Heavy Panzer Detachment in Normandy.

Eleven SS Tiger commanders at Kursk later served as Tiger commanders in the 101st SS Heavy Panzer Detachment in Normandy; three more Tiger commanders in the detachment in Normandy had served in other crew positions at Kursk.

At the start of the Normandy Campaign, the 101st SS Heavy Panzer Detachment had forty-five Tigers assigned; thirty-seven were operational, with the remaining eight in some stage of repair. Those forty-five Tigers, each with a five-man crew, would therefore have had 225 crewmen authorized. Based on this study and the biographies included, 13.7% of the Tiger crewmen in the detachment had fought in Tigers at Kursk. Perhaps more significantly, at Normandy roughly thirty-one percent of the Tiger commanders in the 101st SS Heavy Panzer Detachment had cut their teeth at Kursk.

Another unit that made its mark in Normandy was the 102nd SS Heavy Panzer Detachment. Created on paper on March 23, 1943, the demands from the SS Main Leadership Office in Berlin immediately came into conflict, as Sepp Dietrich, then commander of the *Leibstandarte*, balked and requested a meeting with the Führer. That and the upcoming offensive delayed formation until the middle of July. As the Tiger company of the *Leibstandarte* was the base organization for the 101st, the Tiger company of the *Das Reich* became the base company for the 102nd. In August, the detachment was attached to the *Das Reich* and remained so until October 1943, when it deployed back to Augustdorf, Germany. On November 4, 1943, the SS Main Leadership Office designated that the Tiger company in the *Das Reich* would be placed under an organization to be called the 102nd SS Heavy Panzer Detachment (the headquarters to have Field Post Number 56085). The unit would have three Tiger companies: the 1st Company (Field Post Number 13693), the 2nd Company (Field Post Number 12748), the 3rd Company (Field Post Number 12764), and a maintenance company (Field Post Number 58263).[30]

The detachment began deploying to Argentan, Normandy, in December 1943. Its authorized strength on June 1, 1944, was forty-six Tiger I panzers. During the Normandy campaign the detachment fought in significant battles, including the Battle of Hill 112 on July 10–11, 1944. The detachment was subordinated to 10th SS Panzer Grenadier Division *Hohenstauffen* on July 9, 1944, and to the 9th SS Panzer Grenadier Division *Frundsberg* on August 2, 1944.

Fifty-six SS Tiger crewmen that fought in the Kursk Offensive later fought with the 102nd SS Heavy Panzer Detachment in Normandy.

Seventeen SS Tiger commanders at Kursk later served as Tiger commanders in the 102nd SS Heavy Panzer Detachment in Normandy; one more Tiger commander in the detachment in Normandy had served in another crew position at Kursk.

Based on the biographies of these Tiger crews, 23.9% of the Tiger crewmen in the 102nd SS Heavy Panzer Detachment had fought in Tigers at Kursk. An even greater proportion, some 39.1% of the Tiger commanders in this unit in Normandy had fought at the Kursk Offensive in the Tiger crews of the 2nd SS Panzer Corps. One source credits the 102nd SS Heavy Panzer Detachment with destroying 227 tanks and twenty-eight antitank guns during the period July 10 through August 20, 1944, in Normandy.[31]

On September 22, 1944, the Waffen-SS renamed the shattered 101st SS Heavy Panzer Detachment the 501st SS Heavy Panzer Detachment. The unit had only one Tiger tank left, but the Tiger I was not going to be the centerpiece of the new unit—that would come with the arrival of the Tiger II, known by most as the King Tiger. The first four King Tigers arrived on October 17, 1944, and six more came in the following day. As before, the detachment would be organized with forty-five panzers.[32]

The unit soon received an important mission, although secrecy was so tight that most men would not know about the operation until the day before it began. The detachment was attached to the 1st SS Panzer Regiment in the 1st SS Panzer Division *Leibstandarte Adolf Hitler* on December 14, 1944—its mission would be to spearhead the German Sixth SS Panzer Army's attack into the Ardennes to shatter the American front, capture the major supply port at Antwerp, and possibly cause a stalemate in the west. *Operation Wacht am Rhein* (Operation Watch on the Rhine) was a pipe dream, but for the next several days the old veterans of the detachment told the youngsters what had happened at Kursk—and what could happen in the Ardennes once the Tigers got rolling.

The villages of Honsfeld, Büllingen, Stavelot, Trois Ponts, and La Gleize subsequently became forever linked with the 501st SS Heavy Panzer Detachment and the 1944 Ardennes Offensive. At least twelve Tiger crewmen that fought at Kursk also fought at the Battle of the Bulge and with Army Group South in 1945, at which time the unit had, on March 15, 1945, thirty-two King Tigers on hand, of which eight were operational.[33] These crewmen included:

Hein Bode: commanded King Tiger 112 in the First Platoon in the 1st Company
Jürgen Brandt: commanded King Tiger 131 in the Third Platoon of the 1st Company
Heinz Buchner: commanded King Tiger 121 in the Second Platoon of the 1st Company
Siegfried Fuss: commanded a King Tiger
Ewald Mölly: commanded Tiger 232 in the Third Platoon of the 2nd Company
Karl Müller: commanded King Tiger 223 in the Second Platoon of the 2nd Company
Kurt Sowa: commanded King Tiger 222 in the Second Platoon of the Second Company
Franz Staudegger: commanded King Tiger 123 in the Second Platoon of the 1st Company
Werner Wendt: commanded King Tiger 133 in the Third Platoon of the 2nd Company

Meanwhile, the 102nd SS Heavy Panzer Detachment lost its final Tiger on September 1, 1944. The remaining personnel withdrew to the SS Panzer Replacement Detachment at Sennelager; now designated the 502nd SS Heavy Panzer Detachment, the unit received its initial six King

Tigers on December 27, 1944. From mid-February 1945 to March 6, 1945, further arrivals of King Tigers increased unit strength to thirty-one Tiger II tanks. All of them were operational on March 15, 1945.[34] The detachment saw its first combat beginning March 22, 1945, near Küstrin, on the Oder Front; it ended the war attempting to escape from the Halbe Pocket on May 1, 1945.

Thirty-six SS Tiger crewmen that fought in the Kursk Offensive later fought with the 502nd SS Heavy Panzer Detachment on the Oder Front at the end of the war:

Kurt Baral: commanded King Tiger 121 in the Second Platoon of the 1st Company
Willy Biber: commanded King Tiger 321 in the Second Platoon of the 3rd Company
Kurt Hellwig: commanded King Tiger 222 in the Second Platoon of the 2nd Company
Gerhard Kaempf: commanded King Tiger 123 and later 124 in the Second Platoon of 1st Company
Alois Kalss: commanded King Tiger 101 in the 1st Company
Franz Kraml: commanded King Tiger 112 in the First Platoon of the 1st Company
Walter Reibold: commanded King Tiger 123 in the Second Platoon of the 1st Company
Wilhelm Schmidt: commanded a King Tiger in the 1st Company
Konrad Schweigert: commanded a King Tiger

The last King Tiger tanks lost during the war were destroyed near the Kummersdorff automotive proving grounds just south of Berlin in May 1945. That was ironic, as the dream of the German panzer corps for the Tiger had started—in part—at the same location in the vehicle's infancy in May 1942.

Conclusions

The Battle of Kursk—more specifically the tank battle near Prokhorovka on July 11–12, 1943—was not the largest tank battle in history; that honor probably goes to the Battle of Brody in the Ukraine in late June 1941, when some 4,250 Soviet and German tanks battled during the opening phase of *Operation Barbarossa* and of them 1,100 were destroyed. Kursk was, on repeated reflection, the most interesting large scale tank battle ever fought. There are several reasons for this. First, as has been discussed, there was widespread argument on the German side to even conduct the attack. Second, the depth and lethality of the Soviet defenses have been analyzed as the most formidable antitank killing fields in history: during the first half of July the Red Army defended a total of 190 miles in depth, deployed 503,663 antitank mines interspersed with 439,348 anti-personnel mines, dug 5,700 miles of trenches, and deployed some 1,910,361 soldiers, 5,128 tanks, and 25,013 artillery/antitank/mortar weapon systems. The Germans had less than half the men, sixty percent as many tanks, and forty percent as much artillery, and still they attacked, and kept attacking for eleven days.

Third, Kursk was the combat birthplace of significant new weapons. It was really the first use of substantial numbers of Tiger tanks; although they had many, many maintenance issues, the roughly two hundred Panther tanks that debuted at Kursk showed that this new model of panzer would become a formidable opponent. A cousin of the Tiger, the heavy tank destroyer "Ferdinand," made its debut as well, with some ninety of these vehicles in action with Army Group Center in the northern pincer.

Finally, Kursk validated that a Waffen-SS panzer corps could be one of the most powerful fighting elements of the Wehrmacht after that concept was first evaluated at Kharkov in February–March 1943. The 2nd SS Panzer Corps at the Kursk Offensive turned that initial success into a trend and opponents of Germany began to study these significant ground units that were not part of the German Army but proved their ferociousness nonetheless.

It is always perilous to make conclusions based on small populations. Our sample size of the Waffen-SS troopers of the Tiger tank crews in the 2nd SS Panzer Corps at Kursk is small—less than 250 men. However, the three Tiger companies at Kursk represented, at the time, 100% of all Tiger crews then in the frontline units of the Waffen-SS. What Heinrich Himmler's military learned from the experience at Kursk would undoubtedly shape the future of the Tiger tank in the *Leibstandarte*, *Das Reich*, and *Totenkopf* divisions, and any other Waffen-SS Tiger formation for the rest of the war. Therefore, what can we conclude about these men and their performance during this battle?

The SS Tiger Crews at Kursk Never Quit Despite a High Level of Battle Ferocity

Ferocity (fəräsədē)
the state or quality of being ferocious.

Ferocious (fə-rō-shəs)
exhibiting or given to extreme fierceness and unrestrained violence and brutality; extremely intense; showing fury or malignity in looks or actions.

This study would like to introduce a concept concerning the level of battle ferocity. Quite simply, every soldier involved in combat has an *expectation* of the character and conduct of the fighting about to take place—how ferocious it will be. This expectation is based on previous combat experience, where on the battlefield the soldier is fighting, what other soldiers have discussed about combat, the soldier's own opinion of equipment, tactics, leaders, and comrades on his own side, and the soldiers' opinions on the same categories concerning the enemy.

For example, does the enemy employ really brutal weapons, such as flamethrowers and massive amounts of artillery? If yes, then many soldiers will conclude that this is extremely vicious. Does the enemy routinely kill prisoners? Again, that would be considered extreme fierceness. Does the enemy attempt to close with the opposing side and finish the fight by killing with knives, entrenching tools, machetes, and other slash and smash weapons? Or even strangling or beating to death with their bare hands? Many soldiers view hand-to-hand combat as unrestrained fury.

Casualties play a role; the higher friendly casualties are the more ferocious the fighting is perceived. The way in which soldiers die can add to ferocity. Burning alive inside a tank, or losing both legs to a mine and taking six hours to die in agony are horrible ways to go. If losses are few and spread out over time they are viewed much differently than when one's comrades die in bunches. Also factoring in are the soldiers' assessment of the terrain over which the battle is taking place, the noise level of the fight, the temperature and the weather—in short, everything that contributes to the fighting being ferocious.

Soldiers will form their initial expectations of the level of battle ferocity before the battle begins. Then, after the fighting commences, each soldier will continuously reassess that initial expectation with reality as combat unfolds. The fighting may be so fierce, sudden, and continuous that the soldier is in react mode most of the time, but likely, at some point every day, the soldier will make one of three general conclusions about the ferocity of the battle:

This is more ferocious than I thought. We are getting beat. Lots of our soldiers have been killed or wounded, and I may well be next no matter how careful I am. Second platoon lost half the men last night in hand-to-hand combat. My equipment is breaking or being destroyed. There is so much artillery I can't hear myself think. The temperatures are going to kill me; my feet hurt so badly maybe I have trench foot. The food is terrible; I wonder if I have diarrhea?

In general, the soldier is concluding that the battle is more violent, brutal, and painful than the soldier thought it would be, or more ferocious than the last time the soldier made this assessment. In its worst case, the ferocity of battle causes the soldier to become convinced that sooner or later he will be killed.

This is about the same as I thought. The enemy is not ten feet tall, but they can and do inflict losses on us. If I do my job we will hopefully be alright, we will probably win, and I will get home in relatively good shape. There are about the number of friendly casualties as I expected. This new tank can take some hits and still keep rolling. I still have a level of nervousness, but I can survive. War is hell and I won't tell my grandkids how bad it was, but at least I might make it out to someday have grandkids.

This isn't so bad—a lot less terrible than I thought it would be. The only soldiers who are getting killed on our side are those doing stupid things. Lots of the enemy are dying. My equipment is saving my life. It is not as noisy as I thought it would be. My training got me ready for this. Not only will we win, and I'll make it, but we'll be home by Christmas if this keeps up.

Concerning the level of battle ferocity, this is a constant assessment made by every soldier. It can change in a minute, or it can remain the same over a lengthy period of time. Some of the soldier's input concerning battle ferocity is rational and some of it is not. This is because some things in war appear rational, others appear irrational, and still others seem to be arational outside the domain of reason. Every soldier thinks and assesses differently.

Why is the level of battle ferocity important to understand? **In the offense, if a critical mass of attackers believe that the battle is too ferocious, they will stop moving forward and hunker down in an attempt to weather the storm until that ferocity lessens; in the defense, if a critical mass of defenders believe that the battle is too ferocious, they will cease defending and either surrender, withdraw to a position of reduced ferocity, or retreat.**

The level of battle ferocity is not just another restatement of the idea of a "culminating point" that Carl Clausewitz introduced in his work *On War* in the 1800s. That valid concept, in this study's opinion, had more to do with a higher level of war—the operational. Clausewitz believed that at this level of war, the strength of the attacker in the advance was constantly being diminished by several causes: the necessity of the attacking army to guard the terrain in its rear to preserve its line of communication and supply; losses in combat and through disease; the ever increasing distance from the fighting force from its various depots of supplies and reinforcements; the peeling away of offensive forces to conduct sieges and blockades of fortresses; forces leaving an alliance; and any relaxation of efforts (possibly caused by overconfidence).

The combination of those events, according to Clausewitz, was that at some point not only could the attacker not continue the advance, but that the attacker could not even halt in place and defend what had already been conquered, but rather, withdraw to some previous line of defense that was more favorable.

The level of battle ferocity is a tactical term, and throughout military history there are a multitude of examples of its effect. Pickett's Charge, on July 3, 1863, the third and final day of the Battle of Gettysburg, involved an infantry assault of approximately 11,500 Confederate soldiers from Robert E. Lee's Army of Northern Virginia against 6,500 Union troops of Maj. Gen. George Meade's Army of the Potomac. The assault was preceded by an artillery bombardment of 150 Confederate guns, the largest grand battery ever assembled on the North American continent and probably the loudest artillery fire of the war. Some seventy-five Union cannon responded until ordered to cease fire and conserve ammunition; thus, at its height 225 guns in an area 1.5 miles by 1.5 miles volleyed and thundered.

The nine brigades of attacking troops began at Seminary Ridge in the west and covered more than three-quarters of a mile—initially slightly downhill and then uphill—crossing the Emmitsburg Road and seizing Cemetery Ridge, manned by Federal units. The assault of the nine brigades of Confederate infantry was vulnerable to Union cannon fire the entire time and casualties immediately mounted, growing larger as the Confederates drew closer to their objective. Some 125 to 250 yards before reaching the enemy, Confederate infantry were forced to cross the sunken Emmitsburg Road that had a rail fence on the west side and a post-and-board fence on the east. Both fences were not only in range of Union artillery firing case, cannister, and double cannister rounds—designed to blow apart enemy infantry formations—but also were in range of Union small arms fire. To make matters worse, the Confederates were now being hit by enfilade fire from both flanks. Amid all this shot and shell, Lee's infantry would have to climb over or tear down these fence obstacles while under fire so the momentum of the attack could be maintained.

John M. Priest, author of *Into the Fight: Pickett's Charge at Gettysburg*, analyzed the battle and came to some amazing conclusions. First, he analyzed casualty information. Two of the major Confederate elements in the charge were Maj. Gen. George Pickett's Division on the right and that of Brig. Gen. James Johnston Pettigrew on the left. Excluding losses from artillery, Pickett's Division suffered 2,376 casualties, of which 750 were wounded and captured and 613 unwounded captured (1,363 total prisoners). Pettigrew's Division lost 1,433 casualties, of which 223 were wounded and captured and 535 unwounded captured (758 total prisoners).[1]

Second, he compared the numbers of those captured with a baseline of casualties throughout the war: given the numbers of troops involved and the frontages of the attack, "normally" seventeen percent of the casualties would be killed, sixty-six percent would be wounded, and seventeen percent would be captured (both wounded prisoners and not). Therefore Pickett could have been expected to have lost 403 prisoners and Pettigrew some 243. However, both units at Pickett's Charge suffered more than three times the number of expected prisoners.[2]

The historian continued: "Union and Confederate accounts clearly state that most of the captured were found in the Emmitsburg Road and in the killing zone between the Road and the Federal line. The fact that captured men outnumbered the killed and wounded indicates that many did not leave the cover of the roadbed."[3]

This critical mass of Confederate attackers, once they had reached the Emmitsburg Road, believed that the battle was too ferocious; they stopped moving forward and hunkered down in an attempt to weather the storm until that ferocity lessened, which came in the form of being taken prisoner of war.

Kursk was also a ferocious fight with a high level of battle ferocity. Almost by definition, the fighting between Germany and the Soviet Union fits the definition of an extremely high level of battle ferocity. We understand that this perception may not have been universal among the soldiers fighting at Kursk. So let us examine a few characteristics of the fighting from the point of view of the Tiger crews in the 2nd SS Panzer Corps.

The Tiger crews in the division understood at the basic level that their mission was to spearhead attacks north of the panzer corps, penetrate enemy defenses, destroy enemy mobile reserves (which generally would be tanks), and push forward about 100 kilometers to link with forces from Army Group Center coming south. Such an ambitious mission could be expected to suffer ferocious casualties, but did it?

The following shows the number of killed and wounded among the Tiger crews from the three companies. Those who later died of wounds are included for the date that they received those grievous wounds as that day when their comrades saw them fall. It does not include selected support troops from the companies, nor does it include panzer grenadier casualties to the units the Tigers supported. In addition, none of the Tiger crewmen in the three companies surrendered during the Kursk Offensive.

July 5   13th (Heavy) Company: 2 killed, 4 wounded
           8th (Heavy) Company: 2 killed, 8 wounded
           9th (Heavy) Company: 1 wounded
July 6   13th (Heavy) Company: 1 wounded
           8th (Heavy) Company: 5 wounded

	9th (Heavy) Company: no casualties
July 7	13th (Heavy) Company: no casualties
	8th (Heavy) Company: 5 killed, 7 wounded
	9th (Heavy) Company: no casualties
July 8	13th (Heavy) Company: no casualties
	8th (Heavy) Company: 1 wounded
	9th (Heavy) Company: 4 killed
July 9	13th (Heavy) Company: 1 killed
	8th (Heavy) Company: no casualties
	9th (Heavy) Company: no casualties
July 10	13th (Heavy) Company: 1 wounded
	8th (Heavy) Company: no casualties
	9th (Heavy) Company: no casualties
July 11	13th (Heavy) Company: 2 wounded
	8th (Heavy) Company: 1 killed, 2 wounded
	9th (Heavy) Company: no casualties
July 12	13th (Heavy) Company: 1 killed
	8th (Heavy) Company: 2 wounded
	9th (Heavy) Company: 1 killed, 1 wounded
July 13	13th (Heavy) Company: 1 wounded
	8th (Heavy) Company: no casualties
	9th (Heavy) Company: no casualties
July 14	13th (Heavy) Company: no casualties
	8th (Heavy) Company: no casualties
	9th (Heavy) Company: no casualties
July 15	13th (Heavy) Company: 1 wounded
	8th (Heavy) Company: 1 killed, 1 wounded
	9th (Heavy) Company: no casualties

These overall casualties were incurred as follows: 13th (Heavy) Company—four killed, ten wounded; 8th (Heavy) Company—nine killed, twenty-two wounded; and 9th (Heavy) Company—five killed and two wounded. Eighteen killed is an average of one or two per day and thirty-two wounded is almost three per day. Companies had zero casualties in sixteen days of battle: four days for the 13th (Heavy) Company, four days for the 8th (Heavy) Company, and eight days for the 9th (Heavy) Company. This study has concluded that these are not indicative for a level of high battle ferocity for the Tiger crews and is probably less than the crews expected before the battle began.

A separate analysis concerning the loss of company officers might yield interesting results if some of them had served for quite a long time in the unit or were acknowledged brave individuals, such as winners of the Knight's Cross and higher grades of that award. It appears that none of the officers killed in the three Tiger companies examined belonged to either category. This was unlike the following summer in Normandy. When super Tiger commander Michael Wittmann was killed in action on August 8, 1944, near Saint-Aignan-de-Cramesnil, Normandy, that news skyrocketed throughout the Waffen-SS as a true morale breaker. On the other hand, combat branch officers in both the Waffen-SS and the German Army understood that their imperative was to lead their units from the front against the enemy, which made their positions extremely vulnerable to death or serious wounds.

What about Tigers destroyed and damaged? A high number would contribute to a perceived high level of battle ferocity. From the experience of the Tigers at Kharkov most, if not all, Tiger crewmen in the 2nd SS Panzer Corps at Kursk probably believed that the Tiger was the best tank in the world. Not many had served in a Tiger crew during the fighting at Kharkov, but the ones that did and the soldiers who had fought in crews in other models of panzers knew that Tigers were damaged almost every day of the fighting at Kharkov, although most were returned to action within forty-eight hours. It was possible for the enemy to totally destroy a Tiger, but that would be a rare occurrence. What was more likely to happen was that if a Tiger had been damaged and could not move, and if the battle lines moved backward, the enemy could capture that Tiger, which of course would be a total loss. But as long as you were advancing, losing a Tiger in that manner was not going to happen.

Those expectations of battle ferocity concerning destroyed and damaged Tigers appear to be right on the mark. The following shows the number of Tigers totally destroyed and those that were non-operational (i.e., they had some level of damage that forced them to the rear to be fixed by mechanics). Disabled Tigers caused by mechanical failure, not by enemy munitions, are not counted, nor are Tigers that were hit and sustained minor armor damage, but not enough impairment to leave the battlefield:

July 5   13th (Heavy) Company: 0 Tigers destroyed; 10 Tigers damaged
          8th (Heavy) Company: 0 Tigers destroyed; 4 Tigers damaged
          9th (Heavy) Company: 0 Tigers destroyed; 4 Tigers damaged
July 6   13th (Heavy) Company: 0 Tigers destroyed; 4 Tigers damaged
          8th (Heavy) Company: 0 Tigers destroyed; 4 Tigers damaged
          9th (Heavy) Company: 0 Tigers destroyed; 4 Tigers damaged
July 7   13th (Heavy) Company: 0 Tigers destroyed; 2 Tigers damaged
          8th (Heavy) Company: 1 Tiger destroyed; 1 Tiger damaged
          9th (Heavy) Company: 1 Tiger destroyed; 2 Tigers damaged
July 8   13th (Heavy) Company: 0 Tigers destroyed; 2 Tigers damaged
          8th (Heavy) Company: 0 Tigers destroyed; 0 Tigers damaged
          9th (Heavy) Company: 0 Tigers destroyed; 2 Tigers damaged
July 9   13th (Heavy) Company: 0 Tigers destroyed; 0 Tigers damaged
          8th (Heavy) Company: 0 Tigers destroyed; 0 Tigers damaged
          9th (Heavy) Company: 0 Tigers destroyed; 0 Tigers damaged
July 10 13th (Heavy) Company: 0 Tigers destroyed; 0 Tigers damaged
          8th (Heavy) Company: 0 Tigers destroyed; 0 Tigers damaged
          9th (Heavy) Company: 0 Tigers destroyed; 2 Tigers damaged
July 11 13th (Heavy) Company: 0 Tigers destroyed; 2 Tigers damaged
          8th (Heavy) Company: 0 Tigers destroyed; 0 Tigers damaged
          9th (Heavy) Company: 0 Tigers destroyed; 0 Tigers damaged
July 12 13th (Heavy) Company: 1 Tiger destroyed; 0 Tigers damaged
          8th (Heavy) Company: 0 Tigers destroyed; 0 Tigers damaged
          9th (Heavy) Company: 0 Tigers destroyed; 0 Tigers damaged
July 13 13th (Heavy) Company: 0 Tigers destroyed; 0 Tigers damaged
          8th (Heavy) Company: 0 Tigers destroyed; 1 Tiger damaged
          9th (Heavy) Company: 0 Tigers destroyed; 10 Tigers damaged
July 14 13th (Heavy) Company: 0 Tigers destroyed; 0 Tigers damaged
          8th (Heavy) Company: 0 Tigers destroyed; 0 Tigers damaged
          9th (Heavy) Company: 0 Tigers destroyed; 0 Tigers damaged
July 15 13th (Heavy) Company: 0 Tigers destroyed; 0 Tigers damaged
          8th (Heavy) Company: 0 Tigers destroyed; 4 Tigers damaged
          9th (Heavy) Company: 0 Tigers destroyed; 2 Tigers damaged

Examining the destroyed and damaged Tigers, we see that one Tiger per company was hit so badly that it was declared a total loss: **1312** in the 13th (Heavy) Company, **S24** in the 8th (Heavy) Company, and **914** in the 9th (Heavy) Company. A second Tiger in the 13th (Heavy) Company was stripped of parts to make other Tigers operational, but that was a non-violent administrative decision. Concerning battle damage, on July 5, 1943, the 13th (Heavy) Company sustained ten damaged Tigers, as did the 9th (Heavy) Company on July 13. At the end of those two days the Tiger crews in both companies may well have questioned their assumptions concerning the level of battle ferocity, but their fears were probably soon allayed, as losses the following day for each were much lower.

In fact, it appears that in sixteen days companies experienced no temporary losses of Tigers and included six days for the 13th (Heavy) Company, six days for the 8th (Heavy) Company, and four days for the 9th (Heavy) Company. On those days of no damage clearly the Tiger crews observed a very low level of battle ferocity.

If, in fact, the Tiger crewmen perceived that the Kursk Offensive represented a relatively low level of battle ferocity for themselves, they undoubtedly would have been shocked when the offensive was called off. While we do not have the results of post operation questionnaires—the armies of the day not being big into that—we do have comments from one of these crewmen. Several decades after the battle, retired *Bundeswehr* Brigadier General Kendziora, who had commanded a Tiger in the 8th (Heavy) Company at Kursk as a young man, was interviewed for an extensive study on the battle. General Kendziora concluded his remarks by saying: "When we were ordered to retreat, I believe on the 16th, no one on our level understood this and we were very embittered by it."[4]

The Tiger Crews Developed Their Own Combat Decision-Making Cycle

One might assume that such a radical new type of panzer, with a radical new type of cannon, might have a radical, new type of specially trained, hand selected, combat experienced crew. Such was not the case. Only about one-sixth of the men (38) in the three Tiger companies had previous *panzer* combat experience in any model of tank, which we can determine based on the paucity of the award of the Panzer Battle Badge in Silver prior to Kursk. Still fewer had previous combat experience in a Tiger. On the plus side, a majority of the crewmen had seen extensive combat in infantry and other branches, so in some respects that provided experience in skills required in those branches. Having said that, assigning former Luftwaffe soldiers to what was hoped to be a revolutionary weapons system seems to have been irrational.

Regardless of source or level of previous experience, the crewmen seemed to have bonded sufficiently to rule the battlefield for much of the 2nd SS Panzer Corps offensive, but what exactly does "bonded" mean? This study proposes using a term that did not come into fashion until several decades later: the Waffen-SS Tiger crews at the Kursk Offensive developed their own type of combat decision making cycle of *observe—orient—decide—act* to engage and destroy enemy threats arrayed against them faster than those threats could destroy the Tiger. The proof is in the numbers: only three Tiger tanks in the corps were written off as total losses during the July 5–15 period; the rest were evacuated to the rear and repaired, often several times, and put back into action.

The "OODA Loop" concept, developed by US Air Force Col. John Richard Boyd after the Korean War in the early 1950s, was designed to describe how a single decision maker could act faster than his opponent—in Boyd's case the decision maker being a fighter pilot. Practicing what he preached, Boyd became the head of the Academic Department of the US Air Force Weapons School at Nellis Air Force Base; in addition to instructing he authored the tactics manual for the school. However, it was in the air that John Boyd earned the nickname "Forty Second Boyd," derived from his standard challenge to every student that beginning from a position of disadvantage he could defeat any opposing pilot in air combat in less than forty seconds.

The Tiger crews were on the ground and not in the air. And there were five men in the crew, rather than one pilot, and each had to make decisions in his area of expertise in real time, and often without waiting for orders, so how did these crews achieve this? First, the Tiger tank, as a piece of equipment, facilitated destroying threats faster than those threats could destroy the Tiger. At Kursk, the power of the main gun of a Tiger could engage and destroy enemy tanks hundreds of meters before those tanks could close on the Tiger. Second, the armor plate not only protected the vehicle and crew, but it also served—wholly unintended—as a sensor of enemy fire. At Kursk, Tigers routinely were hit every day by dozens of enemy projectiles that failed to penetrate the armor. What these hits did achieve was to alert the crew of the general direction and type of enemy fire that was striking their tank. For instance, an antitank rifle bullet strike was much less severe than a 45 mm antitank gun shell strike, which in turn was different than the strike from a projectile out of the 76.2 mm gun on a T-34.

The role of the tank commander also added to the effort to shorten (read quicken) the OODA Loop. Photographs of Tigers at Kursk often show the vehicle commander standing in the cupola, with often the top half of his torso exposed. This provided the commander an excellent ability to see in all directions around the Tiger, either with the naked eye, or with binoculars that all Tigers had on board. This was in contrast to many Soviet tank commanders that often had to ride completely inside the turret because in the models of the T-34/76 at Kursk the commander doubled as the gunner, thereby degrading target acquisition by putting too many duties on the commander.

There was a downside to commanders riding high in the turret, of course. During the offensive ten Tiger commanders were wounded in action and six were killed. While not all these men were struck in an exposed region of their body, the position was a dangerous one.

The main sight gave the Tiger gunner an advantage in the OODA Loop race. On the Tiger, the gunner's sight had a twenty-eight degree field of view, while the sight in the T-34/76 provided only about fourteen degrees field of view. In practical terms, this feature allowed the German gunner to see more width on the battlefield than his Soviet counterpart could. More advantages accrued from this disparity. The German gunner had a higher reliability to hit the target with his first round, but his superior sight also assisted him in *not* shooting rounds that would have no effect. This combination lowered the probability that the Soviets would detect the Tiger, as the less main gun rounds—effective or ineffective—a tank fires the less chance the tank will be spotted by enemy units.

But perhaps most significant to achieve a quick combat decision making cycle was the intercom system. Every crewman, except the loader, could hear what every other crewman was saying.[5] Thus, when the gunner heard the Tiger commander announce the presence of several enemy T-34s at a certain range, without being told he knew what type of round to fire given the threat, distance, and even the preference in similar previous situations of the commander. The driver—often one of the most experienced men in the crew—upon hearing the same report from the commander knew to immediately seek a small depression so as to reduce the portion of the Tiger visible to the enemy, or in what direction to orient the vehicle so as to create the critical oblique angle between the front slope of the Tiger and the enemy which would increase the effective thickness of the armor without waiting for an order.

Not every Tiger crew could achieve the same results, especially as each engagement had many variables and some gunners were just better than others. But those crews that could achieved spectacular effects, such as the crew of Tiger **1325**, consisting of Franz Staudegger, Heinz Buchner, Walter Henke, Gerhard Waltersdorf, and Herbert Stellmacher did on July 8, 1943, at Teterevino (North). On that day John Boyd might have called their Tiger: "Ten Second 1325."

The Tiger crews of the 2nd SS Panzer Corps at Kursk clearly accomplished their tactical task of destroying prodigious quantities of Soviet tanks, although as Colonel (Retired) Wolfgang Schneider concludes: "The high scores in defeating many Soviet tanks [at Kursk] originated from bad Soviet tactics."[6] While Colonel Schneider has a valid point, this study would assert that it was the superior observe—orient—decide—act combat decision making cycle in use by the Tiger crews that forced many of those Soviet tanks into positions of disadvantage from which they adopted suboptimal tactics and techniques that then led to their demise.

Having said that, the decision making cycle, and even the Tiger itself, would not save all of them. Some seventy-one of the 2nd SS Panzer Corps Tiger crewmen at the Kursk Offensive would not survive the war.

The Waffen-SS Failed to Develop a Panzer Branch

The Waffen-SS had a fatal flaw: it did not have a panzer (armor) branch as the Army had established in 1935, despite the fact that by 1941, the leadership of the Waffen-SS desired to establish panzer units. Therefore, the Waffen-SS did not formulate and promulgate its own panzer doctrine, but simply borrowed from the German Army panzer troops and organizations. That could be overcome by using someone else's manuals, but other aspects of not having its own panzer branch could not be.

The Waffen-SS began World War II with no panzer divisions. That would soon change according to Oberst a.D. Wolfgang Schneider: "After the French campaign in 1940, the SS decided also to build up armor units, starting with tank regiment *Leibstandarte*. The main initiatives for this came from Hausser and Dietrich. To create this, the panzer companies of the Waffen-SS came from Sturmgeschütz units (for example, Michael Wittmann) and regular Waffen-SS infantry units. This was also one reason that the performance of SS armor was rather limited with respect to efficiency and kill rates. But they never had their own panzer school. The NCOs and officer candidates attended courses at the Army Panzer School, with its own training platoons and groups. That means that they did not have its own armor (Panzer) command. The *Inspekteur der Panzertruppen* [Guderian] also took care of the SS armor units."[7]

By the end of the war the Waffen-SS fielded seven panzer divisions: the 1st, 2nd, 3rd, 5th, 9th, 10th, and 12th. At Kursk, the 1st, 2nd, and 3rd were still developing as panzer grenadier divisions, but would officially become panzer divisions just a few months after the battle. At their apex development, each Waffen-SS panzer division was authorized in the tables of organization and equipment one panzer regiment of two panzer battalions and a total of nine panzer companies. In addition to those forces the Waffen-SS fielded six panzer grenadier divisions, but these units were a different kettle of fish. On paper the 4th, 11th, 16th, 17th, 18th, and 23rd panzer grenadier divisions each had an organic panzer detachment (read battalion), but these organizations frequently fielded assault guns—which were overseen by the artillery branch—instead of panzers.

That was a lot of panzers, and many of them were some of the best in the world, notably the Mark V Panthers and Mark VI Tigers. At Kursk, the Waffen-SS fielded about a third of the Tiger tanks involved. As to the Mark V Panther, it was just coming online and the Waffen-SS had none of these at Kursk—all 200 were assigned to the army's 39th Panzer Regiment that would fight with the army's *Großdeutschland* Panzer Grenadier Division in the army's 48th Panzer Corps that operated to the west of the 2nd SS Panzer Corps.

At Kursk, with no overarching panzer branch to monitor and influence personnel decisions, the absence of such an organization came home to roost. In October 1942, the Waffen-SS high command decided to convert the Second Battalion of the SS Fast Rifle Regiment *Langemarck*

(*Schnelles-SS-Schützen-Regiment Langemarck*), sometimes referred to as SS Infantry Regiment 4 *Langemarck*, into a Second Battalion of the 2nd Panzer Regiment of the *Das Reich*. Originally formed on February 25, 1941, from the 4th Death's Head Standard and armed almost exclusively with Czech weapons—but no tanks—it transferred to the 2nd SS Infantry Brigade in late May 1941 for proposed anti-partisan duties in the upcoming invasion of the Soviet Union. The regiment conducted these operations in the German Ninth Army area before being withdrawn to Krakow, Poland, in December due to high losses. The Second Battalion, with most of the heavy companies, air landed at the airfield of Yukhnov, near Kaluga, on December 26, 1941, and was attached to the 19th Panzer Division.

By April 14, 1942, the battalion transferred back to Germany because of extremely ferocious casualties. Now part of the *Das Reich*, the Second Battalion began to convert to a motorized battalion structure that did not include panzers. The conversion of infantrymen of the *Langemarck* to panzer crews meant that of the 132 panzers in the *Das Reich* at Kursk, there would be these soldiers spread throughout the Mark III (long barrel) panzers, Mark IV (long barrel) panzers, eighteen captured T-34 tanks, and fourteen Mark VI Tigers in the regiment's Second Battalion. For the 8th (Heavy) Company, it meant that twelve Tiger crewmen had started in the infantry of the *Langemarck*, never served in another model panzer, and began their tank service in the November–December 1942 time frame.

The establishment of a Waffen-SS panzer branch could have monitored this situation for a more logical assignment pattern. In addition, it could have weighed in concerning Luftwaffe transfers. Seven former Luftwaffe airmen were transferred from that service to the units in this study—three to the 13th (Heavy) Company and four to the 8th (Heavy) Company—arriving at their new homes on April 9, 1943. Why were any of them sent to the most powerful panzer companies in the Waffen-SS? How many Luftwaffe soldiers were sent to the other panzer companies in the three divisions we do not know; one would hope that this information was presented to Paul Hausser—even though enlisted personnel assignments rarely received the attention of a corps commander—given the expected enormous reliance that was being placed in this weapons system.

A third area that the Waffen-SS would have benefitted from a panzer branch was concerning attendance of personnel at developmental schools and courses back in Germany in general and attendance at leadership schools, known as *SS-Junkerschulen*, and located in locations such as Bad Tölz and Braunschweig in particular. These institutions had a tough mission. The Germany Army sought potential officers of good breeding and character who had at least graduated from what we would call high school (secondary school) and may have even passed the *Abitur*, the entrance examination that qualified a German student to enter a university. The weeding out process was really done by the young soldier's regiment in which he served—in particular his regimental commander.

A good example was German Army officer Martin Steglich, born in 1915 in Silesia, who joined the 27th Infantry Regiment on October 1, 1936, at Rostock—not because he was from the area, but because he had interviewed with regimental commander Colonel Kurt Tippelskirch, who found the young man of high character. Tippelskirch left shortly afterward to an assignment in the General Staff in Berlin. He would later command an infantry division, a corps, and three different armies, but it was not a case of attaching his star to the general, as Martin Steglich never served under him again. Then came Colonel Friedrich Mieth, who told the young soldier to master all the tactics and weapons of the regiment. Colonel Mieth would go on to command an infantry division, then a corps, winning the Knight's Cross with Oak Leaves—the same decoration that Martin would later receive—before Mieth was killed in action in 1944. Thus, Martin began his quest to become an officer. That arrived when he was commissioned as a second lieutenant on April 1, 1939. As the war had not yet started, the timing of his various leadership schools was not affected by wartime requirements.[8]

In contrast, the Waffen-SS valued other characteristics, such as perceived *loyalty* and honor driven by an attitude of paying any price to reach an objective. Thus, to become an officer was not dependent on education level or social standing, and the Waffen-SS had their own leadership schools that taught an officer aspirant. While this egalitarian system fostered much mutual respect between many officers and enlisted men, it did not come without a price. Of all Waffen-SS officer candidates accepted before 1938, some forty percent had only an elementary school education—by American standards finishing the eighth grade.[9] On the other hand, nine soldiers for whom the information is known in this study passed the *Abitur*, indicating college level aptitude.

Created in 1936, these Waffen-SS schools, influenced greatly by Paul Hausser, initially used German Army training methods, with former German Army officers as instructors. The candidate was required to obtain a written recommendation from his commander and undergo a political and racial screening process to determine eligibility for a commission—something the German Army never would have done. In addition to height requirements, the potential officer normally had to serve for at least six months to a year in the enlisted ranks prior to being considered for a place at the *SS-Junkerschule*; combat experience was desired.

However, the exact timing of attendance was flexible, and here is where the absence of a Waffen-SS panzer branch hurt at Kursk. In examining the durations of schools for many soldiers it appears that the typical candidate would be absent from his unit from three to five months for the school, travel time, possibly some leave, and perhaps some other training back in Germany. As mentioned, a report dated July 1, 1943, verifies that nine Tiger crewmen from the 8th (Heavy) Company were back in Germany for Waffen-SS leadership training during the Kursk Offensive.[10] We may assume that some number of Tiger crewmen from the other two companies were in similar situations. Obviously an organization does not want to shut down training, but for the expected premier ground combat system in the force for the anticipated most significant tank battle of the year a little creative scheduling would seem to have been in order.

Did Heinz Guderian have some level of oversight over Waffen-SS panzer units? Yes, but it was a bridge too far to expect an Army general to issue instructions on individual attendance at leadership schools and concerning all the other personnel decisions made by another branch of service.

However—and this does not concern Tiger tanks—Heinz Guderian and Paul Hausser may not have tracked individual attendance at schools, but both certainly knew that almost half their panzer soldiers would not be in Russia for the offensive due to another reason. Two of the SS panzer regiments were sending entire battalions of crews back to Germany in June to train on the new Mark V Panther. Both generals knew the duration of the training and they both knew that these hundreds and hundreds of men would not be present during the Kursk Offensive. Did they discuss this before the offensive, and if so did they consider alternatives, such as sending the crews back to Germany in August, when the offensive presumably would have been completed?

Typically an Armor (Panzer) Branch organization would be responsible for many facets of tanks and the crew that operated them. This would include managing and providing oversight for the unit structure of the force, acquisition of new equipment, conduct of individual training and education, distribution of armor/panzer personnel throughout the force, deployment of individual soldiers and officers, and professional development of armor/panzer officers and enlisted personnel. In addition, the branch had a role in helping to develop and update selected manuals—and sometimes even authoring them. For the Waffen-SS, establishing a panzer branch would have required coming to a detailed understanding of the scope and goals of the organization with Inspector General of Panzer Troops Heinz Guderian, and once that relationship was cemented developing a memoranda of understanding with German Army panzer branch leaders to obtain a synergy in working together. Establishing a panzer branch would not have won the war for Germany, but it would have made Waffen-SS panzer units, training, and leadership much more effective.

The Complexity of Enemy Tank Kill Claims

Since the advent of the tank in the Great War, tank and antitank crews have attempted to quantify the number of enemy tanks they engaged in battle, and more importantly, that they destroyed in combat. It has been a very difficult task. The battlefield is a confusing environment. Tank-on-tank fights can be over in just a few seconds, and usually there is not adequate time to "admire one's work," as other enemy tanks and antitank guns are trying to engage you. With a Tiger, the range at which an enemy tank can be destroyed could sometimes be 1,500 meters and even farther, and at that distance the details of damage inflicted on a target can often be difficult to ascertain. And as this study has shown, not every tank believed destroyed "stayed" destroyed and many returned to the battlefield, which would negate the claim of destroying the vehicle in the first place.

Within the Wehrmacht, it appears that tank commanders were most likely to receive credit for an enemy tank destroyed, with gunners often—but not always—credited with a "kill" as well. German intelligence officers, while wanting to give credit where credit is due, had to be careful in not double counting destroyed enemy tanks by adding the numbers of the tank commander and tank gunner, when in reality they were destroying the same vehicle. These officers sometimes believed that accurate kill figures could be as little as fifty percent of that claimed.

Kill totals were often included in the supporting documents for higher decorations: the grades of the Knight's Cross of the Iron Cross and the German Cross in Gold. However, the intent of those supporting documents was to ensure a particular soldier received the award, so inflation—no matter how slight—cannot be ruled out in some cases. It also appears that enlisted soldiers may have been overlooked in the award process.

At the risk of over-crediting or under-crediting the accomplishments of some very competent soldiers mentioned in this work, here are a few general figures of note:

Soldier	Kursk Success	Overall Wartime Success
13th (Heavy) Company		
Jürgen Brandt (KIA)	Unknown	@47 tanks, commander
Heinz Buchner	@22 tanks, gunner	@51 tanks, gunner/commander
Helmut Gräser	@10 tanks, gunner	Unknown
Heinrich Kling	@18 tanks & 27 antitank guns, commander	@46 tanks & >27 antitank guns, commander
Walter Lau	0 tanks, loader	@26 tanks, gunner
Franz Staudegger	@22 tanks, commander	@35 tanks, commander
Karl-Heinz Warmbrunn	@18 tanks & 27 antitank guns, gunner	@57 tanks & >27 antitank guns, gunner
Helmut Wendorff (KIA)	Unknown	@84 tanks
Michael Wittmann (KIA)	@35 tanks & >28 antitank guns, commander	@138 tanks & @132 antitank guns, commander
Balthasar Woll	@25 tanks & >2 antitank guns, gunner	@80 tanks, gunner
8th (Heavy) Company		
Kurt Baral (KIA)	>13 tanks, commander	Unknown
Wolfgang Birnbaum	Unknown	>8 tanks, Gunner
Paul Egger	Not Present	@101 tanks, commander
Artur Glagow	Unknown	@51 tanks, commander

Julius Hinrichsen	0, gunner	@22 tanks, gunner
Gerhard Kaempf	Unknown	@46 tanks, gunner/commander
Alois Kalss (KIA)	Unknown	@54 tanks, commander
Walter Knecht	Unknown	@20 tanks, commander
Jakob Kuster	@13 tanks, gunner	Unknown
Kurt Meyer	@6 tanks, gunner	@47 tanks, gunner
Karl Skerbinz	@3 tanks, gunner	@26 tanks, commander
Heinz Tensfeld (KIA)	Unknown	@10 tanks, commander
Heinrich Warnick	Not Present	@77 tanks & 44 antitank guns, gunner

9th (Heavy) Company

Fritz Biermeier (KIA)	Unknown	@31 tanks, commander
Ludwig Lachner	>2 tanks, gunner	Unknown
Artur Privatzki	Unknown	@12 tanks, gunner/commander
Wilhelm Schroeder (KIA)	@2 tanks, commander	@Unknown

Perhaps the most accurate conclusion to be made concerning tank kills is that these soldiers, and many others, were highly skilled, and possessed a marked advantage against almost any enemy tank crew that they faced.

The Myth of the Master Race

A bedrock tenet of Nazi ideology concerned a master race (*Übermensch*, *Herrenrasse*, or *Herrenvolk*) in which individuals of Nordic or Aryan descent would not only be deemed the highest form of life in a racial hierarchy, but also would control everyone else. The term sprang from German (although he later claimed pure Polish descent) philosopher Friedrich Nietzsche in his 1883 book *Thus Spoke Zarathustra*, which also posited the death of God. In it a new master race would give meaning to life on earth and create new values within the vacuum of no God, within a framework where the *Übermensch* are always correct.

Nowhere in Nazi Germany was the concept of master race stronger than in the Waffen-SS. First, the organization relied on the Hitler Youth to indoctrinate the youth in Germany. The Hitler Youth were viewed as ensuring the future of Nazi Germany, even if they had to give their lives in the process. Indoctrination included Nazi ideology and racism, although there was greater emphasis on physical fitness, hardness, and military training than there was on academic study. On September 21, 1935, in a speech to 50,000 members of the Hitler Youth at the gigantic stadium of the Nazi party rally grounds in Nürnberg, Hitler provided his vision for young people in Germany: "What we want of our German youth is different to what was wanted in the past. In our eyes the German youth of the future must be slim and trim, swift as a greyhound, tough as leather, and hard as Krupp steel. We have to educate a new type of person so that our People are not destroyed by the symptoms of the degeneration of our time."

That was phase one for a future Waffen-SS soldier, and almost all of the Tiger crewmen in the 2nd SS Panzer Corps that could have been in the organization (i.e., born between 1918 and 1925) were. Phase two was meeting strict physical standards for admission. All of the crewmen for whom that data is known met the requirements.[11]

But Himmler and the SS were not through attempting to control the entire lives of all their soldiers. Entrants into the Waffen-SS had to produce formal genealogical documents to show that their ancestors were Aryan from about 1800, and in the case for a commissioned officer farther back than that.

That was an administrative pain, but then it started to get personal. When a Waffen-SS enlisted man or officer desired to marry, not only he, but also his fiancée, were required to submit another Aryan family history that also included the cause of death for deceased direct ancestors. It did not take a genius to figure out that the SS Race and Settlement Office, to which the papers were submitted, was concerned that hereditary diseases would not be passed along to future generations. We have no information how many marriages the SS Race and Settlement Office disapproved, but it was many.

In response numerous SS soldiers fought back against the system. A Tiger crewman associated with this project submitted the required paperwork and was told that his fiancée's height of under 160 centimeters (less that 5'2") was considered too "un-Aryan" to be a proper bride for an SS soldier. The trooper was having none of it and found a trusted farmer from his hometown to provide enough quality pork products to bribe an *SS-Untersturmführer* who took care of the issue and the happy couple walked down the aisle—Himmler and the SS Race and Settlement Office none the wiser.

Then the Nazis attempted to reduce the influence of God from the lives of their Waffen-SS soldiers. As with many bad ideas it started slowly. Waffen-SS personnel were encouraged to abandon their formal affiliation with the Roman Catholic or Protestant church, the two largest religious denominations in the Fatherland. They did this by making a third designation more attractive—that of *Gottgläubig*, "believing in God." It was not an overall rejection of the concept of God, but rather Deism, in which this creator did not intervene in the universe; this, of course, left that duty to the National Socialist state. Personnel forms had an area in which the soldier's religion was designated and the majority of files, but not all, reflected the abbreviation "ggl." What we do not know is if each soldier actually changed his religious beliefs or went along to avoid potential ramifications of staying in a church. The Nazis were not so blind as to encourage Waffen-SS soldiers to become atheists, but unlike the German Army, they did not have chaplains in German Waffen-SS units, although they did have chaplains in several foreign Waffen-SS formations.[12]

After the war, former *SS-Obergruppenführer* Paul Hausser claimed that the soldiers of the Waffen-SS were alike in many—if not most—respects to their comrades-in-arms in the German Army. In fact, the title of Hausser's book *Soldaten wie andere auch* translates to "Soldiers like any other." Of course, Hausser was talking about a very large sample of men: during the conflict the Waffen-SS was composed of more than 900,000 soldiers (including foreign volunteers), fielded thirty-eight divisions, and lost 314,000 soldiers killed in action or who died of wounds.[13] Those were not the only losses; Walter Krüger, commander of the *Das Reich* at Kursk, did not wait around at the end of the war to see if Waffen-SS soldiers would be treated like any other and committed suicide in Lithuania on May 22, 1945.

It got little better in postwar Germany. Many survivors of the conflict were ostracized after the war for being members of the Waffen-SS, which was deemed at the International Military Tribunal at Nürnberg to have been a criminal organization due to its linkage to the Nazi Party, as well as proven direct involvement in numerous war crimes and crimes against humanity.

The postwar German government jumped in and held that the SS as a whole was a criminal organization. Thus, throughout Germany, former Waffen-SS members were denied many of the rights afforded to other German military veterans, including pensions. Some of these soldiers were hounded so badly that they legally changed their names. The study found no instances at Kursk where these crewmen committed war crimes during the battle, although there seem to be numerous instances where they received shabby treatment after the war by their own countrymen. Any professional boxer who gets his bell rung as many times in his forty-nine losses in sixty-eight fights such as Bobby Warmbrunn did has to figure out there must be a better way to make a living.

Did hundreds of officers in the Waffen-SS commit crimes against humanity? Yes; almost everyone would agree that serving as an officer at a Nazi concentration or extermination camp would be a crime against humanity, although the severity of that crime seems to be determined by whether the viewer is a proponent of German law that preferred to blame those men who actually killed people, versus American law of basic criminal conspiracy that allows for everyone involved in a crime to be punished for acts that their co-criminals actually committed. An extensive review of SS commissioned officers published in 1999 identified 967 officers that served in one or more concentration camps during the period 1934–1945. As that study documented through official personnel files, some 415 of these officers also served in Waffen-SS divisions at some point during the war. *Quod Erat Demonstrandum.*[14]

Did Waffen-SS units ever commit war crimes? Yes—many; a good example was at Malmedy, Belgium, during the Battle of the Bulge. Numerous accounts showed that elements of Battle Group Peiper of the 1st SS Panzer Division *Leibstandarte SS Adolf Hitler* transported eighty-four unarmed, captured American soldiers to a snowy field outside the village and killed them with machine gun fire. The Waffen-SS killed more captured US soldiers at other parts of the battlefield and after the war, the United States organized a trial at Dachau which became known as the Malmedy massacre trial (US vs. Valentin Bersin, et al.), May through July 1946. Seventy-four former Waffen-SS soldiers, including Josef Dietrich, Hermann Priess, and Joachim Peiper—all of whom played prominent roles concerning the Kursk Offensive—went on trial. The court convicted seventy-three SS men, sentencing Peiper to death, Dietrich to life, and Priess to twenty years.[15] None of the forty-three death sentences were ever carried out and by 1956 all of the convicted men had been set free.

There were many reasons for the sentences to be reduced. One of the most glaring was reported by American Army Col. Willis M. Everett Jr., who had been detailed to serve as the defense team chief. Col. Everett came to the conclusion that prior to trial many of the defendants had been threatened with violence and some had been victims of violence that included driving burning matches under fingernails, beatings, and kicking selected defendants in the testicles, as well as light deprivation and insufficient rations.[16] The whole procedure was a mess, leaving everyone dissatisfied.

Closer to Kursk, Joachim Peiper and his Third Battalion of the 2nd SS Panzer Grenadier Regiment retook the village of Krasnaya Polyana during the Battle of Kharkov in February 1943. Reportedly after discovering that a German medical detachment there had been killed and mutilated Peiper had the villagers rounded up and shot. Two other villages, Semyonovka and Yefremovka, received the "blowtorch" treatment on February 17, 1943, when Peiper's battalion killed 872 inhabitants—burning some 240 of them to death in the church of Yefremovka.[17] Perhaps as a result Joachim Peiper's unit received the unofficial moniker the "Blowtorch Battalion."

That the Waffen-SS committed war crimes is not shocking, given the lengthy efforts that Nazi Germany used in an attempt to produce an army of *Übermensch*. One would logically expect that *every* Waffen-SS soldier would have shot prisoners, "blowtorched" villages, and treated everyone else they came across as subhumans. The shocking conclusion is that despite all the efforts to indoctrinate them as small children, weed out potential soldiers that did not fit certain racial characteristics, control whom they could marry, and turn them into soldiers "swift as a greyhound, tough as leather, and hard as Krupp steel," so many Waffen-SS soldiers—such as most of the ones in the three Tiger companies of the 2nd SS Panzer Corps—did not become murderers. Too many in the overall Waffen-SS did; but more did not, which is proof that Heinrich Himmler's dream of the Waffen-SS as *Herrenvolk*, who would all do what had to be done, was just a myth.

This study did not find any conclusive evidence that any of the Tiger crewmen in the 13th (Heavy) Company, the 8th (Heavy) Company, or the 9th (Heavy) Company participated in war crimes during the Kursk Offensive, Battle of the Bulge, the Battle of Kharkov, or any other location during the war. However, several men in the sample may well have been involved: Fritz Biermeier (when assigned to the guard troops (*Wachkommando*) at the Dachau concentration camp in the 1930s, and later when assigned to Battle Group Jeckeln in 1942); Heinz Freiberger (when assigned to the guard troops at the Buchenwald concentration camp in 1939); and Heinrich Kling (when assigned to the 12th *Totenkopf Standarte* in Poland in 1939). Having said that, none of them were ever brought up on charges after the war, although Biermeier was already dead.

The Tiger crewmen weren't saints, and almost every one of them was directly involved in the killing of enemy soldiers—that was their job. They did not like every superior in their chain of command, although they revered some; and they may have thought that the decision makers back in Berlin had no idea what was going on at the front—which of course many of them in cushy jobs on Prinz-Albrecht-Straße (the location of the SS headquarters in Berlin) did not. When wounded, they tried to remain with their company because they knew if they did not it would be difficult to ever return to their comrades and they would be assigned somewhere else.

They also were not "soldiers like any other," as Paul Hausser opined. They were not the best soldiers in World War II—not by a long shot. But they probably were the best disciplined as far as carrying out the orders of their superiors. When those orders were evil, because these soldiers had been indoctrinated for more than a decade concerning all facets of life, too many just followed those commands and subsequently paid the price.

But when those orders were typical combat instructions to attack a prepared, dug in, superior sized force such as in eleven days in July 1943, they—in their awesome Tiger tanks utilizing a superior combat decision making cycle—made everyone aware of exactly where Kursk was, and forced every Soviet T-34 tank crew on that battlefield to fear an increased level of battle ferocity that led many of the enemy to panic, which resulted in their destruction.

For those 264 hours at Belgorod, Beresov, Bykovka, Ivanovka, Klyuchi, and Prokhorovka, the SS Tiger crews were on the hunt. They were indeed as strong as Krupp steel. The arithmetic of the battlefield—the force ratios and Lanchester laws for calculating the relative strengths of opposing forces—gave them no chance to win. But still, they had no concept of defeat because they were individuals fighting side-by-side with and for their friends, not as robots programmed by a cold, vicious ideology to be supermen, and for these reasons there is much to be learned from them.

Appendix 1

Kursk Battlefield Locator

In text (English)	Russian	German WWII Equivalent
Andreyevka	Андреевка	Andrejewka
Belenikhino	Беленихино	Belenikhino
Belgorod	Белгород	Belgorod
Beresov	Березов	Beresoff
Beregovoye	Береговое	Beregowoje
Bolshaya Mayachki	Большая Маяцки	Bolshaya Majatschki
Budy	Буди	Budy
Bykovka	Быковка	Bykowka
Cherkasy	Черкаси	Tscherkassy
Donetsk	Донецьк	Stalino
Gonki	(now Zhdanov)	Gonki
Gryaznoye	Грязное	Gresnoje
Ivanovka	Ивановка	Iwanowka
Ivanovskiy Vyselok	Ивановский Выселок	Iwanowski-Wysselok
Kalinin	Калинин	Kalinin
Kartashevka	Карташевка	Kartaschewka
Kharkov	Харьков	Charkow
Kiev	Киев	Kiew
Klyuchi	Ключи	Kljutschi
Kochetovka	Кочетовка	Kochetowka
Kolontaiv	Колонтаїв	Kolontajew
Komsomol'skiy	Комсомольский	Komsomolets
Korocha	Короча	Korosch
Korotych	Коротич	Korotitsch
Kozlovka	Козловка	Koslowka
Krapivenskiye Dvory	Крапивенские Дворы	Krapinsklje Dvory
Krasnyy Oktyabr'	(Doesn't exist today)	Krassny Oktjabr
Kursk	Курск	Kursk
Lipovyy Donets River	Липовый донец	Fluss Lipowij Donez

Luchki (North)	Лучки	Lutschki (Nord)
Luchki (South)	Лучки	Lutschki (Süd)
Maloyablonovo	Малояблоново	Mal Jablonowo
Malyye Mayachki	Малые Маячки	Mal Majatschki
Mikhaylovka	Михайловка	Michailowka
Nepkhayevo	Непхаево	Nepchajewo
Novoselovka	Новоселовка	Nowosselowka
Oktiabrskii Sovkhoz	Октябрьск	Oktjabrskij
Ol'shanka Stream	Ольшанка	Olshanka
Ozerovskiy	Озерскийв	Oserowskij
Pavlove	Павлове	Pawlowo
Pervomais'k	Первомайськ	Perwomajsk
Petrovka	Петровка	Petrowka
Pokrovka	Покровка	Pokrowka
Pravorot'	Прावороть	Praworot
Prelestnoye	Прелестное	Prelessnoje
Prokhorovka	Прохоровка	Prochorowka
Psel River	Псел	Fluss Pssel
Pushkarnoye	Пушкарное	Puschkarnoje
Rakovo	Раково	Rakowo
Ryl'skiy	Рыльский	Rylskij
Shopino	Шопино	Schopino
Siverskyi Donets River	Сіверський Донець	Fluss Sewerski Donez
Skorodnoye	Скородное	Skorodnoje
Smorodino	Смородино	Smorodino
Solotinka River	Солотинка	Fluss Ssalotinka
Sovodskoye	(Doesn't exist today)	Ssawodskoje
Soschenkov	(Doesn't exist today)	Ssoschenkoff
Stary Oskol	Старый Оскол	Staryi Oskol
Storozhevoye	Сторожевое	Storoshewoje
Streletskoye	Стрелецкое	Strelezkoje
Stepanivka	Степанівка	Stepanovka
Sukhosolotino	Сухосолотино	Ssuch Ssolotino
Ternovka	Терновка	Ternowka
Teterevino (North)	Тетеревино	Teterewino (Nord)
Teterevino (South)	Тетеревино	Teterewino (Süd)
Tomarovka	Томаровка	Tomarowka
Vasil'yevka	Васильевка	Wassiljewka
Vesëlyy	Веселый	Wesselyj
Vinogradovka	Виноградовка	Winogradowka
Visloye	Вислое	Wissloje
Vorskla River	Ворскла	Fluss Worksla
Voronezh	Воронеж	Woronesh
Yakhontov	(Doesn't exist today)	Jachontoff
Yakovlevo	Яковлево	Jakowlewo
Yamki farm	Ямки	Jamki
Yasnaya Polyana	Ясная Поляна	Jasnaja Poljana
Yerik	Ерик	Jerik
Zhimolestnoye	Жимолостное	Shilomostnoje
Zhuravlinyi	(now Rediny Dvory)	

It should be noted that with every passing year the metropolis of Belgorod keeps growing in population and area. The population was about 41,000 residents in 1950 and 79,000 in 1960. In 1989, the census measured the population at 300,408; this increased to 337,030 in 2002; 356,402 in 2010; and 391,554 in 2018.

Each year more terrain of the battlefield is swallowed up to the north of the city; much of the terrain fought over on July 5, 1943, is no longer recognizable, or even remembered by the citizenry, as almost no one alive in Belgorod today lived there during the Kursk Offensive.

Appendix 2

Crew Members Not Present for Duty

The following is a partial listing of personnel that have been thought to have been present for duty during the Kursk Offensive but who were, in fact, not present as part of Tiger crews during the battle, and were located as shown.

8th (Heavy) Company

Edenstrasser, Oswald	SS Panzer Training and Replacement Regiment at Beneschau
Egger, Paul	9th Preparatory Course for Reserve Officer Applicants
Einbeck, Aribert	9th Preparatory Course for Officer Applicants
Hafner, Leo	9th Preparatory Course for Reserve Officer Applicants
Kiekbusch, Ernst	5th Preparatory Course for Officer Applicants
Klink, Hans	8th Preparatory Course for Officer Applicants
Kritz, Hugo	Mayon-le-Caen, France for Panther training
Kruse, Herbert	2nd Preparatory Course for Reserve Officer Applicants
Marquardt, Otto	9th Preparatory Course for Reserve Officer Applicants
Nagel, Hellmut	9th Preparatory Course for Reserve Officer Applicants
Schmitz, Karl-Heinz	9th Preparatory Course for Reserve Officer Applicants
Wüster, Rudolf	Light wheeled vehicle driver and company clerk

9th (Heavy) Company

Klingenbeck, Rudolf	Maintenance and Recovery Platoon, 9th (Heavy) Company

Appendix 3

Unit Field Post Numbers

The following field post numbers [FPN] (*Feldpostnummer*) are associated with Tiger units mentioned in this study. These numbers are frequently found in personnel files and official unit documents.

13th (Heavy) Company	**48165**
8th (Heavy) Company	**58505**
9th (Heavy) Company	**48786**
101st SS Heavy Panzer Detachment	59450A
1st Company	59450B
2nd Company	59450C
3rd Company	59450D
Maintenance Company	59450D
501st SS Heavy Panzer Detachment	59450A
1st Company	59450B
2nd Company	59450C
3rd Company	59450D
Maintenance Company	59450D
102nd SS Heavy Panzer Detachment	56085
1st Company	13693
2nd Company	12748
3rd Company	12764
Maintenance Company	58263
502nd SS Heavy Panzer Detachment	56085
1st Company	13693
2nd Company	02707
3rd Company	12764
Supply Company	44546
Workshop Company	58263

Appendix 4

Waffen-SS Ranks

Waffen-SS	German Army	US Army	British Army
Commissioned Officer Grades			
SS-Hauptsturmführer	Hauptmann	Captain	Captain
SS-Obersturmführer	Oberleutnant	1st Lieutenant	1st Lieutenant
SS-Untersturmführer	Leutnant	2nd Lieutenant	2nd Lieutenant
Non-Commissioned Officer Grades			
SS-Sturmscharführer	Stabsfeldwebel	Sergeant Major	Regimental Sergeant Major
SS-Standartenoberjunker	Oberfähnrich	(Officer Candidate program)	None
SS-Hauptscharführer	Oberfeldwebel	Master Sergeant	Battalion Sergeant Major
SS-Oberscharführer	Feldwebel	Technical Sergeant	Company Sergeant Major
SS-Junker	Fähnrich	(Officer Candidate program)	None
SS-Scharführer	Unterfeldwebel	Staff Sergeant	Platoon Sergeant Major
SS-Unterscharführer	Unteroffizier	Sergeant	Sergeant
SS-Rottenführer	Obergefreiter	Corporal	Corporal
Enlisted Man Grades			
SS-Sturmmann	Gefreiter	None	Lance Corporal
SS-Oberschütze	Oberschütz	Private First Class	None
SS-Schütze	Schütze	Private	Private

Photo Gallery

Beresov

German aerial photograph of a battlefield taken on July 7, 1943, showing the nature of the rolling terrain. Top of photo is north. Belgorod is two photos of this size off the bottom edge. Scale is approximately 1:37, 500. Photo taken by the 4th Flight of the 121st Long Range Reconnaissance Group flying Junkers Ju 88s based in Seshcha. Dark areas are thick woods. Beresov village is marked [name added by author] in the upper center. The thin, white line immediately right of the village is a road leading north from Belgorod to Yakovlevo. The bright line running lower right to middle left is a large antitank ditch; another ditch, with more straight lines, is just below and to the right of Beresov. *Balkas* (gullies) can be clearly seen throughout the terrain. What are not seen are hulks of destroyed German tanks. The Russians primarily used antitank guns in this vicinity. The fight for this area occurred on July 5, and the battle has now moved north. *Source: National Archives, Records Group 373, Photo GX-3527-SK-34, dated 7 July 1943*

German aerial photograph of the battlefield taken on July 7, 1943, immediately north of the Beresov photo. The top of the photo is north. Scale is approximately 1:37, 500. The village of Bykovka is upper left; that of Smorodino is center right [both names added by author]. Under magnification, left (west) of Bykovka can be seen several hulks of destroyed Soviet tanks, possibly destroyed on July 5 by the 13th (Heavy) Company. *Source: National Archives, Records Group 373, Photo GX-3527-SK-33, dated 7 July 1943*

German aerial photograph of the battlefield taken on July 15, 1943. This location near Prokhorovka has been called the high water mark of the Kursk Offensive, although the advance north of the Psel River, led by the 9th (Heavy) Company, gained more ground. The 2nd SS Panzer Corps never captured Prokhorovka, but did briefly hold Oktiabrskii Sovkhoz. The photo was taken by the 2nd Flight of the 11th Long Range Reconnaissance Group flying Messerschmitt Bf 110s, based in Kharkov. Scale is approximately 1:27, 000. *Source: National Archives, Records Group 373, Photo GX-3734-SK-61, dated 15 July 1943*

A Waffen-SS sand table exercise before the Kursk Offensive. Numerous exercises and rehearsals were designed to familiarize the officers with the terrain over which they would fight and the decisions they might have to make at various points on the battlefield. A complete system of fortifications identical to what the Soviets had at the village of Beresov was built near Kharkov for mock attacks. *Source: National Archives, SS-Kriegsberichter Photograph Collection 1940–44, Anton Ahrens #154*

SS General Wilhelm Bittrich was quoted as saying: "I once spent an hour and a half trying to explain a situation to Sepp Dietrich with the aid of a map. It was quite useless. He understood nothing at all." That may have been true, but Dietrich knew how to lead soldiers. *Source: National Archives, SS-Kriegsberichter Photograph Collection 1940–44, Gunter D'Alquen #02*

SS General Josef Dietrich awarding Iron Crosses. Note that several soldiers are smiling and laughing; a former sergeant in the Great War, Dietrich knew how to use humor with fellow soldiers. *Source: National Archives, SS-Kriegsberichter Photograph Collection 1940–44, Paul Augustin #22A*

Josef "Sepp" Dietrich shaking hands at a formation of assault gunners. *Source: National Archives, SS-Kriegsberichter Photograph Collection 1940–44, Paul Augustin #24*

SS General Walter Krüger (*left*) exiting an observation aircraft. Commander of the *Das Reich* at Kursk, he would commit suicide in May 1945 to avoid Soviet capture. *Source: National Archives, SS-Kriegsberichter Photograph Collection 1940–44, Friedrich Zschäckl #32*

SS General Hermann Priess (right) commanded the *Totenkopf* at Kursk. Slightly behind him is Otto Baum, who commanded a Battle Group in the *Totenkopf* at Kursk. *Source: National Archives, SS-Kriegsberichter Photograph Collection 1940–44, Hans Cantzler #8A*

A wartime photo of SS General Paul Hausser, later mounted with a clipped signature of the general. The officer immediately right of Hausser is Sylvester Stadler. Given Stadler's Knights Cross and rank insignia, the photo was taken in April 1943. Hausser is still wearing a bandage over his right eye, under the black eyepatch; he had been severely wounded in the face and lost his right eye in battle near Gjatsch on October 14, 1941. Given the size of the bandage, one wonders what effect it may have had on Hausser at Kursk. *Source: Photo obtained from SJS Militaria in Nova Scotia*

Unloading Tigers from a train, probably heading for *Das Reich* in April 1943. *Source: National Archives, SS-Kriegsberichter Photograph Collection 1940–44, Hermann Grönert #21*

Signed photo of SS General Theodor Wisch; he took command of SS Panzer Grenadier Division *Leibstandarte Adolf Hitler* after Josef Dietrich departed. Wisch commanded the division until August 20, 1944, when he was seriously wounded in Normandy. Wisch died on January 11, 1995. *Source: Photo obtained from Donley Auctions*

Applying a camouflage paint scheme to a *Das Reich* Tiger. *Source: National Archives, SS-Kriegsberichter Photograph Collection 1940–44, Hermann Grönert #26*

Freshly painted camouflage for *Das Reich* Tigers. Vehicles have the wider combat tracks, instead of the narrower tracks used when the tanks are on railcars; this indicates that they are not just off the transport train. *Source: National Archives, SS-Kriegsberichter Photograph Collection 1940–44, Hermann Grönert #7*

Das Reich Tiger; the vehicle number has not yet been painted on the turret. *Source: National Archives, SS-Kriegsberichter Photograph Collection 1940–44, Hermann Grönert #41*

Leibstandarte panzers off the side of the road at Kursk. *Source: National Archives, SS-Kriegsberichter Photograph Collection 1940–44, Johan King #69*

Tiger from the 13th (Heavy) Company in *Leibstandarte* and dismounted infantrymen at Kursk. *Source: National Archives, SS-Kriegsberichter Photograph Collection 1940–44, Max Büschel #7A*

Tiger crew from the 13th (Heavy) Company standing outside their vehicle during a break in the fighting at Kursk. Several miles in the distance burning vehicles can be seen. At the crewmen's feet are numerous 88 mm shell casings. The men are dirty, but are extremely relaxed. There appear to be nine kill rings on the gun tube. One secondary source states that this is Tiger **1312** in the First Platoon of the 13th (Heavy) Company, but the study could not confirm this. It could also be the crew of **1301** after Jürgen Brandt took over the vehicle when Heinz Kling was wounded on July 10. *Source: National Archives, SS-Kriegsberichter Photograph Collection 1940–44, Max Büschel #145*

Another view of one of the crewmen from the 13th (Heavy) Company in soft cap and camouflage uniform. He appears to have grease on his face; his last wash up was probably before the offensive began.
Source: National Archives, SS-Kriegsberichter Photograph Collection 1940–44, Max Büschel #140

Tiger from the 13th (Heavy) Company in *Leibstandarte* and dismounted infantrymen at Kursk. *Source: National Archives, SS-Kriegsberichter Photograph Collection 1940–44, Max Büschel #7A*

Same incident from the 13th (Heavy) Company. The soldier sitting on 88 mm gun is probably the loader; the man sitting on the driver's hatch is likely the driver, and the soldier slouched on the right is most likely the gunner. Damage to the vehicle is probably engine or transmission. While this could have initially come from a mine, the vehicle does not appear to be in a minefield because the infantry is walking too closely to it. That and the positions of the crew indicate that no one is worried about a possible air attack. *Source: National Archives, SS-Kriegsberichter Photograph Collection 1940–44, Max Büschel #230*

Tiger **1313** in the First Platoon of the 13th (Heavy) Company at Kursk. A noted Tiger historian believes that gunner *SS-Unterscharführer* Heinrich Knöss is standing in the commander's cupola. The flag is to assist German aircraft to identify the vehicle as friendly. *Source: National Archives, SS-Kriegsberichter Photograph Collection 1940–44, Max Büschel #13A*

Tiger **1311** (lead) and Tiger **1332** (following) at Kursk. In **1311**, the man halfway in the cupola on the left of the turret appears to be *SS-Obersturmführer* Waldemar Schütz, while the soldier on the right side of the turret in front of the rectangular hatch cover is *SS-Panzerschütze* Walter Lau. In **1332**, in the commander's cupola, is *SS-Oberscharführer* Max Marten. The other men standing on Max's Tiger are infantrymen. *Source: National Archives, SS-Kriegsberichter Photograph Collection 1940–44, Max Büschel #179*

Tiger **1314** of the First Platoon. The tank commander in the cupola is *SS-Oberscharführer* Fritz Hartel. He was commissioned an officer shortly after Kursk. *Source: National Archives, SS-Kriegsberichter Photograph Collection 1940–44, Max Büschel #180*

Grenadiers of *Leibstandarte* in an enemy antitank ditch at Kursk. Obviously any panzer driving into this obstacle will have a difficult time getting out and likely need recovery vehicles. *Source: National Archives, SS-Kriegsberichter Photograph Collection 1940–44, Max Büschel #198*

Joachim Peiper at Kursk. He and his unit, the Third Battalion of the 2nd SS Panzer Grenadier Regiment, were side by side with the 13th (Heavy) Company on several pivotal days of the offensive. Peiper was a hard man. He moved to Traves, in eastern France, in 1972. Four years later, on the night of July 13–14, 1976, multiple unknown attackers firebombed his house. Peiper was killed in the melee; his remains were subsequently buried at the St. Anna Church in Schondorf am Ammersee in Bavaria. *Source: National Archives, SS-Kriegsberichter Photograph Collection 1940–44, Johan King #27*

8th (Heavy) Company Tigers of *Das Reich* with assault guns at Kursk; note the smoke plume. *Source: National Archives, SS-Kriegsberichter Photograph Collection 1940–44, Hans Cantzler #20A*

A *Das Reich* attack column prepares to move out on July 5 during the Kursk Offensive. The front Tiger is **S31** of the Third Platoon of the 8th (Heavy) Company. The soldier in the commander's cupola is Alois Kalss. The three Mark III panzers could belong to the panzer regiment headquarters or one of the regular panzer companies. The tank in the center rear of the photo may be a captured T-34. The photograph was taken by Kurt Baral in **S32**. *Source: Rüdiger Warnick from photos given to him by the nephew of Kurt Baral*

The four Tigers of the Third Platoon in the 8th (Heavy) Company at a short halt at the beginning of the Kursk Offensive on July 5. The three soldiers wearing helmets at the right may be from SS Panzer Grenadier Regiment *Der Führer. Source: Rüdiger Warnick from photos given to him by the nephew of Kurt Baral*

Tigers **S33** (*front*) and **S34** (*rear*) on July 5, just after crossing the first antitank ditch north of Rakovo. The commander in **S33** is Johann Reinhardt. The commander in **S34** is difficult to see, but is believed to be Artur Ulmer. Photograph taken by Kurt Baral in **S32**. Johann Reinhardt was killed in action on August 25, 1943, northwest of Korotych, Ukraine. He was posthumously awarded the German Cross in Gold on September 25, 1943. His remains have never been identified, but may be buried among the unknowns at the German War Cemetery in Kiev. Artur Ulmer was seriously wounded on July 7, and died of his wounds at a field hospital on July 15, 1943. *Source: Rüdiger Warnick from photos given to him by the nephew of Kurt Baral*

Tiger **S02** being recovered on July 5 near Beresov after being immobilized by an enemy antitank mine. Photograph was taken by the radio operator Hans Haselböck. Two Sd.Kfz.9 recovery half-tracks are pulling **S02** (that has its turret to the rear) by use of towing cables, while a third appears to be pushing the stricken panzer from the rear. *Sorce: Hans Haselböck through Rüdiger Warnick*

In the deployment on the first day of the Kursk Offensive. A crew member of **S32** in the Third Platoon of the 8th (Heavy) Company. Tigers are advancing through a narrow ravine to avoid enemy detection as they move. Large flags on the turret are to identify vehicles as German to friendly aircraft. *Source: Rüdiger Warnick from the nephew of a Tiger crew member in the 8th (Heavy) Company*

Kurt Baral and Tiger **S32** in the Third Platoon of the 8th (Heavy) Company on July 5, south of Beresov. Photo was taken by a comrade. The unit has just descended the ridge to the front. At the end of the war on April 19, 1945, shortly after becoming the acting commander of the 3rd Company of the 502nd SS Heavy Panzer Detachment, Kurt was killed by a burst of enemy machine gun fire while climbing into his King Tiger in a wooded area near the village of Briesen. *Source: Rüdiger Warnick from photos given to him by Kurt Baral's nephew*

Das Reich on the march at Kursk. Variety of vehicles are in a *balka*, a large ravine. Numerous *balkas* crisscrossed the battlefield and served as assembly areas in which to reorganize. *Source: National Archives, SS-Kriegsberichter Photograph Collection 1940–44, Max Büschel #25*

The crew of Tiger **S32** eating in a wooded area. The photograph is marked on the rear as July 6, 1943. The soldier in the center is Kurt Baral. The scene is probably from an assembly area early in the day before the attack, as Baral was wounded in the head by shrapnel later during the day. The forest is a good size; note the Tiger to the rear that has been covered with branches for concealment. *Source: Rüdiger Warnick from photos given to him by the nephew of Kurt Baral*

Tiger **S11** in the early days of the Kursk Offensive. The radio operator's hatch is open, indicating that the crew does not expect artillery fire. Two infantrymen (or combat engineers) have a field-made ladder with which to climb into tank ditches or lay across narrow ones to negotiate. The village is very likely Bykovka, and if so this is July 6, 1943. *Source: National Archives, SS-Kriegsberichter Photograph Collection 1940–44, Hermann Grönert #89*

Another view of Tiger **S11** at the same location. The soldier to the right is carrying a flamethrower. Four crewmen can now be seen. The soldier in the commander's cupola appears to be *SS-Obersturmführer* Philipp Theiss. The loader in the hatch on the left top of the turret is unidentified, as is the radio operator crouching on top of the hull deck near his hatch. Sitting to the right, closest to the driver's hatch, is driver *SS-Rottenführer* Eduard Arzner. *Source: National Archives, SS-Kriegsberichter Photograph Collection 1940–44, Hermann Grönert #89A*

The 8th (Heavy) Company rolling through Bykovka on July 6, 1943. Closest is Tiger commander *SS-Hauptsturmführer* Herbert Zimmermann. *Source: National Archives, SS-Kriegsberichter Photograph Collection 1940–44, Hermann Grönert through Wawrzyniec Markowski*

Tiger **S21** of the Second Platoon just past Bykovka on July 6, 1943. The two panzer grenadiers from SS Panzer Grenadier Regiment *Der Führer* are a machine gun crew. On the Tiger, the black smudge on the front of the turret just left of the 88 mm main gun is an indicator that the gunner has fired a very large number of rounds through the coaxial machine gun in the battle! *Source: National Archives, SS-Kriegsberichter Photograph Collection 1940–44, Hermann Grönert through Wawrzyniec Markowski*

8th (Heavy) Company advancing in the early afternoon on July 6. The village to the south in the background is Bykovka. Photo comparisons indicate that the closest Tiger is probably **S13**. If so, that is probably *SS-Unterscharführer* Franz Kraml in the commander's cupola. *Source: National Archives, SS-Kriegsberichter Photograph Collection 1940–44, Hermann Grönert #90*

Tiger **S12** shown in an iconic Kursk windmill photograph. The commander in the cupola is probably SS-*Unterscharführer* Konrad Schweigert. The flag draped on top of the turret is to assist in identification from the air. This photo was taken on July 6. *Source: National Archives, SS-Kriegsberichter Photograph Collection 1940–44, Hermann Grönert #91*

Tiger **S13** advancing with infantry on July 6. In the commander's cupola is *SS-Unterscharführer* Franz Kraml.
Source: National Archives, SS-Kriegsberichter Photograph Collection 1940–44, Hermann Grönert #93

Closeup of **S13** outside of Bykovka on July 6. Commander *SS-Unterscharführer* Franz Kraml is obviously hamming it up for the *SS-Kriegsberichter* war photographer snapping the picture. Tiger commanders had too much to do to carry a Luger pistol and point with it. The two infantrymen are probably rolling their eyes at the thought. The small devil was painted on the turret of every Tiger in the company. According to Knight's Cross winner Will Fey: "A tank man of *Das Reich* panzer regiment found a strange metal figure in the streets of Kharkov after the battle in March 1943. He transferred to the Tiger company in April 1943 and showed his new comrades this lucky emblem of the 'Jumping Devil' and it was adopted by the whole company." *Source: National Archives, SS-Kriegsberichter Photograph Collection 1940–44, Hermann Grönert #94*

Infantrymen from *Das Reich* rest in an antitank ditch. The men appear to be on a hill; the size of the forest to their front hints that these woods are near Smorodino. *Source: National Archives, SS-Kriegsberichter Photograph Collection 1940–44, Hermann Grönert #96*

Tiger **S11** has just engaged the enemy, and from the explosion cloud it appears that they have hit an enemy vehicle. The photo was taken July 6. *Source: National Archives, SS-Kriegsberichter Photograph Collection 1940–44, Hermann Grönert #104*

Tiger **S11** is in the foreground. Based on photo sequencing this is just after **S11** knocked out an enemy tank. An aerial observer will tell the ground troops what is ahead. This photo was taken on July 6. *Source: National Archives, SS-Kriegsberichter Photograph Collection 1940–44, Hermann Grönert #105*

Taken seconds after the one with the aircraft, the crew of **S11** is still inside the panzer and the explosion cloud of the target has grown in size. Photo taken on July 6. *Source: National Archives, SS-Kriegsberichter Photograph Collection 1940–44, Hermann Grönert #106*

Tiger **S13** at Kursk with a soldier in front of it. He may be looking for mines—probably taken on July 6. The commander is cautiously peering out of the cupola with just the top of his hat visible. If this is an actual minefield, SS war photographer Hermann Grönert is standing in the middle of it! *Source: National Archives, SS-Kriegsberichter Photograph Collection 1940–44, Hermann Grönert #109*

Tiger **S24** in the thick of the battle; armored vehicles can be seen to the front. The gunner and commander have swung turret to the right, possibly to engage a target. Depending on what that is, the driver may move forward and steer to the right to place the thickest armor toward the enemy. This photograph had to be taken before noon on July 7, as **S24** became a total loss at that time. *Source: National Archives, SS-Kriegsberichter Photograph Collection 1940–44, Hermann Grönert #131*

The crew of **S13** at Kursk transferring 88 mm main gun ammunition. This is an emergency situation, as **S13** is getting ammunition from another Tiger while combat can be seen to the front. Both vehicles are stationary and extremely vulnerable at this moment. Probably taken on July 7 near Ozerovskiy. *Source: National Archives, SS-Kriegsberichter Photograph Collection 1940–44, Hermann Grönert #132*

Tiger **S21** in action just to the left of **S13** as a transfer of 88 mm main gun ammunition is taking place. *SS-Obersturmführer* Walter Reininghaus, commander of **S24**, is looking east toward the rail line from Belgorod to Prokhorovka on July 7. *Source: National Archives, SS-Kriegsberichter Photograph Collection 1940–44, Hermann Grönert #133*

Tiger **S02** viewed on July 7. *SS-Hauptsturmführer* Herbert Zimmermann (with headset) is the tank commander; to the front is *SS-Rottenführer* Kurt Meyer, who will be the gunner. This is no joyride. Company commander Zimmermann has just had **S01** shot out from under him. He has transferred to **S02** and has a new gunner, Meyer. The two are riding in the hatch together so they can see the battlefield and compare what they are seeing—sort of a test ride. *Source: National Archives, SS-Kriegsberichter Photograph Collection 1940–44, Hermann Grönert #134*

Tiger **S23** with its turret to the right. All the crew is inside, probably in the process of firing. *SS-Oberscharführer* Kurt Hellwig is the commander. *Source: National Archives, SS-Kriegsberichter Photograph Collection 1940–44, Hermann Grönert #136*

Tiger **S23** and two other Tigers. The photo is of the same engagement, but shows spacing between the three panzers. In this configuration they can support one another, especially against multiple threats, which the 8th (Heavy) Company faced almost every day of the Kursk Offensive. *Source: National Archives, SS-Kriegsberichter Photograph Collection 1940–44, Hermann Grönert #137*

Tiger **S32** during the Kursk Offensive. Kurt Baral is in the commander's cupola. The soldier standing in the loader's hatch appears to have minor facial wounds. *Source: Rüdiger Warnick from photos given to him by the nephew of Kurt Baral*

Tiger **S32** was just to the rear of the front at the village of Ozerovskiy to repair engine damage on July 9, 10, and 11, so this photo was taken on one of those days. Shadows indicate midday; open terrain indicates that *Das Reich* is not concerned about enemy air attacks. A winch can be seen in the background that appears to be affixed to the engine compartment area. Kurt Baral (*right*) and another crewman are listening to a portable, hand-crank record player. It could be theirs, or it could belong to the maintenance soldiers; such a record player was worth its weight in gold at the front! *Source: Rüdiger Warnick from photos given to him by the nephew of Kurt Baral*

Das Reich soldiers in a captured antitank ditch at Kursk. The sloping side on the left would be in the direction from which the enemy was expected to advance. Troops look tired, but not at their limit of effort. Believed to be dated July 10. An interesting detail is that only one personal weapon, a Mauser rifle (*right*), is visible. It is possible that these men are vehicle crews. *Source: National Archives, SS-Kriegsberichter Photograph Collection 1940–44, Max Büschel #29*

Tiger **S01** on July 11, 1943, during the Kursk Offensive. Given the battle history of this Tiger, which had it in maintenance much of the time, the photo is probably July 11. The individual in the commander's cupola may be the gunner; if so, it is *SS-Rottenführer* Julius Hinrichsen. *Source: National Archives, SS-Kriegsberichter Photograph Collection 1940–44, Hermann Grönert #170*

Taken on July 11, 1943, this photo shows **S01**, the commander's Tiger in the 8th (Heavy) Company, and two vehicles from the command group of the 2nd Panzer Regiment. The Mark III panzer in the center has turret number R11. *Source: National Archives, SS-Kriegsberichter Photograph Collection 1940–44, Hermann Grönert #171*

Tiger **S01** following Mark III at Kursk, probably on July 11. The photo does not show the face of the soldier in the commander's cupola. Regardless of whether this is the Tiger commander or the gunner temporarily serving as the commander, he will be unable to effectively communicate with the crew as he is wearing no headset. *Source: National Archives, SS-Kriegsberichter Photograph Collection 1940–44, Hermann Grönert #180*

Tiger commander Kurt Baral in front of his vehicle **S32** sometime during Kursk. The dark spots are mud; it has rained that day or the day before. *Source: Rüdiger Warnick from photos given to him by the nephew of Kurt Baral*

The end of the 88 mm cannon with the muzzle brake removed. The weapon has experienced massive damage and will have to be replaced. A high explosive round may have exploded while leaving the tube, or the muzzle brake was hit by enemy fire. *Source: National Archives, SS-Kriegsberichter Photograph Collection 1940–44, Max Büschel #178*

Supposedly Tiger **914** of the 9th (Heavy) Company. Tiger historian Ian Michael Woods believes this was taken on July 5. The turret number is faintly visible just in front of the spare track blocks and helmets on the side of the turret. Tiger **914** in the First Platoon, commanded by Richard Müller, was hit by Soviet artillery rounds on July 7, 1943, near Smorodino during the day and became a total loss. *Source: National Archives through Ian Michael Woods*

Tiger **921** of the 9th (Heavy) Company at Kursk. In the cupola is commander Heinz Quade; the gunner (with his right arm on the turret top) is Artur Privatzki; and astride the 88 mm main gun is loader Franz Hilgert. There was a regulation forbidding crewmen from sitting on the gun tube of the 88 mm to prevent even the slightest misalignment of the system, but this edict was widely disregarded. On Hill 308 near Kolontaiv, in the Ukraine, on August 31, 1943, an enemy antitank round struck the cupola on the Tiger that Hilgert was driving, shearing off the structure, killing commander Heinz Quade, and wounding the other two crewmen in the turret. Franz took charge, restarted the engine, and drove the vehicle to safety. *Source: National Archives, SS-Kriegsberichter Photograph Collection 1940–44, Hans Cantzler #15A*

Two Tigers from the 9th (Heavy) Company following an assault gun loaded with grenadiers on top. We do not know the turret numbers of these Tigers, but several veterans of the company maintained after the war that an assault gun had accidentally fired on Tiger **901**, killing company commander Wilhelm Schroeder, on July 8, 1943. Could any of these vehicles in this photograph have been involved later in that incident? *Source: National Archives, SS-Kriegsberichter Photograph Collection 1940–44, Hans Cantzler #10*

Fritz Hartel was the commander of Tiger **1314** in the First Platoon at the Kursk Offensive. He was posted missing in action on December 30, 1943, near Berdychiv-Khazhyn in the Ukraine. There is some confusion concerning the date, as the German War Grave Commission lists December 1, 1943. His remains have never been discovered. *Source: National Archives, RuSHA Files, Roll C50*

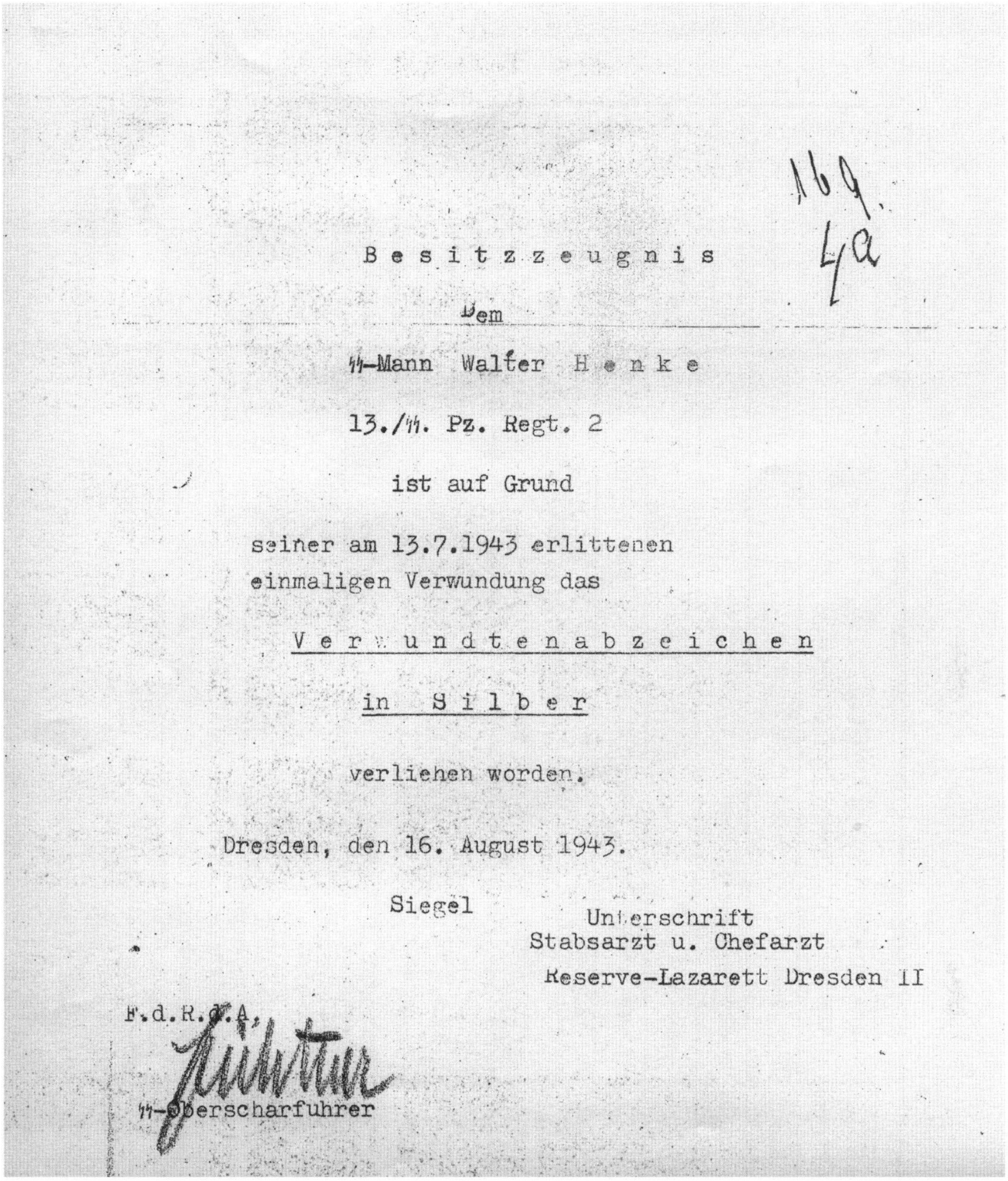

B e s i t z z e u g n i s

Dem

ᛋᛋ-Mann Walter H e n k e

13./ᛋᛋ. Pz. Regt. 2

ist auf Grund

seiner am 13.7.1943 erlittenen
einmaligen Verwundung das

V e r w u n d t e n a b z e i c h e n

in S i l b e r

verliehen worden.

Dresden, den 16. August 1943.

Siegel   Unterschrift
          Stabsarzt u. Chefarzt
          Reserve-Lazarett Dresden II

F.d.R.d.A.

ᛋᛋ-Oberscharführer

Copy of an award certificate for the Wound Badge in Silver to Walter Henke in his SS personnel file. Below his name is his unit. The initial wound occurred on 13.7.1943 (July 13, 1943). The award was made at a military hospital in Dresden on August 16, 1943. A senior SS enlisted man has signed in lieu of a doctor. Walter Henke served as a loader in Tiger **1325** in the second Platoon of the 13th (Heavy) Company during the Kursk Offensive until he was seriously wounded in the eye on July 13. He survived the war. *National Archives, SS Enlisted Personnel Files, Roll G033*

George "Panzergeneral" Lötzsch served in the Second Platoon in the 13th (Heavy) Company as the commander of Tiger **1323** at the Kursk Offensive. He later commanded a Tiger I in Normandy and a Tiger II in the Battle of the Bulge. *Source: National Archives, RuSHA Files, Roll D5142*

Reimers Heinrich
Landarbeiter
11.5.24   T
Schnepke/Hann.
SS-Uscha.   C
Normandie   8.44

Heinrich "Hein" Reimers served as the driver of Tiger **1301** in the Headquarters Platoon of the 13th (Heavy) Company at the Kursk Offensive. He was killed in action on August 8, 1944, in Gaumesnil, Normandy, serving in the 2nd Company of the 101st SS Heavy Panzer Detachment as the driver for Michael Wittmann when their Tiger 007 was engaged by Sherman Firefly tanks from Squadron A of the 1st Northamptonshire Yeomanry. He is buried in the same grave as Michael Wittmann. *Source: German Red Cross (Deutschen Roten Kreuz) Missing Persons Bureau*

Rolf Schamp commanded Tiger **1324** in the Second Platoon of the 13th (Heavy) Company during the Kursk Offensive. Becoming an officer on June 21, 1944, he was assigned to the 17th SS Panzer Grenadier Division *Götz von Berlichingen* on November 1, 1944, serving in the panzer detachment. He survived the war, living later in Weilburg, in Hesse, until his death on July 14, 2007. *Source: National Archives, RuSHA Files*

Wenzel Reinhard
o.A.
8.8.23   U
Jlmenau/Thür.
Gfr.   C
Aachen   12.44

Rolf Schamp played a key but often overlooked role in Franz Staudegger's destruction of twenty-two attacking enemy tanks near Teterevino (N) on July 8, 1943, for which he received the Knight's Cross of the Iron Cross. Schamp and his Tiger protected Staudegger's flank, a perfect by-the-book tactic of putting the success of the unit ahead of personal achievement. *Source: Author's archives, originally from Rolf Schamp*

Reinhart Wenzel served as a loader in Tiger **1324** in the Second Platoon of the 13th (Heavy) Company during the Kursk Offensive. He later served in the 501st SS Heavy Tank Detachment in the Ardennes, where he was killed in action near Malmedy, Belgium, on December 24, 1944. He is buried at the German War Cemetery in Lommel, Belgium, in Block 12 in Grave 362. *Source: German Red Cross (Deutschen Roten Kreuz) Missing Persons Bureau*

Michael Wittmann began the Kursk Offensive as the leader of the Third Platoon of the 13th (Heavy) Company and assumed acting command of the company on July 11, 1943; during the period he commanded in **1331**, **1324**, and possibly other Tigers. One of the most accomplished panzer commanders in the war, he was killed in action on August 8, 1944, in Gaumesnil, Normandy, when his Tiger 007 was engaged by Sherman Firefly tanks firing 17-pound guns from Squadron A of the 1st Northamptonshire Yeomanry. His remains, and those of his crew, lay in an unmarked grave near the site of his death for four decades. His remains are at the German War Cemetery in La Cambe, Normandy, in Plot 47, Row 3, in Grave 120G, along with the rest of his crew. *National Archives, SS Officer Personnel Files, Roll 003C*

1944 photograph of Michael Wittmann with the Knight's Cross of the Iron Cross with Oak Leaves. He would receive the Swords to this award on June 26, 1944. *National Archives, courtesy of George Nipe*

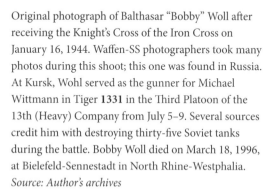

Original photograph of Balthasar "Bobby" Woll after receiving the Knight's Cross of the Iron Cross on January 16, 1944. Waffen-SS photographers took many photos during this shoot; this one was found in Russia. At Kursk, Wohl served as the gunner for Michael Wittmann in Tiger **1331** in the Third Platoon of the 13th (Heavy) Company from July 5–9. Several sources credit him with destroying thirty-five Soviet tanks during the battle. Bobby Woll died on March 18, 1996, at Bielefeld-Sennestadt in North Rhine-Westphalia. *Source: Author's archives*

Another original photograph of Balthasar Woll after receiving the Knight's Cross of the Iron Cross. This example also came out of Russia. In 1944, he transferred to the Third Company of the 101st SS Heavy Panzer Detachment as the commander of Tiger 335. Soon after the invasion in Normandy his panzer was involved in a fight near Bayeux, hitting three British Churchill tanks, but an Allied fighter-bomber struck the tank with rockets, killing three of the crew and seriously wounding Woll, and sending him back to Germany for further medical care. Balthasar Woll would survive the war. *Source: Author's archives*

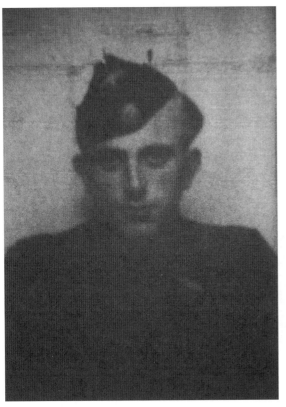

Max Bläsing served as the driver in Tiger **S02** in the Headquarters Platoon of the 8th (Heavy) Company and was wounded on the first day of the battle. He later served as a driver in the 1st Company of the 102nd SS Heavy Panzer Detachment in 1944 at Normandy and as a King Tiger driver in the 1st Company of the 502nd SS Heavy Panzer Detachment at the Oder Front in 1945. Max Bläsing died in Backnang, Baden-Württemberg, on July 16, 1998. *Source: National Archives, RuSHA Files, Roll A512*

Max Bläsing (*left*) and Julius Hinrichsen (*right*) in the Ukraine in June 1943. At Kursk, Bläsing served as the driver in Tiger **S02** in the 8th (Heavy) Company, while Hinrichsen served as the gunner in **S01** and **S02**. Bläsing would later serve as a driver in the 1st Company of the 102nd SS Heavy Panzer Detachment in 1944, and as a driver in the 1st Company of the 502nd SS Heavy Panzer Detachment at the Oder Front in 1945. Hinrichsen later fought in Normandy with the 102nd SS Heavy Panzer Detachment. He was credited in many sources as destroying a total of twenty-two enemy tanks in the conflict. Both men survived the war. *Source: Rüdiger Warnick from photos given to him by the nephew of Kurt Baral*

Berthold "Percussion Cap" Fink drove a Tiger in the 8th (Heavy) Company at Kursk. He was later assigned to the 2nd Company in the 102nd SS Heavy Panzer Detachment as a driver and fought at Hill 112 at Normandy in July 1944. In 1945, Fink drove King Tiger 123 in the Second Platoon of the 1st Company in the 502nd SS Heavy Panzer Detachment on the Oder Front; he is also believed to have been a driver for King Tiger 111. On April 28, 1945, he was among the last handful of King Tigers in the detachment to attempt to break out from the near encirclement of what would become known as the Halbe Pocket. His Tiger made it to the village of Beelitz on May 1, 1945, before it ran out of fuel and the crew blew it up. *Source: Berthold Fink through Rüdiger Warnick*

1944 photograph of Tiger commanders Will Fey (*left*), Paul Egger (*center*), and Artur Glagow (*right*). Only Glagow was at the Kursk Offensive. Because the Waffen-SS had no panzer branch to centralize assignments and schooling Egger was sent back to Germany to a leadership course before the offensive began, thus missing one of the pivotal tank battles of the war. Egger likely destroyed more than 100 enemy tanks in the war, while Fey is often credited with seventy-three kills. *Source: Author's archives, originally from Paul Egger*

Artur Glagow, 8th (Heavy) Company, was the gunner in Tiger **S21**, in the Second Platoon in the Kursk Offensive. He was later listed as missing in action on August 19, 1944, in Normandy, but was actually captured. He survived the war and passed away in 1998. *Source: National Archives, RuSHA Files, Roll B5171*

Erich Holzer, a loader in the 8th (Heavy) Company at Kursk. Later assigned to the 1st Company of the 102nd SS Heavy Panzer Detachment as the loader in Tiger 111, he was killed in action near Caen, France, on June 27, 1944, during an air attack. He is buried at the German War Cemetery at Noyers-Pont-Maugis, France, in Block 4 (Grave 1834) among 26,843 German war dead, of which 4,880 are from World War II. *National Archives, SS Enlisted Personnel Files, Roll H027*

Jörg Hermann
Schüler
12.10.24   J
Hindelwangen/Baden
SS-Uscha.
Soissons-Laon 8.44

Hermann Jörg was a driver for Tiger **S12** at the Kursk Offensive. Later assigned to the 2nd Company of the 502nd SS Heavy Panzer Detachment, he was likely killed in action on August 28, 1944, in the Soissons-Laon area of France; his remains appear to have never been found. *Source: German Red Cross (Deutschen Roten Kreuz) Missing Persons Bureau*

One of the greatest tank gunners in World War II, Gerhard Kaempf is credited by many for knocking out forty-six enemy tanks. Because he was an enlisted man he did not receive the same level of high publicity that commissioned officers often did. At Kursk, Kaempf was the gunner in both Tiger **S31** and Tiger **S22**. In the final month of the war on the Oder Front, Gerhard Kaempf commanded King Tiger 123 in the Second Platoon of 1st Company in the 502nd SS Heavy Panzer Detachment and was on one of the last remaining Tigers to attempt to break out of the Halbe Pocket south of Berlin on April 28, 1945. *Source: Gerhard Kempf through Rüdiger Warnick*

At Kursk, Alois Kalss commanded Tiger **S31** and was the commander of the Third Platoon of the 8th (Heavy) Company. He was wounded on July 5 but remained with the unit. Awarded the Wound Badge in Gold on August 23, 1943, Kalss assumed temporary command of the 8th (Heavy) Company on September 18, 1943, and was awarded the German Cross in Gold on September 23, 1943—in part for his performance at Kursk. Alois Kalss was officially listed as missing in action on May 2, 1945. His remains have never been identified. *Source: Mark Yerger through George Nipe*

Walter Knecht fought at the Kursk Offensive as a commander of Tiger **S22** in the Second Platoon. He later served in the 3rd Company of the 102nd SS Heavy Panzer Detachment in Normandy, commanding Tiger 323. On the Oder Front Walter commanded King Tiger 113 and Tiger 132 in the 1st Company of the 502nd SS Heavy Panzer Detachment. Knecht was wounded in the eye on March 22, 1945, near Alt Tucheband, just west of Küstrin; he was wounded again four days later near Gorgast by an enemy artillery shell, but medics took Knecht to an aid station and he survived. During the war Walter Knecht is believed to have destroyed twenty enemy tanks; he is also believed to have been wounded five times. *Source: Hans Haselböck through Rüdiger Warnick*

An Austrian, Franz Kraml commanded Tiger **S13** in the First Platoon of the 8th (Heavy) Company at Kursk. He later commanded Tiger 112 in the 1st Company of the 102nd SS Heavy Panzer Detachment in Normandy in 1944 and later commanded King Tiger 112 in the First Platoon of the 1st Company in the 502nd SS Heavy Panzer Detachment on the Oder Front at the end of the war. *Source: Franz Kraml's son through Rüdiger Warnick*

Karl Heinz Lorenz. After his death the Wehrmacht issued the family an Honor Roll Clasp on September 19, 1943, for his service. He is shown here with the German Cross in Gold that he received on April 17, 1943; he was also promoted to *SS-Hauptsturmführer* on April 20, 1943, which dates the photograph to about that time. *Source: Mark Yerger through George Nipe*

Bei den schweren Kämpfen im Osten fiel an der Spitze einer Panzer-Komp., die er für den durch Verwundung ausgefallenen Kommandeur übernommen hatte, unser hoffnungsvoller, lebensfroher Sohn, Enkel und Neffe, mein unvergeßlicher Verlobter,

Karl=Heinz Lorenz

SS-Hauptsturmführer u. Regiments-Adjutant in der Waffen-SS

Inh. d. EK. 1 u. 2, d. Deutschen Kreuzes in Gold, des Infanterie- u. Panzer-Sturmabz i. Silber und des Verwundetenabz. in Silber

* 3. 7. 1917   † 7. 7. 1943

Heinr. Lorenz, Musikdir.; Grete Lorenz, geb. Brokmann; Johanna Pflüger, geb. Brokmann; Val. Pflüger; Carl u. Amanda Lorenz; Christa Klaft als Braut.

Bielefeld, Poststr. 49, Bad Oeynhausen, Schwarzach (Niederb.), Wächtersbach b. Frankfurt a. M.

Public death notice for Karl Lorenz. Lorenz served as the acting commander of the 8th (Heavy) Company on July 7, after the company commander was wounded. After assuming command he jumped into Tiger **S24** and moved ahead of the company, crossing a railroad embankment east of Kalinin. At 1200 hours the tank received a direct hit from an antitank gun that instantly killed Karl-Heinz Lorenz. Karl-Heinz left behind a wife, Christa. His remains were never transferred to a German War Cemetery. *National Archives, SS Officer Personnel Files, Roll 277A*

Walter Reininghaus commanded Tiger **S21** as the Second Platoon leader. He took temporary command of the company on July 15 and may have commanded another Tiger. Reininghaus is believed to have later served on the division staff of the *Das Reich* and later in the 9th SS Panzer Division *Hohenstaufen*. He survived the war. *National Archives, SS Officer Personnel Files, Roll 021B*

Nienke Arno
Arbeiter
28.6.24   X
Tilsit/Ostpr.
SS-Rottf.
Osten   3.45

Arno Nienke served as a Tiger driver in the 8th Heavy Company at Kursk. As an *SS-Rottenführer*, he was killed in action on March 27, 1945, near Gorgast, Brandenburg, just west of Küstrin, as the driver for *SS-Untersturmführer* Willy Biber in King Tiger 311. *Source: German Red Cross (Deutschen Roten Kreuz) Missing Persons Bureau*

Fritz Schmid served as the driver in Tiger **S12** in the 1st Platoon of the 8th (Heavy) Company at the Kursk Offensive. He subsequently transferred to the 1st Company of the 102nd SS Heavy Panzer Detachment and later to the 1st Company of the 502nd SS Heavy Panzer Detachment; it appears that he served in the recovery and maintenance sections in both. Fritz Schmid probably was killed in action during the Halbe breakout on April 30, 1945. *Source: Rüdiger Warnick*

Red Cross Missing in Action card for Fritz Schmid. *Source: German Red Cross (Deutschen Roten Kreuz) Missing Persons Bureau*

Schmid Fritz
Bauschlosser
8.2.23   A
Plattling/Ndby.
Uscha.
Berlin   3.45

Wilhelm Schmidt served in the 10th Company of SS Infantry Regiment 4 (motorized) *Langemarck* until October 1942, when the second battalion of the regiment became the second battalion of the *Das Reich* panzer regiment. Schmidt was assigned as the commander of Tiger **S24** in the Second Platoon during the Kursk Offensive. He served later at Normandy with the First Platoon in the 1st Company of the 102nd SS Heavy Panzer Detachment, where he commanded Tiger 114, and later with the 1st Company of the 502nd Heavy Panzer Company, where he commanded King Tiger 112. He was badly wounded on April 25, 1945, in the Halbe Pocket. After the war Wilhelm Schmidt ran a shoe store before he died in 1961. *Source: Rüdiger Warnick from photos given to him by his daughter*

Für die innige Teilnahme anläßlich des Heldentodes meines lieben Mannes und unseres Sohnes, Schwiegersohnes, Bruders u. Schwagers

SS-Obersturmführers

Heinz Tensfeld

danken in stiller Trauer:

Lieselotte Tensfeld geb. Wrede
Willy Tensfeld SS-Brigadeführer u. Generalmajor der Pol., z. Zt. i. Felde und Frau Dolly geb. Willandsen
Ingeburg Tensfeld
Friedrich Wrede u. Frau Minna geb. Bönicke
Frau Ilse Wrede geb. Tahlow
und alle Verwandten.

Hamburg, Dezember 1943

Official public death announcement for Heinz Tensfeld, listing members of his family, starting with his wife Liselotte. Heinz Tensfeld was the commander of Tiger **S11** and the First Platoon in the 8th (Heavy) Company from July 11, 1943. Tensfeld later became the acting commander of the company and was killed in action on November 16, 1943, near Gralimki, Ukraine, south of Kiev. *National Archives, SS Officer Personnel Files, Roll 175B*

Heinrich Warnick in 1944. He drove a Tiger I in the *Das Reich* Tiger company at Kharkov, but then transferred to the Second Battalion and was at transition training for the Panther tank during the Kursk Offensive. Many veteran panzer crewmen were training on the Panther in France and Germany in July 1943—a self-inflicted wound because of a lack of an armored branch in the Waffen-SS. He went on to become a very accomplished gunner; several sources credit him with destroying seventy-seven enemy tanks. Heinrich Warnick survived the war; he died on June 22, 2008, at Neuendettelsau, in Middle Franconia, near the city of Ansbach. *Source: Rüdiger Warnick*

A former Luftwaffe soldier in *Jagdgeschwader 52*, Eduard Woll served as the driver of Tiger **S14** in the First Platoon of the 8th (Heavy) Company at Kursk. He was later assigned to the 1st Company of the 102nd SS Heavy Panzer Detachment at Normandy, where he was the driver of Tiger 132. In October 1944, the unit was designated the 1st Company of the 502nd SS Heavy Panzer Detachment; in this unit he drove King Tigers 101, 102, and 121. Eduard Woll was in one of the last remaining Tigers to attempt to break out of the Halbe Pocket south of Berlin on April 28, 1945. *Source: N. Woll through Rüdiger Warnick*

A photo in the SS personnel file of Fritz Biermeier. At Kursk, he served as the commander of the 9th (Heavy) Company through July 8, 1943, and in this position also commanded Tiger **901** in the Headquarters Platoon. On that day he was elevated to the command of the Second Battalion of the 3rd Panzer Regiment and he departed the company. Fritz Biermeier was killed in action near Modlin, Poland, on October 11, 1944; his remains were initially buried at a temporary German cemetery at Modlin at Field B in Grave Number 3. After the war his remains were reinterred in an end grave at the German War Cemetery at Nowy Dwór Mazowiecki, near Modlin, Poland. *National Archives, SS Officer Personnel Files, Roll 069*

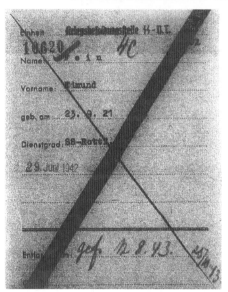

A card from the SS personnel file on Edmund Fein; the large X on the card indicates he has been killed or is missing; "gef. 12.8.43" indicates he fell on August 12, 1943. Edmund Fein commanded Tiger **913** in the First Platoon of the 9th (Heavy) Company during the Kursk Offensive. A month later, at about 1700 hours on August 12, 1943, he was killed in action by a Soviet heavy antitank gun (possibly a Lend-Lease 90 mm cannon from the US) near Pavlove, in the Ukraine; his remains have never been found. *Source: National Archives, SS Enlisted Personnel Files, Roll D007*

Norbert Kochesser served as a loader on a Tiger in the 9th (Heavy) Company at Kursk. He was killed in action on July 30–31, 1943, assaulting the fortified defenses at Hill 213.9 east of Stepanivka, on the Mius front. The company likely conducted a hasty burial of his remains on August 2. Norbert is probably buried with the unknown remains in the German War Cemetery at Kharkov in which rest the remains of 47,322 German soldiers. *Source: National Archives, RuSHA Files, Roll D040*

Hans Lampert commanded Tiger **934** in the Third Platoon of the 9th (Heavy) Company during the Kursk Offensive. He was killed in action on July 30–31, 1943, in fierce combat at Hill 213.9 east of Stepanivka, on the Mius front, as he tried to evacuate his Tiger that was on fire and about to explode. The company conducted a hasty burial of his remains on August 2, but that location remains unknown. *Source: National Archives, RuSHA Files, Roll D0488*

Ferdinand Lasser, gunner 9th (Heavy) Company. He was one of fourteen Austrian Tiger crewmen in the study. *Source: Archive Kraml via R. Warnick*

Lasser Ferdinand
o.A.
3.5.11   P
Österreich
SS-Uscha.
Küstrin   3.45

Ferdinand Lasser, gunner 9th (Heavy) Company. In late March 1945, while a member of the 1st Company of the 502nd SS heavy Panzer Detachment, he was reported missing in action. *Source: German Red Cross (Deutschen Roten Kreuz) Missing Persons Bureau*

Alois Mücke, 9th (Heavy) Company. A radio operator, he was killed in action on July 31, 1943, assaulting Hill 213.9 east of Stepanivka, on the Mius front. An Iron Cross Second Class was awarded to him posthumously on November 10, 1943. *Source: National Archives, RuSHA Files, Roll E079*

Below: Artur Privatzki was the gunner in Tiger **921** in the Second Platoon; he may also have served as a gunner in Tiger **933**. He survived the war. Taken June 27, 1943, at Budy (southwest of Kharkov) before the 9th (Heavy) Company moved north to attack positions. *National Archives, SS-Kriegsberichter Photograph Collection 1940–44, through Wawrzyniec Markowski*

At Kursk Karl Sandler commanded a Tiger in the 9th (Heavy) Company. At the end of the war he was wounded in action on April 10 in Vienna as part of an infantry battlegroup comprised of dismounted panzer crews whose vehicles had been destroyed earlier. He survived the war. *Source: National Archives, RuSHA Files, Roll F145*

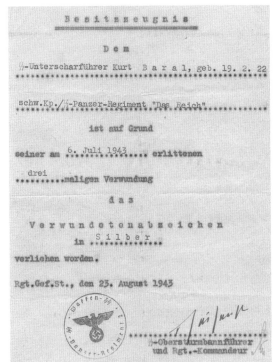

An award document for the Wound Badge in Silver for three wounds to Kurt Baral. The wounds occurred on July 6, 1943. It usually took several weeks for the paperwork to go through, and in this case *SS-Obersturmbannführer* Hans-Albin von Reitzenstein signed the document on August 23, 1943. *Source: Rüdiger Warnick from photo given to him by Kurt Baral's nephew*

Well-worn award document for the Panzer Battle Badge in Silver to Emil Weissfloch. Regimental commander *SS-Obersturmbannführer* Hans-Albin von Reitzenstein signed the document on August 4, 1943. These documents usually took several weeks to process, indicating that the award was for his service at Kursk. *Source: Rüdiger Warnick from family of Emil Weissfloch*

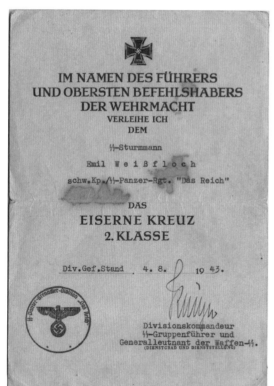

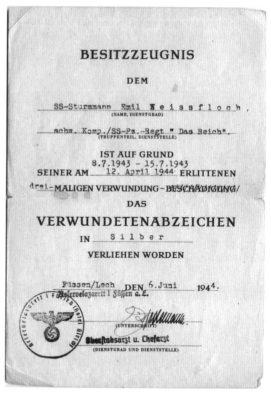

Award document for the Iron Cross Second Class to Emil Weissfloch. Division commander *SS-Gruppenführer* Walter Krüger signed the document on August 4, 1943. These documents also took several weeks to process, indicating that the award was for his service at Kursk. *Source: Rüdiger Warnick from family of Emil Weissfloch*

Award document for the Wound Badge in Silver for three wounds on different days to Emil Weissfloch. The wounds occurred on July 8 and July 15, 1943, at Kursk, and a later wound on April 12, 1944. When a wound resulted in the soldier being evacuated to a hospital a physician often signed the award. *Source: Rüdiger Warnick from family of Emil Weissfloch*

Times were tough after the war for many of the Tiger men. Karl-Heinz Warmbrunn took on the fighting name Robert "Bobby" Warmbrunn and became a professional heavyweight boxer in 1947. Over his sixteen-year career he had fourteen wins, forty-nine losses, and five draws. A club level fighter, he lost his last sixteen bouts before hanging up the gloves on October 5, 1963, after losing to Adolf Mensinger by knockout at the *Fellbacher Stadthalle* in Fellbach, a small village outside of Stuttgart. He then lived in Munich at Leopoldstaße 109, near the Englischer Garten, becoming a sports instructor. *Source: BoxRec Website, Boxing's Official Record Keeper*

Endnotes

Introduction

[1] Ian Michael Wood, *Tigers of the Death's Head*, Mechanicsburg, Pennsylvania: Stackpole Books, 2013, p. 40.

[2] The original German designation for the tank was *Panzerkampfwagen VI Ausführung H*, but in March 1943, the Army redesignated it *Panzerkampfwagen VI Ausführung E*. The military's ordnance inventory designation for the Tiger was *Sonderkraftfahrzeug* [Sd.Kfz.181] (Special purpose Motor Vehicle 181). Source: Bob Carruthers, translator and editor, *Tiger I: Official Wartime Crew Manual (The Tigerfibel)*, Henley in Arden, England: Coda Books, 2011, p. 4.

[3] Christopher A. Lawrence, *Kursk: The Battle of Prokhorovka*, Sheridan, Colorado: Aberdeen Books, 2015, 756.

[4] Multiple discussions with World War II US Army veterans.

[5] Carruthers, *Tiger I: Official Wartime Crew Manual (The Tigerfibel)*, p. 4.

[6] Thirty-one Tigers in the 505th Heavy Panzer Detachment in the 9th Army; 42 Tigers in the 503rd Heavy Panzer Detachment with the 3rd Panzer Corps, twelve Tigers in the *Großdeutschland* Panzer Grenadier Division; and the thirty-five Tigers in the 2nd SS Panzer Corps. There were an additional eighty-nine Ferdinand Tiger turretless antitank assault guns in the 653rd and 654th Heavy Army Tank-Hunter Detachments with the 9th Army.

[7] Speech given to West Point cadets of the Class of 1974 at a tank gunnery range at Fort Knox, Kentucky, in July 1971, during a week of summer armor gunnery training. The speaker, Deputy Post Commander of Fort Knox Brig. Gen. George S. Patton, son of the famous World War II commander, used more colorful language in the description.

Dedication

[1] *Rasse-und-Siedlungs-Hauptamt (RuSHA) Files*, Microfilm Publication A3343, Series RS, National Archives and Records Administration (NARA): College Park, Maryland, Roll G592; and numerous discussions with Rüdiger Warnick.

The Tiger Tank

[1] Thomas L. Jentz and Hilary L. Doyle, *Germany's Tiger Tanks: D. W. to Tiger I: Design, Production & Modifications*, Atglen, Pennsylvania: Schiffer Military History, 2000, p. 32.

[2] *Unternehmen Barbarossa* was named after German King and Holy Roman Emperor Friedrich Barbarossa. Originally termed Friedrich I, he received the name "Barbarossa" by northern Italian cities for his red beard. In Germany his beard was also red, and he was known as Kaiser Rotbart. Born in 1122, in the district of Swabia, near modern day Stuttgart, he drowned on June 10, 1190, in the Göksu/Saleph River near Silifke Castle in southern Turkey while leading the Third Crusade. By legend, after his death his spirit returned to Germany to sleep in a hidden chamber under the Kyffhäuser hills, awaiting the country's hour of greatest need, when he would emerge once again from under the hill to lead his people. Adolf Hitler, who undoubtedly had a hand in naming the operation, may have believed that the invasion of the Soviet Union in June 1941 would turn into Germany's hour of greatest need—it did.

[3] Bob Carruthers, *Tiger I in Combat*, Henley in Arden, England: Coda Books, 2011, Chapter 3.

[4] David Porter, *Das Reich at Kursk*, London, England: Amber Books, 2011, p. 85.

[5] Jentz and Doyle, *Germany's Tiger Tanks: D. W. to Tiger I: Design, Production & Modifications*, p. 31.

[6] Andrew Hills, "Panzerkampfwagen VI Tiger, Sd.Kfz.181, 'Tiger 1'" Tank Encyclopedia, http://www.tanks-encyclopedia.com/ww2/nazi_germany/Panzer-VI_Tiger.php

[7] Jentz and Doyle, *Germany's Tiger Tanks: D. W. to Tiger I: Design, Production & Modifications*, p. 69.

[8] Ibid., p. 23.

[9] Egon Kleine and Volkmar Kühn, *Tiger: The History of a Legendary Weapon 1942–45*, Winnipeg, Canada: J. J. Fedorowicz Publishing, 2004, pp. 1–8; and Waldemar Trojca, *Tiger, 1942–1943, Technical and Operational History, Volume 1*, Katowice, Poland: Model Hobby Publishing, 2010, p. 7.

[10] Kleine and Kühn, *Tiger: The History of a Legendary Weapon 1942–45*, p. 8; and Trojca, *Tiger, 1942–1943*, pp. 9–11.

[11] Jentz and Doyle, *Germany's Tiger Tanks: D. W. to Tiger I: Design, Production & Modifications*, p. 69.

[12] The Tiger cost 250,800 *Reichsmark*; a Panther cost 117,000 *Reichsmark*, while the Panzer Mark IV had a price tag of 103,462 *Reichsmark*, making the Panther the most economical choice to replace the Mark IV—except the Tiger was a stand-alone vehicle and not designed to replace any existing German tank. Source: Anders Frankson and Niklas Zelterling, *Kursk 1943: A Statistical Analysis*, London: Frank Cass Publishing, 2000, p. 61.

[13] Carruthers, *Tiger I: Official Wartime Crew Manual (The Tigerfibel)*, p. 4; and Kleine and Kühn, *Tiger: The History of a Legendary Weapon 1942–45*, p. 9.

[14] Carruthers, *Tiger I in Combat*, Chapter 3.

[15] Ibid.

[16] Wolfgang Schneider, *Totenkopf Tigers*, Winnipeg, Canada: J. J. Fedorowicz, 2011, p. 91.

[17] Military Intelligence Division, *Tactical and Technical Trends Number 34*, Washington, DC: War Department, 23 September 1943, p. 17.

[18] Thomas L. Jentz, *Germany's Tiger Tanks, Tiger I and Tiger II: Combat Tactics, Volume 3*, Atglen, Pennsylvania: Schiffer Publishing, 1997, p. 10.

[19] Ibid.

[20] Jentz, *Germany's Tiger Tanks, Tiger I and Tiger II: Combat Tactics, Volume 3*, p. 10; and Jentz and Doyle, *Germany's Tiger Tanks: D. W. to Tiger I: Design, Production & Modifications*, p. 71.

[21] Jentz, *Germany's Tiger Tanks, Tiger I and Tiger II: Combat Tactics, Volume 3*, p. 11.

[22] Ibid.

[23] Patrick Agte, *Michael Wittmann and the Tiger Commanders of the Leibstandarte*, Winnipeg, Canada: J. J. Fedorowicz, 1996, p. 152.

[24] Jentz, *Germany's Tiger Tanks, Tiger I and Tiger II: Combat Tactics, Volume 3*, p. 36.

[25] Agte, *Michael Wittmann and the Tiger Commanders of the Leibstandarte*, 132; and Schneider, *Totenkopf Tigers*, p. 93.

[26] Jentz, *Germany's Tiger Tanks, Tiger I and Tiger II: Combat Tactics, Volume 3*, p. 11.

[27] Christopher W. Wilbeck, *Sledgehammers: Strengths and Flaws of Tiger Tank Battalions in World War II*, Bedford, Pennsylvania: The Aberjona Press, 2004, pp. 32–33.

[28] Wilbeck, *Sledgehammers*, pp. 32–33.

[29] Ibid.

[30] Ibid.

[31] Ibid.

[32] David Schranck, *Thunder at Prokhorovka: A Combat History of Operation Citadel, Kursk, July 1943*, Solihull, England: Helion & Company, 2013, p. 100.

[33] But not always. The base of the formation, doctrinally, was formed by Panther tanks and at Kursk only the *Großdeutschland* Division had them. On the northern pincer Walter Model's plan of attack was to breach the enemy lines with his infantry. Once this had occurred Model would order his panzer reserve to exploit the success and move into the open area south of the Russian positions. The breach never occurred.

[34] General Heinz Guderian, *Panzer Leader*, translated by Constantine Fitzgibbon, Washington, DC: Zenger Publishing, 1979, p. 290.

[35] Walther-Peer Fellgiebel, *Die Träger des Ritterkreuzes des Eisernen Kreuzes 1939–1945*, Friedberg, FRG: Podzun-Pallas Verlag, 1986, p. 298.

[36] Günter Wegmann, *Die Ritterkreuzträger der Panzertruppe*, Band 1: Albert–Eysser, Bissendorf, Germany: Biblio Verlag, 2004, pp. 270–273.

[37] *Rieger Orgelbau* website, http://www.rieger-orgelbau.com/

[38] Glatter-Götz, Familie, Oesterreichisches Musiklexicon online, https://www.musiklexikon.ac.at/ml/musik_G/Glatter-Goetz_Familie.xml

[39] *Rieger Orgelbau* website, http://www.rieger-orgelbau.com/

[40] Wolfgang Schneider, *Totenkopf Tigers*, p. 85.

[41] Lawrence, *Kursk: The Battle of Prokhorovka*, p. 1, 369.

[42] Schranck, *Thunder at Prokhorovka*, p. 43.

[43] Lawrence, *Kursk: The Battle of Prokhorovka*, p. 1, 369.

[44] Ibid., p. 1, 351.

[45] Ibid., p. 270.

[46] Schranck, *Thunder at Prokhorovka*, p. 38.

[47] Lawrence, *Kursk: The Battle of Prokhorovka*, p. 1, 349.

[48] Ibid., pp. 1, 358–1, 360.

[49] Railroad Armor: Soviet Armored Trains in WW2, http://www.wio.ru/rr/ww2sov.htm

[50] Rüdiger Warnick and Stephan Cazenave, *Tiger! Von schwere Kompanie/SS-Pz.Rgt.2 bis s. SS-Panzerabteilung 102/502*, Bayeux, France: Editions Heimdal, 2008, p. 127.

[51] Lawrence, *Kursk: The Battle of Prokhorovka*, p. 200.

[52] Ibid., pp. 199–200.

[53] Ibid., pp. 391–392.

[54] Schranck, *Thunder at Prokhorovka*, p. 149.

[55] Lawrence, *Kursk: The Battle of Prokhorovka*, p. 206.

[56] Schranck, *Thunder at Prokhorovka*, p. 75.

[57] Carruthers, *Tiger I: Official Wartime Crew Manual (The Tigerfibel)*, p. 103.

[58] Email conversation between Oberst a. D. Wolfgang Schneider and the author, January 24, 2018. Also concerning key communications, the Tiger company commander did not have a separate communications link to the artillery. Instead, a forward observer (FO) artillery officer accompanied the company in a halftrack vehicle, which can sometimes be seen in wartime photographs. One of the FO's radios was on the same frequency as the tank commander's. When he would hear a request for artillery fire on the radio, the FO would transmit this call for fire on a separate radio set to the artillery command post. At that location the decision would be made on whether the request would be executed. If the range to the artillery command post became too great—for example, because the Tiger company was rapidly advancing—the FO would halt his vehicle, erect a special long range antenna, and communicate from a stationary position that generally made communications clearer over the air.

[59] Jentz and Doyle, *Germany's Tiger Tanks: D. W. to Tiger I: Design, Production & Modifications*, p. 51.

[60] Carruthers, *Tiger I: Official Wartime Crew Manual (The Tigerfibel)*, p. 82.

[61] Military Intelligence Division, *Tactical and Technical Trends Number 34*, p. 17.

[62] Carruthers, *Tiger I: Official Wartime Crew Manual (The Tigerfibel)*, p. 66.

[63] Military Intelligence Division, *Tactical and Technical Trends Number 34*, p. 16.

[64] Email discussion with Oberst a. D. Wolfgang Schneider, June 18–19, 2019; and Jentz and Doyle, *Germany's Tiger Tanks: D. W. to Tiger I: Design, Production & Modifications*, p. 53.

[65] Carruthers, *Tiger I: Official Wartime Crew Manual (The Tigerfibel)*, p. 59.

[66] Ibid., p. 15.

[67] Trojca, *Tiger, 1942–1943*, p. 298.

[68] David Porter, *Das Reich at Kursk*, p. 123.

[69] Ben Hollingum, "Ferocious Beast: Six Little-Known Facts About the Tiger Tank, " *MHN, Military History Now Website*, https://militaryhistorynow.com/2015/02/27/ferocious-beast-six-little-known-facts-about-the-tiger-tank/

[70] Robert Forczyk, *Kursk 1943: The Southern Front*, Campaign 305, Oxford, England: Osprey Publishing, 2017, p. 19.

[71] Email with Oberst a. D. Wolfgang Schneider, July 9, 2019.

[72] Ibid.

[73] David Porter, *Das Reich at Kursk*, p. 125.

Battle of Kursk Overview

[1] A Soviet *front* was roughly equivalent to a Western formation of an army group, in that it contained three to five armies. However, a *front* also had its own army-sized tactical fixed wing air organization that was directly subordinated to the *front* commander. During the war, in general terms, Soviet ground units were smaller in size than those in other nations.

[2] John W. Osborn Jr., "Joseph Stalin's Paranoid Purge, " *Warfare History Network*, November 1, 2018, https://warfarehistorynetwork.com/daily/wwii/joseph-stalins-paranoid-purge/

[3] Dermot Bradley and others, *Die Generale des Heeres, 1921–1945*, Band 6: Hochbaum—Klutmann, Bissendorf, Germany: Biblio Verlag, 2002, pp. 157–159.

[4] Ibid. Hoth died on January 25, 1971, in Goslar. He was buried at Goslar at the Friedhof Feldstraße in Section 11, Grave 23/24. The head stone was removed in 2015.

[5] Andreas Schulz, Günter Wegmann, and Dieter Zinke, *Die Generale der Waffen-SS und der Polizei*, Band 2: Hachtel—Kutschera, Bissendorf, Germany: Biblio Verlag, 2005, pp. 79–90.

[6] Hausser died on December 21, 1972, in Munich. He was buried in the Waldfriedhof in Section 455-W in Grave 24-A/B.

[7] Forczyk, *Kursk 1943: The Southern Front*, p. 7.

[8] Lawrence, *Kursk: The Battle of Prokhorovka*, Sheridan, pp. 31–32; and Field Marshal Erich von Manstein, *Lost Victories*, edited and translated by Anthony G. Powell, Novato, California, Presidio Press, 1984, pp. 423–428.

[9] Charles W. Sydnor, *Soldiers of Destruction: The SS Death's Head Division, 1933–1945*, Princeton, New Jersey: Princeton University Press, 1977, pp. 268–280.

[10] Sydnor, *Soldiers of Destruction*, p. 278.

[11] Interior lines is a condition in warfare where lines of movement and communication, and routes of resupply for a defender of a salient, are shorter than those of the attacker on the outside. For example, with interior lines a defender can shift forces quicker from one location to another than the attacker can, because the attacking forces must drive around a longer perimeter of the salient.

[12] Not that the Führer needed any adrenalin; several sources, including physicians that are expert in the field, believe that his physician, Dr. Theodore Morrell, gave Hitler almost daily injections of a mix of cocaine and opioids. Born on July 22, 1886, in Münzenberg in Hesse, Morrell died at Tegernsee, Bavaria, on May 26, 1948.

[13] George H. Stein, *The Waffen-SS: Hitler's Elite Guard at War*, Ithaca, New York: Cornell University Press, 1966, p. 206.

[14] Lawrence, *Kursk: The Battle of Prokhorovka*, pp. 47 and 50.

[15] Forczyk, *Kursk 1943: The Southern Front*, 7.

[16] Lawrence, *Kursk: The Battle of Prokhorovka*, pp. 47 and 51.

[17] Ibid., pp. 53–54.

[18] Interestingly, the Voronezh Front appears to have deployed its forces in July to counter *Operation K*, rather than the final dispositions of Army Group South before the offensive. This would add fuel to the fire that the Soviets knew many of the details of the upcoming offensive due to agents and spies in various German headquarters.

[19] Forczyk, *Kursk 1943: The Southern Front*, p. 7.

[20] Lawrence, *Kursk: The Battle of Prokhorovka*, pp. 60–62.

[21] Trojca, *Tiger, 1942–1943*, pp. 349–351.

[22] Guderian, *Panzer Leader*, p. 306.

[23] Lawrence, *Kursk: The Battle of Prokhorovka*, p. 65. Thus, the OKH committed a cardinal sin in armored warfare. "Order, re-order, chaos" is a situation in which the original operation's order is changed—which happens quite frequently—but if that second, subsequent order is changed once again chaos will develop, as not all key leaders will be "on the same sheet of music."

[24] Lawrence, *Kursk: The Battle of Prokhorovka*, pp. 66–69; and Guderian, *Panzer Leader*, pp. 306–307. In his recollections after the war Guderian believed that the conference had been on May 3, 1943.

[25] Trojca, *Tiger, 1942–1943*, p. 298.

[26] Guderian, *Panzer Leader*, pp. 306–307.

[27] According to Guderian, the two officers came fairly close to conducting a duel over the affair but clearer heads prevailed. For numerous examples of antagonism between German Army commanders in World War II see *2,000 Quotes From Hitler's 1, 000-Year Reich*.

[28] The 51st Panzer Detachment and the 52nd Panzer Detachment, which between them had the 200 Panthers at the Kursk Offensive, had delivery of the tank delayed. The two detachments arrived only on June 30 and July 1, and had almost no time to conduct reconnaissance, or to learn anything about the terrain and enemy they were expected to fight. Both were attached to the Panzer Grenadier Division *Großdeutschland* in the 48th Panzer Corps, west of the 2nd SS Panzer Corps.

[29] Guderian, *Panzer Leader*, pp. 306–307; and Trojca, *Tiger, 1942–1943*, p. 298.

[30] Lawrence, *Kursk: The Battle of Prokhorovka*, p. 67.

[31] Von Manstein, *Lost Victories*, p. 447.

[32] Werner Baumbach, *The Life and Death of the Luftwaffe*, translated by Frederick Holt, New York: Coward-McCann, Inc., 1960, p. 199. Remark made by Werner Baumbach to Heinrich Himmler.

[33] The German military had many, many excellent tacticians, perhaps equal to or more than any other nation in World War II. Germany also had some outstanding operational level of war thinkers such as Erich von Manstein, Karl Dönitz, Walter Wever (although he died in 1936), and Erwin Rommel. But Germany did not have a single competent strategic thinker in the same category as Josef Stalin, Franklin Roosevelt, Winston Churchill, or George C. Marshall.

[34] Guderian, *Panzer Leader*, pp. 308–309.

[35] Hitler ignored Jeschonnek. Although the Luftwaffe would acquit itself fairly well in *Operation Citadel*, Jeschonnek became morose over the situation and path of the war. On the night of August 17–18, 1943, Allied bombers struck German rocket testing facilities at Peenemünde, on the Baltic coast. Receiving reports that 200 enemy aircraft were approaching Berlin, Jeschonnek ordered Berlin's air defenses to open fire. They did, but the aircraft turned out to belong to the Luftwaffe, responding to the Allied raid. Jeschonnek, at a Luftwaffe headquarters at Goldap, East Prussia, on realizing his error retired to his quarters and shot himself. He is buried at Gołdap, Warmian-Masurian Voivodeship, Poland.

[36] Lawrence, *Kursk: The Battle of Prokhorovka*, pp. 74–75.

[37] Ibid., pp. 162–163.

[38] Theodor Wisch died on January 11, 1995, in Norderstedt, in Schleswig-Holstein. He is buried in Barsbüttel at the Stadtfriedhof.

[39] Andreas Schulz and Dieter Zinke, *Die Generale der Waffen-SS und der Polizei*, Band 6: Ullmann—Zottmann, Bissendorf, Germany: Biblio Verlag, 2012, pp. 398–409; Lawrence, *Kursk: The Battle of Prokhorovka*, pp. 1, 295, 1, 314–1, 315; and Rudolf Lehmann, *Die Leibstandarte*, Band III, Osnabrück, FRG: Munin Verlag, 1982. Lehmann wrote that there were eleven Tigers present on July 2. Lehmann served as the operations officer for SS Panzer Grenadier Division *Leibstandarte Adolf Hitler* during the Kursk offensive. He died one year after his book was published; and Jentz, *Germany's Tiger Tanks, Tiger I and Tiger II: Combat Tactics, Volume 3*, p. 90.

[40] Jentz, *Germany's Tiger Tanks, Tiger I and Tiger II: Combat Tactics, Volume 3*, pp. 24, 28, 72.

[41] Ian Michael Wood, 4 (s) Kompanie, SS-Panzer Regiment 1, February and July 1, 1943, List.

[42] Trojca, *Tiger, 1942–1943*, p. 298.

[43] Andreas Schulz, Günter Wegmann and Dieter Zinke, *Die Generale der Waffen-SS und der Polizei*, Band 2, pp. 610–618; Lawrence, *Kursk: The Battle of Prokhorovka*, 1295, pp. 1, 314–1, 315; and Jentz, *Germany's Tiger Tanks, Tiger I and Tiger II: Combat Tactics, Volume 3*, p. 90.

[44] Jentz, *Germany's Tiger Tanks, Tiger I and Tiger II: Combat Tactics, Volume 3*, pp. 24, 28, 73.

[45] Rüdiger Warnick and Stephan Cazenave, *Tiger!* p. 118.

[46] Lawrence, *Kursk: The Battle of Prokhorovka*, pp. 1, 314–1, 315; and Jentz, *Germany's Tiger Tanks, Tiger I and Tiger II: Combat Tactics, Volume 3*, p. 90.

[47] Jentz, *Germany's Tiger Tanks, Tiger I and Tiger II: Combat Tactics, Volume 3*, pp. 24, 28, 73.

[48] Lawrence, *Kursk: The Battle of Prokhorovka*, pp. 1, 314–1, 315; and Jentz, *Germany's Tiger Tanks, Tiger I and Tiger II: Combat Tactics*, p. 90.

[49] George M. Nipe, *Blood, Steel, and Myth: The II. SS-Panzer-Korps and the road to Prochorowka, July 1943*, Stamford, Connecticut: RZM Imports, 2011, pp. 26, 31.

[50] Lawrence, *Kursk: The Battle of Prokhorovka*, pp. 1, 295, 1, 314–1, 315.

[51] Nipe, *Blood, Steel, and Myth*, pp. 30–34.

[52] Jentz, *Germany's Tiger Tanks, Tiger I and Tiger II: Combat Tactics, Volume 3*, p. 79.

[53] The idea to include a terrain analysis in the book comes from Capt. Benjamin R. Simm's wonderful article "Analysis of the Battle of Kursk" in *Armor Magazine* March–April 2003, http://ciar.org/ttk/mbt/armor/armor-magazine/armor-mag.2003.ma/2kursk03.pdf

Daily Battle Actions
July 5, 1943

[1] The original source document for the day's activities of all three divisions is the *Kriegstagebuch Nr. 6, Generalkommando II. SS-Panzer-Korps, Textband 1.6.1943-2.8.1943*, complied by the corps operations officer Ia, for 5.7.1943, which is found at the National Archives and Records Administration (NARA), Records Group T-354, Roll 605, beginning with Frame 000484. This document is the final determinant for all times used in this study.

² Lawrence, *Kursk: The Battle of Prokhorovka*, p. 389.

³ Schranck, *Thunder at Prokhorovka*, pp. 47, 97.

⁴ Information provided by the *Bundesarchiv–Militärarchiv* in Freiberg (Germany's military archives), June 7, 2018, indicates that at the time of the battle the regiment had the official designation of 1st Panzer Regiment, and only later did this change to 1st SS Panzer Regiment.

⁵ Lehmann, *Die Leibstandarte*, Band III, pp. 229–234.

⁶ Ibid.

⁷ Agte, *Michael Wittmann and the Tiger Commanders of the Leibstandarte*, p. 74.

⁸ Lehmann, *Die Leibstandarte*, Band III, pp. 234–243; and Franz Kurowski, *Panzer Aces: German Tank Commanders of WWII*, translated by David Johnston, Mechanicsburg, Pennsylvania, Stackpole Books, 2004, p. 304.

⁹ Agte, *Michael Wittmann and the Tiger Commanders of the Leibstandarte*, p. 74.

¹⁰ Schranck, *Thunder at Prokhorovka*, pp. 42–81; Wolfgang Schneider, *Tigers in Combat II*, Winnipeg, Canada: J. J. Fedorowicz, 1998, p. 105; Nipe, *Blood, Steel, and Myth*, pp. 65–76; Lawrence, *Kursk: The Battle of Prokhorovka*, p. 394; Lehmann, *Die Leibstandarte*, Band III, p. 241; and Franz Kurowski, *Panzer Aces: German Tank Commanders of WWII*, p. 305.

¹¹ Lawrence, *Kursk: The Battle of Prokhorovka*, p. 423; Franz Kurowski, *Panzer Aces: German Tank Commanders of WWII*, p. 306; and *SS Officer Personnel Files*, Microfilm Publication A3343, Series SSO, National Archives and Records Administration (NARA): College Park, Maryland, Roll 179A (Kling, Heinrich, 10-Sep-1913), write-up for the award of the German Cross in Gold.

¹² Lawrence, *Kursk: The Battle of Prokhorovka*, p. 399.

¹³ Information from the *Bundesarchiv–Militärarchiv* in Freiberg (Germany's official military archives), June 7, 2018, indicates that at the time of the battle the regiment had the official designation of 2nd Panzer Regiment, and only later did this change to 2nd SS Panzer Regiment.

¹⁴ Paul Carrell, *Scorched Earth: Hitler's War on Russia, Volume 2*, London: George G. Harrap & Co., 1970, p. 60.

¹⁵ Lawrence, *Kursk: The Battle of Prokhorovka*, p. 391.

¹⁶ Schranck, *Thunder at Prokhorovka*, 59; Lawrence, *Kursk: The Battle of Prokhorovka*, p. 392; and Trojca, *Tiger, 1942–1943*, p. 327.

¹⁷ Wolfgang Schneider, *Das Reich Tigers*, Winnipeg, Canada: J. J. Fedorowicz, 2006, pp. 84–87; Nipe, *Blood, Steel, and Myth*, pp. 77–80; Otto Weidinger, *Division Das Reich im Bild*, Osnabrück, FRG: Munin-Verlag GMBH, 1981, p. 226; and Schranck, *Thunder at Prokhorovka*, p. 38.

¹⁸ Wolfgang Schneider, *Tigers in Combat II*, p. 143; Schranck, *Thunder at Prokhorovka*, p. 55; and Lawrence, *Kursk: The Battle of Prokhorovka*, pp. 390–394, 399.

¹⁹ Julius Hinrichsen, "Meine Dienstzeit bei der 8./schweren Kompanie des 2. SS-Panzerregiments 'Das Reich,'" Website: *schwere SS-Panzer Abteilung 102 / 502*, http://www.ss-panzer.de/Geschichten/geschichten.html

²⁰ Rüdiger Warnick, Personnel List of Panzer Regiment in the 2nd SS Panzer Division *Das Reich*.

²¹ Lawrence, *Kursk: The Battle of Prokhorovka*, p. 399.

²² Information from the *Bundesarchiv–Militärarchiv* in Freiberg (Germany's official military archives), June 7, 2018, indicates that at the time of the battle the regiment had the official designation of 3rd Panzer Regiment, and only later did this change to 3rd SS Panzer Regiment.

²³ In the Wehrmacht, a *Rollbahn* was the term used to designate a road that would be advantageous for use in an attack, both for the initial attack and also for resupply. Interestingly enough, Col. John N. Abrams, as the commander of the 11th Armored Cavalry Regiment in the US Army in Germany in the late 1980s, also used the term in tactical operations of his unit. Col. Abrams, who later retired as a four star general, was the son of former US Army Chief of Staff Creighton W. Abrams.

[24] Wolfgang Vopersal, *Soldaten, Kämpfer, Kameraden: Marsch und Kämpfe der SS-Totenkopfdivision*, *Band 3*, Osnabrück, FRG: Selbstverlag der Truppenkameradschaft der 3. SS-Panzer-Division e. V., 1987, p. 333.

[25] Wolfgang Schneider, *Totenkopf Tigers*, p. 84; Schranck, *Thunder at Prokhorovka*, pp. 45, 49; and Nipe, *Blood, Steel, and Myth*, pp. 80–85.

[26] Ian Michael Wood, Personnel List of Panzer Regiment in the 3rd SS Panzer Division *Totenkopf.*

[27] Lawrence, *Kursk: The Battle of Prokhorovka*, p. 400.

[28] Ibid., p. 744.

July 6, 1943

[1] *Kriegstagebuch Nr. 6, Generalkommando II. SS-Panzer-Korps, Textband* for 6.7.1943.

[2] Agte, *Michael Wittmann and the Tiger Commanders of the Leibstandarte*, pp. 76–77; Schranck, *Thunder at Prokhorovka*, p. 97; Lehmann, *Die Leibstandarte*, Band III, p. 243; and *SS Officer Personnel Files*, Microfilm Publication A3343, Series SSO, National Archives and Records Administration (NARA): College Park, Maryland, Roll 179A (Kling, Heinrich, 10-Sep-1913), write up for the award of the German Cross in Gold.

[3] One source says that on this date enemy antitank fire zeroed in on the immobile target, destroying the hull machine gun and blowing off a hatch cover which wounded the loader, *SS-Panzerschütze* Walter Koch. Most other accounts say that Koch was wounded on July 5.

[4] Agte, *Michael Wittmann and the Tiger Commanders of the Leibstandarte*, pp. 76–77; Schranck, *Thunder at Prokhorovka*, p. 56; and Lehmann, *Die Leibstandarte*, Band III, p. 243.

[5] Franz Kurowski, *Panzer Aces: German Tank Commanders of WWII*, p. 307; and Kleine and Kühn, *Tiger: The History of a Legendary Weapon 1942–45*, p. 89.

[6] Lawrence, *Kursk: The Battle of Prokhorovka*, pp. 464, 468–473; Schneider, *Tigers in Combat II*, p. 105; Schranck, *Thunder at Prokhorovka*, pp. 103, 113; Franz Kurowski, *Panzer Aces: German Tank Commanders of WWII*, p. 307; and *SS Officer Personnel Files*, Microfilm Publication A3343, Series SSO, National Archives and Records Administration (NARA): College Park, Maryland, Roll 179A (Kling, Heinrich, 10-Sep-1913), write-up for the award of the German Cross in Gold.

[7] Kleine and Kühn, *Tiger: The History of a Legendary Weapon 1942–45*, p. 89.

[8] Lawrence, *Kursk: The Battle of Prokhorovka*, p. 476.

[9] Paul Carrell, *Scorched Earth*, p. 66.

[10] Lawrence, *Kursk: The Battle of Prokhorovka*, pp. 464–466; Schneider, *Das Reich Tigers*, p. 87; and Schneider, *Tigers in Combat II*, p. 143.

[11] Lawrence, *Kursk: The Battle of Prokhorovka*, p. 477.

[12] Lawrence, *Kursk: The Battle of Prokhorovka*, pp. 464, 473–474; and Schranck, *Thunder at Prokhorovka*, 98.

[13] Schneider, *Totenkopf Tigers*, p. 85; and Schneider, *Tigers in Combat II*, p. 205.

[14] Lawrence, *Kursk: The Battle of Prokhorovka*, p. 477.

[15] Ibid., p. 744.

July 7, 1943

[1] *Kriegstagebuch Nr. 6, Generalkommando II. SS-Panzer-Korps, Textband* for 7.7.1943.

[2] Lawrence, *Kursk: The Battle of Prokhorovka*, pp. 527–530; Agte, *Michael Wittmann and the Tiger Commanders of the Leibstandarte*, p. 77; Schneider, *Tigers in Combat II*, p. 105; and Lehmann, *Die Leibstandarte*, Band III, pp. 245–249.

[3] Franz Kurowski, *Panzer Aces: German Tank Commanders of WWII*, p. 308.

[4] Lawrence, *Kursk: The Battle of Prokhorovka*, p. 536.

[5] *SS Officer Personnel Files*, Microfilm Publication A3343, Series SSO, National Archives and Records Administration (NARA): College Park, Maryland, Roll 277A (Lorenz, Karl-Heinz, 03-Jul-1917).

[6] Warnick and Cazenave, *Tiger!*, pp. 154–155; and Lawrence, *Kursk: The Battle of Prokhorovka*, p. 643.

[7] Schneider, *Das Reich Tigers*, pp. 87, 108, 114, and 119.

[8] Ibid.

[9] Lawrence, *Kursk: The Battle of Prokhorovka*, p. 537.

[10] Schneider, *Totenkopf Tigers*, p. 93; Wood, *Tigers of the Death's Head*, p. 48.

[11] "Operational figures for 4 (s) Panzer Kompanie and 9 Panzer Kompanie during 1943" list provided by Ian Michael Wood.

[12] Lawrence, *Kursk: The Battle of Prokhorovka*, p. 477.

[13] Ibid., p. 744.

[14] Schranck, *Thunder at Prokhorovka*, p. 145.

July 8, 1943

[1] *Kriegstagebuch Nr. 6, Generalkommando II. SS-Panzer-Korps, Textband* for 8.7.1943.

[2] Schranck, *Thunder at Prokhorovka*, p. 173.

[3] Agte, *Michael Wittmann and the Tiger Commanders of the Leibstandarte*, p. 77; Lawrence, *Kursk: The Battle of Prokhorovka*, pp. 622–625; Schneider, *Tigers in Combat II*, p. 105; Schranck, *Thunder at Prokhorovka*, pp. 178–179, 190; and Lehmann, *Die Leibstandarte*, Band III, p. 251.

[4] Agte, *Michael Wittmann and the Tiger Commanders of the Leibstandarte*, pp. 77–79; and Schranck, *Thunder at Prokhorovka*, p. 177. Schranck maintains that the Soviets lost seventeen tanks.

[5] Lawrence, *Kursk: The Battle of Prokhorovka*, p. 641.

[6] Schneider, *Das Reich Tigers*, pp. 108–110, 114.

[7] Schneider, *Das Reich Tigers*, pp. 108–110, 114; and Lawrence, *Kursk: The Battle of Prokhorovka*, pp. 628–630.

[8] Lawrence, *Kursk: The Battle of Prokhorovka*, p. 642.

[9] Schranck, *Thunder at Prokhorovka*, p. 174.

[10] Email discussion with Ian Michael Wood, June 18–19, 2019.

[11] Ibid.

[12] Schneider, *Totenkopf Tigers*, pp. 93–94; and Schranck, *Thunder at Prokhorovka*, p. 177.

[13] Lawrence, *Kursk: The Battle of Prokhorovka*, p. 643.

[14] Ibid., p. 744.

July 9, 1943

[1] *Kriegstagebuch Nr. 6, Generalkommando II. SS-Panzer-Korps, Textband* for 9.7.1943.

[2] Agte, *Michael Wittmann and the Tiger Commanders of the Leibstandarte*, p. 97; Schneider, *Tigers in Combat II*, p. 105; Lawrence, *Kursk: The Battle of Prokhorovka*, pp. 724–726; and Lehmann, *Die Leibstandarte*, Band III, p. 253.

[3] Lawrence, *Kursk: The Battle of Prokhorovka*, p. 733.

[4] Schneider, *Das Reich Tigers*, p. 114.

[5] Lawrence, *Kursk: The Battle of Prokhorovka*, p. 734.

[6] Schneider, *Totenkopf Tigers*, pp. 94–95; Schneider, *Tigers in Combat II*, p. 205.

[7] Wood, *Tigers of the Death's Head*, p. 48.

[8] Lawrence, *Kursk: The Battle of Prokhorovka*, p. 734.

[9] Ibid., 744.

July 10, 1943

[1] *Kriegstagebuch Nr. 6, Generalkommando II. SS-Panzer-Korps, Textband* for 10.7.1943.

[2] Lehmann, *Die Leibstandarte*, Band III, p. 254.

[3] Lawrence, *Kursk: The Battle of Prokhorovka*, pp. 740–742; Schneider, *Tigers in Combat II*, p. 105; and Lehmann, *Die Leibstandarte*, Band III, p. 254.

[4] The author was close friends with Martin Steglich, who was sent back to Germany, flown out of the Demyansk pocket in 1942 to brief Hitler on the conditions at the front. He spent several hours with Hitler, including lunch, during which then Lieutenant Steglich recalled that wine was served in his honor, although he could not recall seeing if Hitler consumed any. He also remarked that in the inner sanctum officers saluted with the verbal greeting "*Acht-Acht.*" Lieutenant Steglich asked a senior officer the meaning of the greeting and was told that it was code for H-H, the letters being the eighth (H) letter of the alphabet. Apparently Hitler had no problem with this, as the greeting was said in his presence. The author asked him if he had any anxiety briefing Hitler and he replied that while Hitler did not seem fond of the generals he related well to young soldiers. He asked Lieutenant Steglich what the daily supply was for ammunition, what items of machinery or weapons did not work in the cold, what supplies he needed, and other company level questions. Lieutenant Steglich also recalled that he instinctively felt uneasy about Josef Goebbels and Martin Bormann, who stood off to the side and did not say anything.

[5] Ian Michael Wood, 4 (s) Kompanie, SS-Panzer Regiment 1, February and July 1, 1943 List.

[6] Lawrence, *Kursk: The Battle of Prokhorovka*, p. 747.

[7] Lawrence, *Kursk: The Battle of Prokhorovka*, p. 742; Schneider, *Das Reich Tigers*, p. 114; and Nipe, *Blood, Steel, and Myth*, pp. 260–261; and Schneider, *Tigers in Combat II*, p. 143.

[8] Lawrence, *Kursk: The Battle of Prokhorovka*, p. 748.

[9] Nipe, *Blood, Steel, and Myth*, p. 268; Lawrence, *Kursk: The Battle of Prokhorovka*, pp. 750–754; and Schneider, *Totenkopf Tigers*, pp. 94–95.

[10] Nipe, *Blood, Steel, and Myth*, p. 268; Lawrence, *Kursk: The Battle of Prokhorovka*, pp. 750–754; Schneider, *Totenkopf Tigers*, pp. 94–95; and Schneider, *Tigers in Combat II*, p. 205.

[11] Lawrence, *Kursk: The Battle of Prokhorovka*, p. 746.

[12] Ibid., p. 744.

July 11, 1943

[1] *Kriegstagebuch Nr. 6, Generalkommando II. SS-Panzer-Korps, Textband* for 11.7.1943.

[2] Schneider, *Tigers in Combat II*, p. 105.

[3] *Kriegstagebuch Nr. 6, Generalkommando II. SS-Panzer-Korps, Textband* for 11.7.1943, *Zuzammenstellung der Ist, Verflegungs- und Gefechtsstärken mit Stand von 11.7.43.*

[4] Agte, *Michael Wittmann and the Tiger Commanders of the Leibstandarte*, Winnipeg, p. 97; Schneider, *Tigers in Combat II*, p. 105; Lehmann, *Die Leibstandarte*, Band III, pp. 260–262; and Franz Kurowski, *Panzer Aces: German Tank Commanders of WWII*, p. 311.

[5] Ibid.

[6] *SS Officer Personnel Files*, Microfilm Publication A3343, Series SSO, National Archives and Records Administration (NARA): College Park, Maryland, Roll 179A (Kling, Heinrich, 10-Sep-1913), write-up for the award of the German Cross in Gold.

[7] Lawrence, *Kursk: The Battle of Prokhorovka*, p. 762.

[8] *Kriegstagebuch Nr. 6, Generalkommando II. SS-Panzer-Korps, Textband* for 11.7.1943, *Zuzammenstellung der Ist, Verflegungs- und Gefechtsstärken mit Stand von 11.7.43.*

[9] Schneider, *Das Reich Tigers*, pp. 114 and 119.

[10] Warnick and Cazenave, *Tiger!* p. 158.

[11] Schneider, *Das Reich Tigers*, p. 119.

[12] Lawrence, *Kursk: The Battle of Prokhorovka*, p. 763.

[13] *Kriegstagebuch Nr. 6, Generalkommando II. SS-Panzer-Korps, Textband* for 11.7.1943, *Zuzammenstellung der Ist, Verflegungs- und Gefechtsstärken mit Stand von 11.7.43.*

[14] Schneider, *Totenkopf Tigers*, p. 95.

[15] Lawrence, *Kursk: The Battle of Prokhorovka*, p. 761.

[16] Ibid., p. 922.

[17] Ibid., p. 744.

July 12, 1943

[1] *Kriegstagebuch Nr. 6, Generalkommando II. SS-Panzer-Korps, Textband* for 12.7.1943.

[2] Lawrence, *Kursk: The Battle of Prokhorovka*, pp. 922–923.

[3] Paul Carrell, *Scorched Earth*, p. 82. *Schwerpunkt* is easiest to define as point of main effort; the area in which the fate of the battle is most likely to be determined.

[4] Lawrence, *Kursk: The Battle of Prokhorovka*, pp. 929–940; and Kleine and Kühn, *Tiger: The History of a Legendary Weapon 1942–45*, p. 63.

[5] Trojca, *Tiger, 1942–1943*, p. 300.

[6] Agte, *Michael Wittmann and the Tiger Commanders of the Leibstandarte*, pp. 98–99; and Nipe, *Blood, Steel, and Myth*, pp. 329–332; and Ben Wheatley, "A Visual Examination of the Battle of Prokhorovka, " Journal of Intelligence History, Volume 18, 2019, Issue 2, www.tandfonline.com/doi/full/10.1080/16161262.2019.1606545

[7] Lawrence, *Kursk: The Battle of Prokhorovka*, p. 955.

[8] Nipe, *Blood, Steel, and Myth*, p. 347.

[9] Lawrence, *Kursk: The Battle of Prokhorovka*, p. 956.

[10] Wolfgang Vopersal, *Soldaten, Kämpfer, Kameraden*, p. 382.

[11] Ibid., p. 384.

[12] "Operational figures for 4 (s) Panzer Kompanie and 9 Panzer Kompanie during 1943" list provided by Ian Michael Wood.

[13] Schneider, *Totenkopf Tigers*, p. 96; and Schneider, *Tigers in Combat II*, p. 205.

[14] Lawrence, *Kursk: The Battle of Prokhorovka*, p. 954.

[15] Schranck, *Thunder at Prokhorovka*, p. 516.

[16] Wolfgang Vopersal, *Soldaten, Kämpfer, Kameraden*, p. 391.

July 13, 1943

[1] *Kriegstagebuch Nr. 6, Generalkommando II. SS-Panzer-Korps, Textband* for 13.7.1943.

[2] Agte, *Michael Wittmann and the Tiger Commanders of the Leibstandarte*, p. 99.

[3] Agte, *Michael Wittmann and the Tiger Commanders of the Leibstandarte*, p. 99; Schneider, *Tigers in Combat II*, p. 106; and Lawrence, *Kursk: The Battle of Prokhorovka*, p. 966.

[4] Lawrence, *Kursk: The Battle of Prokhorovka*, p. 976.

[5] Schneider, *Das Reich Tigers*, p. 119; Schneider, *Tigers in Combat II*, p. 143.

[6] Lawrence, *Kursk: The Battle of Prokhorovka*, p. 977.

[7] Schneider, *Totenkopf Tigers*, p. 97; and Schneider, *Tigers in Combat II*, p. 205.

[8] Lawrence, *Kursk: The Battle of Prokhorovka*, p. 975.

July 14, 1943

[1] *Kriegstagebuch Nr. 6, Generalkommando II. SS-Panzer-Korps, Textband* for 14.7.1943.

[2] *Unternehmen Roland* appears to have been named for Roland, the bravest and most loyal of the dozen legendary Knights who served Charlemagne, King of the Franks, from 768, and Emperor of the Romans from 800 to his death in 814. One legend states that Roland stood 8 feet tall and carried a magical sword named Durendal that had belonged a millennium before to Hector of Troy. A powerful warrior, Roland was concerned with winning honor and fame, rather

than gaining power in Charlemagne's court. Roland was killed in battle against Muslim forces in 778, near Roncesvalles, in the Pyrenees Mountains.

[3] Agte, *Michael Wittmann and the Tiger Commanders of the Leibstandarte*, Winnipeg, p. 99; and Schneider, *Tigers in Combat II*, p. 106.

[4] Lawrence, *Kursk: The Battle of Prokhorovka*, p. 1, 087.

[5] *Kriegstagebuch Nr. 6, Generalkommando II. SS-Panzer-Korps, Textband* for 14.7.1943; SS-Panzer-Grenadier-Division "Das Reich" *Tagesmeldung.*

[6] Schneider, *Das Reich Tigers*, p. 128; and Schneider, *Tigers in Combat II*, p. 143.

[7] Lawrence, *Kursk: The Battle of Prokhorovka*, p. 977.

[8] Schneider, *Totenkopf Tigers*, p. 97; and Schneider, *Tigers in Combat II*, p. 205.

[9] Lawrence, *Kursk: The Battle of Prokhorovka*, p. 1, 084.

July 15, 1943

[1] *Kriegstagebuch Nr. 6, Generalkommando II. SS-Panzer-Korps, Textband* for 15.7.1943.

[2] Agte, *Michael Wittmann and the Tiger Commanders of the Leibstandarte*, p. 99.

[3] Lawrence, *Kursk: The Battle of Prokhorovka*, p. 1, 088.

[4] Schneider, *Das Reich Tigers*, p. 128; and Schneider, *Tigers in Combat II*, p. 143.

[5] Lawrence, *Kursk: The Battle of Prokhorovka*, p. 1, 093.

[6] Schneider, *Totenkopf Tigers*, p. 97.

[7] Lawrence, *Kursk: The Battle of Prokhorovka*, p. 1085.

[8] Trojca, *Tiger, 1942–1943*, p. 301.

Battle Rosters

[1] Rüdiger Warnick and Stephan Cazenave, *Tiger!* p. 119.

Crew Member Biographies
13th (Heavy) Company

[1] *SS Enlisted Personnel Files*, Microfilm Publication A3343, Series SSEM, National Archives and Records Administration (NARA): College Park, Maryland, Roll A026.

[2] Ibid., Roll A027.

[3] Ibid., Roll A071.

[4] Ibid.

[5] Franz Kurowski, *Panzer Aces: German Tank Commanders of WWII*, p. 304.

[6] Volksbund Deutsche Kriegsgräberfürsorge e.V. website; Gräbersuche online: Arthur Bernhardt.

[7] *SS Enlisted Personnel Files*, Microfilm Publication A3343, Series SSEM, National Archives and Records Administration (NARA): College Park, Maryland, Roll B007; Bodo Langer; and Gregory A. Walden, *Tigers in the Ardennes: The 501st Heavy SS Tank Battalion in the Battle of the Bulge*, Atglen, Pennsylvania: Schiffer Publishing, 2014, p. 111.

[8] *SS Enlisted Personnel Files*, Microfilm Publication A3343, Series SSEM, National Archives and Records Administration (NARA): College Park, Maryland, Roll B042; and Trojca, *Tiger, 1942–1943*, p. 297.

[9] *SS Enlisted Personnel Files*, Microfilm Publication A3343, Series SSEM, National Archives and Records Administration (NARA): College Park, Maryland, Roll B042.

[10] Walden, *Tigers in the Ardennes*, p. 114; Schneider, *Tigers in Combat II*, p. 108; and Volksbund Deutsche Kriegsgräberfürsorge e.V. website; Gräbersuche online: Jürgen Brandt.

[11] *SS Officer Personnel Files*, Microfilm Publication A3343, Series SSO, National Archives and Records Administration (NARA): College Park, Maryland, Roll 107 (Buchner, Heinz, 3-May-1924.)

¹² Ibid.

¹³ Multiple discussions with John Moore, a pre-eminent researcher of the Waffen-SS for several decades.

¹⁴ Rüdiger Warnick, Personnel List of Panzer Regiment in the 2nd SS Panzer Division *Das Reich*.

¹⁵ Agte, *Michael Wittmann and the Tiger Commanders of the Leibstandarte*, p. 432.

¹⁶ Volksbund Deutsche Kriegsgräberfürsorge e.V. website; Gräbersuche online: Franz Enderl.

¹⁷ *SS Enlisted Personnel Files*, Microfilm Publication A3343, Series SSEM, National Archives and Records Administration (NARA): College Park, Maryland, Roll A231; and Agte, *Michael Wittmann and the Tiger Commanders of the Leibstandarte*, p. 187.

¹⁸ Volksbund Deutsche Kriegsgräberfürsorge e.V. website; Gräbersuche online: Max Gaube; and Agte, *Michael Wittmann and the Tiger Commanders of the Leibstandarte*, p. 216.

¹⁹ Volksbund Deutsche Kriegsgräberfürsorge e.V. website; Gräbersuche online: Georg Gentsch; *SS Enlisted Personnel Files*, Microfilm Publication A3343, Series SSEM, National Archives and Records Administration (NARA): College Park, Maryland, Roll E016.

²⁰ Bodo Langer; and Agte, *Michael Wittmann and the Tiger Commanders of the Leibstandarte*, pp. 156, 292.

²¹ *SS Enlisted Personnel Files*, Microfilm Publication A3343, Series SSEM, National Archives and Records Administration (NARA): College Park, Maryland, Roll E056.

²² *Rasse-und-Siedlungs-Hauptamt (RuSHA) Files*, Microfilm Publication A3343, Series RS, National Archives and Records Administration (NARA): College Park, Maryland, Roll B5358.

²³ *SS Officer Personnel Files*, Microfilm Publication A3343, Series SSO, National Archives and Records Administration (NARA): College Park, Maryland, Roll 179A (Gruber, Helmut, 25-Apr-1925; *SS Lists*, Microfilm Publication A3343, Series SS, National Archives and Records Administration (NARA): College Park, Maryland, Roll A016, List #5429; and Agte, *Michael Wittmann and the Tiger Commanders of the Leibstandarte*, p. 104.

²⁴ Volksbund Deutsche Kriegsgräberfürsorge e.V. website; Gräbersuche online: Helmut Gruber.

²⁵ *Rasse-und-Siedlungs-Hauptamt (RuSHA) Files*, Microfilm Publication A3343, Series RS, National Archives and Records Administration (NARA): College Park, Maryland, Roll C50; Volksbund Deutsche Kriegsgräberfürsorge e.V. website; Gräbersuche online: Fritz Hartel.

²⁶ *SS Enlisted Personnel Files*, Microfilm Publication A3343, Series SSEM, National Archives and Records Administration (NARA): College Park, Maryland, Roll G033.

²⁷ *SS Enlisted Personnel Files*, Microfilm Publication A3343, Series SSEM, National Archives and Records Administration (NARA): College Park, Maryland, Roll G040; and discussions with John Moore, a pre-eminent researcher of the Waffen-SS for several decades.

²⁸ *Rasse-und-Siedlungs-Hauptamt (RuSHA) Files*, Microfilm Publication A3343, Series RS, National Archives and Records Administration (NARA): College Park, Maryland, Roll C417; and Agte, *Michael Wittmann and the Tiger Commanders of the Leibstandarte*, p. 268.

²⁹ Ibid.

³⁰ Volksbund Deutsche Kriegsgräberfürsorge e.V. website; Gräbersuche online: Johann Höld; Schneider, *Tigers in Combat II*, p. 108.

³¹ *Rasse-und-Siedlungs-Hauptamt (RuSHA) Files*, Microfilm Publication A3343, Series RS, National Archives and Records Administration (NARA): College Park, Maryland, Roll C425; and Agte, *Michael Wittmann and the Tiger Commanders of the Leibstandarte*, p. 132.

³² *SS Enlisted Personnel Files*, Microfilm Publication A3343, Series SSEM, National Archives and Records Administration (NARA): College Park, Maryland, Roll H060; Volksbund Deutsche Kriegsgräberfürsorge e.V. website; Gräbersuche online: Martin-Gerhard Iwanitz.

³³ Multiple discussions with John Moore.

³⁴ Bodo Langer.

[35] Volksbund Deutsche Kriegsgräberfürsorge e.V. website; Gräbersuche online: Kurt Kleber; Schneider, *Tigers in Combat II*, p. 111; and Agte, *Michael Wittmann and the Tiger Commanders of the Leibstandarte*, pp. 315, 316.

[36] *SS Officer Personnel Files*, Microfilm Publication A3343, Series SSO, National Archives and Records Administration (NARA): College Park, Maryland, Roll 179A (Kling, Heinrich, 10-Sep-1913).

[37] Ibid.

[38] Ibid.

[39] Ibid.

[40] Ibid.

[41] *SS Officer Personnel Files*, Microfilm Publication A3343, Series SSO, National Archives and Records Administration (NARA): College Park, Maryland, Roll 179A (Kling, Heinrich, 10-Sep-1913); Schneider, *Tigers in Combat II*, pp. 112, 266.

[42] *SS Enlisted Personnel Files*, Microfilm Publication A3343, Series SSEM, National Archives and Records Administration (NARA): College Park, Maryland, Roll 187A.

[43] Multiple discussions with John Moore.

[44] *SS Enlisted Personnel Files*, Microfilm Publication A3343, Series SSEM, National Archives and Records Administration (NARA): College Park, Maryland, Roll J044; multiple discussions with John Moore.

[45] *SS Enlisted Personnel Files*, Microfilm Publication A3343, Series SSEM, National Archives and Records Administration (NARA): College Park, Maryland, Roll K073.

[46] Bodo Langer; and Agte, *Michael Wittmann and the Tiger Commanders of the Leibstandarte*, pp. 187, 432, 433.

[47] Bodo Langer.

[48] Multiple discussions with John Moore.

[49] *Rasse-und-Siedlungs-Hauptamt (RuSHA) Files*, Microfilm Publication A3343, Series RS, National Archives and Records Administration (NARA): College Park, Maryland, Roll D5142.

[50] Agte, *Michael Wittmann and the Tiger Commanders of the Leibstandarte*, p. 451.

[51] Walden, *Tigers in the Ardennes*, p. 117.

[52] *Rasse-und-Siedlungs-Hauptamt (RuSHA) Files*, Microfilm Publication A3343, Series RS, National Archives and Records Administration (NARA): College Park, Maryland, Roll D5142.

[53] Bodo Langer; and Trojca, *Tiger, 1942–1943*, p. 318.

[54] Agte, *Michael Wittmann and the Tiger Commanders of the Leibstandarte*, pp. 187, 291.

[55] Multiple discussions with John Moore.

[56] Volksbund Deutsche Kriegsgräberfürsorge e.V. website; Gräbersuche online: Heinz Owczarek.

[57] Volksbund Deutsche Kriegsgräberfürsorge e.V. website; Gräbersuche online: Heinrich Reimers; *SS Enlisted Personnel Files*, Microfilm Publication A3343, Series SSEM, National Archives and Records Administration (NARA): College Park, Maryland, Roll O081; and Agte, *Michael Wittmann and the Tiger Commanders of the Leibstandarte*, p. 291.

[58] *SS Enlisted Personnel Files*, Microfilm Publication A3343, Series SSEM, National Archives and Records Administration (NARA): College Park, Maryland, Roll P035.

[59] Multiple discussions with John Moore.

[60] *SS Officer Personnel Files*, Microfilm Publication A3343, Series SSO, National Archives and Records Administration (NARA): College Park, Maryland, Roll 069B (Schamp, Rolf, 22-Sep-1921.); Series of Letters from Rolf Schamp to a Herr Richter dated 1 September 1999 and 25 July 2000; Agte, *Michael Wittmann and the Tiger Commanders of the Leibstandarte*, p. 565.

[61] *SS Enlisted Personnel Files*, Microfilm Publication A3343, Series SSEM, National Archives and Records Administration (NARA): College Park, Maryland, Roll Q029.

[62] Multiple discussions with John Moore.

[63] Ibid.

[64] *SS Officer Personnel Files*, Microfilm Publication A3343, Series SSO, National Archives and Records Administration (NARA): College Park, Maryland, Roll 108B (Schütz, Waldemar, 9-Oct-1913); and Trojca, *Tiger, 1942–1943*, p. 311.

[65] *SS OfficerPersonnel Files*, Microfilm Publication A3343, Series SSO, National Archives and Records Administration (NARA): College Park, Maryland, Roll 108B (Schütz, Waldemar, 9-Oct-1913.)

[66] *SS Officer Personnel Files*, Microfilm Publication A3343, Series SSO, National Archives and Records Administration (NARA): College Park, Maryland, Roll 108B (Schütz, Waldemar, 9-Oct-1913); and Gregory T. Jones, *Panzerheld: The Story of Hauptsturmführer Michael Wittmann, The Greatest Tank Commander of World War Two*, Self-Published, 1993, p. 41.

[67] *SS Officer Personnel Files*, Microfilm Publication A3343, Series SSO, National Archives and Records Administration (NARA): College Park, Maryland, Roll 141B (Söffker, Roland, 13-Nov-1923); Report from American Consul, Hamburg to Secretary of State, Washington, Subject: Possible 212 (A) (33) Ineligibility, (SOEFFKER, ROLAND WOLFGANG KARL HEINZ), 17 November 1987, at https://www.cia.gov/library/readingroom/docs/HITLER%2C%20ADOLF%20%20%28DI%29%20%20%20VOL.%201_0096.pdf

[68] *SS Officer Personnel Files*, Microfilm Publication A3343, Series SSO, National Archives and Records Administration (NARA): College Park, Maryland, Roll 141B (Söffker, Roland, 13-Nov-1923).

[69] *Rasse-und-Siedlungs-Hauptamt (RuSHA) Files*, Microfilm Publication A3343, Series RS, National Archives and Records Administration (NARA): College Park, Maryland, Roll F5388; and Walden, *Tigers in the Ardennes*, p. 117.

[70] Schneider, *Tigers in Combat II*, p. 262.

[71] *SS Enlisted Personnel Files*, Microfilm Publication A3343, Series SSEM, National Archives and Records Administration (NARA): College Park, Maryland, Roll S022; multiple discussions with John Moore.

[72] Multiple discussions with John Moore.

[73] *SS Enlisted Personnel Files*, Microfilm Publication A3343, Series SSEM, National Archives and Records Administration (NARA): College Park, Maryland, Roll T048.

[74] *SS Enlisted Personnel Files*, Microfilm Publication A3343, Series SSEM, National Archives and Records Administration (NARA): College Park, Maryland, Roll T050.

[75] *SS Enlisted Personnel Files*, Microfilm Publication A3343, Series SSEM, National Archives and Records Administration (NARA): College Park, Maryland, Roll T050; Schneider, *Tigers in Combat II*, p. 258; and Agte, *Michael Wittmann and the Tiger Commanders of the Leibstandarte*, pp. 189, 316, 339.

[76] BoxRec Website, Boxing's Official Record Keeper, Robert Warmbrunn, http://boxrec.com/en/boxer/28302

[77] *SS Officer Personnel Files*, Microfilm Publication A3343, Series SSO, National Archives and Records Administration (NARA): College Park, Maryland, Roll 236B (Wendorff, Helmut Max, 20-Oct-1920.)

[78] Ibid.

[79] *SS Officer Personnel Files*, Microfilm Publication A3343, Series SSO, National Archives and Records Administration (NARA): College Park, Maryland, Roll 236B (Wendorff, Helmut Max, 20-Oct-1920.); Schneider, *Tigers in Combat II*, pp. 104, 109, 110; and Volksbund Deutsche Kriegsgräberfürsorge e.V. website; Gräbersuche online: Helmut Wendorff.

[80] Gregory A. Walden, *Tigers in the Ardennes*, p. 114.

[81] *SS Enlisted Personnel Files*, Microfilm Publication A3343, Series SSEM, National Archives and Records Administration (NARA): College Park, Maryland, Roll, T075; Volksbund Deutsche Kriegsgräberfürsorge e.V. website; Gräbersuche online: Reinhart Wenzel.

[82] *SS Enlisted Personnel Files*, Microfilm Publication A3343, Series SSEM, National Archives and Records Administration (NARA): College Park, Maryland, Roll U021; and Warnick and Cazenave, *Tiger!* pp. 309, 427.

[83] Other contenders for the crown of the most skilled German tank commander include Kurt Knispel, Otto Carius, Walter Kniep, Karl Korner, Hans Sandrock, Ernst Barkmann, Franz Bäke, Paul Egger, and perhaps Will Fey.

[84] On March 19, 1945, Westernhagen was relieved of command of the 501st SS Heavy Panzer Detachment in Hungary; his replacement was Heinz Kling. Later in the day the command reported that the staff car in which von Westernhagen was riding on the way to headquarters had been destroyed by a Russian air attack and that he was dead. In actuality he had committed suicide by gunshot.

[85] Joe Ekins died on February 1, 2012, in Kettering, Northamptonshire.

[86] Jones, *Panzerheld*; *SS Officer Personnel Files*, Microfilm Publication A3343, Series SSO, National Archives and Records Administration (NARA): College Park, Maryland, Roll 003C (Wittmann, Michael, 22-Apr-1914); and Schneider, *Tigers in Combat II*, pp. 109, 112.

[87] Agte, *Michael Wittmann and the Tiger Commanders of the Leibstandarte*, p. 134.

[88] Multiple discussions with Oberst a.D. Wolfgang Schneider, March–June 2019.

[89] Agte, *Michael Wittmann and the Tiger Commanders of the Leibstandarte*, p. 291.

[90] Ibid., p. 291.

[91] Gerd Nietrug, *Die Ritterkreuzträger des Saarlandes 1939–1945*, Zweibrücken, Germany: VDM Heinz Nickel, 2004.

[92] *SS Enlisted Personnel Files*, Microfilm Publication A3343, Series SSEM, National Archives and Records Administration (NARA): College Park, Maryland, Roll U030; Interview with Bobby Wohl dated 1991, https://web.archive.org/web/20110812002455/http://panzer4520.yuku.com/forum/viewtopic/id/1300#.UxMYZPR5PNA.

8th (Heavy) Company

[1] *SS Officer Personnel Files*, Microfilm Publication A3343, Series SSO, National Archives and Records Administration (NARA): College Park, Maryland, Roll 008 (Allwinn, Egon, 19-Feb-1922); and Warnick and Cazenave, *Tiger!* p. 208.

[2] *SS Officer Personnel Files*, Microfilm Publication A3343, Series SSO, National Archives and Records Administration (NARA): College Park, Maryland, Roll 008 (Allwinn, Egon, 19-Feb-1922).

[3] *Rasse-und-Siedlungs-Hauptamt (RuSHA) Files*, Microfilm Publication A3343, Series RS, National Archives and Records Administration (NARA): College Park, Maryland, Roll A57.

[4] Warnick and Cazenave, *Tiger!*, pp. 71, 169; Volksbund Deutsche Kriegsgräberfürsorge e.V. website; Gräbersuche online: Eduard Arzner.

[5] *Rasse-und-Siedlungs-Hauptamt (RuSHA) Files*, Microfilm Publication A3343, Series RS, National Archives and Records Administration (NARA): College Park, Maryland, Roll A128; and Warnick and Cazenave, *Tiger!* pp. 17, 77, 309, 427.

[6] *Rasse-und-Siedlungs-Hauptamt (RuSHA) Files*, Microfilm Publication A3343, Series RS, National Archives and Records Administration (NARA): College Park, Maryland, Roll A129.

[7] *SS Officer Personnel Files*, Microfilm Publication A3343, Series SSO, National Archives and Records Administration (NARA): College Park, Maryland, Roll 031, (Baral, Kurt, 19-Feb-1922.)

[8] Ibid.

[9] Wolfgang Schneider, *Das Reich Tigers*, p. 328; and Warnick and Cazenave, *Tiger!* p. 419.

[10] *Rasse-und-Siedlungs-Hauptamt (RuSHA) Files*, Microfilm Publication A3343, Series RS, National Archives and Records Administration (NARA): College Park, Maryland, Roll A500; and Warnick and Cazenave, *Tiger!* pp. 300, 427, 445, 473, 491.

[11] Ibid.

[12] Warnick and Cazenave, *Tiger!* p. 201; and Rüdiger Warnick, Personnel List of Panzer Regiment in the 2nd SS Panzer Division *Das Reich*.

[13] Ibid.

[14] Warnick and Cazenave, *Tiger!*, p. 17; and *Rasse-und-Siedlungs-Hauptamt (RuSHA) Files*, Microfilm Publication A3343, Series RS, National Archives and Records Administration (NARA): College Park, Maryland, Roll A512.

[15] Rüdiger Warnick, Personnel List of Panzer Regiment in the 2nd SS Panzer Division *Das Reich*.

[16] *SS Enlisted Personnel Files*, Microfilm Publication A3343, Series SSEM, National Archives and Records Administration (NARA): College Park, Maryland, Roll B025; and Warnick and Cazenave, *Tiger!* pp. 72, 196, 309, 406, 491.

[17] *Rasse-und-Siedlungs-Hauptamt (RuSHA) Files*, Microfilm Publication A3343, Series RS, National Archives and Records Administration (NARA): College Park, Maryland, Roll A5290; and Rüdiger Warnick, Personnel List of Panzer Regiment in the 2nd SS Panzer Division *Das Reich*.

[18] *Rasse-und-Siedlungs-Hauptamt (RuSHA) Files*, Microfilm Publication A3343, Series RS, National Archives and Records Administration (NARA): College Park, Maryland, Roll A5332.

[19] *Rasse-und-Siedlungs-Hauptamt (RuSHA) Files*, Microfilm Publication A3343, Series RS, National Archives and Records Administration (NARA): College Park, Maryland, Roll A5332; Warnick and Cazenave, *Tiger!* pp. 177, 196; and Rüdiger Warnick, Personnel List of Panzer Regiment in the 2nd SS Panzer Division *Das Reich*.

[20] Warnick and Cazenave, *Tiger!* p. 320.

[21] *Rasse-und-Siedlungs-Hauptamt (RuSHA) Files*, Microfilm Publication A3343, Series RS, National Archives and Records Administration (NARA): College Park, Maryland, Roll B355; and Warnick and Cazenave, *Tiger!* pp. 406, 427, 471, 491.

[22] *Rasse-und-Siedlungs-Hauptamt (RuSHA) Files*, Microfilm Publication A3343, Series RS, National Archives and Records Administration (NARA): College Park, Maryland, Roll B466; and Warnick and Cazenave, *Tiger!* pp. 309, 422, 427, 485, 491.

[23] Rüdiger Warnick, Personnel List of Panzer Regiment in the 2nd SS Panzer Division *Das Reich*.

[24] *SS Enlisted Personnel Files*, Microfilm Publication A3343, Series SSEM, National Archives and Records Administration (NARA): College Park, Maryland, Roll D078. Another George Wilhelm Gallinat, born the exact same date, died on February 3, 1942, near Timonzevo/Rshev, and should not be confused with the correct soldier in this study.

[25] *Rasse-und-Siedlungs-Hauptamt (RuSHA) Files*, Microfilm Publication A3343, Series RS, National Archives and Records Administration (NARA): College Park, Maryland, Roll B5171; Warnick and Cazenave, *Tiger!* p. 397; and Wolfgang Schneider, *Das Reich Tigers*, p. 328.

[26] Warnick and Cazenave, *Tiger!* p. 77.

[27] *SS Enlisted Personnel Files*, Microfilm Publication A3343, Series SSEM, National Archives and Records Administration (NARA): College Park, Maryland, Roll E036; Warnick and Cazenave, *Tiger!* p. 320; and Rüdiger Warnick, Personnel List of Panzer Regiment in the 2nd SS Panzer Division *Das Reich*.

[28] *SS Enlisted Personnel Files*, Microfilm Publication A3343, Series SSEM, National Archives and Records Administration (NARA): College Park, Maryland, Roll E039.

[29] *SS Enlisted Personnel Files*, Microfilm Publication A3343, Series SSEM, National Archives and Records Administration (NARA): College Park, Maryland, Roll F011; and Warnick and Cazenave, *Tiger!*, pp. 71, 196.

[30] Ibid.

[31] Volksbund Deutsche Kriegsgräberfürsorge e.V. website; Gräbersuche online: Alfred Grupe.

[32] *SS Enlisted Personnel Files*, Microfilm Publication A3343, Series SSEM, National Archives and Records Administration (NARA): College Park, Maryland, Roll F011.

[33] *SS Enlisted Personnel Files*, Microfilm Publication A3343, Series SSEM, National Archives and Records Administration (NARA): College Park, Maryland, Roll F030; Volksbund Deutsche Kriegsgräberfürsorge e.V. website; Gräbersuche online: Benno Hackbarth; and Email from Rüdiger Warnick on June 30, 2019.

[34] *SS Enlisted Personnel Files*, Microfilm Publication A3343, Series SSEM, National Archives and Records Administration (NARA): College Park, Maryland, Roll F070; and Warnick and Cazenave, *Tiger!* pp. 23, 196, 492.

[35] Ancestry.com, Hans Xaver Haselböck.

[36] Email from Rüdiger Warnick, June 30, 2019.

[37] *SS Lists*, Microfilm Publication A3343, Series SS, National Archives and Records Administration (NARA): College Park, Maryland, Roll A0002, List # 0680; Warnick and Cazenave, *Tiger!* pp. 302, 427; Rüdiger Warnick, Personnel List of Panzer Regiment in the 2nd SS Panzer Division *Das Reich*; and Wolfgang Schneider, *Das Reich Tigers*, p. 332.

[38] Julius Hinrichsen, "Meine Dienstzeit bei der 8./schweren Kompanie des 2. SS-Panzerregimentes "Das Reich,"" Website: *schwere SS-Panzer Abteilung 102 / 502*, http://www.ss-panzer.de/Geschichten/geschichten.html

[39] Rüdiger Warnick, Personnel List of Panzer Regiment in the 2nd SS Panzer Division *Das Reich*.

[40] *SS Enlisted Personnel Files*, Microfilm Publication A3343, Series SSEM, National Archives and Records Administration (NARA): College Park, Maryland, Roll G071.

[41] Warnick and Cazenave, *Tiger!* p. 165.

[42] *SS Enlisted Personnel Files*, Microfilm Publication A3343, Series SSEM, National Archives and Records Administration (NARA): College Park, Maryland, Roll G078; and Warnick and Cazenave, *Tiger!* pp. 17 and 72.

[43] *SS Officer Personnel Files*, Microfilm Publication A3343, Series SSO, National Archives and Records Administration (NARA): College Park, Maryland, Roll 109A, (Hoffmann, Richard, 29-Jul-02.)

[44] *SS Enlisted Personnel Files*, Microfilm Publication A3343, Series SSEM, National Archives and Records Administration (NARA): College Park, Maryland, Roll H010; Warnick and Cazenave, *Tiger!* p. 196; Volksbund Deutsche Kriegsgräberfürsorge e.V. website; Gräbersuche online: Bruno Hofmann; and Rüdiger Warnick, Personnel List of Panzer Regiment in the 2nd SS Panzer Division *Das Reich*.

[45] *SS Enlisted Personnel Files*, Microfilm Publication A3343, Series SSEM, National Archives and Records Administration (NARA): College Park, Maryland, Roll H027; Warnick and Cazenave, *Tiger!* pp. 309, 316, 494; Rüdiger Warnick, Personnel List of Panzer Regiment in the 2nd SS Panzer Division *Das Reich*; and Volksbund Deutsche Kriegsgräberfürsorge e.V. website; Gräbersuche online: Eric Holzer.

[46] *SS Enlisted Personnel Files*, Microfilm Publication A3343, Series SSEM, National Archives and Records Administration (NARA): College Park, Maryland, Roll H051; and Rüdiger Warnick, Personnel List of Panzer Regiment in the 2nd SS Panzer Division *Das Reich*.

[47] *SS Enlisted Personnel Files*, Microfilm Publication A3343, Series SSEM, National Archives and Records Administration (NARA): College Park, Maryland, Roll H061; and Warnick and Cazenave, *Tiger!* pp. 300, 422.

[48] *SS Enlisted Personnel Files*, Microfilm Publication A3343, Series SSEM, National Archives and Records Administration (NARA): College Park, Maryland, Roll I004; Rüdiger Warnick, Personnel List of Panzer Regiment in the 2nd SS Panzer Division *Das Reich*; and Warnick and Cazenave, *Tiger!* pp. 303 397.

[49] Post-war letter from Gerhard Kaempf to Rüdiger Warnick. Kaempf and Rüdiger's grandfather, served in the Third Platoon together at Kursk; letter shown to author on June 30, 2019.

[50] Ibid.

[51] Warnick and Cazenave, *Tiger!* pp. 17, 71, 160, 491; and Wolfgang Schneider, *Das Reich Tigers*, pp. 328, 332, 427.

[52] Warnick and Cazenave, *Tiger!* pp. 74, 201, 309, 337, 427; *SS Officer Personnel Files*, Microfilm Publication A3343, Series SSO, National Archives and Records Administration (NARA): College Park, Maryland, Roll 149A (Kalss, Alois, 18-Feb-1920); Veit Scherzer, *Himmlers militärische Elite, Die höchst dekorierten Angehörigen der* Waffen-SS, *Band 1 Adam–Kauth*, Bayreuth, Verlag Veit Scherzer, 2004, p. 530; Wolfgang Schneider, *Das Reich Tigers*, p. 307.

[53] Lawrence, *Kursk: The Battle of Prokhorovka*, pp. 119, 392, 934.

[54] Email conversation with Oberst a. D. Wolfgang Schneider, September 12, 2018; *SS Enlisted Personnel Files*, Microfilm Publication A3343, Series SSEM, National Archives and Records Administration (NARA): College Park, Maryland, Roll I057.

[55] Warnick and Cazenave, *Tiger!* p. 165.

[56] Schneider, *Das Reich Tigers*, pp. 328, 332.

[57] *Rasse-und-Siedlungs-Hauptamt (RuSHA) Files*, Microfilm Publication A3343, Series RS, National Archives and Records Administration (NARA): College Park, Maryland, Roll D152; and Warnick and Cazenave, *Tiger!* pp. 309, 427.

[58] Ancestry.com, August Koppelkamp.

[59] *SS Enlisted Personnel Files*, Microfilm Publication A3343, Series SSEM, National Archives and Records Administration (NARA): College Park, Maryland, Roll K005.

[60] *SS Enlisted Personnel Files*, Microfilm Publication A3343, Series SSEM, National Archives and Records Administration (NARA): College Park, Maryland, Roll K005; Warnick and Cazenave, *Tiger!* pp. 427, 491; and Rüdiger Warnick, Personnel List of Panzer Regiment in the 2nd SS Panzer Division *Das Reich*.

[61] *Rasse-und-Siedlungs-Hauptamt (RuSHA) Files*, Microfilm Publication A3343, Series RS, National Archives and Records Administration (NARA): College Park, Maryland, Roll D290; and Warnick and Cazenave, *Tiger!* p. 427.

[62] *SS Enlisted Personnel Files*, Microfilm Publication A3343, Series SSEM, National Archives and Records Administration (NARA): College Park, Maryland, Roll K080; and Warnick and Cazenave, *Tiger!* pp. 309, 427.

[63] Volksbund Deutsche Kriegsgräberfürsorge e.V. website; Gräbersuche online: Ferdinand Lasser.

[64] *SS Enlisted Personnel Files*, Microfilm Publication A3343, Series SSEM, National Archives and Records Administration (NARA): College Park, Maryland, Roll L002; Rüdiger Warnick, Personnel List of Panzer Regiment in the 2nd SS Panzer Division *Das Reich*; Warnick and Cazenave, *Tiger!* pp. 309, 422; and Ancestry.com, Albert Laumbacher.

[65] *SS Officer Personnel Files*, Microfilm Publication A3343, Series SSO, National Archives and Records Administration (NARA): College Park, Maryland, Roll 277A (Lorenz, Karl-Heinz, 03-Jul-1917.)

[66] Email from Rüdiger Warnick, June 30, 2019.

[67] Rüdiger Warnick, Personnel List of Panzer Regiment in the 2nd SS Panzer Division *Das Reich*.

[68] Ibid.

[69] *SS Officer Personnel Files*, Microfilm Publication A3343, Series SSO, National Archives and Records Administration (NARA): College Park, Maryland, Roll 308A (Menninger, Waldemar, 03-Apr-1925); and *Rasse-und-Siedlungs-Hauptamt (RuSHA) Files*, Microfilm Publication A3343, Series RS, National Archives and Records Administration (NARA): College Park, Maryland, Roll D466.

[70] Rüdiger Warnick, Personnel List of Panzer Regiment in the 2nd SS Panzer Division *Das Reich*.

[71] Warnick and Cazenave, *Tiger!* p. 175.

[72] *SS Enlisted Personnel Files*, Microfilm Publication A3343, Series SSEM, National Archives and Records Administration (NARA): College Park, Maryland, Roll L089; Warnick and Cazenave, *Tiger!* pp. 309, 427, 491; and Rüdiger Warnick, Personnel List of Panzer Regiment in the 2nd SS Panzer Division *Das Reich*.

[73] *SS Enlisted Personnel Files*, Microfilm Publication A3343, Series SSEM, National Archives and Records Administration (NARA): College Park, Maryland, Roll M058; and Warnick and Cazenave, *Tiger!* p. 182.

[74] "Anton Mühldorfer: Obituary," *Mittelbayerische Zeitung Regensburg*, 21. November 2018; *SS Enlisted Personnel Files*, Microfilm Publication A3343, Series SSEM, National Archives and Records Administration (NARA): College Park, Maryland, Roll M058; and Warnick and Cazenave, *Tiger!* pp. 71, 300, 309, 375, 377, 422, 427.

[75] Rüdiger Warnick, Personnel List of Panzer Regiment in the 2nd SS Panzer Division *Das Reich*, courtesy of John Moore; Schneider, *Das Reich Tigers*, pp. 266–269; and Warnick and Cazenave, *Tiger!* pp. 429, 436, 437.

[76] Warnick and Cazenave, *Tiger!* p. 196; Rüdiger Warnick, Personnel List of Panzer Regiment in the 2nd SS Panzer Division *Das Reich*.

[77] *SS Enlisted Personnel Files*, Microfilm Publication A3343, Series SSEM, National Archives and Records Administration (NARA): College Park, Maryland, Roll O022.

[78] *SS Officer Personnel Files*, Microfilm Publication A3343, Series SSO, National Archives and Records Administration (NARA): College Park, Maryland, Roll 006B, (Ramm, Heinz, 6-Mar-22) and Rüdiger Warnick, Personnel List of Panzer Regiment in the 2nd SS Panzer Division *Das Reich*.

[79] *SS Officer Personnel Files*, Microfilm Publication A3343, Series SSO, National Archives and Records Administration (NARA): College Park, Maryland, Roll 009B (Ratter, Albert, 05-Jun-1909.)

[80] *Rasse-und-Siedlungs-Hauptamt (RuSHA) Files*, Microfilm Publication A3343, Series RS, National Archives and Records Administration (NARA): College Park, Maryland, Roll E5317.

[81] Ibid.

[82] Rüdiger Warnick, Personnel List of Panzer Regiment in the 2nd SS Panzer Division *Das Reich*.

[83] *Rasse-und-Siedlungs-Hauptamt (RuSHA) Files*, Microfilm Publication A3343, Series RS, National Archives and Records Administration (NARA): College Park, Maryland, Roll F5352; Volksbund Deutsche Kriegsgräberfürsorge e.V. website; Gräbersuche online: Johann Reinhardt; and Warnick and Cazenave, *Tiger!* pp. 170, 181.

[84] *SS Officer Personnel Files*, Microfilm Publication A3343, Series SSO, National Archives and Records Administration (NARA): College Park, Maryland, Roll 021B (Reininghaus, Walter, 16-Feb-1904.)

[85] Ibid.

[86] Warnick and Cazenave, *Tiger!* p. 187.

[87] Warnick and Cazenave, *Tiger!* p. 15; *SS Officer Personnel Files*, Microfilm Publication A3343, Series SSO, National Archives and Records Administration (NARA): College Park, Maryland, Roll 021B (Reininghaus, Walter, 16-Feb-1904.)

88 Warnick and Cazenave, *Tiger!* p. 77; and Rüdiger Warnick, Personnel List of Panzer Regiment in the 2nd SS Panzer Division *Das Reich.*

89 Warnick and Cazenave, *Tiger!* pp. 17, 422.

90 Rüdiger Warnick, Personnel List of Panzer Regiment in the 2nd SS Panzer Division *Das Reich.*

91 Ibid.

92 *Rasse-und-Siedlungs-Hauptamt (RuSHA) Files*, Microfilm Publication A3343, Series RS, National Archives and Records Administration (NARA): College Park, Maryland, Roll F194; and Warnick and Cazenave, *Tiger!* p. 17.

93 Ibid.

94 Volksbund Deutsche Kriegsgräberfürsorge e.V. website; Gräbersuche online: Werner Schäfer.

95 *Rasse-und-Siedlungs-Hauptamt (RuSHA) Files*, Microfilm Publication A3343, Series RS, National Archives and Records Administration (NARA): College Park, Maryland, Roll F400; and Warnick and Cazenave, *Tiger!* pp. 309, 427; Rüdiger Warnick, Personnel List of Panzer Regiment in the 2nd SS Panzer Division *Das Reich.*

96 *SS Officer Personnel Files*, Microfilm Publication A3343, Series SSO, National Archives and Records Administration (NARA): College Park, Maryland, Roll 085B, (Schmidt, Georg, 13-Apr-25); and Rüdiger Warnick, Personnel List of Panzer Regiment in the 2nd SS Panzer Division *Das Reich.*

97 Warnick and Cazenave, *Tiger!* p. 309; Schneider, *Das Reich Tigers*, pp. 296, 332; and Rüdiger Warnick, Personnel List of Panzer Regiment in the 2nd SS Panzer Division *Das Reich.*

98 Warnick and Cazenave, *Tiger!* pp. 309, 427.

99 Warnick and Cazenave, *Tiger!* p. 158; and Volksbund Deutsche Kriegsgräberfürsorge e.V. website; Gräbersuche online: Heinz Schöneberg.

100 *SS Officer Personnel Files*, Microfilm Publication A3343, Series SSO, National Archives and Records Administration (NARA): College Park, Maryland, Roll 125B (Schweigert, Konrad, 24-Mar-1920); and Warnick and Cazenave, *Tiger!* p. 22.

101 Warnick and Cazenave, *Tiger!* p. 22.

102 *SS Officer Personnel Files*, Microfilm Publication A3343, Series SSO, National Archives and Records Administration (NARA): College Park, Maryland, Roll 130B, (Seidel, Heinz, 7-Jan-24); and Warnick and Cazenave, *Tiger!* p. 208.

103 Ancestry.com, Heinz Seidel.

104 Warnick and Cazenave, *Tiger!* pp. 256, 300, 422, 427; and *SS Enlisted Personnel Files*, Microfilm Publication A3343, Series SSEM, National Archives and Records Administration (NARA): College Park, Maryland, Roll R 071.

105 Ancestry.com, Karl Skerbinz.

106 *Rasse-und-Siedlungs-Hauptamt (RuSHA) Files*, Microfilm Publication A3343, Series RS, National Archives and Records Administration (NARA): College Park, Maryland, Roll F5348; and "Im Gespräch: Günter Skribelka, " *Deutsche Militärzeitschrift (DMZ)*, September–Oktober 2018, Nr. 35, Berchtesgaden, Germany.

107 Warnick and Cazenave, *Tiger!* pp. 17, 71, 377, 427.

108 Warnick and Cazenave, *Tiger!* p. 427; and Rüdiger Warnick, Personnel List of Panzer Regiment in the 2nd SS Panzer Division *Das Reich.*

109 *SS Officer Personnel Files*, Microfilm Publication A3343, Series SSO, National Archives and Records Administration (NARA): College Park, Maryland, Roll 175B, (Tensfeld, Heinz, 11-May-1919).

110 Warnick and Cazenave, *Tiger!* p. 175.

111 *SS Officer Personnel Files*, Microfilm Publication A3343, Series SSO, National Archives and Records Administration (NARA): College Park, Maryland, Roll 175B, (Tensfeld, Heinz, 11-

May-1919); and Horst Scheibert, *Die Trager der Ehrenblattspange des Heeres und der* Waffen-SS, Friedberg, Germany: Podzun-Pallas-Verlag, 1986, p. 126.

[112] Warnick and Cazenave, *Tiger!* p. 79.

[113] Ibid., pp. 14–15.

[114] Ibid., p. 79.

[115] Rüdiger Warnick, Personnel List of Panzer Regiment in the 2nd SS Panzer Division *Das Reich*.

[116] Warnick and Cazenave, *Tiger!* pp. 309, 427; and *SS Enlisted Personnel Files*, Microfilm Publication A3343, Series SSEM, National Archives and Records Administration (NARA): College Park, Maryland, Roll S062.

[117] Warnick and Cazenave, *Tiger!* Ibid., pp. 309, 389.

[118] *SS Enlisted Personnel Files*, Microfilm Publication A3343, Series SSEM, National Archives and Records Administration (NARA): College Park, Maryland, Roll T016; Volksbund Deutsche Kriegsgräberfürsorge e.V. website; Gräbersuche online: Artur Ulmer; and Rüdiger Warnick, Personnel List of Panzer Regiment in the 2nd SS Panzer Division *Das Reich*.

[119] *Rasse-und-Siedlungs-Hauptamt (RuSHA) Files*, Microfilm Publication A3343, Series RS, National Archives and Records Administration (NARA): College Park, Maryland, Roll G374.

[120] *SS Enlisted Personnel Files*, Microfilm Publication A3343, Series SSEM, National Archives and Records Administration (NARA): College Park, Maryland, Roll T046; and email from Rüdiger Warnick June 25, 2019.

[121] Warnick and Cazenave, *Tiger!* pp. 77, 309, 427, 492.

[122] Email from Rüdiger Warnick, June 30, 2019.

[123] Volksbund Deutsche Kriegsgräberfürsorge e.V. website; Gräbersuche online: Heinz Wilken.

[124] *Rasse-und-Siedlungs-Hauptamt (RuSHA) Files*, Microfilm Publication A3343, Series RS, National Archives and Records Administration (NARA): College Park, Maryland, Roll G5384; and Warnick and Cazenave, *Tiger!* pp. 77, 309, 427, 474.

[125] *SS Enlisted Personnel Files*, Microfilm Publication A3343, Series SSEM, National Archives and Records Administration (NARA): College Park, Maryland, Roll U044; and Warnick and Cazenave, *Tiger!* pp. 156, 196.

[126] *Rasse-und-Siedlungs-Hauptamt (RuSHA) Files*, Microfilm Publication A3343, Series RS, National Archives and Records Administration (NARA): College Park, Maryland, Roll G5491; and Warnick and Cazenave, *Tiger!* pp. 309, 427.

[127] Ancestry.com, Joachim Zimbehl.

[128] *SS Officer Personnel Files*, Microfilm Publication A3343, Series SSO, National Archives and Records Administration (NARA): College Park, Maryland, Roll 023C, (Zimmermann, Herbert, 19-Feb-1922).

[129] *SS Officer Personnel Files*, Microfilm Publication A3343, Series SSO, National Archives and Records Administration (NARA): College Park, Maryland, Roll 023C, (Zimmermann, Herbert, 19-Feb-1922); Mark Yerger, *German Cross in Gold, Holders of the SS and Police Volume 2*, "*Das Reich*" *Karl-Heinz Lorenz to Herbert Zimmermann*, San Jose, California: R. James Bender Publishing, 2005, pp. 336–337.

[130] Warnick and Cazenave, *Tiger!* p. 152.

9th (Heavy) Company

[1] Schneider, *Totenkopf Tigers*, p. 121; and Volksbund Deutsche Kriegsgräberfürsorge e.V. website; Gräbersuche online: Hans-Ludwig Bachmann.

[2] Warnick and Cazenave, *Tiger!* p. 334.

[3] Rüdiger Warnick, Personnel List of Panzer Regiment in the 2nd SS Panzer Division *Das Reich*.

⁴ Trojca, *Tiger, 1942–1943*, p. 385.

⁵ *SS Officer Personnel Files*, Microfilm Publication A3343, Series SSO, National Archives and Records Administration (NARA): College Park, Maryland, Roll 066 (Biber, Willy, 8-Jun-1915); Warnick and Cazenave, *Tiger!* pp. 415, 427, 436; multiple discussions with John Moore, a preeminent researcher of the Waffen-SS for several decades; and Schneider, *Das Reich Tigers*, p. 267.

⁶ *SS Officer Personnel Files*, Microfilm Publication A3343, Series SSO, National Archives and Records Administration (NARA): College Park, Maryland, Roll 069 (Biermeier, Fritz, 19-May-1913.)

⁷ *SS Officer Personnel Files*, Microfilm Publication A3343, Series SSO, National Archives and Records Administration (NARA): College Park, Maryland, Roll 069 (Biermeier, Fritz, 19-May-1913); and Scherzer, *Himmlers militärische Elite*, p. 115.

⁸ Ibid.

⁹ Ibid.

¹⁰ Volksbund Deutsche Kriegsgräberfürsorge e.V. website; Gräbersuche online: Fritz Biermeier.

¹¹ Schneider, *Totenkopf Tigers*, p. 246.

¹² *SS Enlisted Personnel Files*, Microfilm Publication A3343, Series SSEM, National Archives and Records Administration (NARA): College Park, Maryland, Roll B022; and Volksbund Deutsche Kriegsgräberfürsorge e.V. website; Gräbersuche online: Franz Böhm.

¹³ *SS Enlisted Personnel Files*, Microfilm Publication A3343, Series SSEM, National Archives and Records Administration (NARA): College Park, Maryland, Roll D007; Schneider, *Totenkopf Tigers*, p. 110; and Volksbund Deutsche Kriegsgräberfürsorge e.V. website; Gräbersuche online: Edmund Fein.

¹⁴ Ian Michael Wood, Personnel List of Panzer Regiment in the 3rd SS Panzer Division *Totenkopf.*

¹⁵ Ibid.

¹⁶ Schneider, *Totenkopf Tigers*, p. 121.

¹⁷ *SS Enlisted Personnel Files*, Microfilm Publication A3343, Series SSEM, National Archives and Records Administration (NARA): College Park, Maryland, Roll G077.

¹⁸ Ibid., Roll G078.

¹⁹ Ibid.

²⁰ *SS Officer Personnel Files*, Microfilm Publication A3343, Series SSO, National Archives and Records Administration (NARA): College Park, Maryland, Roll 101A (Hock, Fritz, 18-Jul-24).

²¹ Schneider, *Totenkopf Tigers*, p. 110; and Volksbund Deutsche Kriegsgräberfürsorge e.V. website; Gräbersuche online: Franz Hofer.

²² *SS Enlisted Personnel Files*, Microfilm Publication A3343, Series SSEM, National Archives and Records Administration (NARA): College Park, Maryland, Roll SSEM I058; Ancestry.com: Hans Georg van Kerkom; and Ian Michael Wood, Personnel List of Panzer Regiment in the 3rd SS Panzer Division *Totenkopf.*

²³ *Rasse-und-Siedlungs-Hauptamt (RuSHA) Files*, Microfilm Publication A3343, Series RS, National Archives and Records Administration (NARA): College Park, Maryland, Roll D040; and Volksbund Deutsche Kriegsgräberfürsorge e.V. website; Gräbersuche online: Norbert Kochesser.

²⁴ Ian Michael Wood, 9. Kompanie Zug Führeren List.

²⁵ A personnel file at NARA could not be found on him.

²⁶ *SS Enlisted Personnel Files*, Microfilm Publication A3343, Series SSEM, National Archives and Records Administration (NARA): College Park, Maryland, Roll K006.

²⁷ *SS Enlisted Personnel Files*, Microfilm Publication A3343, Series SSEM, National Archives and Records Administration (NARA): College Park, Maryland, Roll K030; and Schneider, *Totenkopf Tigers*, p. 200.

[28] *SS Enlisted Personnel Files*, Microfilm Publication A3343, Series SSEM, National Archives and Records Administration (NARA): College Park, Maryland, Roll K059; and Ian Michael Wood, Personnel List of Panzer Regiment in the 3rd SS Panzer Division *Totenkopf*.

[29] *SS Enlisted Personnel Files*, Microfilm Publication A3343, Series SSEM, National Archives and Records Administration (NARA): College Park, Maryland, Roll K063; and Ian Michael Wood, Personnel List of Panzer Regiment in the 3rd SS Panzer Division *Totenkopf*.

[30] *Rasse-und-Siedlungs-Hauptamt (RuSHA) Files*, Microfilm Publication A3343, Series RS, National Archives and Records Administration (NARA): College Park, Maryland, Roll D0488; and Volksbund Deutsche Kriegsgräberfürsorge e.V. website; Gräbersuche online: Hans Jakob Lampert.

[31] A personnel file at NARA could not be found on him.

[32] Volksbund Deutsche Kriegsgräberfürsorge e.V. website; Gräbersuche online: Friedrich Johann Lau.

[33] A personnel file at NARA could not be found on him.

[34] Ibid.

[35] Ibid.

[36] Volksbund Deutsche Kriegsgräberfürsorge e.V. website; Gräbersuche online: Hermann Mocnik.

[37] *Rasse-und-Siedlungs-Hauptamt (RuSHA) Files*, Microfilm Publication A3343, Series RS, National Archives and Records Administration (NARA): College Park, Maryland, Roll E079.

[38] Volksbund Deutsche Kriegsgräberfürsorge e.V. website; Gräbersuche online: Ludwig Müller.

[39] Volksbund Deutsche Kriegsgräberfürsorge e.V. website; Gräbersuche online: Richard Müller.

[40] *SS Enlisted Personnel Files*, Microfilm Publication A3343, Series SSEM, National Archives and Records Administration (NARA): College Park, Maryland, Roll N004.

[41] *SS Enlisted Personnel Files*, Microfilm Publication A3343, Series SSEM, National Archives and Records Administration (NARA): College Park, Maryland, Roll N044; and Schneider, *Totenkopf Tigers*, p. 200.

[42] A personnel file at NARA could not be found on him.

[43] *SS Enlisted Personnel Files*, Microfilm Publication A3343, Series SSEM, National Archives and Records Administration (NARA): College Park, Maryland, Roll O044; and Ian Michael Wood, Personnel List of Panzer Regiment in the 3rd SS Panzer Division *Totenkopf*.

[44] Ian Michael Wood, Personnel List of Panzer Regiment in the 3rd SS Panzer Division *Totenkopf*.

[45] *SS Officer Personnel Files*, Microfilm Publication A3343, Series SSO, National Archives and Records Administration (NARA): College Park, Maryland, Roll 398A (Quade, Heinz, 31-May-21). Schneider, *Totenkopf Tigers*, p. 121; and Ian Michael Wood, 9. Kompanie Zug Führeren List.

[46] *SS Officer Personnel Files*, Microfilm Publication A3343, Series SSO, National Archives and Records Administration (NARA): College Park, Maryland, Roll 069 (Rathsack, Willi, 2-Jan-20).

[47] *SS Officer Personnel Files*, Microfilm Publication A3343, Series SSO, National Archives and Records Administration (NARA): College Park, Maryland, Roll 069 (Rathsack, Willi, 2-Jan-20); and Ian Michael Wood, 9. Kompanie Zug Führeren List.

[48] *SS Officer Personnel Files*, Microfilm Publication A3343, Series SSO, National Archives and Records Administration (NARA): College Park, Maryland, Roll 069 (Rathsack, Willi, 2-Jan-20); and Warnick and Cazenave, *Tiger!* pp. 302, 310, 381.

[49] "9 Kompanie Zug Führeren, " provided by Ian Michael Wood; Warnick and Cazenave, *Tiger!* p. 330; and Volksbund Deutsche Kriegsgräberfürsorge e.V. website; Gräbersuche online: Willi Rathsack.

[50] A personnel file at NARA could not be found on him.

[51] *SS Officer Personnel Files*, Microfilm Publication A3343, Series SSO, National Archives and Records Administration (NARA): College Park, Maryland, Roll 028B (Richter, Wilfried, 9-May-

15); and Franz Thomas und Günter Wegmann, *Die Ritterkreuzträger der Deutschen* Wehrmacht *1939–1945, Teil I: Sturmartillerie*, Osnabruck, FRG: Biblio Verlag, 1985, pp. 230–231.

[52] Thomas und Wegmann, *Die Ritterkreuzträger der Deutschen* Wehrmacht *1939–1945, Teil I: Sturmartillerie*, pp. 230–231; Schneider, *Totenkopf Tigers*, p. 103; and Klaus Schneider, *Spuren der "Nibelungen 1945,"* Potsdam, Germany, Kurt Vowinckel Verlag, p. 120.

[53] A personnel file at NARA could not be found on him.

[54] *Rasse-und-Siedlungs-Hauptamt (RuSHA) Files*, Microfilm Publication A3343, Series RS, National Archives and Records Administration (NARA): College Park, Maryland, Roll F145; and Ian Michael Wood, 9. Kompanie Zug Führeren List.

[55] Ibid.

[56] *SS Enlisted Personnel Files*, Microfilm Publication A3343, Series SSEM, National Archives and Records Administration (NARA): College Park, Maryland, Roll P082.

[57] A personnel file at NARA could not be found on him.

[58] Ian Michael Wood, 9. Kompanie Zug Führeren List.

[59] *SS Officer Personnel Files*, Microfilm Publication A3343, Series SSO, National Archives and Records Administration (NARA): College Park, Maryland, Roll 103B (Schroeder, Wilhelm, 23-Apr-98); and Mark C. Yerger, *Allgemeine-SS: The Commands, Units, and Leaders of the Allgemeine-SS*, Atglen, Pennsylvania, Schiffer Publishing, 1997, pp. 83, 146, 178–179 and 182.

[60] Ian Michael Wood, *Tigers of the Death's Head*, p. 47.

[61] Ian Michael Wood, 9. Kompanie Zug Führeren List.

[62] *SS Officer Personnel Files*, Microfilm Publication A3343, Series SSO, National Archives and Records Administration (NARA): College Park, Maryland, Roll 105B (Schüffler, Heinz Karl, 10-Apr-21); and Ian Michael Wood, 9. Kompanie Zug Führeren List.

[63] *SS Officer Personnel Files*, Microfilm Publication A3343, Series SSO, National Archives and Records Administration (NARA): College Park, Maryland, Roll 105B (Schüffler, Heinz Karl, 10-Apr-21); and Volksbund Deutsche Kriegsgräberfürsorge e.V. website; Gräbersuche online: Heinz Karl Schüffler.

[64] Ian Michael Wood, *Tigers of the Death's Head*, p. 153.

[65] *SS Enlisted Personnel Files*, Microfilm Publication A3343, Series SSEM, National Archives and Records Administration (NARA): College Park, Maryland, Roll R037; and Volksbund Deutsche Kriegsgräberfürsorge e.V. website; Gräbersuche online: Werner Schweitzer.

[66] Ian Michael Wood, Personnel List of Panzer Regiment in the 3rd SS Panzer Division *Totenkopf*; and Ancestry.com: Friedrich Wilhelm Selonke.

[67] *SS Enlisted Personnel Files*, Microfilm Publication A3343, Series SSEM, National Archives and Records Administration (NARA): College Park, Maryland, Roll S055; and Ian Michael Wood, Personnel List of Panzer Regiment in the 3rd SS Panzer Division *Totenkopf*.

[68] A personnel file at NARA could not be found on him.

[69] *SS Enlisted Personnel Files*, Microfilm Publication A3343, Series SSEM, National Archives and Records Administration (NARA): College Park, Maryland, Roll T059; and Ian Michael Wood, Personnel List of Panzer Regiment in the 3rd SS Panzer Division *Totenkopf*.

[70] *SS Enlisted Personnel Files*, Microfilm Publication A3343, Series SSEM, National Archives and Records Administration (NARA): College Park, Maryland, Roll T077.

[71] Schneider, *Totenkopf Tigers*, p. 246.

[72] *SS Enlisted Personnel Files*, Microfilm Publication A3343, Series SSEM, National Archives and Records Administration (NARA): College Park, Maryland, Roll U055.

[73] *SS Enlisted Personnel Files*, Microfilm Publication A3343, Series SSEM, National Archives and Records Administration (NARA): College Park, Maryland, Roll U058. However, information on him could not be located on the roll.

Analysis

[1] Not only Waffen-SS combat vehicle commanders were at risk. In a discussion with the author in 1991, Bruno Kahl discussed his own experience during the Kursk offensive. In command of the 216th *Sturmpanzer* Detachment, consisting of forty-five "Grizzly Bear" 150 mm assault guns—part of the 656th Panzer Jäger Regiment in the northern pincer of the attack—Bruno was in the commander's hatch of one of his assault guns. A neighboring gun received a hit from a Soviet antitank gun and a piece of steel flew off the target, striking Kahl in the mouth. Major Kahl spit his many damaged teeth out into a handkerchief and later took them to an aid station to see if they could be put back in. Dentists could not save the teeth, but Bruno received a nice set of dentures as a consolation prize. Three weeks later Bruno Kahl's superiors submitted him for the award of the Oak Leaves to the Knight's Cross he had already received earlier in the year. He received the Oak Leaves on August 8, 1943.

[2] Stein, *The Waffen SS: Hitler's Elite Guard at War*, p. 12.

[3] Ibid., 13.

[4] Ibid., p. 14.

[5] Email conversation between Oberst a. D. Wolfgang Schneider and the author, January 24, 2018.

[6] Schneider, *Totenkopf Tigers*, p. 177.

[7] Ibid.

[8] LTC John R. Angolia, *For Führer and Fatherland: Military Awards of the Third Reich*, San Jose, California: Roger James Bender, 1976, pp. 337–338.

[9] Discussion of the author with Lieutenant General Heinz-Georg Lemm, *Bundeswehr* Retired, recipient of the Knight's Cross of the Iron Cross with Oak Leaves and Swords; and with Colonel Martin Steglich, *Bundeswehr* Retired, recipient of the Knight's Cross of the Iron Cross with Oak Leaves, at the annual *Ritterkreuzträger* gathering in 1990.

[10] Angolia, *For Führer and Fatherland*, p. 343.

[11] Ibid., pp. 350–357.

[12] Ibid., pp. 358–363.

[13] Ibid., pp. 364–365.

[14] Ibid., pp. 328–330.

[15] Angolia, *For Führer and Fatherland*, p. 259; and Michael F. Tucker, *German Combat Badges of the Third Reich, Volume 1 Heer & Kriegsmarine*, Richmond, Virginia: Winidore Press, p. 222.

[16] Ibid.

[17] Ibid.

[18] Angolia, *For Führer and Fatherland*, pp. 85–87; and Tucker, *German Combat Badges of the Third Reich, Volume 1*, pp. 53–61.

[19] *SS Enlisted Personnel Files*, Microfilm Publication A3343, Series SSEM, National Archives and Records Administration (NARA): College Park, Maryland, Roll R037.

[20] Email conversation with Oberst a. D. Wolfgang Schneider July 9, 2019.

[21] Angolia, *For Führer and Fatherland*, pp. 85–87; and Tucker, *German Combat Badges of the Third Reich, Volume 1*, pp. 53–61.

[22] Angolia, *For Führer and Fatherland*, pp. 109–113.

[23] Angolia, *For Führer and Fatherland*, pp. 81–83; and Tucker, *German Combat Badges of the Third Reich, Volume 1*, pp. 8–12.

[24] Angolia, *For Führer and Fatherland*, pp. 92–96; and Tucker, *German Combat Badges of the Third Reich, Volume 1*, pp. 96–100.

[25] Schneider, *Totenkopf Tigers*, p. 2.

[26] Carruthers, *Tiger I: Official Wartime Crew Manual (The Tigerfibel)*, p. 5.

[27] Ian Michael Wood, *Tigers of the Death's Head*, p. 4; and Schneider, *Totenkopf Tigers*, p. 2.

[28] Nipe, *Blood, Steel, and Myth*, p. 28.

[29] S./SS-Panzer Regiment "Das Reich," "Erfassung der SS-Führerbewerber," 1.7.1943.

[30] Warnick and Cazenave, *Tiger!* p. 248.

[31] Waldemar Trojca, *Tiger, 1942–1945, Technical and Operational History, Volume 3*, Katowice, Poland: Model Hobby Publishing, 2017, p. 141.

[32] Schneider, *Tigers in Combat II*, p. 262.

[33] Thomas Jentz, *Panzertruppen: The Complete Guide to the Creation & Combat Employment of Germany's Tank Force 1943–1945, Volume 2*, Atglen, Pennsylvania: Schiffer Military History, 1996, p. 247.

[34] Ibid.

Conclusions

[1] John M. Priest, "Pickett's Charge, " Essential Civil War Curriculum, https://www.essentialcivilwarcurriculum.com/picketts-charge.html

[2] Ibid.

[3] Ibid.

[4] Lawrence, *Kursk: The Battle of Prokhorovka*, p. 1, 232.

[5] Jentz and Doyle, *Germany's Tiger Tanks: D. W. to Tiger I: Design, Production & Modifications*, p. 53.

[6] Email conversation between Oberst a.D. Wolfgang Schneider and the author, January 24, 2019.

[7] Ibid., May 23, 2019.

[8] Numerous discussions by the author with Martin Steglich from July 1989 to February 1993 in Germany.

[9] Stein, *The Waffen SS: Hitler's Elite Guard at War*, p. 13.

[10] S./SS-Panzer Regiment "Das Reich," "Erfassung der SS-Führerbewerber," 1.7.1943.

[11] Personnel files for the Tiger crewmen revealed the height for fifty of them. The tallest man was Franz Staudegger at 190 cm (6' 2.8"); the shortest were Werner Hoberg, Paul Jadzewski, and Karl Heinz Grothum who were 168 cm (5'6.1"). The average height of the Tiger crewmen was 5'8.2" tall. The median height was 5'9.4". By way of comparison, a *PBS* source states that when the United States entered World War II young American men averaged 5'9" tall—almost 2 inches taller, on average, than the young Germans, primarily in the German Army, that they were fighting. Additionally, during the war the US Army Quartermaster Corps kept logs concerning the sizes of clothes that were issued; they found that the average male inductee was 5'8" tall and weighed 144 pounds; an inch taller and eight pounds heavier than his father and uncles had been in the Great War. The World War II GI had a 33.25" chest measurement and 31" waist measurement, but could expect to add an inch to his chest and gain anywhere from five to twenty pounds during training because he was exercising more and eating "three squares" a day. It should be remembered that armored units are not looking for the tallest soldiers, as tanks are relatively cramped and men too large can be at a severe disadvantage when in combat.

[12] Perhaps the most interesting situation was in the 13th *Waffen* Mountain Division of the SS *Handschar*, a Croatian anti-partisan division that had a large contingent of Balkan Muslims. As such it had several Catholic chaplains and Muslim Imams!

[13] Lieutenant Colonel Rüdiger Overmans, *Deutsche militärische Verluste im Zweiten Weltkrieg*, Oldenbourg 2000, p. 266.

[14] French L. MacLean, *The Camp Men: The SS Officers Who Ran the Nazi Concentration Camp System*, Atglen, Pennsylvania: Schiffer Publishing, 1999.

[15] *Records of US Army War Crimes Trials in Europe: United States of America v. Valentin Bersin, et al., War Crimes Case 6–24, May 16–18, 1946*, Washington, DC: National Archives, 2003.

[16] "War Crimes: Clemency, " *Time Magazine*, January 17, 1949.

[17] Danny S. Parker, *Hitler's Warrior: The Life and Wars of SS Colonel Jochen Peiper*, Cambridge, Massachusetts; Da Capo Press, 2014, pp. 356–357.

Bibliography

Primary source documents

Kriegstagebuch Nr. 6, Generalkommando II. SS-Panzer-Korps, Textband 1.6.1943–2.8.1943, National Archives and Records Administration (NARA), Records Group T-354, Roll 605.

Military Intelligence Division, Tactical and Technical Trends Number 34, Washington, DC: War Department, 23 September 1943.

Rasse-und-Siedlungs-Hauptamt (RuSHA) Files, Microfilm Publication A3343, Series RS, National Archives and Records Administration (NARA): College Park, Maryland.

SS Enlisted Personnel Files, Microfilm Publication A3343, Series SSEM, National Archives and Records Administration (NARA): College Park, Maryland.

SS Officer Personnel Files, Microfilm Publication A3343, Series SSO, National Archives and Records Administration (NARA): College Park, Maryland.

Secondary source books

Agte, Patrick. *Michael Wittmann and the Tiger Commanders of the Leibstandarte*, Winnipeg, Canada: J.J. Fedorowicz, 1996.

Angolia, LTC John R. *For Führer and Fatherland: Military Awards of the Third Reich*, San Jose, California: Roger James Bender, 1976.

Baumbach, Werner. *The Life and Death of the Luftwaffe*, translated by Frederick Holt, New York: Coward-McCann, Inc., 1960.

Bradley, Dermot and others. *Die Generale des Heeres, 1921–1945, Band 6: Hochbaum—Klutmann*, Bissendorf, Germany: Biblio Verlag, 2002.

Carrell, Paul. *Scorched Earth: Hitler's War on Russia*, Volume 2, London: George G. Harrap & Co., 1970.

Carruthers, Bob, translator and editor. *Tiger I: Official Wartime Crew Manual (The Tigerfibel)*, Henley in Arden, England: Coda Books, 2011.

Fellgiebel, Walther-Peer. *Die Träger des Ritterkreuzes des Eisernen Kreuzes 1939–1945*, Friedberg, FRG: Podzun-Pallas Verlag, 1986.

Forczyk, Robert. *Kursk 1943: The Southern Front*, Campaign 305, Oxford, England: Osprey Publishing, 2017.

Guderian, General Heinz. *Panzer Leader*, translated by Constantine Fitzgibbon, Washington, DC: Zenger Publishing, 1979.

Jentz, Thomas L. *Germany's Tiger Tanks, Tiger I and Tiger II: Combat Tactics*, Volume 3, Atglen, Pennsylvania: Schiffer Publishing, 1997.

Jentz, Thomas L. and Hilary L. Doyle. *Germany's Tiger Tanks: D. W. to Tiger I: Design, Production & Modifications*, Atglen, Pennsylvania: Schiffer Military History, 2000.

Jones, Gregory T. *Panzerheld: The Story of Hauptsturmführer Michael Wittmann, The Greatest Tank Commander of World War Two*, Self-Published, 1993.

Kleine, Egon and Volkmar Kühn. *Tiger: The History of a Legendary Weapon 1942–45*, Winnipeg, Canada: J.J. Fedorowicz Publishing, 2004.

Kurowski, Franz. *Panzer Aces: German Tank Commanders of WWII*, translated by David Johnston, Mechanicsburg, Pennsylvania, Stackpole Books, 2004.

Lawrence, Christopher A. *Kursk: The Battle of Prokhorovka*, Sheridan, Colorado: Aberdeen Books, 2015.

Lehmann, Rudolf. *Die Leibstandarte, Band III*, Osnabrück, FRG: Munin Verlag, 1982.

MacLean, French L. *The Camp Men: The SS Officers Who Ran the Nazi Concentration Camp System*, Atglen, Pennsylvania: Schiffer Publishing, 1999.

MacLean, French L. *2,000 Quotes From Hitler's 1,000-Year Reich*, Atglen, Pennsylvania: Schiffer Publishing, 2007.

von Manstein, Field Marshal Erich. *Lost Victories*, edited and translated by Anthony G. Powell, Novato, California, Presidio Press, 1984.

Nietrug, Gerd. *Die Ritterkreuzträger des Saarlandes 1939–1945, Zweibrücken*, Germany: VDM Heinz Nickel, 2004.

Nipe, George M. *Blood, Steel, and Myth: The II. SS-Panzer-Korps and the Road to Prochorowka, July 1943*, Connecticut: RZM Imports, 2011.

Overmans, Lieutenant Colonel Rüdiger. *Deutsche militärische Verluste im Zweiten Weltkrieg*, Oldenbourg 2000.

Parker, Danny S. *Hitler's Warrior: The Life and Wars of SS Colonel Jochen Peiper*, Cambridge, Massachusetts; Da Capo Press, 2014.

Porter, David. *Das Reich at Kursk*, London, England: Amber Books, 2011.

Records of US Army War Crimes Trials in Europe : United States of America v. Valentin Bersin, et al., War Crimes Case 6-24, May 16–18, 1946, Washington, DC: National Archives, 2003.

Scheibert, Horst. *Die Trager der Ehrenblattspange des Heeres und der Waffen-SS*, Friedberg, Germany: Podzun-Pallas-Verlag, 1986.

Scherzer, Veit. *Himmlers militärische Elite, Die höchst dekorierten Angehörigen der Waffen-SS, Band 1 Adam–Kauth*, Bayreuth, Verlag Veit Scherzer, 2004.

Schneider, Klaus. *Spuren der "Nibelungen 1945,"* Potsdam, Germany, Kurt Vowinckel Verlag.

Schneider, Wolfgang. *Das Reich Tigers*, Winnipeg, Canada: J. J. Fedorowicz, 2006.

Schneider, Wolfgang. *Tigers in Combat II*, Winnipeg, Canada: J. J. Fedorowicz, 1998.

Schneider, Wolfgang. *Tiger Im Kampf: Die Einsätze in der Normandie*, Uelzen, Germany: Schneider Armour Research, 2004.

Schneider, Wolfgang. Totenkopf Tigers, Winnipeg, Canada: J. J. Fedorowicz, 2011.

Schranck, David. *Thunder at Prokhorovka: A Combat History of Operation Citadel, Kursk, July 1943*, Solihull, England: Helion & Company, 2013.

Schulz, Andreas, Günter Wegmann and Dieter Zinke. *Die Generale der Waffen-SS und der Polizei, Band 2: Hachtel–Kutschera*, Bissendorf, Germany: Biblio Verlag, 2005.

Schulz, Andreas and Dieter Zinke, *Die Generale der Waffen-SS und der Polizei, Band 6: Ullmann–Zottmann*, Bissendorf, Germany: Biblio Verlag, 2012.

Stein, George H. *The Waffen-SS: Hitler's Elite Guard at War*, Ithaca, New York: Cornell University Press, 1966.

Sydnor, Charles W. *Soldiers of Destruction: The SS Death's Head Division, 1933–1945*, Princeton, New Jersey: Princeton University Press, 1977.

Thomas, Franz und Günter Wegmann. *Die Ritterkreuzträger der Deutschen Wehrmacht 1939–1945, Teil I: Sturmartillerie*, Osnabruck, FRG: Biblio Verlag, 1985.

Trojca, Waldemar. *Tiger, 1942–1943, Technical and Operational History, Volume 1*, Katowice, Poland: Model Hobby Publishing, 2010.

Trojca, Waldemar. *Tiger, 1942–1945, Technical and Operational History, Volume 3*, Katowice, Poland: Model Hobby Publishing, 2017.

Trojca, Waldemar and Gregor Trojca. *Tigers and Königstiger of the LSSAH and s.SS-Pz.Abt. 101/501*, Katowice, Poland: Model Hobby Publishing, 2016.

Tucker, Michael F. *German Combat Badges of the Third Reich, Volume 1 Heer & Kriegsmarine*, Richmond, Virginia: Winidore Press.

Vopersal, Wolfgang. Soldaten, *Kämpfer, Kameraden: Marsch und Kämpfe der SS-Totenkopfdivision, Band 3*, Osnabrück, FRG: Selbstverlag der Truppenkameradschaft der 3. SS-Panzer-Division e. V., 1987.

Walden, Gregory A. *Tigers in the Ardennes: The 501st Heavy SS Tank Battalion in the Battle of the Bulge*, Atglen, Pennsylvania: Schiffer Publishing, 2014.

Warnick, Rüdiger and Stephan Cazenave, *Tiger! Von schwere Kompanie/SS-Pz.Rgt.2 bis s.SS-Panzerabteilung 102/502*, Bayeux, France: Editions Heimdal, 2008.

Wegmann, Günter. *Die Ritterkreuzträger der Panzertruppe, Band 1*: Albert–Eysser, Bissendorf, Germany: Biblio Verlag, 2004.

Weidinger, Otto. *Division Das Reich im Bild*, Osnabrück, FRG: Munin-Verlag GMBH, 1981.

Wilbeck, Christopher W. *Sledgehammers: Strengths and Flaws of Tiger Tank Battalions in World War II*, Bedford, Pennsylvania: The Aberjona Press, 2004.

Wood, Ian Michael. *Tigers of the Death's Head*, Mechanicsburg, Pennsylvania: Stackpole Books, 2013.

Yerger, Mark C. *Allgemeine-SS: The Commands, Units and Leaders of the Allgemeine-SS*, Atglen, Pennsylvania, Schiffer Publishing, 1997.

Magazine and newspaper articles

"Anton Mühldorfer: Obituary, " *Mittelbayerische Zeitung Regensburg*, 21. November 2018.

"Im Gespräch: Günter Skribelka, " *Deutsche Militärzeitschrift* (DMZ), September–Oktober 2018, Nr. 35, Berchtesgaden, Germany.

"War Crimes: Clemency, " *Time Magazine*, January 17, 1949.

Unpublished sources

Series of Letters from Rolf Schamp to a Herr Richter dated 1 September 1999 and 25 July 2000.

Warnick, Rüdiger. Personnel List of Panzer Regiment in the 2nd SS Panzer Division *Das Reich*.

Wood, Ian Michael. 4 (s) Kompanie, SS-Panzer Regiment 1, February and July 1, 1943 List.

Wood, Ian Michael. "Operational figures for 4 (s) Panzer Kompanie and 9 Panzer Kompanie during 1943" List.

Wood, Ian Michael. Personnel List of Panzer Regiment in the 3rd SS Panzer Division *Totenkopf*.

Websites

Ancestry.com, www.ancestry.com

Glatter-Götz, Familie, Oesterreichisches Musiklexicon online, https://www.musiklexikon.ac.at/ml/musik_G/Glatter-Goetz_Familie.xml

Andrew Hills, "Panzerkampfwagen VI Tiger, Sd.Kfz. 181, 'Tiger 1'" Tank Encyclopedia, http://www.tanks-encyclopedia.com/ww2/nazi_germany/Panzer-VI_Tiger.php

Julius Hinrichsen, "Meine Dienstzeit bei der 8./schweren Kompanie des 2. SS-Panzerregiments 'Das Reich,'" Website: schwere SS-Panzer Abteilung 102 / 502, http://www.ss-panzer.de/Geschichten/geschichten.html

Ben Hollingum, "Ferocious Beast—Six Little-Known Facts About the Tiger Tank, " MHN, Military History Now Website, https://militaryhistorynow.com/2015/02/27/ferocious-beast-six-little-known-facts-about-the-tiger-tank/

Interview with Bobby Wohl dated 1991, https://web.archive.org/web/20110812002455/http://panzer4520.yuku.com/forum/viewtopic/id/1300#.UxMYZPR5PNA

John W. Osborn Jr., "Joseph Stalin's Paranoid Purge, " Warfare History Network, November 1, 2018, https://warfarehistorynetwork.com/daily/wwii/joseph-stalins-paranoid-purge/

John M. Priest, "Pickett's Charge, " Essential Civil War Curriculum, https://www.essentialcivilwarcurriculum.com/picketts-charge.html

Rail-road Armor: Soviet Armored Trains in WW2, http://www.wio.ru/rr/ww2sov.htm

Rieger Orgelbau website, http://www.rieger-orgelbau.com/

Volksbund Deutsche Kriegsgräberfürsorge e.V. website; Gräbersuche online, www.volksbund.de/home.html

Index

Historians and contributors
Agte, Patrick, 9
Cazenave, Stephan, 10
Doyle, Hilary L., 9
Forczyk, Robert, 9
Glantz, David, 7, 9
House, Jonathan, 7, 9
Jentz, Thomas L., 9
Kleine, Egon, 9
Kuhn, Volkmar, 9
Langer, Bodo, 10
Lawrence, Christopher, 9, 10
MacLean, David G., 13
Moore, John P., 9
Nietrug, Gerd, 109
Nipe, George, 9, 10
Pallud, Jean Paul, 108
Priest, John M., 166
Reitlinger, Gerald, 153
Romanych, Marc, 9
Schneider, Wolfgang, 9, 10, 26, 153, 154, 171
Schranck, David, 9
Spielberger, Walter J., 9
Sydnor, Charles W., 34
Trojca, Waldemar, 9
Warnick, Rüdiger, 10, 13, 117, 134, 159
Wood, Ian Michael, 10, 145, 147, 225
Yerger, Mark, 239

American Personalities
Boyd, John Richard, 169, 170
Eisenhower, Dwight D, 31
Everett, Willis M. Jr., 177
Lee, Robert E., 165
Marshall, George C., 257
Meade, George, 165
Pettigrew, James Johnston, 166
Pickett, George, 170
Roosevelt, Franklin D., 31, 257

British personalities
Churchill, Winston, 31
Ekins, Joe, 108
Gordon, Douglas, 108
Montgomery, Bernard, 31

French personalities
Napoleon Bonaparte, 154

Italian personalities
Mussolini, Benito, 37, 107

Soviet personalities
Rokossovsky, Konstantin, 31, 32
Stalin, Josef, 31, 32, 257
Vatutin, Nikolai, 32
Zhukov, Georgy, 31

German military, war production, and political personalities (non-SS)
Aders, Erwin, 16
Baumbach, Werner, 37
Brauchitsch, Walter von, 33, 158
Christern, Hans, 21
Clausewitz, Carl, 165
Glatter-Götz, Josef von, 21, 22
Glatter-Götz, Josef von (senior), 22
Göring, Hermann, 159
Guderian, Heinz, 6, 21, 29, 35, 36, 37, 40, 171, 173
Himmler, Heinrich, 14, 35, 119, 153, 159, 163, 175, 176, 177
Hitler, Adolf, 6, 16, 17, 21, 29, 33, 34, 35, 36, 37, 38, 64, 72, 104, 107, 108, 153, 155, 156, 175
Hoth, Hermann, 21, 32, 33, 34, 35, 55, 69, 152
Jeschonnek, Hans, 37, 257
Jodl, Alfred, 33, 34, 36
Keitel, Wilhelm, 36, 37
Kempf, Werner, 152

Kleist, Ewald von, 33
Kluge, Günther von, 31, 35, 36, 37, 72
Lüttichau, Hannibal von, 21
Manstein, Erich von, 31, 32, 33, 34, 35, 36, 37, 40, 72, 257
Mieth, Friedrich, 172
Model, Walter, 35, 36, 37, 55, 152, 225
Nietzsche, Friedrich, 175
Paulus, Friedrich von, 37
Porsche, Ferdinand, 16, 17
Rieger, Franz, 22
Rudel, Hans-Ulrich, 47
Speer, Albert, 17, 36
Speidel, Hans, 34
Steglich, Martin, 172, 261, 262
Thomale, Wolfgang, 17
Tippelskirch, Kurt, 172
Wilhelm II, Kaiser, 156
Zeitzler, Kurt, 33, 34, 35, 36

Senior Waffen-SS personnel
Baum, Otto, 62, 191
Becker, Helmuth, 61
Bittrich, Wilhelm, 121, 189
Bochmann, Georg, 58
Dietrich, Josef, 38, 50, 92, 102, 108, 160, 171, 177, 189, 190, 193
Hausser, Paul, 32, 34, 40, 42, 46, 55, 79, 171, 172, 173, 176, 178, 192
Jeckeln, Friedrich, 138
Jüttner, Hans, 158
Krüger, Walter, 39, 47, 135, 176, 191, 252
Kunstmann, Eugen, 39, 58
Ostendorff, Werner, 117
Peiper, Joachim, 53, 97, 177, 203
Priess, Hermann, 39, 62, 138, 177, 191
Reitzenstein, Hans-Albin von, 39, 53, 54, 251
Schönberger, Georg, 38
Stadler, Sylvester, 192
Tensfeld, Willy, 133, 134, 244
Vogt, Fritz, 95
Wessel, Jürgen, 92
Westernhagen, Heinz von, 108, 268
Wisch, Theodor, 38, 46, 64, 107, 193, 258

Waffen-SS tank crewmen (not in Tigers at Kursk)
Edenstrasser, Oswald, 182
Egger, Paul, 10, 13, 121, 134, 159, 174, 182, 236, 267

Einbeck, Paul, 182
Fey, Will, 212, 236, 267
Hafner, Leo, 182
Kiekbusch, Ernst, 182
Klingenbeck, Rudolf, 182
Klink, Hans, 182
Kritz, Hugo, 182
Kruse, Herbert, 182
Marquardt, Otto, 182
Nagel, Hellmut, 182
Schmitz, Karl-Heinz, 182
Warnick, Heinrich, 12, 175, 245
Wüster, Rudolf, 182

Waffen-SS Tiger crewmen at Kursk
Allwinn, Egon, 86, 109, 110
Arzner, Eduard, 74, 85, 110, 209
Asmussen, Heinrich, 86, 110, 157
Aspöck, Max, 110
Augst, Otto, 82, 91
Aumüller, Leopold, 83, 91
Bachmann, Hans-Ludwig, 89, 137
Baral, Kurt, 7, 8, 50, 86, 110, 111, 134, 151, 162, 174, 204, 205, 207, 208, 218, 219, 223, 251
Baumann, Otto Ernst, 89, 137
Bender, Paul, 53, 83, 91, 157
Berges, Kurt, 83, 91
Bernhardt, Arthur, 71, 82, 92, 150
Biber, Willy, 88, 126, 137, 138, 162, 242
Biermeier, Fritz, 58, 71, 87, 138, 147, 155, 156, 157, 175, 178, 246
Bingert, Walter, 53, 83, 92
Birnbaum, Wolfgang, 86, 111, 112, 122, 157, 174
Bittner, Gottlob, 86, 112
Bläsing, Max, 47, 85, 112, 151, 235
Blattmann, Karl, 88, 139
Bode, Hein, 89, 139, 161
Böhm, Franz, 89, 139
Boehmer, Hans-Joachim, 85, 112, 113
Börker, Willi, 86, 113, 151
Brandt, Jürgen, 50, 81, 83, 92, 93, 156, 157, 161, 174, 197
Braubach, Gunther, 83, 93
Buchner, Heinz, 83, 93, 161, 170, 174
Bürvenich, Klaus, 46, 82, 93, 151
Bullay, Ludwig, 86, 113
Cantow, Helmut, 84, 113, 151
Elmer, Franz, 83, 93
Enderl, Franz, 59, 82, 93, 150

Esslinger, Johannes, 85, 114
Fein, Edmund, 88, 139, 141, 246
Fink, Berthold, 86, 114, 157, 236
Frank, Hans, 89, 139
Franz, Josef, 89, 139
Freiberger, Heinz, 86, 114, 178
Frenzel, Wilfried, 47, 86, 114, 115, 150
Frielau, 89, 139
Fuss, Siegfried, 83, 93, 94, 161
Gaube, Max, 46, 83, 94
Gallinat, Georg, 47, 84, 115, 151
Gebhardt, 85, 115
Gentsch, Georg, 84, 94, 150
Glagow, Artur, 85, 115, 174, 236, 237
Gleissner, Erich, 86, 115
Gnerlich, Helmut, 86, 115
Göckl, Josef, 58, 88, 139, 150
Gräser, Helmut, 69, 83, 94, 174
Graf, Ewald, 82, 94
Grothum, Karl Heinz, 84, 94, 279
Gruber, Helmut, 84, 95
Grüner, Günther, 89, 140
Grupe, Alfred, 85, 115
Grupe, Günther, 85, 116
Grupe, Karl, 85, 116
Hackbarth, Benno, 116
Hans, Peter, 87
Hartel, Fritz, 82, 95, 201, 228
Haselböck, Hans, 85, 116, 134, 151, 206
Heering, Max, 117
Hellwig, Kurt, 86, 117, 162, 217
Henke, Walter, 74, 83, 95, 151, 170, 229
Hepe, Werner, 84, 95
Hilgert, Franz, 89, 140, 226
Hinrichsen, Julius, 47, 84, 117, 118, 157, 175, 221, 235
Hitz, Fritz, 88, 140
Hoberg, Werner, 89, 140, 279
Hobohm, Hagbert, 118, 85, 86
Hock, Fritz, 89, 114
Höflinger, Hans, 84, 96
Höld, Hans, 83, 96
Hofer, Franz, 88, 141
Hoffmann, Hans-Joachim, 89, 141
Hoffmann, Richard, 87, 118
Hofmann, Bruno, 71, 87, 118, 151
Holzer, Erich, 87, 118, 119, 237
Hurlbrink, Dieter, 87, 119
Iwanitz, Martin-Gerhard, 83, 96

Jadzewski, Paul, 85, 119, 279
Jörg, Hermann, 85, 119, 238
Jung, Siegfried, 82, 96
Kaempf, Gerhard, 13, 24, 85, 86, 114, 119, 120, 137, 162, 175, 238
Kalss, Alois, 14, 47, 85, 86, 114, 120, 121, 126, 127, 134, 151, 154, 155, 156, 157, 158, 162, 175, 204, 239
Kaschlan (Kaschlun), Gerhard, 84, 96, 97
Kendziora, Alfred Ernst, 87, 121, 169
Kerkom, Hans-Georg van, 89, 141
Kirschner, Gustav, 46, 83, 97, 151
Kleber, Kurt Quax, 71, 84, 97
Kling, Heinrich, 45, 46, 50, 55, 67, 71, 81, 97, 98, 99, 102, 107, 151, 155, 156, 157, 174, 178, 197, 268
Klingenbeck, Rudolf, 182
Klötzer, Hans, 87
Knecht, Walter, 85, 112, 122, 157, 175, 240
Knöss, Heinrich, 82, 98, 200
Koch, Walter, 46, 83, 98, 151, 260
Kochesser, Norbert, 89, 141, 247
Köhler, Walter, 58, 71, 87, 88, 141, 142, 146, 154
König, Ewald, 84, 98, 99
Köppen, Otto, 88, 142
Koppelkamp, August, 84, 122
Kraml, Franz, 85, 122, 123, 162, 211, 212, 240
Kranz, Herbert, 88, 142
Krichel, Friedrich Robert, 123
Kronmüller, Willy, 88, 142, 144
Kühnke, Wolfgang, 89, 142
Küster, Karl, 88, 142
Kuster, Jakob, 50, 86, 123, 151, 175
Lachner, Ludwig, 88, 137, 142, 175
Lampert, Hans, 89, 143, 247
Lange, Helmut, 84, 99
Lasch, Fritz, 90, 143
Lasser, Ferdinand, 87, 123, 248
Lau, Friedrich Johann, 90, 143
Lau, Walter, 82, 83, 99, 174, 200
Laumbacher, Albert, 87, 123
Lechner, Rudi, 99
Lein, Fritz, 89, 143
Lieber, Karl, 83, 99, 151
Lötzsch, Georg, 53, 71, 82, 99, 100, 230
Lorenz, Karl-Heinz, 53, 54, 84, 86, 124, 130, 150, 156, 241
Lotter, Wilhelm, 51, 87, 124, 151
Lucht, Walter, 88, 143

Lünser, Alfred, 84, 100
Märker, Werner, 47, 125, 150
Malsch, Erwin, 87, 125
Marten, Max, 83, 100, 200
Matthäi, Hans Joachim, 89, 143
Menninger, Waldemar, 125
Meyer, Kurt, 47, 84, 85, 125, 151, 175, 217
Mocnik, Hermann, 88, 143
Möller, Heinz, 46, 100
Mölly, Ewald, 55, 82, 100, 161
Mohrbacher, Kurt, 85, 126
Mücke, Alois, 90, 143, 249
Mühldorfer, Anton, 85, 126
Müller, Karl, 84, 161
Müller, Ludwig, 58, 150
Müller, Richard, 54, 151, 225
Münch, Walter, 88, 142, 144
Nienke, Arno, 87, 126, 242
Obenaus, Werner, 86, 126
Osha, Fritz, 90, 144
Owczarek, Heinz, 46, 84, 101, 150
Pleger, Ernst, 87, 126
Pollmann, Kurt, 67, 83, 151
Privatzki, Artur, 89, 144, 175, 226, 249
Probst, Willi, 88, 144
Quade, Heinz, 88, 89, 140, 144, 145, 151, 154, 226
Ramm, Heinz, 86, 127
Rathsack, Willi, 72, 89, 145, 148, 151, 154
Ratter, Albert, 84, 127
Reibold, Walter, 86, 127, 128, 162
Reimers, Heinrich, 82, 101, 231
Reinhardt, Johann, 86, 128, 156, 205
Reininghaus, Walter, 47, 79, 84, 85, 128, 129, 151, 216, 242
Reissmann, Herbert, 87, 129
Rex, Hans, 88, 89, 146
Richter, Wilfried, 74, 87, 146, 155
Röpstorff, Willi, 84, 101
Rose, Walter, 84, 101
Ross, Hans, 86, 129
Rudolph, Fritz, 89, 146
Sandler, Karl, 90, 146, 250
Sandmeier, Erwin, 87, 129, 151
Sauer, Gerhard, 87, 129
Schäfer, Ernst, 54, 86, 129, 150
Schäfer, Georg, 48, 90, 147, 151
Schäfer, Karl, 87, 129, 130
Schäfer, Werner, 54, 86, 130, 151
Schamp, Rolf, 57, 59, 82, 96, 101, 231, 232

Schindhelm, Heinz, 84, 102
Schleusner, Horst, 85, 130
Schmid, Fritz, 85, 130, 243
Schmidt, Georg, 87, 130
Schmidt, Wilhelm, 86, 130, 131, 162, 244
Schnabel, Ludwig, 85, 131
Schneider, Siegfried, 84, 102
Schöneberg, Heinz, 67, 86, 131, 151
Schreyer, Gunther, 90, 147
Schroeder, Wilhelm, 58, 87, 88, 142, 147, 175, 227
Schüffler, Karl, 71, 87, 189, 148, 154
Schütz, Waldemar, 46, 64, 82, 93, 102, 103, 106, 108, 151, 157, 200
Schulze-Berge, Karl, 88, 148
Schumacher, Alfred, 84, 102
Schweigert, Konrad, 85, 131, 162, 211
Schweitzer, Werner, 90, 148, 157
Seidel, Heinz, 87, 131, 132
Selonke, Friedrich, 88, 148
Skerbinz, Karl, 85, 132, 175
Skribelka, Günter, 86, 132
Söffker, Roland, 84, 103
Sowa, Kurt, 83, 103, 157, 161
Staudegger, Franz, 13, 57, 64, 83, 93, 95, 103, 104, 155, 158, 161, 170, 174, 232, 279
Stellmacher, Herbert, 83, 104, 170
Stemann, Franz, 54, 86, 133, 151
Stolzenberg, Horst, 87, 133
Sümnich, Paul, 84, 99, 104, 157
Stuttenecker, Johann, 87, 133
Tasler, Alois, 89, 148
Tensfeld, Heinz, 67, 74, 85, 133, 134, 175, 244
Theiss, Philipp, 67, 79, 84, 85, 133, 134, 150, 209
Theunis, Emil, 87, 134
Trautmann, Heinz, 87, 134, 135, 157, 158
Ulmer, Artur, 86, 135, 150, 205
Ullrich, Paul, 87, 135
Vögler, Ernst, 72, 90, 148, 150
Walter, Herbert Erich, 87, 135
Waltersdorf, Gerhard, 83, 104
Warmbrunn, Karl-Heinz, 71, 81, 104, 105, 106, 157, 174, 176, 252
Wehr, Erwin, 90, 148, 149
Weissfloch, Emil, 87, 135, 151, 251
Wendorff, Helmut, 45, 59, 82, 93, 99, 105, 151, 154, 155, 174
Wendt, Werner, 64, 82, 106, 161
Wenzel, Reinhart, 82, 106, 232
Werner, Felix, 90, 149

Wilfling, Anton, 87, 135

Wilken, Heinz, 54, 84, 135, 150

Wimmer, Georg, 90, 149

Winkler, Peter, 83, 106

Wittmann, Michael, 13, 14, 46, 48, 50, 59, 67, 69, 81, 82, 83, 96, 97, 98, 99, 100, 101, 107, 108, 109, 154, 155, 156, 160, 167, 171, 174, 231, 233, 234

Wohlgemuth, 81, 108

Woll, Balthasar, 19, 83, 109, 155, 174, 234

Woll, Eduard, 85, 136, 245

Zacharias, Rudolf, 71, 87, 136, 151

Zieten, Georg, 89, 149

Zimbehl, Joachim, 87, 136

Zimmermann, Herbert, 47, 53, 67, 84, 133, 134, 136, 137, 151, 156, 209, 217

Zimmermann, Ludwig, 58, 88, 149, 150